INSIDE LITTLE BRITAIN

Matt would like to dedicate this book to David.
David would also like to dedicate this book to David.

INSIDE LITTLE BRITAIN

Matt Lucas, David Walliams
& Boyd Hilton

EBURY
PRESS

First published in Great Britain 2006

1 3 5 7 9 10 8 6 4 2

Ebury Press, an imprint of Ebury Publishing.
Random House, 20 Vauxhall Bridge Road, London SW1V 2SA

Random House Australia (Pty) Limited
20 Alfred Street, Milsons Point, Sydney, New South Wales 2061, Australia

Random House New Zealand Limited
18 Poland Road, Glenfield, Auckland 10, New Zealand

Random House (Pty) Limited
Isle of Houghton, Corner of Boundary Road and Carse O'Gowrie, Houghton, 2198,
South Africa

Random House Publishers India Private Limited
301 World Trade Tower, Hotel Intercontinental Grand Complex, Barakhamba Lane,
New Delhi 110 001, India

The Random House Group Limited Reg. No. 954009

www.randomhouse.co.uk

A CIP catalogue record for this book is available from the British Library.

ISBN 9780091912314 (after Jan 2007)
ISBN 0091912318

Mixed Sources
Product group from well-managed
forests and other controlled sources
www.fsc.org Cert no. TT-COC-2139
© 1996 Forest Stewardship Council

Printed and bound in Great Britain by Clays, St Ives PLC

Picture credits: pages 24, 68, 70, 75, 78, 85, 135, 142, 151, 211, 323, 363, 369, 377, 394
© Adam Lawrence; pages 18, 35, 66, 92, 174, 186, 192, 199, 205, 220, 290, 337, 353,
366, 401 © Boyd Hilton; page 399 © Victoria Dawe/Comic Relief ; page 342 © Sam
Taylor-Wood ; pages 27, 29, 51, 115, 164, 215, 235, 237, 240, 244, 304, 351, 380, 396
taken from Matt Lucas's and David Walliams's private collections.

Acknowledgements

Thanks to

Kevin McGee, Diana and Ralph Lobatto, Kathleen and Peter Williams, Julie Larter, Katy Carmichael, Robin Dashwood, Caroline Aherne, Neil Tennant, Chris Lowe, Paul Stevens at ICM, Conor McCaughan and Melanie Rockcliffe at Troika, Barbara Charone and Moira Bellas at MBC.

All the people who worked so hard on *Little Britain* Live, especially Paul Putner, Samantha Power, Geoff Posner, Jeremy Sams, Phil McIntyre, Paul Roberts and everyone at Phil McIntyre Entertainments, Tony Harpur, Gareth Weeks, Peter Waller, Cosmo Williams.

Everyone who worked on the *Little Britain* TV show, especially Myfanwy Moore, Jon Plowman, Graham Linehan, Steve Bendelack, Matt Lipsey, Declan Lowney, Annie Hardinge, Lisa Cavalli-Green, Stuart Murphy, Jane Root, Jana Bennett, Peter Fincham and Lorraine Heggessey.

Professor Greg Whyte, everyone at Comic Relief especially Richard Curtis, Kevin Cahill, Peter Bennett-Jones, Vanessa Russo and Katie Morrison, everyone at the BBC who worked on *Little Britain*'s Big Swim especially Rachael Gosling, Alastair Cook and Robert Davis.

Everyone at Ebury especially Andrew Goodfellow, Hannah MacDonald, Jake Lingwood, Di Riley and Sarah Bennie, and copy-editor Mari Roberts.

Lesley, Ron and Phil Hilton, Cameron Smith, Boyd's colleagues at *Heat*, especially Mark Frith, Cliff Longridge, Kay Ribeiro, Lucie Cave and Kevin McCreeth, Robert Kirby at PFD.

Contents

Preface

This is the story of Matt Lucas and David Walliams refracted through the lens of the strangest, most extraordinary year in their lives. In October 2005, *Little Britain* embarked upon a journey across Great Britain. Matt and David were set to perform nearly 150 dates over a nine-month period. They sold out a year in advance. Dozens more shows were added; their first arena dates were thrown in. All in all, they would be performing to over 800,000 people. It became the biggest live comedy tour ever.

They didn't know what to expect. They were worried they might both go mad. Friends told them they would probably never talk to each other ever again. The idea of performing hundreds of shows in quick succession was too much to take in. They had mixed feelings of queasy dread and giddy excitement. This tour would be the culmination of their plan for *Little Britain*: to progress from radio to television to a big live show. But it had to work; they had to give the fans what they wanted. Even though there would be a huge team working behind the scenes, when the curtain went up, Matt and David would be held responsible.

They were also faced with knowing that their lives were about to be put on hold; they'd be away from their friends and families and homes, while at the same time coming to terms with a level of success and fame they had never experienced before. Matt was desperate to have his partner Kevin with him as much as possible throughout it all. David would have loved to have someone special to share everything with too. Instead, rather a lot of his time would be spent yearning for one particular woman.

Amid these hundreds of shows, and all the attention they would be receiving in papers, magazines, and unofficial, inevitably inaccurate, biographies, they were aware that it may never be like this again. This was their time, and they needed to cherish and remember it. To chronicle how it really was, and how they got there in the first place. Which is how this book came about.

Part One

1

Autumn 2005: 7 weeks to go

Matt answers the door of David's flat. I'm immediately distracted by the state of his face. He's got two large pieces of tissue paper stuck to his cheeks, one on each side, and there's blood seeping through them. He clocks my expression. 'Hello, friend!' he says merrily. 'Notice anything odd about my face?'

He's joking, but also stressed out. In about twenty minutes' time he's due to be photographed by dozens of paparazzi and film crews on the red carpet leading up to the Opera House, Covent Garden, and he ruefully explains that he's just burst some spots. I try to think of something comforting to say but I know that the press would love to get hold of pictures of Matt in this state. Instead I just say, 'What happened?'

It turns out that Matt's skin often erupts at inopportune moments. Usefully, Matt and David have got a make-up artist on hand to help them look their best in front of the TV cameras and still photographers. 'Excuse me while I get this seen to,' says Matt. Matt's boyfriend Kevin is here, a model of calm, reassuring support.

David lives in a small but beautifully interior-designed Belsize Park one-bedroom flat, themed round the colour pink. It's verging on flamboyant, but with judicious lighting and lots of velvety materials the space feels luxurious and classy. On the wall hangs a large print of a photograph of the actor Sir Michael Gambon by David's friend Sam Taylor-Wood, from whom he bought his vintage Mercedes car. The Michael Gambon picture, part of her Crying Men series, is slightly blurred. David tells me his mum complained that it was out of focus.

The last time I was here, a few months ago, there was a *Lost In Translation* film poster where the Gambon print is now. There are little hillocks of DVDs, many of them unopened box-sets, surrounding David's plasma TV. He sees me eyeing them and says he's stocking up on stuff to watch when they go on tour. 'There's going to be a lot of time to fill,' he says.

In fact, they're about to embark upon the biggest live comedy tour ever: over two hundred dates throughout the next fourteen months, breaking only for Christmas and New Year and then the summer.

David is putting the finishing touches to his outfit – black suit, red shirt, black tie – a little bit Franz Ferdinand, but slightly more classically elegant. Matt's in a dark pinstriped suit with white shirt and red tie. They look vaguely coordinated, but not cheesily so.

'What shall we say in our thank-you speech?' asks David, of both myself and his friend and guest for the evening James Corden, an actor he met while filming the TV comedy-drama *Cruise of the Gods* in 2002. 'I could make a joke about sleeping with married women.'

This is a reference to the front-page Sunday tabloid story claiming that David had been named as the 'other man' in an underwear model's divorce papers. She's claiming that her two-night affair with David, or as the legal document calls him 'a well-known public figure', is one of her irreconcilable differences with her husband, but she also makes it quite clear, in the lengthy story she's sold to the paper, that David didn't know she was married when he dallied with her after they met at an Agent Provocateur party. I think it might be quite a good idea for David to show he's not fazed by this woman's kiss-and-tell story and tell him so.

Matt isn't sure. 'I don't know. You'll be giving the story more publicity.'

'Yes, maybe,' says David, 'but if I say something funny about it, it might stop the 3AM girls and everyone else from asking me about it.'

The make-up woman has been busy working on Matt for a few minutes.

He turns round to face us. His skin has gone a pale shade of green. He sees us all looking a bit doubtful, and checks himself out in the mirror. 'It's green. My face is green . . .' None of us know what to say. 'Have you seen this, David? I look awful. I won't be able to go if I'm gonna be in this state.'

'Surely something can be done,' says David.

Kevin says, 'Yeah, just make it paler?'

'Let me have another go,' says the gallant make-up artist. When I first walked in I was surprised she was here. Now I'm wondering what Matt would have done if she hadn't been. David looks out the window and checks that their car is still waiting. The ceremony is due to start in half an hour, and the journey from Belsize Park to Covent Garden could easily take that long. Kevin sits next to Matt as the make-up is applied again.

It's not the BAFTAs they're about to attend – and they know they've won their category – but they are both tense.

I ask David if he knows who else is going to be on their table.

'Not Morrissey,' he says. 'They told us he might show up. But I know he won't. Why would he? He didn't even turn up to do the Brits, and he'd pretty much agreed to do a song with Robbie. So I can't see him coming to the GQ Awards. But it would be lovely to meet him, to be introduced to him and become his friend and be able to go and have tea with him.'

Do you think he likes *Little Britain*?

'I doubt it. I think he finds TV comedy vulgar, doesn't he? Especially anything current. I wonder if he's even seen it . . . If he didn't like it I would cry.' Pause. 'Maybe it's best if he doesn't come.'

James says, 'Isn't Denise on our table?'

David confirms that Denise Van Outen will be there. She's due to present Matt and David's award to them. 'Though apparently there might be some kind of surprise,' he adds. 'Last year we picked up the award from Peter André. He didn't seem to know who we were. He said the award was going to "Little Brian", which I thought was brilliant.'

'They asked us if we had any suggestion of who we'd like to present our award,' says Matt from the make-up corner, where he now looks pasty white, which is an improvement on the green, 'so we said John Inman.'

'John Inman would be great,' says David. 'I mean, he's the guy, isn't he? He's passed the cultural baton down to us. From Kenneth Williams . . . to John Inman . . . to us!'

David knows Inman would be too camp for GQ, and anyway he's been ill recently, and looks very different to how we remember him as Mr Humphries.

'It's always a shock when you see TV stars from your childhood, isn't it? I saw a picture of Batman and Robin today, the actors who played them in the 1960s TV series, and Robin didn't look great . . .' *Batman*, starring Adam West, was one of David's favourite TV shows. He's annoyed that it's not yet available on DVD.

'I've got the film, which was a spin-off of the TV series. There's a brilliant scene in it where Batman's running with a bomb on a pier and he needs to throw it over the edge and he sees some ducks in the water so he can't throw it. He doesn't want to murder the ducks! And Adam West has got this over-the-top earnestness.'

During the slow journey from bloody cheeks to powdery white, Matt is in good humour, and everyone else – David, Kevin, myself and James – is trying to be calm, making sure that Matt's face is merely a mini-crisis rather than a full-blown one. There are no publicists, agents, managers or any other kind of professional entourage around to add to the excitement of the situation, apart from, of course, the make-up artist, who is proving to be the hero of the night. 'There,' she announces. 'I think it's okay.'

Matt stands up and offers his face for appraisal. 'It looks fine,' says Kevin. That's all Matt needs to hear.

The people-carrier pulls up in front of the Opera House, Covent Garden. Bryan Ferry, Bob Geldof and Simon Cowell are walking up the red carpet.

Those of us in the car who haven't been nominated for an award wait while Matt and David climb out and offer themselves to the cameras. No one seems to notice anything unusual about Matt's cheeks. Then we hurry round the back of the red carpet to the lobby, where, standing by the camera crews, are Matt and David's publicists, Barbara Charone and Moira Bellas. They also handle pop acts, including Charlotte Church, REM and Madonna, and until recently Elton John. BC and Moira are looking after Charlotte Church tonight.

As we make our way to our table, David points to a tanned young man in a dark suit and asks if that is Jamie Redknapp. David met him after the Comedy Awards last year. David was driving into a car park and Jamie spotted him and said, 'Well done on those Comedy Awards last night,' to which he couldn't think of a more suitable response than: 'Ooh, thanks. Well . . . keep kicking those balls!' David's not the slightest bit interested in football, and often has to sit in quiet contemplation while Matt, a devoted Arsenal fan, engages in complicated conversations with people about the latest developments in the football world. I am an Arsenal fan too, so many of my conversations with Matt at least begin with a discussion of their news. David finds the urge to bond over sport mystifying, but he's clearly slightly jealous too. Jenson Button is also in the room. David asks me who he is.

Denise Van Outen is sitting at the table with a girlfriend of hers when we arrive. David sits next to Denise and ushers me to sit next to him. Then just as Matt and Kevin are about to sit down on the other side of the table, up pops Matt's old friend Philip Salon. Matt introduces me to Philip, who I met recently at the *Little Britain* wrap party, where he told me about his fondness for car-boot sales and haggling 'like a good Jew'. Salon is wearing a red velvet jacket with no shirt underneath. He asks me what I think of his look and I tell him it's certainly bold and brave. It's an outfit that a chiselled 20-year-old Adonis might carry off. Salon isn't such a man. But this is all part of his maverick image. He's going to go half-naked and he doesn't give a shit. He does seem to have an entirely hairless chest. I assume it must have been waxed.

Philip has been one of Boy George's friends for years and was featured as a character in his autobiographical musical *Taboo*, in which Matt played legendary performance artist Leigh Bowery.

Kevin sits next to Salon, and Matt next to him. Some people from GQ are also there. 'Where are your friends?' Matt asks Philip, and Philip explains that they'll be arriving later for the party element of the evening because he wasn't sure if there would be enough room for them at the table. There wouldn't have been. Just as I wonder who these friends might be, Philip asks me how I know Matt and David. I tell him I've known them for five or six years. I tell him I'm writing a book about them. 'Oh,' he says. 'So you'll be writing about this?'

I glance round the room again, and spot Burt Bacharach, Sam Taylor-Wood, Paula Abdul, Gordon Ramsay, Davina McCall, Alicia Silverstone, Eva Herzigova, Jerry Hall, Bob Geldof, Bryan Ferry, Carol Vorderman, Gavin Henson, Tess Daly and Vernon Kaye, Nancy Dell'Olio, Fearne Cotton, Chris Moyles, Jay-Z and Dale Winton. It's a better turnout than many televised awards ceremonies. Maybe people feel more at home, more relaxed, without the TV cameras. Matt and David certainly do.

It ends up being quite difficult for me to follow much of what Matt and

David are saying because Philip Salon is such a good talker. He's also peculiarly and entertainingly blunt. He tells me juicy stuff about Boy George within about five minutes of sitting down. Normal awards-show table etiquette would have us still discussing the wine or the menu at this point. While Philip is merrily gabbling about sex, drugs and car-boot sales, I'm half trying to hear what David is talking about with Denise Van Outen. It seems that Denise isn't presenting Matt and David with their award tonight. David is pleading with Denise to tell him who is, but she won't. 'I promised I wouldn't.'

'But I won't tell Matt!' says David, grinning. He always wants to know what's about to happen. Matt likes the moment of surprise, but David prefers to know so he feels less nervous and can concentrate on coming up with something funny to say in his acceptance speech. He asks Denise whether it's a good idea for him to make a jokey reference to the tabloid story about being named in that kiss-and-tell woman's divorce papers. Denise says it might be quite funny, and quite a good way of showing that David isn't taking the story seriously. Matt, walking by on his way to the toilet, repeats his view that he doesn't think it's such a good idea.

When Matt walks off, David asks Denise again who's handing out the award. It must be the fifth time he's asked so far.

Philip Salon is asking me how often I go to synagogue. As I turn back to him to tell him never, Denise whispers something to David. He beams.

'Do you fast at Yom Kippur?' asks Philip Salon.

'No,' I tell Philip. 'I don't believe in God. I'm an atheist Jew. I'm proud to be Jewish but I'm not religious.'

The first course arrives – buffalo mozzarella with grilled artichoke and fig on rocket salad with balsamic vinegar. 'It's always the same, this kind of food, isn't it?' says Philip. 'It'll be lamb for the main course. Have you got any relatives in Israel?'

Matt returns to the table and David stops whispering in Denise Van Outen's ear. By the time Matt is back in his seat, Philip is rather loudly berating me for not wanting to go to Israel. We've somehow got into a discussion about the Israel/Palestine issue. Philip's astonished that, as a Jew, I'm not automatically taking the Israeli side.

Matt looks concerned and leans over to ask Philip something. Philip says, 'I'm just explaining to this anti-Israel Jewish boy here –'

Matt says, 'Oh God, leave him alone.'

David has also caught wind of the conversation and says to Philip that the Palestinians are the oppressed ones in that situation.

I'm grateful to David and Matt for sticking up for me, while I'm also quite enjoying the argument. Matt seems to be about to stand up and walk round the table in my direction. And just as I think he might be about to intervene to make sure Philip and I don't come to blows, I realise that Simon Cowell is standing behind me, chatting to David. Cowell's white shirt is slashed open practically to his waist, to reveal almost as much of his chest as Philip is showing. Simon Cowell tells Matt and David that a forthcoming episode of *The X Factor* features a girl he describes on air as looking like Vicky Pollard.

'We've got our own Vicky,' he tells them. 'You don't mind that we've compared her to Vicky Pollard, do you?' he asks Matt.

'No!' says Matt. 'It's great. In fact, if you want to use a clip I'm sure we can sort something out.'

Matt and David have spotted Pierce Brosnan a few tables away, and point this out to Simon Cowell.

'Look – we're in the same room as James Bond!' says David. Simon says he didn't realise who it was because he's got a huge grey beard. David's a big James Bond fan.

'Do you think he'd know who we are?' asks David.

'Even if he doesn't know who we are,' says Matt, 'I'd still like to meet him.' But just as they're about to wander over in Brosnan's direction, the GQ Men of the Year Awards ceremony begins.

Matt and David's big moment comes fairly early on, after an impressions-filled monologue from host Rory Bremner, Timothy Spall presenting Actor of the Year to Daniel Craig, Jay-Z picking up International Man of the Year from Jade Jagger and Charlotte Church winning Woman of the Year. Then Rory Bremner introduces a very special guest. The Aerosmith rock song 'Dude Looks Like A Lady' blares out of the speakers and Bremner says, 'Please welcome Mr Gary Barlow!' Matt and David look momentarily confused. Then a familiar-looking man in jeans, white shirt, black tie and grey waistcoat walks onstage. It's Robbie Williams.

Matt is visibly thrilled and says, 'Oh brilliant!'

David feigns surprise very well. 'You knew all along, didn't you?' he says to Denise.

'Hello,' says Robbie onstage. 'Judas here!'

In the style of the *Rock Profile* spoof of his former Take That bandmate Gary, he announces that his friends Matt and David have won the Comedians of the Year award.

Matt and David bound onto the stage.

David asks the audience if they enjoyed Robbie's stint wearing a dress in their special Comic Relief Emily and Florence sketch, which prompts a huge cheer. Matt jokingly hails Robbie as 'A little lad with a big talent!'

There's no mention of David's current news story, about being named in that woman's divorce papers. It's totally forgotten.

At the table, while Matt and David and Robbie are having their photos taken, a security man approaches with two new chairs and asks me and James if we can make some space for two new arrivals. A few seconds later Robbie sits next to me, along with his best mate Jonathan Wilkes. Robbie introduces himself to me, shakes my hand and says, 'This is my mate Jonny.' I tell Robbie we met one time previously, at Matt's thirtieth birthday party. I was with Justin Lee Collins, a TV presenter. Robbie says enthusiastically, 'Oh yeah, I remember. He was funny!' Jonny Wilkes seems to be scouring the room on behalf of his friend to check how many potentially irksome journalists there are in the immediate vicinity. I haven't got round to mentioning that I am a journalist. I tell Robbie I'm writing a book about Matt and David. He nods and says, 'Wow,' but I'm not sure if he really hears what I'm saying because Jonny is whispering something in his ear, presumably letting him know that representatives of the 3AM girls and the Bizarre column are here.

I can see that they're already staring at Robbie, working out in their minds the best way to approach him. And he doesn't seem to have any security or entourage with him. Just his best friend.

By the time Matt and David return to the table with their award and have a chat with Robbie, the entire room seems to be staring in our direction.

Four minutes later, Robbie and Jonny decide it's time to leave.

'It's a shame,' David observes as Rob and Jonny hurry off. 'They can't even just sit here for a few minutes enjoying themselves. No wonder he'd rather stay at home with his friends . . .'

'What a lovely surprise though,' says Matt.

Two beautiful young people are approaching the table. A blond boy and a blonde girl dressed in elaborate Regency-period costume. They look about sixteen.

'Ah! You made it! Fabulous!' says Philip Salon. They're Philip's friends, who've arrived just in time to attend the party, and turn out to be brother and sister.

I ask Philip if they're in fancy dress and he, slightly tartly, tells me no, they always dress like this. Always? Well, quite often, he claims. I try to extract from Philip the story of how he knows these two young visions of peculiar, foppish beauty, but get a rather vague answer.

The young fops ask Philip how the evening's going. He tells them it's been okay, that I've been keeping him entertained with my self-hating Jewishness, and he has no idea who most of the people here are.

'I think the party's going to be boring,' he adds.

Matt and Kevin decide to call it a night, and head home.

David doesn't intend to have a particularly late night either, but he gets distracted by Dale Winton at the party. David embraces Dale with elaborate campness, and just says, 'You!' to him. Dale tells David he loves him, thinks he's one of the funniest men he's ever met. David interrupts with: 'One of?'

'I want to go for tea with you in Primrose Hill!' says Dale.

'I can't imagine anything better,' says David.

'Are you pulling my leg?'

'No! Seriously, I love the idea of taking tea with you. Let the whole world see: just the two of us, two single men on the town, having tea and cakes . . .'

Dale and David check they have one another's correct mobile number.

As well as rehearsing for the tour, Matt and David are also finishing off the new series of *Little Britain*, scheduled to begin in mid-November on BBC1, and fitting in press interviews to promote the new series *and* the DVD of the previous series. At one point in the rehearsal schedule they have to meet me in a pub in Primrose Hill so that I can interview them for *Heat*, which is a peculiar moment for all of us. I just pretend I haven't been spending most of my time with them in recent weeks, and crack on with asking them the general questions that readers will want to know, which slightly embarrass- ingly include trying to get them to talk about their celebrity friends. Especially Robbie Williams. *Heat* readers, like most people vaguely interest- ed in fame and popular culture, are fascinated with Robbie. Luckily they come up with some obviously comedic answers – Matt says they fight over Robbie all the time; David adds that if they both want to kiss him at the same time they'll have a bitch-fight over it. Later we get into the topic of newspaper speculation about David and his sexuality. He makes the point that if you're male, famous and not married, they will assume you must be gay. Matt uses the example of Robbie, who has had to read about rumours of his gayness for years, and observes that he's never felt any gay vibes from Rob at all. The rest of the interview gets sidetracked by an in-depth debate on the merits of the current contenders in *The X Factor*.

Later, over lunch, it becomes clear that the unusually unkempt David has a cold and is a bit irritable, while Matt is also tense. Rehearsals for the tour are proving to be tougher than either of them thought they would be. They're having debates about the running order of the sketches. Just when they think they have sorted out a structure for each half of the show, they realise that one element of it doesn't work. They want it to flow slickly from one sketch to the next. They want the costume and scenery changes to fly by almost magically, so the audience can barely tell how they've got from one outfit to the next. But at the moment, sections of the show seem sluggish, they're uncertain if some sketches work in a live situation at all, and they have no idea if their ambitious technical plans can be achieved. This is a live performance that is supposed to feature mass projectile vomiting and an old woman urinating uncontrollably. Opening the show is Matt as Andy, flying down from the ceiling behind a seemingly oblivious David as Lou. They haven't seen any of these elements in action yet. They have one week of technical rehearsals before the tour kicks off to sort all this out. Is this long enough? Matt and David have no idea.

The interview for *Heat* is the fourth one they've done with me for the magazine. I first met Matt and David six years ago when I was invited to sit with them at the *Broadcast* magazine annual awards ceremony. They had been nominated for Best Non-Terrestrial TV Show for their *Rock Profile* series, which went out on satellite channel UKPlay. I was a journalist for a fairly new magazine. I'd written a few gushing reviews of *Rock Profile* in our publication. Despite its tiny budget and extensive use of pop video clips, I thought it was one of the most exciting comedy programmes on TV. Matt and David created lovingly detailed characters based on rock and pop stars like the Bee Gees, Take That and the Chemical Brothers. Often they wouldn't bother trying to imitate their targets at all, but came up with deliberately inappropriate versions of their subjects. Prince, for example, was given the voice and demeanour of a Scottish vagrant. Most of all, the series was an expression of their fascination with the minutiae of pop culture.

They didn't win the *Broadcast* award. Sky One's football drama *Dream Team* did. When host Jonathan Ross announced the winner with the words, 'And the award goes to a programme which has really excelled on a really tight budget,' Matt and David were getting ready to stand up, because, as David puts it, 'No one worked on a tighter budget than us.' They took the disappointment with good grace, though, and were nice to me, inviting me for a few post-show drinks at the nearby Trader Vic's bar in the Hilton Hotel on Park Lane.

It was Matt who stayed out longer than David that night. He told me about a series of live dates he did of a stage version of Vic and Bob's TV panel game *Shooting Stars*, in which he starred as George Dawes. He confessed that the tour wasn't a particularly pleasant experience. I think he was grateful for the chance to vent. We also talked for a long time about our mutual love of television and Arsenal. We did that thing that football fans always do, testing each other with unsubtle references to obscure old players (Brian Marwood! Gus Caesar!) to check the other person really does properly support the team.

Matt later gave me home-made CDs of the entire radio series of *Little Britain*, long before they were released commercially.

One day, after a set-visit to watch them filming the one-off special *Rock The Blind*, David asked if I wanted to share a cab with him into central London. He was going to the YMCA to do some swimming and work out in the gym. I was heading back to the office. We spent most of the cab journey discussing Caroline Aherne, who David told me was a good friend of his, and who I had met before too. He told me Caroline had mentioned me, and that we should all go for dinner some time. David and I swapped mobile phone numbers and I hopped out of the cab overly excited at the prospect of socialising with David Walliams and Caroline Aherne.

That 25-minute cab journey was the start of my friendship with David. After that, I would see him and Matt at regular intervals: at awards ceremonies, at recordings of their new radio or TV shows, at birthday parties and social events such as a gathering at David's flat to celebrate the premiere of *Little Britain* on BBC3, and yes, David did invite me to have dinner with him and Caroline Aherne.

So I guess the cliché about my relationship with Matt and David is that I'm 'the journalist who knows them best'.

Of course, Matt and David's lives have changed immeasurably since I first met them in 2000. They're now the biggest comedy stars in Britain. Their show is watched in dozens of countries. The last series of *Little Britain* was watched by over ten million people. It was among the five most watched shows of the year. They have sold over 3.5 million DVDs. They're undertaking this epic live tour, performing to 800,000 people. They are recognised instantly wherever they go. And David even has his own regular section in the *Sun*'s Bizarre page.

The 'gay-o-meter' has been running as an occasional item in the *Sun*'s Bizarre gossip column for many months. It monitors moments in David's life, or rather the tabloid coverage of his life, or even more specifically his paparazzi picture appearances, and measures the extent to which his behaviour is 'gay'. It's the most prominent example of the press's fascination with David's undeniably camp demeanour and flamboyant personal style, and his fondness for dating a great many sexy women. 'You have got to keep track of the gay-o-meter in the book,' says David. 'It would be good to know how gay I am from one day to the next.' So every time the gay-o-meter appears, David texts me or calls me. Sometimes David appears in Bizarre even when there's no gay-o-meter, like the day when there was a story claiming that David is secretly writing songs with Robbie Williams. 'Utter bollocks as usual,' was David's reply to my text. Then he added, 'But where's the gay-o-meter? I'm feeling incredibly gay today . . .'

And it turns out there's a peculiar, thoroughly unexpected postscript to the bogus story about David writing songs with Robbie Williams. Matt *has* ended up writing a song with Robbie and his team, but we'll get to that later because no one really knows about it yet.

2

On location

'Oh dear . . . Scottie from *Star Trek* has died.'

Producer Geoff Posner, sitting next to David on the back seat of the car, points out that Scottie was pretty old.

'I know. Well, they all seemed pretty old when they did that first *Star Trek* film,' says David. 'You sat there thinking: why would they let octogenarians fly a spaceship? It's just dangerous. It's like the late Roger Moore James Bond films when you just thought: why are they sending an old man into danger like this?'

David was in bed by 10.30 p.m. but then he read some of his book on Chairman Mao which helped send him to sleep on the nervy night before filming. For years he's had problems sleeping. Last night reading about Mao's Long March seemed to help.

'Chairman Mao just marched thousands of them up and down the country till loads of them were dead,' he explains, 'but he never seemed to have a plan of why they were doing it so he just came up with the name the Long March in the middle of it. "Oh, I think we'll call it the Long March."'

David decides to practise his lines with Geoff. It's the last day of location filming. They run through the Lou and Andy dialogue for a sketch in which they're on a boat on the Thames and Andy disappears from his wheelchair and ends up on waterskis to the back of the boat. David asks how they're going to film it, where the cameras will be and how they're going to edit in the special effect of Matt waterskiing.

We arrive at the location base on the South Bank and walk past some extras on the way to David's trailer. David and Matt had been visited on location the previous day by *The South Bank Show*. Sir Melvyn Bragg filmed an introduction to the documentary they're making about *Little Britain*. But Melvyn himself isn't interviewing them for the show. 'He doesn't take part in all of them,' David explains. 'It does take a little bit of the excitement away from it. You'd like to get Melvyn ideally. But he just interviews the really important people. Like Woody Allen.'

Matt pops in to David's trailer to let him know he's arrived. 'I've just had

Meeting Lord Bragg

my first fry-up breakfast of the whole series,' he says. 'I'm trying to eat slightly healthily.'

David has a good look at him. 'You might have lost a bit of weight actually.'

David asks how the filming went yesterday when Matt had to swim in a huge water tank at Pinewood Studios. It was for the punchline shot of another sketch they're filming today at the aquarium, when Andy ends up swimming with the exotic fish.

'It's just a giant swimming pool really. Very deep,' says Matt, 'but it was quite exciting because it's only been there a few months and not that many people have used it.'

'Was it cold?' asks David.

'No, it was 90 degrees. And I had five or six divers with me, taking me step by step. I had to go quite deep.'

'Were you scared?'

'Yeah, I was to start with. Then I was okay once I was in, because it got very technical. Just trying to get myself in the right position to get the shot they wanted, and position myself in front of the green screen. It took hours, because when I eventually did swim into frame they said, "It's great, but we can't tell it's you." So I had to do it all over again. The other weird thing is that the glasses I wear as Andy are really thick prescription lenses which make my eyes look bigger, so I couldn't see anything down there in the water. They have this sound system so you can hear what they want you to do. I said to Geoff, "Just talk me through it and tell me where to go," so it wasn't much of a performance.'

David says he received a text from his friend David Morrissey who's filming *Basic Instinct 2* at Pinewood Studios. 'You could have popped in to see Sharon Stone,' he says to Matt.

'Well, they told me Sharon Stone had been in the pool just before me.'

'Had she pissed in it?' asks David.

'Errm, I didn't ask. But then I didn't need to.'

'Was she naked?'

'Don't know. You'd assume so.' Matt giggles. As he walks back to his own trailer next door we can hear him still giggling.

David catches sight of a tub of moisturiser. 'Wow,' he says to Lisa. 'I've just seen how expensive that moisturiser is and I'm very pleased.'

'Yes,' says Lisa. 'I thought I'd keep the price tag on so you'd know how much we value your skin.'

Lisa Cavalli-Green has worked with Matt and David since *Sir Bernard's Stately Homes*. The budget for the entire series of *Rock Profile* was smaller than the make-up budget for *Little Britain*. But she still has to fight to get the money she needs for Matt and David's increasingly elaborate ideas.

'They *have* given us more money,' she says. 'Reluctantly.'

'I think they half expect us to wear the same costumes and wigs and wear the same make-up that we were using in series one,' says David. 'But I think if you scrimp on the details then it really shows. We are the ones insisting we shoot a different title sequence for each series. I know it's just packaging, but it does make it seem more of an event. It gets people excited about it.'

He explains they have had similar battles over the wig and costume budget for the tour. They've fought for every hairpiece.

As for the tour experience as a whole, David's preparing himself for the worst.

'It'll be miserable. In a way my life will be on hold. It would be difficult to maintain any relationship, wouldn't it? That's why Matt's so lucky that he's got Kevin. Kevin's going to be with him most of the time, I think, but I won't have anyone . . .' He adopts an exaggerated whine: 'Ohh, baby . . . it'll just be you and me!'

Even though David's been linked to numerous women in recent weeks and months, the truth is that he's not seeing anyone right now, despite his best attempts to woo one person in particular. They've been on dates. They talk on the phone a lot, and text a lot, and have kissed, but that's about it. And David doesn't really know if she wants to take the friendship any further. She's a woman who is also quite famous, so he hasn't decided whether we can mention her name in the book.

'Oh God . . .' he says, continuing the put-on whine, 'when will it end? When will the heartache end?'

I tell him I'll be there to keep him company. He thanks me, then says, 'But I want her . . .'

Presumably she can come to visit him.

'Yeah, I hope she does. I just want to hold her in my arms and kiss her.'

He's joking about it, talking in a series of silly, melodramatic voices, but the wistful look on his face betrays the fact that there's a real longing there too.

What David hasn't worked out yet is how he'll deal with the travelling, the staying in hotels, and what he'll do to fill his days. Among the hardest things for him, since he's become instantly recognisable, are those moments in the day when he's on his own and between appointments and engagements. He used to be able to wander around the shops, browsing the racks of HMV, but now he has to weigh up the likelihood of being stopped by people and having his photograph taken when all he wants to do is just relax and be alone with his thoughts. He's keen to emphasise that he's not complaining. He's just talking about the way it is. Every trip out of his flat is complicated now. Everything's complicated.

'At least on tour I'll have my swimming to keep me occupied.' David likes to swim, more than any other sport or way of keeping fit. 'It's a secret at the moment, but I'm going to attempt to swim the Channel.'

I'm suitably dumbstruck, and not sure if he's joking. When?

'Next year. But I have to start the training regime now, and stick to it more or less every day for the next nine months.' He grins and then laughs at the absurdity of it all.

But why?

'A few weeks ago Matt and I were invited to go to Ethiopia by Comic Relief. We didn't want to be filmed. We just wanted to see what it was like for ourselves so we could talk about it in a genuine way to the press when it came to publicising our Comic Relief DVD. And when we were there we couldn't believe what we were seeing; so much suffering – people living in corrugated iron shacks dying of Aids, orphanages where everyone had been sexually abused or raped, and yet somehow they still had great hope. So we were travelling round with Kevin Cahill, the guy who runs Comic Relief with Richard Curtis, and he turned to me at one point and asked, "Is there something you've always wanted to do but never got round to?" And I said, "Well, I like swimming and I've thought maybe one day I could swim the Channel," and he just went, "Okay, you can do it next year for Sport Relief." Maybe I should have thought of something less extreme and time-consuming . . . but when you're in Ethiopia and you're surrounded by all that, you'll agree to almost anything.'

He gets a piece of paper out of his pocket with a timetable of training sessions on it: go to the gym here, swim a hundred lengths there, that kind of thing. There seems to be something every weekday. And some weekends.

So he'll be getting up in the morning, swimming hundreds of lengths, and then doing the same show again and again for nine months. He admits he has no idea how he's going to deal with it, and ponders the possibility that the whole scheme is insane. It feels like he's only really thinking about the consequences of all this now, as he's saying it out loud. 'It might be a *bit* gruelling,' he laughs. 'But I am looking forward to it as well. Not the training, or the rehearsals or all that, but being on tour itself. Matt and I have been wanting to do that for years. And I hope that we'll get a great response. That'll make it all worthwhile. Although we have to come up with a show first.'

Matt returns, already in his grey Andy sweatpants and bedraggled vest, to get his make-up done, just as David is explaining his hopes for the tour.

'You talking about the tour?' asks Matt. David nods. 'Yeah, it will be the realisation of our dream, won't it?' continues Matt. 'Right from the start, right from when we first came up with *Little Britain*, we knew we wanted to do radio, then TV, then live. That was the dream.'

'There,' says Lisa, inspecting the finished version of Lou, with his bad teeth, pasty face and frizzy hair. 'I've made you look shit.'

'What a lovely *day*!' says Diana, Matt's mum.

'Beautiful,' says David's mother Kathleen. 'It doesn't feel like work, does it?'

'It does to us,' says David, laughing. 'This is the third sketch we've filmed today as Lou and Andy. It gets a bit repetitive.'

Matt nods. 'I just did six or seven Marjorie Dawes routines in two days and by the last one I was really tetchy. I didn't feel funny any more.'

'But people won't notice at all when they watch it on the TV,' points out Matt's mum.

'That's the magic of it!' says David. He smiles at her and asks if she's ready for her big moment. She hopes so, and wonders what she'll look like on camera.

David adopts a quiet, flirtatious voice: 'You'll look beautiful. You always do!' Then he bursts out laughing.

Diana is a surprisingly slight woman; slim, with a noticeably good posture. She's sitting very upright on the bench at the side of the boat, in a smart pale turquoise skirt and matching cardigan.

'Oh you always flirt, David!' she says. 'You're awful!'

'I know,' replies David, sounding incongruously smooth while dressed in his Lou curly wig, glasses, bad teeth and tracksuit bottoms. 'I think it's wonderful that we can express our love for each other like this.'

From the comfort of his Andy wheelchair, Matt watches David joking with his mum and giggles uncontrollably.

We're on the boat sailing up and down the Thames while the Lou and Andy sketch is being filmed. It's now a brilliant midsummer's afternoon. A lot of extras are needed to make the boat look like it's full of tourists, so Matt and David have invited their families to star as background artists. Along with their mums, David's dad Peter and his sister Julie are here.

As Matt and David are taken away for another take, their mothers study them closely. Diana asks Kathleen if she'll be going to all the studio recordings next month. Kathleen says David will let her know which ones are likely to be the most enjoyable ones to attend, and she'll probably go to one or two of them. 'Not that any of them won't be enjoyable,' she points out quickly, 'but you know what I mean. Some will be more interesting than others.'

'Oh *yes*,' says Diana. 'Well, we won't be going to all of them. I think Matt was saying that the very last one would be nice to see, because there'll be a little party afterwards too.'

It's as if the mums are making sure that they're being equally supportive.

We're all told to be quiet, before 'Action!' is yelled, the boat starts speeding up the river and the cameras roll. Diana points enthusiastically at the Houses of Parliament, like a real tourist would. Kathleen chats to her husband slightly more vividly than she would if no one was filming.

We can't hear the dialogue that Matt and David as Lou and Andy are saying to each other, but it lasts about thirty seconds and that's that. Cut.

Matt's mum asks me: 'So what kind of book are you writing?' I tell her it's going to be a kind of fly-on-the-wall documentary of a year in their lives. 'I'll be hoping to interview you about Matt's life at some point, if that's all right with you.'

'Ooh really? How *exciting*!' she says, adding great emphasis to the last word, much in the way that Marjorie Dawes would. There's more than a passing resemblance between Diana and Marjorie, not physically, but in their expressions and way of speaking. Diana can get very high-pitched. She seems like Marjorie with all the bitter and twisted elements removed. She says she'll help out with the book in any way she can, and tries to think of some funny stories about Matt. Funny stories would be good, I tell her. And just as the similarities between her and Marjorie are ebbing away slightly, she asks me if I know that she really did take Matt to Weight Watchers when he was a teenager. Matt had mentioned it before. 'Oh yes,' says Diana, 'it's all my fault. But he did start getting heavily overweight. Unfortunately there's a history of obesity in the family, on his paternal grandfather's side.' She

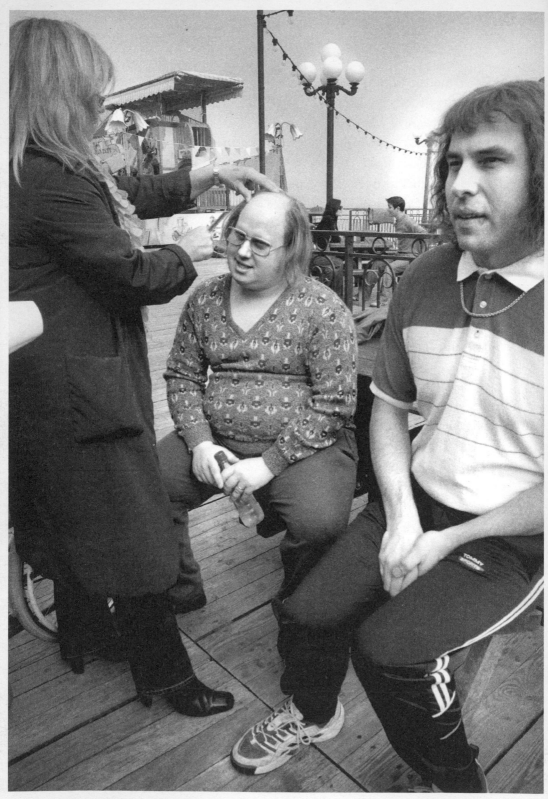

Lou and Andy on location

studies Matt in his distinctly unflattering Andy Pipkin vest. 'Believe it or not, he did very well at Weight Watchers. He took it very seriously and lost a lot of weight.' A pause. 'It's all back on now though!'

Diana wonders if Kathleen will have lots of stories about David.

'I'm sure I can come up with lots of stories,' says David's mum. 'I'm not sure if he'd want me to tell them though!'

David's sister Julie, who very much resembles her mother – both rather jolly, possibly even cheeky, imposing blonde ladies, while David vaguely resembles his toothier father – chimes in and tells me she'll have plenty of embarrassing tales of David's youth to relate, if her mum isn't willing. Like the time David fell in the pool.

'Have you ever seen David swimming?' Julie asks me. 'He's a brilliant swimmer. Has been since school. But when he was about six, and he was riding around our friend's pool on his trike, he just skidded and cycled into the pool.'

'For a while he was just lying there in the pool,' says his mum. 'But I knew he'd be okay because he had his armbands on. In case you think I was a completely heartless mother!'

'But we just thought, oh he's just making a fuss,' laughs Julie. 'We knew he was fine. And there was the other time when we thought he was whining about being hurt. I'd pushed him over onto some rubble and he was crying his eyes out about it, and we all just thought, oh that's David exaggerating as usual. But after the accident in the pool he just carried on crying and claiming he was in pain. And it was days before we eventually took him to the doctor. They X-rayed him and it was only then we realised he'd broken his collarbone.'

David's mum was so mortified she bought him a Matchbox Kojak car.

Later on I mention this story to David. 'Oh yes,' he says, 'and did they tell that story of me falling in the pool as if it was some kind of amusing anecdote?'

Yes. Kind of.

'And did they tell you I'd broken my collarbone?' he says, sipping from a glass of champagne as the boat sails up the Thames and everyone around us – the cast and crew, and extras and family members – enjoy the delights of the wrap party. But I can't work out if his tone is mock indignation or serious indignation. Possibly a bit of both. 'It was really quite distressing,' he adds. 'They just left me there at the bottom of the pool. What does that say?'

The series isn't actually fully wrapped yet because there's all the studio filming to come next month, when they perform six nights of sketches in front of a studio audience at BBC TV Centre. But not all of the location crew will be working on the studio sessions, so Geoff Posner, the series producer, makes a speech thanking everyone for their hard work.

Matt's mum is quaffing champagne and talking about how far Matt and David have come. She remembers seeing their first show together in Edinburgh, which she found shockingly rude. And she supported Matt when he did his first shows as Sir Bernard Chumley, even though she was never very fond of the character. 'Even the TV thing,' she says, '*Sir Bernard's Stately Homes*... I thought was pretty terrible.'

1990

They had seen each other around the place but never met. Then, one evening, as they stood near each other in the doorway of the halls of residence bar, they were introduced by mutual friends. As they shook hands and came face to face for the first time, Matt did his Jimmy Savile, and David camped it up as Frankie Howerd. And that was it. They made each other laugh.

Matt was sixteen, David nineteen. They had both made it to the National Youth Theatre, based in Tufnell Park, north London. The surroundings were drab and functional but the atmosphere was giddy: teenagers away from home, mingling in acting workshops, inevitably having sexual encounters with each other. Except for Matt and David. Who did impressions.

David had noticed Matt before he ever met him, and remembered him mainly because of his bald head. Then someone said to him, 'Oh you've got to meet Matt. He's really funny, with his impressions and stuff,' and David thought, 'I bet he's not that funny, I bet he's just bald and you've mistaken that for funniness.'

As soon as Matt saw David, he was slightly in awe of him. He was only three years older, but at that age three years seems like everything, and Matt felt like a teenager still, whereas David was a grown-up, and quite a glamorous one at that. David would always be smartly dressed, almost foppish. Even then.

Matt would see David around the halls of residence and go up to him and say, 'Go on, do your Frankie Howerd!' and David would sigh, and only half-reluctantly unleash his inner Frankie Howerd. Soon after they had started showing each other their special impressions, Matt saw a dress rehearsal of

Mash and Peas, one of Matt and David's early incarnations as a double act, 1996

the production of *Surrender Dorothy*, in which David turned into a werewolf. He thought David was brilliant.

Matt had acted in school productions, but joining the National Youth Theatre was a big step up. This was a chance to mingle with proper fledgling actors and be among people who, like him, just wanted to perform, and amuse and entertain. Matt had just started, and like all first years at the NYT, was doing an acting course. After taking that course he would be allowed to audition for roles in productions the following year. But David was already a young star of the National Youth Theatre. In the autumn he would be back at Bristol University where he was studying in the respected Drama Department.

They bumped into each other again later that year at a National Youth Theatre production of a play called *Once A Catholic* at the Bloomsbury Theatre, by which time David had unusually long hair, so Matt noticed him from afar and took the opportunity to say hello. David greeted him with a mock superior 'Oh, and who are *you* then?' response.

A year later, back at the NYT halls of residence, Matt and David saw a lot more of each other. David had another big role in an avant garde production of *The Tempest*, partly inspired by Lindsay Kemp and partly by Japanese kabuki. Matt was one of a group of 'kouken' working backstage, all dressed completely in black with black masks against a black backdrop, known as black box theatre.

The director insisted on giving Matt – along with the rest of his backstage colleagues – a hard time. Matt began to think the director was acting like a despot, and he felt that he was encouraging the rest of the company to treat the behind-the-scenes team with contempt. David thought it was wrong that such an obviously talented boy as Matt was only being given a backstage role.

Whatever David did was regarded with great excitement by everyone. One time backstage he set fire to some cotton wool on his foot and ran manically round the dressing room, milking the slapstick scene of his foot being on fire for all it was worth.

Matt thought David was hysterically funny. They bonded over comedy. During lunch breaks they'd watch videos of Vic and Bob, who were just becoming big TV stars. They were both gleefully enthusiastic about television comedy shows past and present. Both had a hunger for anything they thought might be funny. One day they discovered their mutual fondness for *Monty Python*, and through that they found *Ripping Yarns*. And they devoured it.

Matt, thespian, aged thirteen

They studied it all, the bits they liked and the bits they didn't, and tried to figure out how it all worked.

More than that, they used comedy to make each other happy. David knew the director was giving Matt a tough time, so they'd take the piss out of him together.

In the middle of the run of *The Tempest*, Matt took the opportunity to tell David about this comedy character he'd come up with, called Sir Bernard Chumley, and he went as far as to say that one day he'd like to pluck up the courage to stand up and perform as Sir Bernard in front of an audience. Instead of laughing at the notion, David encouraged it.

At the end of the play's run, they swapped addresses and numbers, and Matt was thrilled. He had no doubt that David was going to be the biggest comedian in the country, and he'd become his friend. He'd exchanged numbers with this guy he knew was going to be a huge, huge comedy star, and one day Matt would be able to tell people that he had been in a play with David Walliams. In fact, Matt didn't expect David to contact him. He thought it would be a fleeting friendship, one he'd look back on in years to come when David became famous.

But one day, about two or three weeks later when he was back home, suffering from flu, Matt went downstairs to check his mail and found a postcard from David. To Matt, it seemed so nice of David to remember him and to go out of his way to keep in touch.

Their friendship was cemented when Matt himself arrived at Bristol University's Drama Department. Matt was already interested in applying to Bristol to do his degree, because, just like David had been advised a few years earlier, he had been told that it was a great place for an adventurous young aspiring performer to study. And David went out of his way to encourage Matt, and told him all about life in the Drama Department, who the good lecturers were and which courses to take.

When Matt arrived at Bristol, David sent him a survival pack, which had vegetarian sausage powder mix in it. Matt was touched. It felt like David was going out of his way to look after him.

Soon they started socialising. They went to *Top of the Pops* together to see the Pet Shop Boys singing 'Liberation'. They saw the original theatre production of Jonathan Harvey's *Beautiful Thing*, which helped inspire Matt to come out. They went to see a film called *Totally Fucked Up* by American Indie director Gregg Araki at the Everyman Cinema in Hampstead.

Then one night they were due to meet each other at a comedy club called Punchlines, but on the way there Matt was knocked down by a car. Matt was sent flying, but just about made it to the venue. David found him sitting in the bar, in a daze, drinking a brandy, and insisted on taking him to hospital where he stayed with him all night. Matt was concussed.

Once again David was looking after Matt.

Eventually Matt's mum turned up to take him home. It was the first time she'd met David, and wondered who this lovely young man was who had been so kind and caring to her son.

3

Four weeks to go

David's been sent a package. In it is a set of *Are You Being Served?* DVDs signed by John Inman, a cuddly donkey, chocolates and a *Doctor Who* book focusing on the Daleks.

They're from a female fan who has written an accompanying in-depth letter expressing her love for him, and she has clearly spent a good deal of time researching David's likes. He was brought up on *Are You Being Served?*, and is fascinated by John Inman's story. And he loves *Doctor Who*, and would quite like to be Doctor Who. One day. The chocolates and the donkey are random extras.

'It's a bit scary,' he says, pondering the fan's level of devotion while tucking into the chocolates. The BBC TV Centre dressing room is surprisingly large and luxurious, like something out of a boutique hotel.

The Sunday papers are scattered over the dressing-room sofa. David asks if I've seen the story about an *EastEnders* actor supposedly engaging in lewd conduct in car parks. Or, as the paper put it, he's a 'dogging pervert'. David feels sorry for him. He isn't harming anyone. But he feels even more sorry for the parents.

'You just don't want them to read that kind of stuff,' he explains. 'Even if there was one of those silly kiss-and-tell stories where the girl goes on about how big it is and how she was truly satisfied and all that, you still don't want your mum and dad to have seen that.'

Do you worry about a girl selling a kiss-and-tell story about you to the papers?

'Well, part of me would be mortified. But I don't think it's worth worrying about it too much. You can't stop living your life because of the papers. It's like Robbie knows that any woman he sleeps with might well end up selling the story, but what harm can it do these days? Oh, so he meets women and has sex with them and sometimes that's that. Well, again, it's not illegal, and he's not hurting anyone.'

He thinks the papers are living in a fantasy world where everyone is in perfect monogamous happy heterosexual relationships. It's as if journalists assume that everyone in the country is having normal sex apart from these famous people who are having bad, perverse sex.

David puts 'Everyday Is Like Sunday' on his iPod. He stands up, sways around to the song and then embarks upon an impromptu, full-on, elaborate and ultra-camp dance. Then he stops, gathers his breath and tells me he's had his own legal issues with a newspaper.

'They said I'd had sex with some porn star and it wasn't true, so I pursued it, and so far I've had three legal bills, one for £2,000, one for £5,000 and one for £10,000. It's quite a lot, isn't it? So God knows what it's like if you go to court. And they're asking me if I'd like to go to court, but I'm like, no, it just isn't worth it, because no one even remembers the original article anyway.'

David flicks to a story in the paper claiming that he's bought Supernova Heights. He points out that the house in north London hasn't been called Supernova Heights for many years, not since Noel Gallagher lived there in fact. 'I have bought it,' he confirms. 'I want to call it Superduper Heights. But I'm doing it up completely. It'll be a lot of work. I won't be able to move in till next year, after the tour.'

His only worry is that it's so big he might get lonely. He's thinking of getting a friend to live with him, in the absence of a wife. But he needs them to be tidy.

You could get a cleaner.

'Yeah, or I could get my mum to do it. She still does my washing. Well, some of it. *The South Bank Show* were filming me at my parents' house the other day and I did what I always do, which is give her some of my best shirts to clean and press. I don't trust anyone else to do it. Roz from *The South Bank Show* said they'd go back and film my mum when she'd finished the shirts to check how good they were.'

After they introduce themselves to the audience for this last studio recording of series three, Matt and David invite Matt's mum to stand up and take a bow. Matt says, 'I had a disturbed childhood and no friends so she's done a great job! Give her a round of applause!'

'I tell you he's a lucky boy – he's got no cellulite on that bottom,' observes Ruth in her deep Welsh accent.

David says, 'Yeah, he's got cellulite.'

'No, Matt *hasn't* got any cellulite on that bottom,' clarifies Ruth.

'Really? Are you sure? It's big though!'

'Yes, but I can't get over the fact there's no cellulite.'

'He's very lucky like that.'

'Very lucky!'

Ruth Madoc, veteran actress most famous for her role in the 1980s sitcom *Hi-De-Hi*, is in tonight reprising her role as Dafydd's mum. She is what actors like to call a real pro: disarmingly friendly, jolly and totally lacking in pomposity. It's as if she has no idea she's remotely famous. She's sitting in the dressing room with David, watching Matt filming a Dafydd sketch on the TV screen on the wall. Matt's wearing a spectacularly revealing thong-style outfit which displays most of his buttocks.

She watches Matt act out a scene in which he's become a rent boy and comments that, even though the characters are all very funny, none of them are over-the-top. 'It's very naturalistic . . . the acting. Don't you think?'

Very different from her glory days of *Hi-De-Hi*?

'Oh yes,' Ruth says. 'We were encouraged to go very big. I don't think we even thought about keeping it natural at all!'

David joins Matt on the studio floor to thank the audience for coming.

Matt: 'That was our last studio recording for this series. You may have read rumours that *Little Britain* is coming to an end, but that's not true. We are doing a Christmas Special next year . . . Now we'd like to thank everyone who worked on the series. We can't thank them all by name but . . .'

Shooting *Little Britain* series three, 2005

David: 'We'd like to thank the actors, the make-up people, the costume design – the whole crew. We've been supported by an amazing team. And we'd like to thank you for supporting us and coming along and laughing.'

Matt: 'Yeah, we really appreciate it. And we'll be on tour later in the year so come and see us! Thanks so much. Bye!'

Rapturous applause. Standing ovation.

Back in the dressing room, Matt says, 'It's funny watching the sketches that they don't like . . . There seemed to be quite a few that didn't get many laughs.'

'Yeah, it's difficult when people don't laugh to know why they're not laughing,' says David. 'You can't ask them all individually – 500 people – why they don't laugh. You want to know: was it that you didn't understand it, or was it that you just didn't find it funny?'

1990s

It seemed inevitable. Like it was the natural thing for them to do. Matt and David were hanging out together in the summer of 1994 having a drink in the Gilded Balloon bar in Edinburgh and they both just knew that they should start working together. It almost didn't need to be said, because having got to know each other, become friends and bonded over their impressions and love of TV comedy and disdain for the pretentious theatrical types they encountered at the National Youth Theatre and then at the Bristol University Drama Department, it seemed like the obvious thing to do: form a comedy partnership and come up with a show to put on at the following year's Edinburgh Fringe.

They'd gone to Edinburgh together and seen acts like Armstrong & Miller and Parsons & Naylor and they thought: we could do this. What 'this' meant was play a room of one hundred people doing a 55-minute show.

To Matt and David that was the dream: to get their own show on in Edinburgh, and have one hundred people come to see them on a Saturday night. The idea of it seemed amazing.

They had both gained a certain amount of experience by that time, performing comedy to small audiences.

David formed his first comedy partnership with his friend Jason Bradbury when they were still students at Bristol University. They called themselves Bunce and Burner – David Bunce and Raleigh Burner. Their act was part Fry and Laurie and part Reeves and Mortimer. Their material was fairly surreal but delivered in quite a twee way. In fact it was, by David's own admission, quite wanky. They'd refer to Jean-Luc Godard films and Baudrillard. Quite different to the material they'd see regular stand-up comedians perform. David knew, though, that he didn't want to just be a stand-up. He was more interested in performers like Harry Hill, who did a daft act. But it was hard to please audiences doing characters in a stand-up context, because it seemed they were watching acting. They just wanted to be chatted to about normal things in life like sex and smoking dope and having the munchies.

Matt, though, thought they were wonderful. And he thought maybe he could try his hand on the stand-up circuit too. He had already created his own character: Sir Bernard Chumley.

Matt came up with Sir Bernard after he'd seen Harry Enfield's one-off comedy *Norbert Smith: A Life*. Matt used to walk round the playground at school with a Walkman on, listening to the mono tape recordings he'd made of comedy programmes by connecting his tape recorder to the television. He'd stroll around and memorise dialogue from *Saturday Night Live* and Jasper Carrott and Harry Enfield. He was particularly obsessed with Enfield's creations, and when he listened repeatedly to the theatrical spoof *Norbert Smith*, Matt seized upon a character in it called Sir Donald Stuffy, reminiscent of a real old-school grandiose thespian like Donald Sinden. He was the inspiration for Sir Bernard Chumley.

His brother came up with the name. He used to go to a record shop in Camden called Popbeat, and the guy who worked there had a quirky manner and was called Bernard. Matt's brother invented the surname 'Chumley' for him because he'd read about an eccentric character called Sir Soloman Cholmondely (pronounced Chumley) in an Evelyn Waugh novel and he thought it somehow suited him. Matt adopted the name Sir Bernard Chumley for his ageing actor character and performed it at an audition to get into the National Youth Theatre production of *The Tempest*.

Matt went to see David and Jason do a show at the Comedy Café on Rivington Street in London, and there was a spare spot on the bill so Matt put himself forward. But he hadn't really written a whole routine for Sir Bernard Chumley yet, so it was a bit haphazard and unfocused. What Matt didn't expect was booing. A joke about Sir Bernard having a curry was misinterpreted by the Comedy Café crowd as racist. But before and after the boos, Sir Bernard got a small smattering of laughs too, and that was enough for Matt. He believed he could turn his act into a viable routine for the circuit.

He joined a stand-up comedy course in Archway, north London, run by Ivor Dembina. Among his fellow students were a posh and engaging guy called Louis Mortier, a glam Jewish housewife from Ilford called Pamela Phillips who did a routine which climaxed with the phrase 'and then I got raped', and the funniest person in the group – a bloke who could do funny voices and whose skills annoyed Matt because he made him feel inferior. His name was Paul Putner. Paul and Matt became good friends.

By now, Bunce and Burner had drifted apart. In the end, David felt his act with Jason wasn't going anywhere. They didn't really know who they were and what they were doing.

After taking the comedy course, Matt booked a gig at the Punchlines club in London for 3 October 1992. It would be his first proper stint as a comedian in front of a paying audience.

Matt was so excited when he walked onstage that he proceeded to run around and get out of breath before he even spoke. He also managed to break a cardinal rule of the stand-up comedy world. He took the piss out of one of his fellow performers. Dave Thompson, who later found fame as Tinky Winky on the Teletubbies, was the object of Matt's cheeky bid to get a cheap laugh. And as soon as he'd done it, Matt knew he'd done something awful. Dave said to him, 'How dare you? You never undermine another comic. Never.' Matt was mortified by his own behaviour. But he was only an eighteen-year-old. He made a mistake during his first gig and he'd been taught a lesson. Thompson graciously forgave Matt when he appeared on the same bill as him again the following evening.

Matt booked himself to do two more gigs – one at the VD ('Val Doonican') Clinic in Belsize Park on the Sunday, and then a spot the following Thursday at the Comedy Store. That was his plan. He thought everyone would say he was wonderful and that would be his way to comedy stardom. But after the Sunday gig still felt all over place and unfinished, he postponed the Comedy Store one by six weeks.

But the gigs were starting to go well. He'd come on as Sir Bernard and tell a long anecdote set at a party where the guests included Sir Jimmy Savile (cue impression) and Jim Bowen (cue another impression) about his arse exploding and his shit landing everywhere: 'There was shit on the ceiling, dump on the dining table, poo on the porcelain, and I turned to Felicity Kendal and I said, "Felicity, you've grown a moustache," but she hadn't . . . she just had some poo on her upper lip.'

Matt would also arrive at each venue wearing the wig his parents tried to get him to wear as a child when he lost his hair. Towards the end of Sir Bernard's routine, he would scratch his head so the wig would topple off, and there would be a gasp from the audience.

He didn't have good jokes. His impressions were out of date. But he had this wig, and everyone would remember the sight of Matt scratching it and revealing his baldness . . .

Matt had achieved his ambition, to secure a paid 20-minute set. He was a professional comedian.

Five weeks into Matt's stand-up career, Bob Mortimer was in the audience one night for Matt's set, and was so impressed he asked Matt to come and work with himself and Vic Reeves. He was already being given the chance to appear on TV and be funny.

4

10 October 2005 – 2 weeks to go

David answers the door naked apart from a towel wrapped round his waist. 'Just in time!' he says. 'I've just come out of the shower.'

It's 6.30 a.m. Matt and David have got a hectic day ahead. They're doing a live interview on the Radio 1 *Breakfast Show* at 7.45 a.m. to promote their new DVD. Then it's straight on to Madame Tussauds for the official unveiling of the waxworks models of Matt and David as Lou and Andy, where they'll do a photo shoot for the next day's papers. After that David is going swimming. The afternoon is set aside to rehearse for the live show, before they're due at the *Daily Mirror* Pride of Britain Awards where they're presenting an award to a woman who saved someone's life when they were about to be stabbed to death. She happens to be a huge *Little Britain* fan.

While he gets dressed, David lets me rifle through his fan mail. He lets it build up into a fairly hefty pile then goes through it all and sends replies – to everyone. The letters aren't what I expected. A lot of them are from women expressing how much they fancy David. One such offering goes on for twelve pages and has been written in various different colours of ink over a period of weeks. It relentlessly refers to the sexual feelings she has for David, including imagining seeing pictures of him in white briefs in a state of arousal. The letters often include photos. I notice a snap of David with a fan. It's been included in a letter from the fan's sister who politely asks David to ponder the picture and realise that he could have a fulfilling relationship with her. She is, after all, of 'medium build, with no kids, husband or baggage'. 'Next time you're in the north-west,' suggests the writer, 'why not give her a call and have dinner with her?' Her number is written on the back of the photo. Another woman has had a card made with a screen-grab of David's bottom reproduced within a red heart, with the words 'Scrumptious Botty' printed in large pink letters. Inside the card is a poem, also printed in pink, in which the woman's fantasies about having sex with David are vividly described in rhyming couplets ('I'd rip off your pants in a sexual frenzy . . . you can have me how you want, I'm ever so bendy'). There's also a closely typed letter in the same envelope, in which the writer explains that she hasn't eaten, drunk, slept or 'done toilet' for three days ever since she saw the picture of David's bottom.

Then there are the sad letters. There is one from a woman who talks about how her fondness for David has helped her with her self-harm and depression issues. Another explains that she's recovering from a relationship with a Ricky Martin lookalike who turned out to be a gambler and womaniser and who left her when their son was two weeks old. She plans to have plastic surgery, though she looks perfectly healthy and nice in the photo she's included, which also shows her sweet-looking son, now four years old. She thanks David for coming up with a TV show that she can watch with her son. Another mother writes to explain that her son has autism and that they're about to be thrown out of their home because she can't pay the rent, and she asks, in a roundabout way, if there's any way David can help them out. A 21-year-old bloke has sent a letter outlining his problems with depression, anxiety, panic attacks and lack of sleep. He says that he's a huge fan of Matt and David and that a signed photo of them would make him smile even though he doesn't have much to smile about. It's only in the third paragraph of his letter that he mentions how he tried to commit suicide two weeks previously by taking all his medication pills.

Does every famous person get letters like these?

'I don't know. You just have to try not to take it too personally – they could be writing to any famous person. I think it could drive you mad. Or at least make you very depressed, if you let it get to you. You've got to be nice to them, to reply to them obviously, but you've got to be careful not to get too close otherwise it'll take over your whole life . . .'

In the car on the way to Radio 1, David looks through the papers. Kate Moss is on the front page of the *Mirror*, as they spin out her cocaine story for the third week. David wonders if they keep sticking with this story just so they can print pictures of her looking gorgeous. There's a diagram in the paper showing the links between the 'Primrose Hill set' – Jude Law, Sadie Frost, Sienna Miller, Kate and so on.

'Well, they were married, and so were they,' he says, surveying the links. 'It's not like they've all been swapping partners really. Is it so debauched?'

I ask David if he's prepared for tonight's Pride of Britain Awards.

'I made sure I had a tape of last year's ceremony,' he explains. 'I've never watched it and I wanted to know how it works. It would be awful to come on and misjudge it. You wonder, are we supposed to make a joke or are we just meant to be serious for the whole thing?'

So what are you going to do?

'Because the woman is a *Little Britain* fan, I think that means we should do a few of the voices for her. We just have to make sure we're catering the whole thing to her.'

David catches sight of a man running down the street in sweatpants with a rucksack on his back and a baseball cap on his head.

'You'll never ever see me,' he announces rather dramatically, 'running and carrying a heavy weight on my back. It's not a look I'm ever going to go for . . .'

When we arrive at the Radio 1 building, Louise, the publicist for the company that distributes the *Little Britain* DVD, is waiting. 'Are we all set for the DVD release?' he asks her in an exaggerated tone of excitement. 'What's number one in the DVD chart at the moment? Max and Paddy?'

She's not quite sure what number one is, but does seem quite certain that *Little Britain Series Two* will be at the top of the chart in a week's time.

Just then we catch sight of Matt getting out of his car.

Matt says good morning to all of us and asks if he's late. He's not.

David asks him how his charity gig went last night. Matt, in Marjorie Dawes guise, hosted an auction at a gala for the National Youth Music Theatre, which he belonged to himself as a teenager. Prince Edward is a patron and was there last night, so Matt asked how his mum was.

'Could you see him from the stage?' asks David.

'No, sadly. I couldn't really tell if he was laughing . . . But there was one item I auctioned which was such a treat: tickets to see Amy Nuttall, Christopher Cazenove, Russ Abbot and Julia McKenzie in *My Fair Lady* in Manchester, and you'd get to have cream tea with the stars beforehand. So I was saying, "C'mon, there are middle-class children who need your money."'

David asks if there were many people there he recognised from his time at the National Youth Music Theatre.

'Yes there were. I met people I acted with eighteen years ago when I was thirteen and hadn't seen since. It was quite weird.'

'And what were they like?'

'Well, there was one guy who was like the real star of the company and I know he went into it professionally but it just didn't work out and now he's a market researcher . . . with grey hair . . . it just didn't work out for him.'

'Like me!' says David.

Matt laughs, then says, quite seriously, 'Yeah. It was just weird. It's like all the big stars who were the kids on the posters and who had the right look haven't ended up with the success they wanted.'

A member of the *Breakfast Show* team comes to escort us down to the studio, and reminds them that it's Scott Mills hosting the show this morning instead of Chris Moyles.

'WHAT? Scott Mills?' says David, virtually yelling. He's joking, but the Radio 1 lad looks momentarily terrified.

When they take their places opposite Scott in the studio, Matt immediately says, 'What a pleasure it is not to have to sit here opposite that beery bear Chris Moyles.'

'I always flirt with him outrageously,' says David. 'Is there going to be any flirting today?'

Mills seems momentarily disconcerted. 'We'll just have to see . . .' he says, before moving on. David looks very pleased with this reaction.

On air, Scott plucks up the courage to ask David about the coverage of his private life in the press. Is he, as the papers constantly portray him, a bit of a ladies' man?

'I've just got lots of friends who are girls,' answers David. 'And I'm a bit of an enigma . . . like Cliff Richard.'

Scott asks if blokes feel they have to keep their girlfriends away from David.

Now David's a bit taken aback. 'What, like I'm some kind of predatory animal? No, I don't think so . . . I just have lots of friends who are girls, and people assume I'm going out with them, but usually I'm not. Like Denise Van Outen is one of my friends, but we just stay in and watch *X Factor* together, and we've never been boyfriend and girlfriend.'

Matt grabs hold of the *The X Factor* opportunity and runs with it, discussing his views on the main contenders and providing some relief from the topic of David's private life.

Then Scott goes to the listeners who've called in with questions. The first is a woman from Birmingham who, along with some friends, is staging a pantomime next month entirely using *Little Britain* characters. She's inviting Matt and David to come and see it if they have the time.

Matt tells her that they'd love to but they're going on tour and so it's unlikely they'll make it to the show. David just laughs.

The next caller is a bloke from Wales asking them if they realise that the official sign welcoming people to Llanddewi-Brefi keeps getting stolen. David asks him if he's from Llanddewi-Brefi. He isn't. He's just Welsh. Matt says it's a shame people keep stealing the sign and they should stop. David says the weird thing is that they just looked at a map of Wales and chose the name of the village at random, and now they've ruined the people of Llanddewi-Brefi's lives.

'We can only say sorry.'

In the car on the way to Madame Tussauds, Matt asks David what the plan is for the Pride of Britain event. David says that it's taking place at the LWT studios on the South Bank and that they won't be seated at tables or anything, they'll just be waiting backstage. There'll be a clip about Julia O'Connor, the woman whose award for Outstanding Act of Bravery they are presenting, and then Carol Vorderman will usher them on to give the award to her.

They talk about what to say.

'I think we just gear it towards the winner of the award,' says David. 'Maybe ask her who her favourite characters are or something, and do the voices . . .'

Matt's partner Kevin is waiting outside Madame Tussauds, and a slightly camp man in a suit is standing next to him to welcome Matt and David and escort us all into a room that feels like a boardroom, with a long table and chairs all round it. On the table are pastries, muffins and cakes, bottles of champagne, flasks of coffee and tea and fresh juices.

The camp Tussauds man asks if Matt and David would like to come and see the waxwork models of Lou and Andy.

When he claps eyes on the likeness of himself as Andy in the wheelchair with a lopsided droop at the corner of his mouth, Matt just cackles. And laughs. And cackles a bit more. It not only looks exactly like Matt as Andy, but it's got a creepily life-like quality.

'If you just glanced at it,' says David, 'without really taking in the fact that he's not moving, you'd totally assume it was Matt.'

David's likeness is pretty spot-on too, but it doesn't quite seem as disorientatingly human as Matt's.

The team who made the waxworks are on hand to meet Matt and David, and to make some last-minute adjustments to the hair and make-up and make sure the costumes are hanging correctly.

Matt and David take turns to shake their hands.

'They really are brilliant,' says David.

Back in the room with the muffins and champagne, I ask what they're going to put on their riders for the tour.

'I've asked for bubble wrap. I love it,' says Matt. 'And some M&S melon medleys would be nice. What would you like, David?'

'I don't know. Who gets it? The venue?'

'Yeah, I think so. It's paid for by the venue as a kind of courtesy thing. On the first Vic and Bob tour they had pork pies . . .'

When most acts go on tour, part of the whole deal is an elaborate rider of some kind: a list of items – usually luxury food or drink orders, but sometimes more esoteric demands like a certain item of furniture or an obscure make of scented candle – which has to be ready for them in their dressing room in each venue before the start of each show.

They haven't put much thought into their rider yet.

BC and Moira are back from seeing the waxworks. 'They're creepy!' they say.

Matt's family is here. Diana asks David how his mum is. She tells him she sent her a nice picture of Matt and David in return for a nice picture Kathleen sent to her.

'I'm sure it's very much appreciated,' says David. He gives her a broad smile. 'The mums – you're getting your own spin-off, aren't you?'

Matt's mum laughs. 'It's such a beautiful day,' she says. 'It's a shame we all have to go back to work . . .'

'Well, why do we?' says David. 'Why don't you and I go off together somewhere?'

'Oooh, that would be lovely, David. But you've got work to do. And so have I!'

BC, Moira, Matt and David discuss the promotional events they've got coming up. David asks what time the *Parkinson* recording starts on Thursday. Moira tells him 6 p.m., and that it should be over by eight.

'How weird,' says David. 'Six o'clock seems like a very early start, doesn't it? It feels like a show that should be late-night and erudite. Maybe it's Parky getting old . . .' and he slips into his Parkinson impression: 'Oh yes, it's eight o'clock, I need to go to bed.'

I get a call from David later that night. He and Matt have met the Prime Minister, at the Pride of Britain Awards.

'As soon as we arrived this man came up to us and said Tony Blair would like to meet us. We went ooh! We were quite excited. So we meet him and he does seem to have a big knowledge of our stuff. He even mentions *Rock Profile*. He says, "I remember seeing you on the rock show." He explained that it was his children who are big fans, but that he likes our stuff himself, and I suppose they are of the kind of age who would watch. So he was being very nice and then the photographer came over and I just thought: I've got to do something . . . memorable. We were talking about the show and I said, "Ooh, do you recognise yourself in there anywhere?" He said, "Maybe, but I don't have a camp aide any more . . ." Then the photo was about to be taken so I draped myself over him, and when it was finished Matt says, "You just flirted with the Prime Minister."'

And did he flinch when you put your arm round him?

'No, he was fine. Even when I touched his arse.'

1995

Ten people showed up. In an Edinburgh venue that had 200 seats. Four of the audience phoned the venue beforehand to ask them to delay the start of the show so they could finish watching *EastEnders*. They then decided to play a smaller room with 120 seats packed in on three sides round the stage area, so it felt like the audience was more intimately connected to the show.

The show itself was formless and ramshackle, a bit of an out-of-control mess. But it was a still a big step for Matt and David: at least they'd created a show. They came onstage at midnight and went off at 1 a.m. and something happened in between. That was an exciting achievement for them.

But in addition to Matt and David's midnight show, Matt had agreed to perform in a one-off special show at the Edinburgh Playhouse in the middle of the festival. Addison Cresswell, Jonathan Ross's agent, organised it. Mark Lamarr hosted it, Vic and Bob headlined it, and also on the bill were Sean Locke, Charlie Chuck, and Matt. Harry Hill was supposed to be in the show but couldn't make it at the last minute. The gig was due to start at 11.15 p.m. at the Playhouse, and Matt was also supposed to be doing his show with David at midnight. So the plan was for Matt to go on first at the Playhouse and then dash off in a car waiting to take him to the Assembly Rooms. If he ended up being a few minutes late then so be it, their show would be slightly delayed. He was thrilled to be getting £250 to do the Playhouse gig.

Matt got to the venue and was told that there were sound problems. None of the mics were working, and the venue needed to be tidied up. At 11.40 p.m. nothing was working, so he decided to go do his show with David and then come back to the Playhouse, where he would be fitted into the show whenever it would work. His performance with David didn't go well because Matt was edgy, knowing he had to go back and perform to 3,000 people.

The Playhouse show started an hour and fifteen minutes late, during which time the audience had to wait out in the street. They were understandably pissed off and rowdy. Mark Lamarr dealt with the hecklers very well, but Vic and Bob started to trim their segment down. Matt arrived at the venue out of breath at 1.30 a.m. Addison said, 'You're all right, you've got forty-five minutes. You're fine. Chill. Relax. The audience is a bit lairy but it'll be fine.' Matt thought: Oh, I've got to go on at quarter past two. Not great – but he resigned himself to it.

He was sitting there in the dressing room, just getting his breath back, when he felt a tap on the back, and was told, 'You're on!' He assumed they'd made a mistake. Then he heard the announcer say, 'And now Sir Bernard Chumley!' And he just had to go on.

So he went out there, grabbed the hand-held mic, and he thought: fuck it, this is my moment. So he did his well-rehearsed Sir Bernard Chumley posh old actor routine: 'Wonderful to be here. Wonderful to see all the young people here. I try to stay young myself. I even entered the Young Musician of the Year the other day. He was furious!' Matt got a big laugh. Then he started to do his impressions. Jimmy Savile. Big laugh. Jim Bowen. Hilarity. He did seven minutes of this stuff and was going down brilliantly.

Then he started to do some more esoteric stuff – three or four minutes of slightly less accessible material, before returning to the mainstream, straightforward gags. But the laughter had died away. After two or three more minutes, he realised no one was laughing. They had just stopped.

Then someone shouted, 'Get off!' And about twenty other members of the audience joined in.

Matt didn't hang about. He scarpered within twenty seconds of being booed.

But he was devastated. It was the big comedy show of the festival. More people saw Matt getting booed off that year than saw all of Matt and David's shows. All the comedy critics were there. He came offstage and Addison said, 'It wasn't your fault,' and Vic Reeves said, 'Well, I enjoyed it anyway.' Everyone else left him alone, which is how it is when a comedian gets booed offstage.

Eventually he went to the Gilded Balloon bar and all night people came up to him to offer their condolences and tell him he didn't deserve it. For Matt it was the first time he knew real fear onstage. It was the viciousness of the response that stunned him.

One review said Matt was so bad there were people vomiting in the aisles. The night became a legend among his peers: how a comedian started off his set giddily high and then it all died away, which seemed crueller than just getting booed off at the start. (Matt didn't go back to the Edinburgh Playhouse until ten years later, on this *Little Britain* tour, and as soon as he walked in to the venue, the doorman recognised him from that night. Matt asked if he remembered how badly the evening went for him, and the doorman simply replied, 'Ooh yes.')

Matt got used to being booed off that year, especially when he supported Blur for their brief Seaside Tour. This is how Matt got welcomed into the inner circle of Britpop.

After his first ever rehearsal with Vic and Bob for their TV show in 1994 when he was twenty, Matt was taken to the Groucho by Vic, Bob and *Fast Show* co-creator Charlie Higson. He sat on a sofa with Vic to his left and Bob to his right and they were sounding him out, asking if he was a bit of a ladies' man. They reckoned he was. They also explained to him how they worked, how they liked to find someone young and up-and-coming like Matt, work with them and then when they were ready to fly off on their own, they would happily watch them establish their own career and be ready to find someone else to take under their wing.

As Matt was intently listening to Vic and Bob, an unkempt bloke in his early thirties breathlessly ran in clutching a videotape, shouting: 'Vic! Vic, come and watch this!' This guy, whom Matt had never seen before, took them all upstairs to watch a five-minute video he'd made. His name was Damien Hirst.

When Damien was commissioned to direct the video for Blur's 'Country House' a few weeks' later, he wanted to have a bald man running round evoking the image of Benny Hill, so he asked Vic about the bald guy he was working with. Vic and Bob assumed Hirst meant Matt, although he actually meant Les, who had appeared with them since the days of Vic Reeves's *Big Night Out*. But sure enough, Matt got the job of running round in the Blur video. On the day of filming, bass player Alex James greeted Matt with, 'Oh, Bernard Chumley!' He recognised Matt from his appearance a few weeks earlier on a TV show called *The Beat*, hosted by Gary Crowley. (Matt spent much of the show describing everything he could think of as 'sassy'.) Alex introduced Matt to the rest of the band and he immediately got on well with them. He played a game of table football with drummer Dave Rowntree. At one point, Matt challenged Damon to climb up a rope that was hanging from the ceiling of the sound stage. Damon eagerly climbed 30 feet up the rope. Matt stood there thinking: I hope I'm not responsible for the death of Britpop.

Matt was impressed with how open and honest Blur were. They just wanted to enjoy themselves; to enjoy their success.

After filming the video, Matt got a call from his agent telling him that Blur wanted to see footage of Matt as Bernard Chumley, because they were doing nine warm-up dates round seaside towns for their forthcoming UK tour and they were interested in Matt being the support act. Most bands have to pay their own way when they get a support slot on a big rock tour, but Matt needed to be paid. He accepted £100 a night and travelled on the tour bus with the band.

So Matt went on tour with Blur, at the height of their success, when every week there was another press story about their rivalry with Oasis, when hundreds of screaming girls followed them wherever they went. Matt knew his role was going to be tough. He'd be trying to perform his Bernard Chumley comedy act to teenage fans of the biggest, trendiest band of the moment. On the first night, he told the members of Blur not to watch him. Matt wanted to see how it was going to work, and if it was going to work. But he went down quite well. He performed about twenty minutes of stand-up and got enough laughs. With his confidence boosted, Matt was happy for Blur to watch him the second night. He was booed off after a minute and a half. Every other night of the brief tour he would get booed off. One of the low points was Dunoon in Ayrshire. They were the first band to play there since The Tourists in 1980. Matt was booed off after ninety seconds, accompanied by mass chanting of: 'You fat bastard! You fat bastard!'

In the dressing room after the gig, Matt could see, through a frosted-glass window, dozens of eager Blur fans waiting outside for a glimpse of their heroes. Matt had his Chumley wig on and every time he walked in front of the window he heard screams of 'Damon! Damon!'. Matt decided to pull his wig off. The crowd screamed. They thought they'd discovered that Damon was bald.

When they hit Morecambe, Matt had flu, which he had caught from the air conditioning on the tour bus, and he ended up praying to God that he would go down well. It was the only time he ever prayed before a show. It seemed to work because he received a great response from the crowd.

Despite the nightly stress of trying to amuse twelve-year-old girl Britpop fans, Matt loved the experience of being on tour with Blur, especially the sense of camaraderie. He saw how well Blur treated the people who worked with them. They were a team, going on a journey together. Years later Matt would go to a Blur gig and find the same people still working there. He saw how well they treated their staff and how the staff in turn were grateful.

That was Matt's brief adventure in the world of Britpop. He'd been part of a phenomenon. He didn't think he'd experience that kind of madness ever again.

As for Matt and David's Edinburgh show that year, starting it so late at night meant they had to deal with a lot of drunken audience members. So they adopted an aggressive, abrasive style to deal with them. And threw in lots of raw, rude material. Drunken crowds at midnight expect that kind of thing. Edinburgh that year was also full of sketch troupes and double acts, many of them long since forgotten, so Matt and David felt they had to be unusual and challenging.

The whole show was hosted by Matt as Sir Bernard Chumley, while David played an assistant stage manager called Tony Rodgers – a guy Sir Bernard

David's favourite fancy-dress outfit (1997)

had met somewhere who had escaped from prison, where he was probably in for murder – and he would tell politically incorrect jokes: 'What's the difference between a radical feminist and a bin-liner? A bin-liner gets taken out once a week.'

He had a catchphrase: 'Nice one, lads . . . sorry, women!'

They put a note on the flyer for the show announcing that there would be a free crèche. The show would start with David ambling onstage, and instead of gleefully announcing something like, 'Hi, we're here to entertain you!' he told the audience to be quiet. He'd have a plastic bag in his hand and he'd empty the contents on the floor – a few bits of a jigsaw and a child's shoe and he'd say – 'There you go . . . it's a crèche,' before continuing to berate the audience: 'Will you LISTEN?' he'd shout. 'Oh, it's like banging your head against a brick wall . . .'

To further unsettle the audience they would leave a plate with some half-eaten food onstage, and get rubbish bags from outside the venue and leave bits of garbage in the seats.

They had a character called Erik Estrada, played by David. He was a Bristolian stunt-cock porn star whose opening line was: 'You may not know my face but you will recognise my hot veiny throbbing penis,' and he'd been in porn adaptations of sitcoms like *It Ain't Half Hard Mum* and *Yes Yes Yes Yes YES Minister* and *Filthy Rich and Cuntflap*. David did a performance artist called Simon Geiger, inspired by the rather earnest people they saw at Bristol University Drama Department.

The show turned out to be an Edinburgh Fringe hit, doing well enough to enable them to do one night in the Riverside Studios in London, a 400-seater venue. They sold 385 of those 400 seats, which felt like a triumph in itself.

Matt and David were gaining a reputation, while at the same time they were learning from their peers. They went to see the *League of Gentlemen*, and Matt and David were awestruck. It was on another level.

During that time the likes of Bob Mortimer, Vic Reeves, Chris Morris and Julian Clary came to see the show, and people from Radio 4 came to meet them. And it was all down to their Edinburgh show. Eventually Myfanwy Moore, David's old friend from university, signed them up to do a series of spoofs for the Paramount Comedy Channel.

It was the first time they had a sense there could be a career in what they were doing, that they could be paid for being funny. But they also came very close to splitting up.

During that first show in Edinburgh, they were writing together, rehearsing together, performing together and living together. They shared a small flat for the month-long festival. David was also spending a lot of time with his girl-friend Katy, and she often stayed there too. Matt was on his own, apart from a mouse scuttling round his room, stopping him from getting to sleep. He could hear it behind his bin munching on a plastic bag and every time he lifted the bin the mouse scurried to the other side of the room.

Matt was also smoking a lot of spliffs. With the dope, the excitement of doing his first show in Edinburgh, and the peculiarly competitive, intense atmosphere of the Fringe, Matt was starting to go a bit mad. He started to lose perspective, and began to take himself very seriously, obsessively focusing on the show. If the show went well it would be the best thing ever; if it went badly it would be the end of the world.

It was all too much; too intense. It became clear that they couldn't be friends, professional partners, co-writers *and* flatmates.

A few days after they finished their month in Edinburgh, Matt was perched on the top of the stairs having a conversation with David on the phone, which turned into a quarrel. They had begun to dislike each other during that grim period living together, and they were having disagreements over what they should do next. Matt ended up putting the phone down on him. But within minutes he realised that what they had begun to build together was being jeopardised. He called David back, and they sorted their disagreement out.

Next year, before they went to Edinburgh for the second time with a show, they agreed that they would write the show together, rehearse together and perform together, and they'd probably go out to dinner together after the show. But they wouldn't live together. And it worked perfectly.

5

13 October 2005 – 11 days to go

In the car on the way to *Parkinson*, with Matt, David and Matt's boyfriend Kevin, Matt seems pensive and quiet. Kevin asks how rehearsals are going for the tour.

'Not brilliantly. I didn't really enjoy it today.'

Nothing, it turns out, is ready. The show feels too long and flabby, and they've rehearsed the material so often it doesn't seem very funny any more. And none of Matt's shoes seem to fit. 'Just give me one pair of shoes that fit!' he says, smiling grimly at the absurdity of it all. 'I know it doesn't sound like a big thing, but it plays on your mind . . .'

Well, I say, trying to lighten the mood, at least tonight you get to meet Gloria Hunniford.

'Yes, that's true!' He laughs.

'And Michael Parkinson,' says David. He's looking through the papers.

Matt catches sight of a picture of Ant and Dec. 'They're so huge aren't they – Ant and Dec.'

'Yeah,' agrees David. 'It's like everyone loves them. Like they're untouchable.

Quite rightly, because they are brilliant. It'll be interesting to see what happens to their film.'

Matt asks me if I've heard much about the film. I tell him all I know is that it's called *Alien Autopsy*. Just then Matt remembers it's Yom Kippur, a major Jewish holy day, and makes a phone call to his mum.

David's reading an article conjecturing about the identity of the actor chosen to play the new James Bond, who is to be officially announced next week. He thinks he knows who it is but he can't say.

Matt comes off the phone and asks him why.

David says because the person who told him told him not to tell anyone.

Matt asks him who told him.

David says he can't say who told him either, because he doesn't want to get that person in trouble.

Matt says he thinks he knows who it is who told David.

David says he may do but he still can't talk about it.

Matt drops it.

There's a twenty-second silence before David says, 'I'll tell you later.'

It's almost an argument, but not quite. They both seem to know when they're on the verge of a disagreement, and often they'll tacitly agree to back off. Matt still seems bewildered that David can't talk to him about the new James Bond and David is slightly irritated that Matt doesn't understand why David can't talk about it. But that's as far as it's going to go. They both seem to be aware, even as they're talking, that this is a silly subject to argue about.

When I watch them in meetings with their agents or publicists or promoters or any people trying to persuade them to do stuff, it's usually the case that if one of them disagrees with the other, the one who is most intent on their viewpoint will get their way. Or they'll map out the pros and cons and reach an agreement. But they know one another well enough to realise when one of them really doesn't want to do something, and when that happens the other one will swiftly fall in line. This goes from the tiniest decision about a line in the middle of a sketch in their show to the biggest, most momentous issues.

The car arrives at the ITV tower on the South Bank and we're ushered in by a beaming *Parkinson* staffer, who takes us straight to the set. Matt and David take turns to walk down its famous staircase (David waves his arms in the air and shouts, 'Yes, it's me!') and sit in the revolving chairs on the stage. Their fellow guest Gloria Hunniford arrives and warmly greets Matt and David. The other star of the show, Will Young, is nowhere to be seen. The producer explains that Matt and David will be on first, then Gloria and finally Will, who will perform his new single and will also join Parky and the others for a chat. *Parkinson* is unique among TV chat shows for insisting that all the guests stick around for the entire show. Each act gets its own interview, of course, but they're also encouraged to chip in at appropriate moments during subsequent chats and at the end there's a group discussion where everyone is supposed to join in. 'I can have fun with Will Young,' says David.

After a few moments larking around on Parkinson's set, we're politely encouraged to move to the dressing rooms area. Matt and David are given luxurious separate dressing rooms. They're white and shiny and brightly lit. Not quite as glitzy and comfortable as the star dressing rooms at BBC TV Centre, which are more reminiscent of moody boutique hotel rooms, but they'll do. There's a spread of fruit, sandwiches and some chocolates, plus a copy of *Vogue*, bottles of Molton Brown 'energising bath and shower', and the gift of a special Michael Parkinson-branded Mont Blanc pen, which David finds very funny. Before Matt goes off to enjoy his own room, he apologises to David for probing him about the new James Bond thing.

'I just couldn't say in front of the driver,' says David. Ah, the *driver*. 'You think they're just sitting there driving and not paying any attention but you've got to be careful because they do sell stories to the papers and stuff. I'm not saying I know there was any problem with that specific driver, but just in general you have to be careful.'

'Oh sorry,' says Matt. 'Fair enough. That makes sense. So who is going to be the new James Bond?'

'Well, I've been told it's between Daniel Craig and a young, fairly unknown guy. I can't remember his name . . . he's like twenty-two or something.'

'Really? Daniel Craig would be great, wouldn't he? He's a proper great actor, isn't he? I think that would be really interesting.'

'It would be interesting,' says David. 'And he is brilliant. But I just can't quite see him as Bond; we'll have to wait and see.'

They agree to differ about Daniel Craig as Bond, and Matt says he'll just be relaxing in his dressing room if David needs him at all.

David clicks the TV on in his dressing room. 'Right, let's get Paul O'Grady on.' But he's momentarily distracted by a Sky News entertainment report about Jude Law. 'Oh God – who's he fucked now?'

Before he has a shower and shave, David needs to make a phone call. His parents, sister and her husband are coming to see the recording, and David's booked a table for them to have dinner together afterwards. But he also wants his friend Denise Van Outen to join them, so he calls the Ivy: 'Hello, I'd just like to check about a booking for dinner tonight. It's for David Walliams. Thanks. It's booked for five people but I'd like to have another friend join us if that's possible. [pause] Oh, I see. Well, are they all chairs or is there a banquette? Okay, can she squeeze on to the banquette? It's Denise Van Outen and she's only got a small arse.'

How far in advance, I ask, did he make the booking for a party of five to have dinner on a Thursday night at the Ivy? A few days ago, he says. It's all about having the right number of the right person at the Ivy. Once you're in, that's it. They can usually accommodate. He doesn't think he could just call up on the night and get a table. Well, maybe one for two people. 'But wouldn't it be awful if they suddenly dropped you? If you called up one time and they were like, "Oh sorry, we don't care about you any more . . ."'

He tells me it was Patsy Kensit who taught him how to get a table at the Ivy. She phoned the restaurant and said, 'Hello, this is Patsy Kensit here.' And it worked. So now he tries to remember to say, 'Hello, this is David Walliams here.' It is a little bit embarrassing but worth it.

David emerges from the shower as the *Parkinson* lady pops her head round the door.

'Nearly ready!' she announces, and then adds, 'Michael's in make-up but he sends his regards to you.'

David laughs. 'Good. Well, we'll be seeing him later.'

She leaves to make the same announcement to Matt.

David doesn't do that many impressions on a regular basis. His parents are often imitated, but not gratuitously so, only when he's telling a story about them. I have, however, heard him do Parkinson many times. I've seen him compete with Jonathan Ross over who can do the best, or rather the most exaggerated Parkinson. It's all about going quite deep, gruff, soft Yorkshire, and making lots of extraneous guttural noises.

'I love the idea of Parky sitting there and going [adopts Parky impression] "Uurgh . . . send my regards to David Walliams, and then send them to Matt Lucas too!"'

Then he adds, 'It would be great to pull out right now, wouldn't it?'

His playfulness snowballs as he finishes getting ready and studies himself in the mirror. 'Look at this suit. What a beauty! Wow!' It is a Richard James suit, dark grey, very soft woollen nap. 'You are witnessing something very special,' he says, laughing.

I ask him who else, apart from his family, is coming to witness this beauty. His publicists Barbara Charone and Moira Bellas and his agent Conor should be here.

'BC would work the audience up into a frenzy,' I say, having seen her getting very excited during performances by her clients.

'Yeah, she's a bit like Bubbles. Bubbles Charone!'

He means she's reminiscent of the grotesquely fat and over-the-top *Little Britain* character purely in the way she talks, in the colourful way she expresses herself and in her glitzy enthusiasm. BC speaks with a husky New York drawl, rather than Bubbles's Eurotrash accent. But she does quite happily yell for champagne. And almost everything she says has an exclamation mark at the end. For the record, though, she isn't grotesquely fat. She is, in fact, tiny. Just as David makes the Bubbles comparison, there's a knock on the door and it is BC, with Moira.

'Hey! You look amazing! Fucking amazing!' she says to David.

'Aw, thank you very much. Thank you for coming,' he replies.

'Are you kidding? Would we miss this!'

BC notices me in the corner: 'Hey! How are you? It's the third member of *Little Britain*!'

'Except funnier,' I say, trying to be wry and immediately wishing I hadn't said it in case she thinks I'm being serious. But she cackles appreciatively.

'Do you wanna come and hear the Madonna album on Thursday?' she asks me. Before getting a reply she says to David: 'That is a really good suit.'

David asks if she's seen his family yet. She tells him they're upstairs in the green room.

'They're already getting pissed, are they?' he asks.

'The only shame about tonight is that Matt's mum couldn't be here because it's Yom Kippur,' says BC.

'But you're here. Even though it's Yom Kippur.'

'Yeah I'm Jewish, but I'm not religious. That's a line from a Madonna song . . .'

'I know! "Nothing Fails". From the last album. "I'm in love with you, you silly thing . . ."'

'Don't tell everyone!' yells BC. 'Fuck, you're good, David.'

David giggles. 'That's a great Madonna lyric and one of my favourite Madonna songs.'

'Wait till you hear the new album, David.'

'Well, why don't I have a copy?'

The *Parkinson* assistant producer arrives to gather David and Matt and take them to make-up.

I join BC and Moira in the green room, which resembles an atmospherically lit nightclub lounge, with giant plasma screens dotted throughout. In one dimly lit corner sits a gaggle of handsome young men who could be torn from the fashion pages of Men's *Vogue*. 'Will's people,' says Barbara. She reminisces about her and Moira's rowdy behaviour the last time she came to a *Parkinson* recording. 'It was at Christmas and we were here with Rod Stewart and his friends. We behaved really badly. Lily Savage's people were here and Barbara Windsor's family. They got really annoyed with us . . .'

'Quite rightly so,' says Moira. 'They were trying to watch their people on the show and we were shouting and laughing over the whole thing.'

'Yeah but there are three fucking plasma screens in here,' says BC.

Matt and David's agents Melanie and Conor arrive. They've recently formed their own joint agency and called it Troika.

'Hey, you guys, how's Trotsky going?'

'Trotsky?' Melanie repeats the word.

'Yeah, your company? Isn't that the name? Trotsky?'

'No, it's Troika. Close!'

'Oh,' says BC. 'I knew it was something Russian. Anyway, you guys should get together with us. Maybe on the first night of the tour. We should have a party. I can't wait to see the live show. And I can't wait to see the new series either.'

We suddenly hear the unmistakable tones of Michael Parkinson coming from the speakers all around us. 'Any Will Young fans here?' he asks. Screams and cheers from the audience. 'Good. Do you like *Little Britain*?' Even louder screams and cheers. 'They'll be followed by one of our most beloved broadcasters and an old friend of mine, Miss Gloria Hunniford.'

Parky's introductions over, we settle down and watch the recording.

David and Matt seem relaxed and confident during the interview. Their answers are funny but also genuine and uncontrived. When their segment is over, they stay in their seats onscreen for the rest of the show. Gloria Hunniford is up next, and is talking about her late daughter Caron. Matt and David look calm and respectful and focused on everything that Hunniford is saying. But a whole new, strange thing happens when Will Young joins them. After he sings his new single he walks over to the seated area for his chat with Michael and kisses Gloria hello, shakes Matt's hand, and then before he can do anything else, David puts his finger to his own mouth by way of telling Will to kiss him. Which he does. Happily. They make comedy eyes at each other, and then just as he's about to take the empty seat next to Parky, he scampers over to David instead, sits on his lap and bounces up and down. The studio audience squeals with excitement. The green room explodes in laughter and applause.

'Fucking brilliant,' exclaims BC.

'Wow,' says Mel. 'That'll get them in the papers.'

A few minutes later David makes a joke about seeing Bob Hoskins naked in Will's film and Will says he looks better naked than Hoskins did. David smiles flirtatiously, Will mouths something ambiguous, and they eye each other up to the point where Parkinson says, 'Are we interrupting something?' They end the show by dancing with each other under the closing credits. It is, by general consensus in the green room, the gayest *Parkinson* ever.

Matt and David arrive in the green room to whoops of celebration and appreciation. They're both smiling calmly, as if any second they might whoop with joy or dance a jig of delight but are keeping their emotions in check in case they appear too self-congratulatory. Barbara Charone yells, 'That was just brilliant! Well done, guys!' The rest of us in their support group agree vigorously.

Matt embraces Kevin and says, 'That was fun.' To us he says, 'I was nervous at the start, but quite quickly it just felt like a natural conversation.'

Melanie, Matt's agent, comes over to tell him that it was his best-ever TV interview. 'Seriously, darling, it was just so good,' she says.

I glance at David, who's chatting to his agent Conor. He's talking quickly and gesturing and nodding vigorously. I walk over to offer my congratulations and see that he's glowing with the excitement of it all.

'I could do that every week!' he says.

I ask him if he's surprised at how well it went.

'Yeah. It just feels like one of those milestones . . . and it's a relief that it went well. Because it could always go either way. It's easier than doing Jonathan's show, where essentially he is the star, and that's how it should be. And with Jonathan it's weird because we're friends and we socialise with him, so there's a lot of knowledge of what we're like going on behind his line of questions. In a way it's more natural and easier to be interviewed on TV by someone who doesn't really know you . . .'

And Will Young?

'What a bonus,' says David. 'He was great. I think Parky really thought there was something going on between us.'

I tell him I think there was on Will's part. There was a glint in his eye.

'Hmm . . . cheeky!' And he pokes me in the chest. 'I'm sure he was just joking. It was lovely, though. I bet the *Parky* viewers have never seen anything like that before.'

Matt and David have learned how to do *Parkinson*. I've never seen them happier.

Later that night after David's dinner at the Ivy with his family and Denise Van Outen, we talk on the phone.

His mum loves Denise, thinks she's got such a good sense of humour and, he suggests, would quite like her to be her future daughter-in-law.

He's still on a high after his *Parkinson* triumph and tells me that a lot of people thought that the flirting was quite genuine between him and Will Young. Neil Tennant, the Pet Shop Boy, has already been on the phone, asking what happened afterwards, 'As if I might have got off with him or something.' So David told him, 'Yeah, I fucked him.' To which Neil said 'Really?'

In the end David had to say, 'No, I'm joking.'

Many viewers complained to ITV after this episode of *Parkinson*, variously describing it as "disgraceful", "disgusting" and "degenerate". One claimed that homosexuals didn't have the right to display that kind of behaviour on a mainstream TV channel, before accusing ITV of political correctness and assuming that every other person was a homosexual by inviting so many apparently gay guests onto the same show, and even worse, allowing them to display open lust of a homosexual nature.

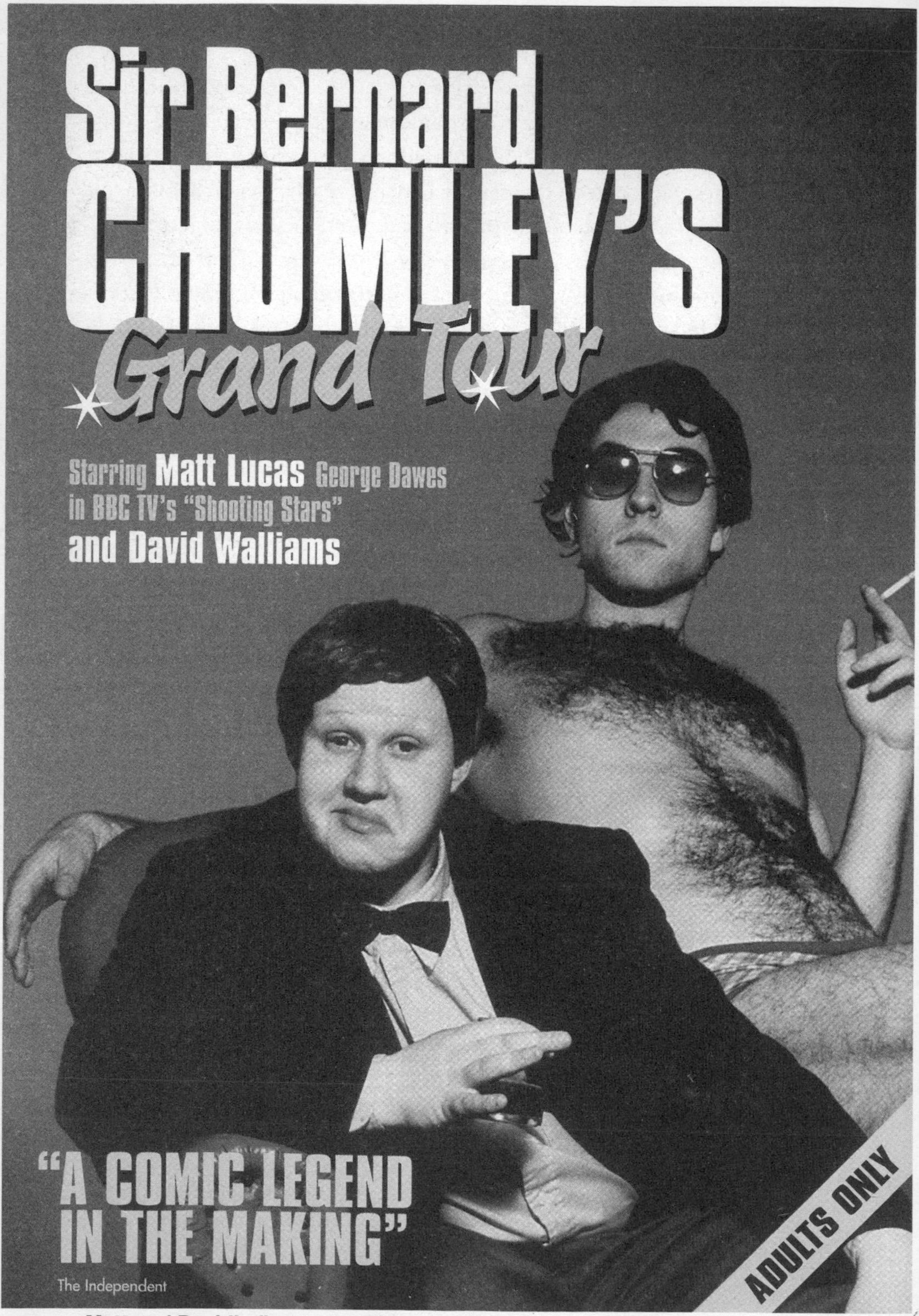

SIR BERNARD CHUMLEY'S Grand Tour

Starring **Matt Lucas** George Dawes in BBC TV's "Shooting Stars" **and David Walliams**

"A COMIC LEGEND IN THE MAKING"

The Independent

ADULTS ONLY

Matt and David's first tour, 1997

Another complainant said that Parkinson should be ashamed of himself for being part of what was little more than a television advert for gayness.

One viewer felt sorry for Gloria Hunniford, surrounded as she was by such campness, and asked plaintively whether it was not possible to avoid showing men kissing each other and having gay love-ins on primetime television.

But perhaps best of all was the person who complained bitterly about Will Young and David Walliams' sickening behaviour in daring to show such a tasteless and unnecessary interest in each other, before going on to express what a pleasure it was at least to watch Matt Lucas.

1996 – Edinburgh

Stephen Merchant came to the show and Matt and David got him out of the audience because they thought he looked quite funny.

It was their second year doing their own comedy show at Edinburgh. If anything, it was even ruder than the first. Matt had left Bristol University and filmed the first series of *Shooting Stars*, having been spotted doing his Sir Bernard routine by Bob Mortimer. David was keen to maintain the new comedy partnership he'd formed with Matt.

When they invited Stephen Merchant onstage, they also tried to get him to take his shoes and socks off. And then his trousers. Merchant wouldn't go that far. But he seemed to enjoy the experience and complimented Matt and David on their anarchic act.

David also performed the character of washed-up children's TV presenter Des Kaye, who opened his bit by throwing lollipops into the crowd. One of them hit Sean Lock in the eye. Lock claimed he was scarred for life by David's lolly.

Despite the injuries, the show got better reviews than the year before. Mostly positive, except one from Ben Thompson in the *Telegraph*, who wrote: 'Lucas and Walliams have torn free of their satirical moorings and are skating headlong into an anal misogynistic cul-de-sac'.

David memorised the line and felt it was the most extraordinary review they would ever get. It also served as a warning that they were getting too rude and needed to pull back a bit.

When *Shooting Stars* was shown, and became a hit, Matt suddenly became noticeably more famous than David. A by-product of the popularity of the instantly recognisable George Dawes was that, for the first time, Matt and David's partnership seemed to many onlookers to be unequal, even though it has always been a 50/50 double act, in which they wrote the material together, came up with ideas together and performed together. But because Matt was on a successful BBC2 series, people began to regard David as his sidekick. The misconception was, for a brief period, tough for David to deal with.

Of course, Matt and David knew the truth.

George Dawes was also starting to affect Matt in an unforeseen way. Audiences for his Bernard Chumley stand-up shows were beginning to expect and want to see George Dawes. But Matt didn't think there was an act in the character of George Dawes. And the Chumley routine survived on the audience not knowing who Matt was, so the character could then turn them round.

Matt also felt that maybe it was time to leave the stand-up circuit and devote himself to his burgeoning relationship with David. He was getting disillusioned with the live scene, where comedians were encouraged to stick to their tried-and-tested routines. You did your best set and you kept doing it, or else you might not be booked again. So the stand-up scene encouraged a certain amount of ennui and frustration, which itself led to a lifestyle of continuous drinking and drug-taking. One night after performing a Bernard Chumley show, Matt found himself lying in bed in a Travel Tavern-type hotel room in Manchester. It was the only room left in the hotel, there was just a little window in the ceiling, and he realised what a lonely life he was leading.

By the end of the year he had finished with the stand-up circuit for good.

6

14 October 2005 – 10 days to go

The day after *Parkinson*, it's back to rehearsals. First, a confusing few days in a room resembling a school gym in the Jerwood Space arts complex in south London, before they move on to Twickenham Studios where they'll have a proper stage.

There are lists on the wall with the running order for each act, and the lists get constantly replaced as they tinker with the line-up of sketches. Paul Putner, supporting cast member along with Samantha Power, describes it as a Rubik's show – every different combination of sketches tried. A puzzle. And they haven't solved it yet. Apparently act two is perfect, but Geoff Posner, the *Little Britain* series producer who is acting as script editor of the live show, watched rehearsals earlier this morning, and threw some new ideas into the act one mix. He wanted to give it a different dynamic.

To add to the confusion, the crew from *The South Bank Show* is here, shuffling around to try to find an appropriate place to film without getting in the way.

Jeremy Sams, the director of the live show, is trying to be positive. 'It's lovely to have an audience. If you want to laugh, please do it loudly.' He admits they're going through an interesting restructuring of act one. 'We're in a certain state of flux, but in a good way,' says Jeremy, who much of the time speaks in something of a loud whisper. He has a special way of being affable, optimistic, warm and jolly, yet firm as he explains what works and what doesn't. *Private Eye* would call him a luvvie. He's also a distinguished and highly respected theatre director, writer, translator, lyricist and composer. He's worked on *Chitty Chitty Bang Bang*, as well as plays by Tom Stoppard and Alan Bennett.

Stage manager Gareth sits behind a desk tapping away flamboyantly on his laptop. Jeremy hovers next to Gareth, watching the cast's every move. Various costumes hang from clothes rails by the far wall. They've been working here for a few days but today is their first full run-through of the whole show. They're not going to bother with any costumes. This is to see how the show feels with the new running order.

'Okay, from the top!' shouts Jeremy.

Jeremy doesn't interrupt the rehearsal at any point. He sits there taking

Matt and David with Paul Putner

notes on his pad, smiling, frequently laughing along with those of us who haven't seen this material every day for the last few weeks. He gets particular pleasure out of Matt's 'traditional Thai song' performance during the TingTong and Dudley sketch. David's Dudley accent sounds quite similar to the voice he uses when he impersonates his dad – his lower-middle-class suburban burr, maybe broadened a notch to reflect Dudley's seedier edge.

The Vicky Pollard sketch that follows, in which she's returning to her old school to be interviewed in assembly by David's trendy teacher, is the biggest challenge for Matt. He has to wheel on a prop of six baby's pushchairs stuck together and then sprint through four or five monologues densely packed with names and cultural references at Vicky's trademark breathless speed while making them audible to an audience of thousands. For the first time today, Matt needs prompting from Gareth. He gets lost in the middle of two of Vicky's rants. He has a lot of names to remember: Trish, Rochelle, Craig Herman, Jade Maguire, Lee Cherry, Michaela Conway, Colleen McGovern. Matt and David spend a lot of time getting the sound of those names right.

Next up is Des Kaye, the bitter and twisted old children's TV presenter character played by David, revived from the first series of *Little Britain*. Des has the first bit of audience participation in the show, inviting two members of the audience – 'one little boy and one . . . little boy' – to play his 'hide the sausage' game. David exclaims, 'So, let's find some contestants!', catches my eye and walks up to me, grinning manically. I'm worried on many levels. I don't particularly want to be filmed by *The South Bank Show* being humiliated by Des Kaye, whatever it is he's about to do, and I'm afraid that if there's some kind of physical molestation involved, then the iPod on which I'm recording will fall out of my pocket. And my glasses might fall off. David seems to notice the blind panic on my face and makes do with his co-star Paul Putner to take the role of the 'attractive boy'; he doesn't bother trying to find someone to stand in for the 'ugly boy', who's really just a bystander. Turns out I was right to be worried. The sketch climaxes with David as Des trying to find the hidden sausage by grappling with his volunteer's crotch and bottom, wrestling him to the ground, trying to pull his trousers down and finally dry-humping him. And he's planning to do this every night of the tour to a young man plucked randomly from the audience.

The final sketch of act one is the vomiting. The weirdest thing about it in rehearsals is watching Matt and David, as Judy and Maggie, extensively simulating the puking action and sound minus the actual physical sick. But I can still sense that the eventual illusion of mass projectile vomiting onstage will be a suitably spectacular way of ending the first act.

The run-through of both acts done, Jeremy gathers the cast to give them his notes, of which the final one is to praise David's performance in the Sebastian/PM sketch: 'I love you having a complete firework display as Sebastian,' he says. 'You can blow up completely. Okay . . . Thank you very much indeed and we'll see each other in Twickers.'

In Twickers, now with just a few days to go until the first night of the tour in Portsmouth, everything seems more fraught. The running order has been fixed, but little else. Costume changes, wig changes, microphones, the big screen backdrop, the videos that play on it, the music, the song and dance routine, the piss that comes out of Mrs Emery, the hydraulics that make Matt fly, the vomit that comes out of the WI ladies, the sets, the props, the lighting – none of it is working properly. Some of it works some of the time,

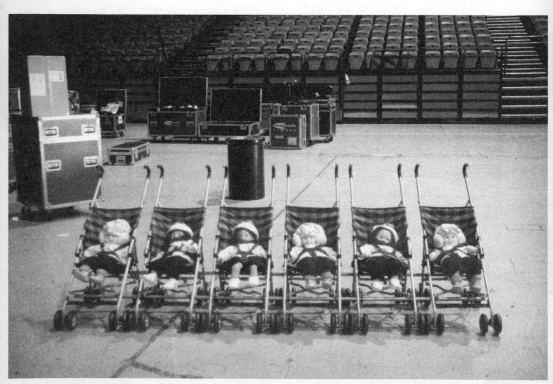

Vicky's kids

but no one has seen all of it working how they hoped it would. And Matt's shoes still don't fit.

Tech people surge around the huge, cavernous space, attending to different bits and pieces of machinery. Tony the tour manager stalks the dark edges of this aircraft hangar of a room, mobile phone pressed to his ear, other hand gesticulating deliberately as he tries to sort out all the problems. Even Gareth, sitting by a desk as always, is grimacing when he usually grins. Jeremy Sams looks over in his direction and tells me, 'He's having a rough time. He's doing at least two jobs at once. He's in a dark place. He's gone over to the dark side.'

The days are long. They've got a week to perfect everything: to get the performances right and all the technical elements working.

While Jeremy is trotting about geeing everyone up, checking this and that, David Arnold, the composer, is fine-tuning the music, especially the closing Dafydd song, which is a big gay disco anthem. He's got to make it more gay.

Lisa, in charge of hair and make-up, introduces me to the wig-master, a tall, distinguished-looking man called Richard Mawbey. She and Matt and Richard start a discussion about the Dafydd wig – a blond spiky number. Is it big enough? 'I think from a distance the Dafydd wig needs to be bigger,' says Lisa. Richard nods. Then he whispers to me conspiratorially, 'See the microphone? The wigs have mics hidden in them. It's very complicated.' Pause. 'This is a one-shot thing.'

Richard has been working with Matt and David since the pilot. 'They came to me and said, "We're working on this show for the BBC but we have no money, can you help us?" And I did everything I could do to make them some great wigs on a very tight budget and they've been tremendously loyal to me ever since.'

I'm transfixed by the immaculate rococo sculpture of his own hair. 'But the ridiculous thing about this tour,' he continues, 'is that even though we've known we're doing it for the last year or so, no one ever seemed available to make the major decisions about what would actually be needed until just as the show was about to open. So I've made about fifty wigs in the last three weeks. Which has been an absolute living nightmare.'

Those last three words seem like a fairly accurate summary of the mood of the moment.

'You see the thing about this show is that if it was a stage play or musical

Rehearsing the finale

they would have a few weeks of previews, where the audiences know that they're still banging it into shape. But with this, they've got a week of rehearsals then they start the tour for real on Monday night. Terrifying.'

The man's a walking theatrical production, and brilliant company. Though I've only known him ten minutes.

'Oh God . . .' says David, smiling, 'what have we done?' He means the show, the tour, everything.

'I wish I had some shoes that fit me,' says Matt.

'I wish we knew how everything was going to work,' says David. They haven't seen the vomit yet. But he's more worried about the pissing. He's not sure if it's going to be visible to the audience. He even considers ditching the whole sketch. 'If it's not working there's no point doing it for the sake of it. We don't have to do everything.'

The director gathers Matt and David for a quick huddle, so I have a chat with Paul and Sam. Sam asks how much of the tour I'm going to observe. I tell her I'm going to be there until Matt and David have gone insane. Paul asks what the title of the book is. He says he likes titles of showbiz memoirs to be a bit mysterious and in-jokey, like David Niven's *The Moon's a Balloon*, so you have to read the book before you find out that the title means. He suggests we could call the book *Where's the Piss Machine?* or *The Vomit's Too Thick.*

They return from the huddle. 'I don't want to sound dramatic,' says Matt, 'but I think this tech week is turning into one of the worst weeks of my life.'

David doesn't know what to say. He lets out a low hum of doubt and anxiety. Eventually he says, 'We could just carry on working on it, trying to get it right over the whole weekend, but I think we really need a day off.'

Matt agrees and they resolve to try to forget about it for their last day of freedom, and enjoy themselves at Ant and Dec's birthday party on Sunday night. Plus they've got one more full dress rehearsal at the venue in Portsmouth on Monday before the first night proper.

Matt adds: 'Oh, you know that shoe problem? We couldn't work out why all the shoes felt so tight. Well, we worked out they were on the wrong feet.'

1997

Fifty weeks after they recorded a pilot, the BBC got round to telling Matt and David that the series wouldn't be commissioned. They'd been trying to come up with pilots for radio shows since they met with people at Radio 4 after their Edinburgh show in 1996. They recorded a pilot called *Sir Bernard's Soirée*, which was their attempt to turn their Sir Bernard Chumley live show into a radio format with a view to eventually making a television series. Every time they asked their agents whether the radio series was a goer, they were told the meeting had been cancelled.

Eventually they realised how the business works: you never get told when they don't want to make your show, you just have to eventually realise that it's not going to happen. After *Sir Bernard's Soirée* they tried another idea, called *Make a Difference with Lucas and Walliams*. Matt got it into his head that he didn't want to record the show in front of a studio audience, which Radio 4 agreed to, but instead of just loose sketches they insisted Matt and David linked everything to give the programme an identity. It was a hodge-podge, anything-goes type of sketch show, full of spoofs, like the Ned Sherrin game show called 'Harridan, Harlot or Whore'. (Matt would impersonate Sherrin's arch theatricality: 'So is this lady a harridan? or a whore?') But also included in that pilot were an Emily Howard sketch, two Dennis Waterman sketches and one with royal reporter Peter André, all characters that would end up in *Little Britain*.

When they finished the pilot of *Make a Difference* and handed it to Radio 4, they eventually received two words of feedback: lacks conviction.

So they had one more go at a radio sketch show. And one more go at coming up with a linking device and an overall theme and identity for it. This time round they knew they didn't want to do the links themselves, so they came up with the idea of getting someone else with an appropriately authoritative voice to do them in the style of an old educational programme, as if the narrator was guiding the listener through the landscape of the characters, like a travelogue. Both being huge *Doctor Who* fans, Matt and David asked Tom Baker to provide that voice, and they thought of a title for the show: *Little Britain*.

Once they'd agreed upon that name for the show, they decided all the sketches should be set in contemporary Britain and all should feature modern British characters. Historical sketches, spoofs of TV and films and aimless monologues were banned. They'd established a set of rules, a format that made sense and had an identity.

As soon as they recorded the pilot, they knew it was significantly better than the ones they'd made before. They knew it was something special.

7

24 October 2005 – Portsmouth: first night

'Do you think U2 do this before the opening night of their tour?' David asks. 'Have a Chinese above a Spar?'

'No, they'd have an Indian,' says Matt. Then he adds: 'It's fine by me. I'd rather have Wagamama's, but this is fine.'

'Oh I'm not complaining,' clarifies David. 'It's just different from what you expect, isn't it?'

'Maybe next time we'll splash out on catering,' says Matt.

'The thing about catering,' observes David, 'is that sometimes the catering just isn't very good. You get horrible food every day.'

We're joined at our unglamorous, unglitzy dinner by Tony, and tour promoter Phil McIntyre, of Phil McIntyre Entertainment, and his can-do sidekick Paul. Phil is, as he would be among the first to point out, one of the most powerful men in British comedy, television and live entertainment. He's an imposing, no-nonsense bloke. He represents Peter Kay, Victoria Wood and Ben Elton. He and Paul have got almost exactly the same way of speaking, which could be summed up as brash Mancunian enthusiasm.

David says he'd rather have Phil on his side than against him. 'I somehow feel you'd happily kill someone on our behalf,' he tells Phil.

Phil beams enigmatically. 'No . . . no . . .' he says. 'Maybe I'd torture them.'

I ask Phil how this tour ranks among all the comedy tours he's ever master-minded.

'Oh it's the biggest,' he says firmly, 'by far. This is the biggest comedy tour ever. And we'll be adding some arena dates soon, which will make it even bigger.'

'It's a record-breaker!' shouts Paul, who's smaller and more nimble than Phil.

'And a money-maker!' adds David, smiling. 'Not that we're doing it for the money.'

'No. And anyway, we're spending all the money on props,' notes Matt.

A friendly waiter takes our drinks order first. Matt and David just want still water. 'No ice,' says David. He hates ice in his water.

Matt is explaining how doing a tour has been part of the *Little Britain* master plan right from the start, in as much as there ever was a master plan. Matt and David have both studied the paths of the comedy acts that influence them, and people like Vic and Bob, and *The Fast Show* and *The League of Gentlemen*, all went on huge national live tours. More important than the size of those shows was the sheer joy of seeing those talents performing live.

'We always wanted to see what we could do with *Little Britain* in a live situation, and part of that was seeing if we could live up to the live comedy shows we'd seen and loved,' says Matt.

The drinks arrive. David's glass of water is half-filled with ice.

This is how we got to Portsmouth, and the Chinese above the Spar.

Nine hours earlier I'm sitting in the front seat of the car, alongside Cosmo, Matt's driver.

'Look, I've got one of these!' Matt announces, fishing a small rectangular tablet from his rucksack. 'Have you seen one?'

I recognise it from pictures I've seen in gadget magazines.

'It's an Archos personal video recorder and you can put TV shows on it, films, photos.'

'Games . . .' says Kevin.

'Look,' says Matt, pressing a button, and up pops the opening titles of

Curb Your Enthusiasm. 'It's the first episode of season five. Downloaded.'

He tells me he can copy it over to my laptop when we get to the hotel if he's got the right leads with him. 'I've also just downloaded *Bar Mitzvah Boy.* Which I've never ever seen. And I've always wanted to . . .'

Matt's also brought a device on tour with him that enables his Apple laptop computer to pick up satellite TV from wherever they are in the world. It then turns the hard disk of the computer into a digital recorder so he can download whichever TV shows he wants. He can also tell his home Sky+ system to record what he wants if he forgets to set it in advance.

'I've also got a new video camera,' he says, handing it to Kevin to record this momentous first drive to the first venue on the first day of the tour. Kevin's been looking at the Archos tablet thing, and places it on the seat between him and Matt. A small collection of sleek gadgets is piling up on the back seat of the car. Matt waits till Kevin is recording on the video camera and makes an announcement: 'Hello, it is Monday the twenty-fourth of October, and today is the first day of our eleven-year-long nationwide tour of *Little Britain.* And sitting in the front of the car are Boyd Hilton, writer of

TV and make-up

our book about a year in our lives, and then there's Cosmo at the wheel, and I'm very nervous, er . . . about the tour.'

'What are you nervous about?' asks Kevin, flicking his long blond hair away from his eyes as the car picks up speed on the motorway.

'About being on tour. I'm nervous about the changes . . . getting in costume in time for the start of the sketches. I'm nervous about the technical elements. I think we've got a good show but I'm nervous that it goes down well. Especially because we'll have critics there tonight, and I don't think they'll be understanding if it goes wrong or if bits of it are weak.'

Matt and David's PR people have specifically invited the *Sun* and the *Mirror*, but no other national newspapers, to cover the show and have a little schmooze with Matt and David afterwards, in the hope of guaranteeing some prominent, positive pieces in the next day's press. Most other national newspapers have also arranged to review the show off their own backs.

Matt's also worried that they're performing characters in the live show that haven't been seen on TV yet. 'That's going to be strange. Like there's a sketch set in a curry restaurant that feels quite different and we're not sure if it'll work in the context of the show.'

He's still not sure, either, if the Mrs Emery pissing sketch is going to work. To start with the management asked if they could just imply the peeing with sound effects. But they said no, they had to actually see the liquid. So they had to build a kind of raft on which the sketch can take place because it's not safe to have water on the stage. 'And we mic in the sound of weeing,' explains Matt, 'like they play in the sound of tap-dancing during *Riverdance.*'

As for the vomit which has to be able to spew up out of the vomit rig, Matt tells me and Kevin that they started off using water, then they mixed it with vegetable soup, cream of chicken soup and water, which really smelt alarming and didn't come out of the pipes properly. Today in the dress rehearsal they're going to try a kind of porridge mixture. Matt says he's glad there won't be any journalists watching the dress rehearsal – there had been requests from the papers so that they could meet their deadlines more easily, but Matt and David said no way.

Kevin asks Matt if he knows the kind of people he's looking for to bring onstage for the Marjorie Dawes sketch.

'I know the kind of person I'm looking for . . . but during the run-throughs, no one has really wanted to come onstage, so that's another thing that feels a bit untested. I think I need to find a proper fat person in the audience each night. Let's just hope there are lots of fatties across Britain.'

Kevin puts the video camera away. I'd forgotten he was filming. Matt is looking through his mail.

'So we got invited to Elton and David's wedding . . .' he says. 'Not the actual ceremony, just the dinner and party afterwards. Well, when I say "just" – it'll obviously be incredible.'

'The invitation was amazing,' says Kevin. 'It just had the date on it and it said "details to follow".'

'It'll be great. I think it's about the most exciting thing I can think of in my entire life,' says Matt.

Every now and then our conversation is punctuated by the faint sound of a slightly alien female voice giving directions. Cosmo has got the Mercedes' satellite navigation on, and it's directing us from Matt's west London flat to Portsmouth. David is being driven simultaneously from his flat in a separate car. They each have their own dedicated driver and car while they're on tour for the next nine months. Cosmo, who is only just taller than Matt, has been chosen to drive him and act as his bodyguard should the need arise. Pete, David's driver, got the job because he's even taller than David. The crew has a bus, while Matt and David's two supporting cast members, Sam and Paul, travel with Tony.

We've been en route since 9 a.m., when Cosmo picked us up from Matt's flat in a rather plain mansion block. He's lived there for years, but he's just had an offer accepted on a big house in a much more central location. He's thrilled. 'I bought my current place just after I'd done a Cadbury's ad and used the money from that. But it's a bit gloomy and drab. It's always felt like I was just lodging there. I never felt I could stamp my own personality on it . . .'

But finding a place he liked has been difficult. 'All these estate agents were gossiping with each other and it was getting in the papers that I was looking for somewhere.' Eventually he and Kevin saw a place in Hampstead they liked. But the estate agent said it hadn't been valued yet, and later he rang them and told them it would cost four and a half million pounds. 'Slightly out of our price range,' laughs Matt. 'And we just thought, why did he show us this lovely house that he knew was out of our range? Anyway, I just happened to see another house in an estate agent's window in Hampstead that wasn't actually in Hampstead but it looked so nice. And we fell in love with it as soon as we saw it.'

Kevin says it's a beautiful house, designed by an architect.

'Yeah, but it's got a lot of floors,' explains Matt, 'and we got my mum in to see it and she goes, "Well, by the time you get to the top floor you've forgotten what you went up there for."'

They're thinking of putting a hot tub on the roof, and getting the ultimate TV satellite system so they can have people round on match days to watch Arsenal wherever they're playing.

'Oh, and you know what?' says Matt. 'This is how nervous I am about the tour: Ant and Dec had a party last night and I totally forgot to go.'

Trying to look on the bright side, Matt says this is all a learning process for him and David.

'I think it was a bit underestimated what we had to do. Maybe we should have done the tech earlier. We were so up against it that any changes we wanted to make creatively felt difficult to do.' He thinks there are some sketches that are a bit weaker than they should be, and he's not entirely sure if the whole show hangs together and makes sense. Suddenly he asks: 'Do you know how much we've spent on wigs?'

I don't, but I remember wig-master Richard outlining with great admiration how Matt and David had refused to scrimp on the wig budget.

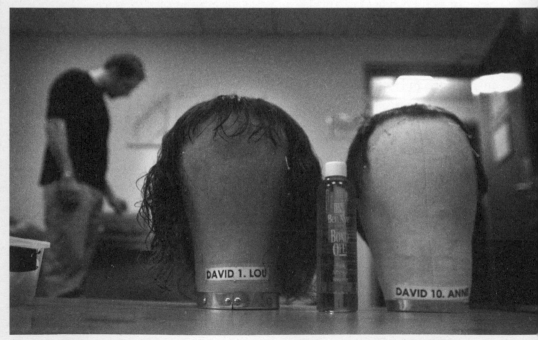

Wigs

'The *Fast Show* tour I think spent about thirteen or fourteen grand on wigs. We've spent nearly a hundred.'

'On wigs?' asks Kevin, with understandable incredulity.

'Yeah, wigs,' says Matt. 'It's worth it, though. And things are gradually getting better with the show.'

Changing the subject, Matt says it's good that I'm going along to the National TV Awards tomorrow night with his and David's mum. He's worried that the mums will be exposed to tabloid journalists.

'I've asked that one of our publicity people, Moira or Barbara, is there to look after them, but it's good that you're there too.'

He's right to be concerned. There will be journalists there who will stop at nothing to get a story. If you work for a tabloid gossip column, the pressure is on for you to find stories about famous people every day. The showbiz reporters are fiercely competing with each other for stories about the same clutch of noteworthy people, which right now includes Matt and David. The tabloid reporters need to get invited to events like the National TV Awards so that they can stock up on stories about TV celebrities that will keep their columns going for a few days at least.

Matt says he never likes to hang around at the after show parties, partly because he dreads having journalists prowling around him for stories and partly because he'd just rather go home and curl up on the sofa with a Bailey's and a packet of crisps.

David, on the other hand, tends to want to socialise with his friends at such events, and always gets bothered by reporters until he decides to leave. Yet really these events are completely tailored to the needs of the gossip columns.

Matt wonders if the stars of *The X Factor* will be at the National TV Awards. 'I'd love Sharon Osbourne to win something. If, God forbid, anything happened to Ozzy, I would like to marry her,' he says. 'Did you see *The X Factor* on Saturday? I love all those boy-band-type blokes who aren't really that good-looking. They wear the clothes that good-looking boys should wear, but actually they're a bit ugly. A pain on the eyes. Aargh! They're hurting my eyes! Get them off!'

'The other guy's good,' says Kevin.

'Shayne? Yeah, he's cute. But I think the binman might win.'

'Chico's quite entertaining,' says Kevin, 'but I don't think he should be there. It's supposed to be about singing.'

'Well,' says Matt, 'it's not about singing, it's about the X factor! Although there are some of them that shouldn't have got this far. Journey South – not my cup of tea to be honest. What's all the fuss about them?'

'They're the new Robson and Jerome,' says Kevin.

At a service station Matt and Kevin buy snacks and drinks and papers. 'These places always make me feel like a kid, like I'm on a trip with my parents,' says Kevin.

While we're at the tills, we notice David is in the same shop. He's looking dapper yet comfortable in a dark, single-breasted suit jacket, black T-shirt and jeans.

'Ooh hullo!' says Matt. 'How are you? How was last night? I forgot about the party! Isn't that terrible? Was it fun?'

'Yeah, it was good,' says David.

Matt suggests that I travel the rest of the way to Portsmouth with David. Before I make the swap, five or six fans stop to get autographs from Matt and David or to get their photographs taken with them.

'Come on, trouble!' says David, ushering me towards his car.

I ask David how his weekend has been.

'Erm, well, Saturday was quite hard: our last chance to rehearse the show. And of course it didn't all go according to plan, so it's a bit scary. Then I went out for dinner on Saturday night with Denise and another friend of hers.'

There's nothing sexual going on between David and Denise, despite some rumours to the contrary in the tabloids. They simply enjoy each other's company. The current person who is occupying most of David's romantic thoughts is a woman he dated a few times last year and with whom he has now become increasingly besotted. He has got to know her pretty well, been on quite a few nights out with her recently, and spent quite a while mesmerised by her at the Pride of Britain Awards, just after he'd got his practice in by flirting with Tony Blair. He also wants to protect the identity of the woman he calls 'her' because at this stage it's all so tentative and uncertain what – if anything – will happen between them. He doesn't want their fledgling friendship getting besmirched by unwanted coverage in the papers, which would inevitably happen because she is also quite famous. So for the purposes of this book we agree that we won't name her. We'll call her 'X'.

'And then I went to Ant and Dec's party last night,' he adds. 'Robbie was there. I gave him DVDs of the new series. And Jimmy Nesbitt, who always makes me laugh. And Denise was there and Kirsty Gallacher and Cat

Deeley. Ant and Dec both turn thirty this year. It was nice. Quite relaxed. It took my mind off the show. And I knew I wouldn't be able to sleep last night, so I stayed quite a while.'

In the end David managed to sleep for a couple of hours. He's just about managing to put the problems with the show out of his mind. He's comforting himself with the thought that the audience will be excited to see the show, and if some technical things go wrong with the changes and the cues they won't be too disappointed. He's happy with the content, and with his and Matt's performances, and if anything does go wrong then hopefully they can have some fun with it.

It's just difficult to know what will work in front of two thousand people. It's difficult to know how to pace the show for that many people. He's got to worry about whether the audience can hear every line. David and Matt were last on tour in 1997, and they were playing to hundreds, not thousands. And while Matt starred in the *Shooting Stars* live show, which played to similar-size audiences, this is all new to David.

'The idea that the whole world is watching is quite scary,' says David. 'That's an exaggeration but you know what I mean. Of course all the tickets are sold already, so even if we get bad reviews it's not the end of the world. I guess we still have to sell tickets for the London dates, and maybe those sales would be affected if the reviews were really bad . . . I think once the show is on, and the reviews start coming in, then it'll be different.'

The London shows – at the Hammersmith Apollo – start next September, and they hope to be in residence there for at least a couple of months.

'I think the tabloids will be fine. But the broadsheets – I don't know. It's quite a broad show. It's not that subtle, is it? But I tell you what the really stressful element of the whole thing is: being backstage. During the show it's going to get so hectic . . . while we're onstage and performing it's calmer because we're in control of it. But backstage there are the wigs and the costumes and the props and sets, and it's just really really stressful.'

He pauses, thinking.

'It's nice that Matt's got someone to share all this with. Do you know what I mean? He's got someone who can see all this, the success, the incredible unreality of it all, and I think that makes it seem more real maybe. I mean I've got my family, and lots of nice friends and everything, but I haven't got that someone intimate I can share all this with. And in all likelihood I'm experiencing the most incredible time of my life.'

I ask him how his relations with X are going.

'I think I'm going to invite her to Elton's wedding. That's got to be the ultimate date, hasn't it?'

Just as we get to the centre of Portsmouth, David says, 'Oh and I got a call from someone at Elton's office today: "Elton wants the dolls. Your *Little Britain* dolls." So I had to gather up all the ones I had in my house and give them to him. So I don't have any left. But obviously I wanted Elton to have them. Well, you would, wouldn't you?' The official *Little Britain* talking dolls of characters such as Lou and Andy and Vicky Pollard are selling out everywhere in the build-up to Christmas.

As for X, he still thinks about her every day. 'She's the kind of person I end up writing poems about.'

You write poems?

'Yeah. Every now and then. Well, I've only ever written them to two people: two women I've been in love with.'

Do you keep them?

'Er no, not really. They're kind of personal. I think I ended up writing them at the point where I was totally without hope. I don't think they're ever going to be collected in a volume.'

David tells me he was reading poetry by Harold Pinter last night. When he was feeling stressed out by the whole idea of the tour.

'Did I tell you I saw Pinter on the day he won the Nobel Prize? It was when I went to the Ivy with my parents after we were on *Parkinson*, and he was having dinner there with people like Simon Gray and Tom Stoppard, and – who's the guy who wrote *Closer*? – Patrick Marber. They were obviously celebrating his prize. I was so tempted to go up to him and congratulate him. But you think no, he'd probably rather be left alone.'

David has a thing about avoiding meeting his heroes. There are some people he holds in such high regard that he'd rather preserve the idea he has of them in his mind than risk having a disappointing encounter with them. He has had the chance to meet Björk and Mike Skinner of The Streets, for example, but bottled out because he loves them so much. In the back of David's mind is the time he did have a run-in with Harold Pinter.

He went to the theatre with Jonathan Ross to see Lee Evans in the Samuel Beckett play *Endgame* in the West End. They'd been given really good seats near the front, and as they sat down David noticed out of the corner of his eye that Harold Pinter was in the same row. He was too close for David to be able to say anything to Jonathan about it, but he was really excited because he is one of David's idols. Then Jonathan started talking quite loudly . . . about the safety curtain. 'Do you think that's the curtain they use for every production at this theatre?' he asked of David. 'Or is it a *special* curtain for this play?' David was just about to enter in to the discussion about the curtain, when Harold Pinter just looked at them, pointedly said, 'Excuse me!' and dramatically got up and moved about ten rows further back, giving up his really good seat to move to a much worse one. It was like he couldn't bear the thought of having to sit next to David and Jonathan Ross gabbling on.

David, though, still hero-worships Pinter.

Pete points out the venue at the end of the street.

'Oh wow. We're here. This is it. I'm quite excited now.'

Picking up on his new lease of life and optimism and general good mood, I ask him what he's most looking forward to about the show.

'The bit I'm most looking forward to is Des Kaye. Getting to play with a nice young man from the audience.' He laughs. 'I did Pete in rehearsals.'

Pete the driver says, 'Yeah, I could feel my belt pop when you grabbed me and I thought my trousers were going to come down.'

'Well, that's the idea. I want to get the trousers round the ankles. Obviously I wasn't going to subject you to that, Pete.'

'No. Thanks for that.' Pete, tall, northern, imposing but gentle, wouldn't look right with his trousers down. He's too dignified for that.

'What I really want is someone wearing tracksuit bottoms. They'll just come straight down. A belt and jeans is a bit difficult.'

'Linda Nolan's had a shit here!' announces David when he surveys his dressing room and its facilities.

There are big tubes of Smarties and Jelly Tots, and bottles of champagne and boxes of chocolates on the dressing table. And lots of bouquets of flowers from friends and well-wishers. He gets his iPod and its speakers out of his bag and sets it up on the dressing table. 'Get The Message' by Electronic pumps out quite loudly.

But it's a rather glum room, with ageing brown/maroon carpets, a couple of ragged chairs and one small window onto which the rain is thrumming gently. It's got a slightly musty smell to it. There's a big mirror surrounded by bare light bulbs, just like all the dressing-room mirrors in the movies. But apart from that, there's nothing glamorous about the place at all.

'They're weird places, aren't they, these regional theatres? I'm sure I've been here before with my mum and dad when I was a kid,' says David. 'It's like a big hall in front of the stage. And I didn't even see the front of the theatre. I expected to see a big marquee with our names on or something, but it feels like we've just found ourselves in this strange little venue. And it's so dark . . .'

I ask if anyone special is coming to see the show tonight.

'Apart from the critics, no. I wanted to let the show bed down. My mum and dad are coming at the weekend. And Erin O'Connor's coming, the model, and Jonathan Ross and family. They've got a country house near Bournemouth. It'll be lovely to see them. It's nice to have guests coming to see the show. I wonder what kind of response Jonathan and his family will get when they arrive at the venue? I imagine people will be quite excited to see them.'

Tony knocks on the dressing-room door and tells David that they've got a little audience gathered for the full dress rehearsal. There are about fifty or sixty people, made up of friends of Gareth, the stage manager, and others rustled up by the theatre. So it's going to be more or less a proper show, just with far fewer people to perform to. David is assured by Tony that there are no journalists there and they'll only be arriving in time for the actual first-night show later on, although the photographer for the tour will be taking pictures. 'Oh, and *The South Bank Show* is here,' he adds.

Roz, the producer from *The South Bank Show*, is in fact hovering in the corridor outside the dressing room. There's just her, a cameraman and a soundman, but it's something else for Matt and David to worry about. When Tony mentions her, she politely says hello and asks David if it's okay to film a bit of behind-the-scenes action in the build-up to the dress rehearsal. David says it's fine but that they need to be careful when they actually start the show because it's going to be pandemonium backstage, with very little space to manoeuvre.

'As long as you don't get in the way,' notes David gently but firmly.

'Oh we won't. We'll just sneak around. You won't notice us,' says Roz.

'That's what they all say,' says David jovially.

Kelly the make-up girl arrives to get David together for the start of the rehearsal. She says she's had 'an interesting weekend'. David asks her what

In the dressing room

she means. She's reluctant to explain. 'Oh come on,' he says. 'Tell us.' Eventually she explains that she's been travelling with the crew on the tour bus and she's having a hard time dealing with the gang of blokes who make up the majority. They're turning out to be smelly and loud and very blokey . . . so she didn't get much sleep.

'I don't want to sound feeble and girly, though. But it's just a bit difficult to deal with. I suppose they're just messing about . . .'

'So they're carousing?' asks David. 'Like pirates . . .'

'Yes,' she says. 'There must be something like thirty of us on that bus. You should come and have a look, David. Or ride on it with us one time.'

'Noooo . . . but thanks!' He laughs. 'Seriously though, if you're not comfortable with it, you should tell Tony and maybe you could travel with him and Sam and Paul. Or we could ask him for you.'

'No, we'll be all right. I'm sure I'll get used to it.'

David gets a text. I can tell it's from X. He's beaming. 'She wishes me good luck,' he says. 'And she's going to try to come and see the show next week.' He's got his wistful voice on. 'Oh God, I can't wait to see her . . .'

His revelry is interrupted when he notices an unopened letter on the table addressed to Jamie Cullum. It says 'confidential' on the front. 'That probably means it's a picture of some girl fan of his, naked.'

Matt comes in to David's dressing room to explain how he's made a couple of CDs to 'play in' while the audience is gathering in the auditorium and waiting for the show to start. 'One of them is a collection of real classic up songs: it's completely conventional with Beatles and Stones and Robbie,' he explains, 'just everything completely up, and I've done another for the interval and afterwards which is *The Dambusters* and the theme from *Thunderbirds* and the William Tell Overture, big British marching music. I think it will be fun and something different. It's all tunes everyone knows. But I still think it underlines that people are coming to see something different and exciting.'

'Okay.' David nods, then notices something. 'Look, I've got a towel.' It's a particularly sad little off-white towel draped on the back of his chair.

'And you've got a fridge,' says Matt. 'I don't have one. So I might have to borrow yours for water and stuff.'

'Oh yeah, of course. It's a bit ridiculous that you haven't got your own fridge. Maybe we should have thought about the rider. It's hardly Elton John, is it?'

When are you going to eat? I ask them.

'I don't know,' says David. 'I'd like to eat before the show, because if you come offstage and eat afterwards that's a sure way of becoming fat, and I don't want to become fat. Especially while I'm training for the Channel swim.'

'Maybe we can get takeaway or something before the show starts,' says Matt.

I still can't believe they haven't sorted out a rider. Tony tells them he will go and get some treats from Marks & Spencer.

Jeremy the director pops his head round the door to say hello, along with Andy the production manager.

David tells Jeremy and Andy that he's worried about the Des Kaye sketch, because he has to play around with a bloke from the audience and there isn't much room onstage. The sketch ends with David dragging his victim backstage. They need to make sure there's enough space to allow David to manoeuvre the audience member behind the curtain without them tripping over any props or bumping into any stagehands. Andy firmly assures him it will be fine and that there's enough room.

'We can't put someone in danger,' reiterates David. 'Especially as it's a member of the public and they could fall off the stage. It just doesn't feel like there's enough room.'

Andy says he'll try to make sure there's enough clear space.

'Okay, thanks. We've just got to be really careful,' says David.

Paul arrives.

'Hey!' he yells in his big, broad, loud Mancunian accent. 'Hey hey hey!'

'Hey hey!' replies David, slightly mimicking Paul's accent.

'Well, here we are!' shouts Paul, grinning broadly. Maybe he doesn't quite shout, but he says it loudly.

'Here we are,' replies David, laughing. 'The winners!' Just the merest exclamation of enthusiasm from Paul makes David laugh. Paul says everything loudly and with huge gusto.

'Good of you to promote the tour by appearing on the front of the paper! Smashing! Great stuff, David!'

'What do you mean?' asks David. 'Who? What paper?'

'The *Standard*,' Paul explains. 'You're on the front, pictured with your latest lay-dee!'

'What do you mean? Doing what?'

Paul explains that it's a photo of David and Denise leaving Ant and Dec's party last night.

'We're on the front page? Really?' says David, mystified. 'That's front-page material? Must be a crappy day for news. What does it say? Have you got a copy? Do I look good?'

Paul doesn't have a copy.

'Well, go and get one then!' says David, laughing.

I ask Paul if he remembers what the headline is.

'Oh "Comedy Love Rat's Latest Squeeze Denise" or something,' he says.

David smiles.

'Well, it was a nice picture.' Paul changes the subject. 'So are you feeling good about the rehearsal?' he asks.

David nods noncommittally.

Paul goes to find Matt, and David ponders the thought of being on the front page of the London *Evening Standard* with Denise Van Outen.

'You know what I really hate,' he says, 'is when a journalist asks what you think about being in the papers with famous women. You know – rather than ask if you're going out with someone, they go round the houses and ask how you're dealing with all the coverage in the papers.'

A tactic I've used many times myself, I sheepishly admit.

'Well really, it's easier just to be asked. "Are you going out with Denise Van Outen?" And you just say, no I'm not, and that's that. There's nothing more that can be said.'

During the full dress rehearsal in front of the mini-audience quite a few things do go wrong. During the curry sketch, in which Matt and David play a couple settling down to eat in a restaurant, there's just one fork between them on the table. Matt makes a joke about it to let the audience in on the mistake. Paul Putner's entrance as a flying bee interrupting the Dennis Waterman sketch is delayed, and David as Dennis says, 'Unprofessional bee! Sack the unprofessional bee!' David gets a couple of lines of dialogue wrong as Linda. The weighing-machine prop in the Marjorie Dawes sketch doesn't work properly. Marjorie's dress falls open at the back. And his Marjorie wig hair gets in his mouth, at which point he says, 'I wouldn't mind but it's not even my own hair.' Similarly, in the Mr Man bit, hairs from Matt's moustache fall off and sneak their way into his mouth, making him cough and splutter. Matt also has trouble finding someone in the front who has sweets for him to steal in the opening Lou and Andy sketch. One of David's two pairs of glasses in the Ray McCooney sketch falls off and he has to pick them up off the stage. And there's a delay before the vomit starts working, and when it does, you can hear a fizzing electric shock somewhere onstage, and the microphones start failing.

But in general it looks like a smooth, slick show. The transitions between sketches feel swift and clever, and the images that play on the giant screen while Matt and David aren't onstage are so engaging you barely notice that they're filling a void of a few seconds to allow the cast to change clothes and wigs. Everyone seems happy with how it's gone, even though watching the show with such a small audience is slightly odd. They are enthusiastic and laughing and applauding all the way through, but it's too small a crowd to generate any atmosphere. Although when David takes all his clothes off as Sebastian, squeals of shock, excitement and disbelief fill the theatre.

As soon as Matt sits down in his dressing room to recover from the dress rehearsal he says, 'One fork! That's funny, isn't it? A fork. A couple coming to eat and there's one fork!'

David stands by the door and says, 'The audience found it quite funny, didn't they? The way we made something of it.'

'Oh yeah, they loved it. But you're looking at it as you come onstage and you think, ah, one fork . . . okay, what do we do now?'

'Yeah, I think those kinds of mistakes aren't too bad. If we can make something funny out of it and the audience doesn't feel uncomfortable. Not that we want anything else to go wrong . . .'

Matt points out that there were people in the audience taking pictures on their mobiles and even filming it. 'Maybe we should have some signs up telling people to turn their phones off or something,' he says. ''Cause they'll film the show and sell it on eBay.'

Just then Tony arrives and tells Matt there's not much they can do about people taking pictures. 'If they try to film it on video cameras,' he says, 'we'll stop them. If we can get to them.'

Tony has another pressing issue to discuss. 'One favour. If it's achievable. The sausage. It would be good to try to make sure you get it back from the audience member . . . Otherwise we lose the sausage.'

'Have we only got one?' asks David.

'We've got two.'

'We should get some more.'

'Yep, but the stupid, strange thing is . . . well, I won't tell you how much the sausages cost.'

'Oh go on,' says Matt.

'Two hundred pounds for two. Basically that's a person for a day plus materials.'

'We could just get a real sausage,' suggests David.

'If you're happy to deal with a real sausage then I can get normal frankfurters,' says Tony.

'No, it's okay, I'll get it back. I can get the sausage back from the boy.'

'Two. Hundred. Pounds,' says Matt. 'We don't need to be paying that kind of money for a prop like that.'

'I know,' agrees Tony. 'We shouldn't be.'

David says, 'Well, I just wasn't aware of that . . .'

'I know, that's why I'm flagging it up . . .'

Matt asks, 'How real does it look?'

David says, 'It doesn't really matter.'

Tony says, 'It does look and feel quite real. It's got that flop to it . . .'

Matt says, 'Two hundred pounds . . .' again.

Tony suggests that David just makes sure he gets the sausage back from his victim in the middle of the sketch.

'You can just say: that's my tea, that is,' says Matt.

BC and Moira arrive. 'Have a seat in this very glamorous dressing room,' says David.

'It was fantastic,' says BC, 'especially the Dafydd song at the end. It was astonishing.'

Moira adds, 'And it was even funny when it went wrong.'

'With the fork!' says BC. 'You guys were hysterical, ad-libbing with the fork. It was really really funny.'

Matt asks how the video screens look, and what the visuals are like during his Dafydd song. He's never seen the video production number that gets projected behind him. I say that the video transitions look great.

David Arnold, the official *Little Britain* composer, is next to arrive.

'What did you think, David?' asks Matt.

'It was so much better than I was expecting,' he answers. 'Nothing big went wrong.'

David brings up the issue of finding a fat woman in the audience to take part in the Marjorie Dawes sketch. Do they need to make sure there's a fat lady in the audience? Matt says he thinks there will be, and if there isn't then he'll use a fat man. David also wonders, in the same sketch, whether it's really necessary for Matt as Marjorie to warn the person who's about to walk onstage and be humiliated by Marjorie that it will be the worst experience of their life.

'I just don't think it's that bad,' says David.

Matt points out that Marjorie does shout, 'You're fat! Fat pig!' at her victim.

Matt then says he couldn't find someone in the front row with sweets for him to steal in the opening Lou and Andy sketch, when Andy gets out of his wheelchair and jumps down from the stage to find some sweets.

'Yes, well, we've got to make sure there are some sweets. Let's get Tony to buy a box of Maltesers every day to give to someone in the front row so we know there'll be some there for you.'

Suddenly the relentlessly positive Paul says, 'Do it! Anything you need to do. Everything about this show reeks of class.' He pauses. 'Though we have fucking spent the money.'

'What, more than you thought we would?'

'Just a bit more.'

'Well, if we need to play maybe one week more of dates to recoup that money then . . .'

'That's all we'd need to do.'

'Of course by then I'll be suicidal,' Matt adds. 'Just with the tedium of doing the show every day.'

'Don't think about it,' says Paul.

Matt says, 'Those giant T-shirts that I give to the fat person each night cost thirty-five quid each. When you multiply that by over a hundred dates it does add up.'

Paul intervenes vehemently. 'Don't do that, Matt. You don't want to do that! Don't think about it. You've got to do it. It's like the sick. They love seeing the sick, even if it is expensive . . . It's a great act one closer. You can't not do it.'

'Yeah,' says Matt, 'and it worked. And it doesn't smell as bad as it did last week. I think it's the difference between the powdered soup and the canned soup. And maybe we could introduce more porridge oats so they stick on us a bit more. Shame it gave me an electric shock! Backstage it was spraying sick everywhere.'

6.35 p.m. We're back in the dressing-room area after the Chinese over the Spar. A bunch of red roses has arrived for Matt and David from Robbie Williams and Jonathan Wilkes. David's also got a box of M&S chocolates from his agent. They're very rich, luxurious chocolates which he happily samples as he waits for showtime. In the corridor are other bouquets of flowers, from their DVD distributors, from their BBC bosses, from BC and Moira, from their friends Lee and Josie, and from *The South Bank Show*. I'm thinking that maybe I should have brought them some flowers or chocolates or something.

The pre-show preparations begin. I'll see these take place in the same order at more or less the same time repeatedly over the next nine months. But this is the first time I see the routine enacted in full.

First Matt and David's individual make-up ladies arrive to do their faces. Then their individual dressers help them put on their respective costumes for the opening sketch: Matt as Andy, David as Lou. This involves them

Extra large

stripping down to their pants. Those of us who happen to be present in the dressing rooms before the start of the show will get to know what Matt and David's bodies are like pretty well over the ensuing months. And that David usually wears briefs, and Matt invariably goes for boxers. David will occasionally do a little camp dance in his underpants. After the costumes are put on, the soundman arrives to fix their microphones. Gareth the stage manager knocks on the door to give them the half-hour warning at around 7 p.m. A ten-minute warning is next, and finally, 'Beginners,' which means everyone should take their place ready to start the show as soon as they get the cue. It takes Matt a few seconds before each show to be strapped into a kind of saddle so that he can be elevated above the stage and flown in behind David in the opening sketch. The show is scheduled to begin at 7.30 p.m. each night, though it usually starts five or ten minutes after that, to allow the sell-out crowds to take their seats.

Moira and BC pop into each of the dressing rooms to tell Matt and David that the journalists from the *Sun* and *Mirror* are here. They've set up laptops and broadband links in the theatre's meeting room so the reporters can write their reviews as soon as the first night finishes and send them for publication the next day.

'We should say hello to them after the show, shouldn't we?' says David.

'That would be great,' says BC. 'You're *so* good! Okay, we're gonna take our seats. Good show!'

'Good show' seems to be the preferred method of wishing good luck to the performers. 'Good luck' seems to be frowned upon. 'Break a leg' feels a bit cheesy.

For a moment, with the publicists having taken their seats, the make-up and costume people having finished their work, and between announcements from Gareth, David is alone in his dressing room with just me for company. I don't have to ask if he's nervous. There's a grimace on his face like a child about to be dragged to his first day at school.

'I feel sick,' he announces. 'It's the wait. I just want the fucking thing to start.'

I tell him that if any of the audience members walked in right now, simply the sight of him in his Lou gear and goofy, curly wig would be enough to make them giggle.

'Yeah,' he sighs. 'I just don't feel very funny right now. I feel sick.'

He's pacing around now. He puts the Pet Shop Boys' 'Left To My Own Devices' on his iPod. 'This is such a spectacular song,' he says. 'I just hope it takes his mind off his nerves. He gets a call on his mobile. From the tone of his answers it sounds like it's Jonathan Ross calling him. I take my opportunity to check on how Matt's doing.

Tony the tour manager is in his dressing room, giving him some Maltesers.

'We need at least ten boxes of these every night,' says Matt, eating. 'Just to be on the safe side.'

Kevin perches on the edge of Matt's chair, slowly rubbing his back. What a difference it must make to have a partner with you at this moment. David arrives at Matt's door to tell him that Jonathan wishes him good luck.

Matt says, 'Shall we have one of those huddles like Madonna does before her shows?'

'And a nice prayer,' says David. He grabs a handful of Maltesers.

As soon as he gets back to his dressing room, David says, 'I just feel like throwing up'. He puts Morrissey's 'Everyday Is Like Sunday' on, and thrusts his body back and forth in time to the lilting melody.

7.25 p.m. I check out the auditorium. There are still some stragglers trying to find their seats but it's about 95 per cent full. About 1,800 people chattering loudly. Roughly equally divided into men and women, which is quite unusual for a comedy event. Comedy often seems to be loved most by blokes. There are some groups of blokes with beer but there are also plenty of gatherings of women. There's also a definite sense of first-night anticipation in the air. I speak to a few people in the stalls. They're thrilled to be the first people in the world to see the show. They're intrigued to know if the performance is going to include the vomiting lady, and if they'll do Bitty, David's breastfeeding adult. I tell them they're going to be disappointed on that last point. Sitting at the front, they're also worried about audience participation. And they can't quite believe they're here, having bought their tickets a year ago.

The supporting actors Samantha and Paul are already hovering backstage, deep in conversation. I ask them if they're nervous. 'Nah,' says Paul. 'It's our job to be the calm ones.'

'Yes, we're calm,' says Sam, slightly unconvincingly.

I go back to the dressing-room area, where Matt and David are standing in the corridor between their two rooms. They wish each other a good show, and march along the chilly corridors towards the stage. Roz and her *South Bank Show* boys are standing in the cramped backstage area. As Matt and David climb the wooden steps onto the rear of the stage, dodging in and out of sections of set, stagehands, and make-up, costume, prop and sound people, I realise what David was worrying about when he said it gets hairily hectic behind the curtain. Matt motions to me to join them as they walk onstage. We're two feet away from the closed curtain. On the other side of it are 1,800 fans of *Little Britain*, waiting to laugh and be entertained. And critics from most of the national newspapers. As Matt is hoisted up towards the ceiling, David pokes me in the chest and says, in his comedy sincere thespian voice, 'Let's make some live comedy.'

The curtains are parted to reveal David standing there as Lou, in his shiny tracksuit bottoms pulled snugly round his crotch. The sound of 1,800 people applauding, cheering and even screaming simultaneously seems to encourage David to make his performance twice as big as it was during the dress rehearsal a few hours ago. And when Matt as Andy hovers into view, high up above the stage and behind David, the response from the crowd is even louder. I glance around at the tour manager, the stage manager, the crew. Everyone backstage is grinning, madly.

1999

Matt and David thought this was going to be their big break in TV: a Channel 4 spoof boyband sitcom called *Boyz Unlimited*, which they had created. They could write it and star in it.

They'd seen a documentary in 1998 called *A Band Is Born* in the BBC2 Modern Times strand, about the creation of a boyband called Upside Down. It was one of those documentaries that everyone with an inclination towards the absurdities of pop culture seems to have watched. Matt and David thought they could write a funny spoof of it, and turned it into an amusing little sketch for the Paramount Comedy channel. Then Hat Trick, one of the most success-ful independent TV production companies of the time, encouraged them to develop the idea into a six-part half-hour series for Channel 4.

Matt and David set about creating the series helped by a writer/producer called Richard Osman, with whom David had worked previously. The idea was that the three of them would write it, Matt and David were going to star in it – as the Gary Barlow and Howard Donald-type figures respectively – and Richard was going to produce it. He took over the business side of things and pitched it himself to Seamus Cassidy, a comedy commissioner at Channel 4. In the writing sessions, Matt thought it was odd that Richard never seemed to look him in the eye. He sensed something might be wrong from the start.

And so it turned out.

Even though the whole show was their idea, when it came to negotiating the contract to make the series, suddenly Matt and David were left floundering with no leverage at all. They'd entered into a working relationship with Osman purely on trust. It felt to them as though he had been aiming to get rid of them from the project all along.

They were devastated. Partly because they felt they'd been screwed over, and partly because they felt they had had an opportunity to forge a working relationship with the biggest comedy production company of the moment.

The most distressing element of the whole experience was a meeting that Matt, David and Richard had with Jimmy Mulville, the head of Hat Trick.

Mulville just started shouting at them. He told Matt and David that he didn't want them on the show, he didn't know who they were, that he'd got the commission from Channel 4 and he didn't want them coming in and ruining it. He told them to take some minor roles in the series, take a script-editing credit and get on with it.

It was a horrible experience for Matt and David. They felt they'd been bullied. Their agent at the time was present, but said nothing. David came out of the meeting nearly in tears.

But Hat Trick still needed Matt and David's signatures to make the series. Matt told them he wouldn't give them his signature because he didn't want to validate their behaviour. He told them they could go ahead and make the programme, but they said, 'No, we need your signatures.' Matt said, 'I don't care . . . it's not about money. I'm just disgusted with your behaviour and I'm not going to give you my signature . . .' So Matt refused to sign and was called up by his agent and he got the impression that if he didn't sign she couldn't guarantee that he'd ever work again.

So he signed, and they were both paid a small amount of money each for their troubles.

Matt went away on holiday and read the *NME* on the plane, which had an interview with Richard Osman as the creator of *Boyz Unlimited*.

Matt was apoplectic. The timing couldn't have been worse. It all happened just after his dad died, the most painful event in his life so far. Now his first big TV break with David was turning out to be a nightmare. He felt totally crushed. He was in such a state of stress that he lost a lot of weight. Bob Mortimer, with whom he was working on *Shooting Stars*, told him just to walk away from the whole thing.

For David, too, it felt like a massive, soul-destroying setback. It was their introduction to the world of television, and they felt strongly that they'd been fucked over in what they perceived to be a ruthless manner.

But they'd learned about the harsh realities of the industry too, and that, much like any business, one had to be tough to stay on top and survive. They also learned about the importance of agents, and contracts, and trusting people, and trusting your judgement. Matt would swear that since then Richard Osman couldn't look him in the eye.

In the end, Matt and David watched *Boyz Unlimited* go out on Channel 4, their names barely connected to it. And they thought it was shit.

David bumped into Richard recently. He's now a successful producer, and was working on the Channel 4 panel game *8 Out of 10 Cats*, on which David was appearing as a panellist. But he just couldn't bring up the *Boyz Unlimited* experience. He knew he would get upset and angry, and he wanted to be happy and confident to perform on the show.

Both Matt and David bumped into Jimmy Mulville in Soho recently, when they were with their friend and colleague Geoff Posner. Mulville offered his hand to Matt and David to shake. There was an embarrassing pause because neither of them wanted to shake his hand. In the end they did, mainly to avoid embarrassing Geoff.

The vomit doesn't work. A squirt of sick here and there, but no gushing fountains of puke. And Matt's microphone cuts out in the middle of a few sketches and each time no one in the crew seems to notice for ages, while of course it's apparent to the entire audience.

Both Matt and David are angry and frustrated as they walk offstage after the anti-climactic non-vomiting end of the first act, but their annoyance is tempered by the fact that in general the show is going down brilliantly. The audience is in an almost constant state of audible elation. David's molestation of a young man from the audience in the Des Kaye sketch brings delighted gasps as they realise that yes, David really is going to wrestle the lad to the floor, pull down his jeans, climb on top and dry-hump him. The mere sight of Vicky Pollard walking onstage with her six prams stuck together is met with near hysteria. So while there is confusion when the audience can't hear what Matt is saying in the Mr Man sketch, and while the vomit failure is mystifying for everyone watching, it somehow doesn't really matter. The 1,800 fans adore the whole spectacle, technical faults and all.

So there's a weird calmness to David's query of 'What went wrong?' to anyone who'll listen as he trots back to his dressing room. And when Matt says, 'No one told me my microphone wasn't working,' he isn't yelling in disbelief. He is instead, seconds later, asking me if the audience is enjoying it as much as it sounds to him onstage. I tell him they're lapping it up, and Matt says, 'Yeah, they're great.'

'It really helps when you've got two thousand people laughing all the time,' says David.

A succession of members of the crew come into the dressing rooms to apologise to Matt and David for the vomit and sound cock-ups, and Matt and David are firm in their request that something be done about both issues.

'There's really no point doing that sketch if the vomit's not going to work,' points out David.

'Shouldn't there just be a back-up mic?' asks Matt.

The soundman explains that there are back-ups but that at the moment the people in the middle of the auditorium working at the sound desk can't communicate with the people backstage with the microphones.

'Why not?' asks David. 'It seems like something that they should be able to do.'

There's no budget for walkie-talkies, explains the soundman.

Right on cue Paul the promoter arrives and says they'll make sure they can communicate with each other. 'It's in hand. Don't worry about it.'

David smiles.

'Fucking brilliant job, guys,' adds Paul. 'Just amazing.'

BC and Moira arrive. 'It's incredible,' drawls BC. 'Just unbelievable.'

She says that in addition to the journalists from the *Sun* and the *Mirror*, there are critics here from the *Independent*, *The Times*, the *Telegraph* and the London *Evening Standard*. And if they're paying any attention to the audience, says Moira, they'll all give it a rave review.

'Well, you never know,' says David calmly. 'They can just as easily ignore what the audience reaction is and decide to slag it off.'

'I bet we get some snidey reviews,' says Matt. 'Especially from the broadsheets. But in the end, does it really matter? Listen to that lot out there. They're having a good time, aren't they?'

'Oh God, they're fucking loving it,' says BC.

'Do you think they'll mention the technical problems?' asks Matt. 'The critics, I mean. Or do you think they'll take the fact that it's the first night into account?'

'I think they might mention the sick not working. It would be weird to ignore it,' says David. 'But I also don't think that should stop them from giving us a good review.'

The second half has a few minor technical hitches. Matt's mic crackles every now and then. Matt and David get a few lines jumbled up during the Dennis Waterman sketch, but the audience loves that. In fact, the applause and cheers just seem to get louder after each sketch. By the time David strips naked for the Sebastian sketch, it feels like all 1,800 of them are practically ecstatic with excitement. The encore of Dafydd's song and the accompanying dance routine and production number inspires a standing ovation.

Failed vomiting aside, it really couldn't have gone much better. Whatever else happens for the rest of this epic tour, Matt and David know they've got a hugely crowd-pleasing show. At least if this first night is anything to go by.

There's an impromptu celebratory gathering in Matt's dressing room. Matt and David have changed out of their revealingly clingy gay Dafydd-sketch outfits and have showered to wash off their make-up, and now they're taking in the approbation of their agents, publicists, tour managers, colleagues and the crew from *The South Bank Show*. Everyone agrees that the show has been a triumph. We're all trying to find different ways of congratulating Matt and David, seizing upon favourite moments. Certain observations are agreed upon: the audience loves it when Matt and David stumble over lines or when they corpse. I've noticed through rehearsals and now in front of an audience that it's usually Matt who corpses, and David goes along with it for a bit, because he knows the audience gets excited. It all adds to the sense of being at a unique occasion. Live. Special. You don't see them making mistakes in the TV show. There's also general agreement that the audience participation bits bring the house down, and that the closing song is a suitably spectacular way of ending the show.

BC says, 'The song, Dafydd's song, is fucking amazing. But the Pet Shop Boys are gonna sue!'

'Well, luckily they're our friends,' says David, 'and I think it's more of a Pet Shop Boys pastiche, or a homage . . .'

Tony arrives with champagne. David's keen to meet and greet the people from the *Mirror* and the *Sun*, so we go along and take champagne with us too.

Polly Hudson from the *Mirror* and Gordon Smart from the *Sun* are bashing away at their laptops in a large hall at the back of the theatre. BC gives them glasses of champagne and jokes that she's getting them drunk so they write gushingly nice reviews. Matt and David introduce themselves to Polly and Gordon and thank them for coming all the way from London to see the show. They're being friendly and charming and trying not to seem too much like they're just after a good review. And it's not really a blatant schmoozing exercise. They both feel it would be rude not to say hello, and they do both appreciate the fact that Polly and Gordon have come to Portsmouth. David also invites the reporters to the hotel afterwards for a post-show drink. BC whispers to me that I should try to lean over Polly's shoulder to check what she's writing. I think she's joking. We agree it would be peculiar for either of these two journalists to slag off a show that has clearly gone down so well with the audience. I suggest, though, that the broadsheet critics won't let the crowd's reaction affect their opinion. BC agrees. 'Oh yeah. They'll fucking slag it off if they feel like it!' Maybe that's why there aren't any broadsheet journalists here in this room.

After meeting the tabloid writers, David and Matt arc keen to get to the hotel, which is at least thirty minutes away by car. They make sure the rest of the cast and crew as well as their agents and publicists know that they'll be having first-night drinks at the hotel bar, and off we go.

The journey from the theatre stage door to Matt and David's cars is short enough, but there's a large gathering of fans waiting to greet them. They were expecting maybe a handful of devotees to wait the half-hour or so after the end of the show to catch a sighting of them, but as we emerge from the back of the theatre in the pouring rain we see fifty or sixty people gathered there. Among the crowd is a group of blokes dressed in Emily and Florence-style drag, waving photos of Matt and David while shouting, 'We are lay-dees!' They've waited so long in the cold and rain that Matt and David are happy to sign autographs, although it's a bit of a scrum. Only one signed item per fan, though, is the rule, enforced firmly by Cosmo and Pete, the drivers/security team. As soon as a fan offers more than one book or programme or DVD to be signed, you know they'll be auctioned off on eBay.

After ten minutes or so of signing, Matt and Kevin get in their car, driven by Cos, and I accompany David in his, driven by Pete.

This will be the default pattern for the rest of the tour. It just seems to make sense for me to keep David company, while Matt and Kevin need their moments alone together after the hectic, tense and exciting day.

As it turns out, David hardly needs my company during the journey from the Portsmouth Guildhall to the hotel. He gets calls on his mobile from Sam Taylor-Wood, Paul Kaye, X, Robbie Williams, Reece Shearsmith, Neil Tennant, and Martin, his old head of drama at Bristol University. They're all asking him how the first night has gone, so I hear him explain seven or eight times that the vomit machine didn't work, the mics had a few failures and they got some lines wrong, but that overall it was fine. And they got a standing ovation. Martin wants David and Matt to give a talk to the current drama students when they start their dates at the Bristol Hippodrome in December. David thinks it's a good idea. He was so inspired when he was at Bristol by any even vaguely famous or successful alumni that he wants the chance to try to inspire the students of the moment.

I hear him discussing a shoot Sam Taylor-Wood recently did of Matt and David for a newspaper interview. David would like a print of the cover shot. (There's some discussion of whether David should pay for it, which he's happy to do, because Sam is clearly offering to do it for free, and also, while she's at it, is there any chance of David getting a print of her famous photo of Kate Moss naked and smoking a cigar, in return for a substantial donation to the charity it was originally taken for?) They also discuss being invited to Elton's wedding. Sam is doing the wedding photos. With Neil Tennant, he mainly ends up explaining the logistics of the tour, how he and Matt have separate cars so they can have independent plans on a day-by-day basis ('Though I woke up this morning, one day in, and thought: what am I going to do with myself?' says David), and then David tells Neil about the Dafydd song and how Pet Shop Boysy it is. Neil's offering to do a remix of it, which David says would be an honour, and they also discuss the possibility of releasing it as a single. I hear Neil suggest in a jolly tone: 'It could be a Christmas number one!' They end the conversation by agreeing that the song works best in the confines of the show. And they discuss Madonna's new album. Neil wants to come and see the show when it arrives in Newcastle, or maybe Manchester. Finally Robbie, David tells me, says he's going to try to come to one of the Southend shows next week. He's trying to arrange a helicopter to bring him to the Southend Cliffs Pavilion.

Checking in doesn't go very well. The woman on reception has no record of David's tour pseudonym (in the tradition of celebrities being checked into hotels under false names for security reasons, David is Mr Brown and Matt is Mr Green). David asks her to check the *Little Britain* party details. In theory, everyone from the *Little Britain* tour, including myself, should be in the hotel's computer system under the same booking. David tells her his real name. Still no luck. You would have thought she might recognise him, but she's got a heavy eastern European accent.

'Oh God,' he says, exasperated, to the hotel employee. 'Well, I'm definitely supposed to be staying in this hotel. I'm not making it up.'

She has a blank, rather disinterested expression. Neither of his names seems to be in her system and that, quite simply, is that. She is resistant to the possibility that there might be some kind of error in her system. No one else from the tour party has arrived yet, so there's not much more David can do, except stand there and get irritated. He wants to dump his bags and clothes in his room, have a quick wash and settle down at the bar for a relaxing drink.

'*Little Britain*? *Little Britain* tour? Can you check that?' he suggests to her. She's squinting at him.

'Little . . .?'

I suggest he asks if she's got a booking under Tony's name. It works. Huge relief.

In the lift up to his room, David says, 'And people wonder where we get our characters from.'

David unpacks a few items to help himself feel at home: his iPod and its speaker system, and his books to read over the next few weeks – new novels by Bret Easton Ellis and Kazuo Ishiguro, *How Mumbo Jumbo Conquered the World* by Francis Wheen and a collection of essays by George Orwell. He spots me eyeing up his books and asks me if I've read Ishiguro's *The Unconsoled*. I haven't. He tells me it is his favourite book of all time.

By his bed are some chocolates left by the hotel as a welcoming treat. He grabs one, then says he really shouldn't eat it.

'I need to lose weight for the swim,' he says, 'or at least get fitter. I think I'm supposed to have a certain amount of fat on me. But I also want to lose weight in time for X coming to see the show next week. I want to look my best for her.' He laughs.

At least he'll be swimming every day, I tell him.

'Yeah . . . maybe I'll go to the gym too . . . just in time for her visit.' He's joking about it, but he's not really smiling much now. 'Oh God. I hate fancying someone too much. It's really unhelpful. You lose all judgement, and it occupies your mind.'

I ask him if she's coming to see the show on her own.

'Er, she's bringing her sister. I asked if her sister looked like her and she said yes, except she's got bigger tits. Well, bring her on!' He stops his efforts at organising his room. 'Right, come on, Trouble, let's have a drink!'

Matt's driver Cos, an indefatigably upbeat man, got rather lost on the way. His satellite navigation system kept conking out. Tony the tour manager is having a chat with the hotel staffer who had trouble checking David in. Paul and Sam, the supporting cast, are already in the bar area with Phil McIntyre and Paul, and Matt's agent Melanie and David's agent Conor. Polly from the *Mirror* and Gordon from the *Sun* are here too, chatting with Barbara Charone and Moira Bellas.

David and I order drinks from the bar. Before we've found a seat, Gordon is greeting us. Gordon is young, friendly, quite trendy, charming and straightforwardly nice. A million miles away from the stereotype of a tabloid hack. He asks David how he's feeling after the first night, and David immediately asks him if the conversation they're about to have is off the record. Gordon says it is totally off the record and that they're just having a private chat. David tells him he's delighted by the response to the first show, that it's very exciting to be on tour. Gordon asks what he thinks about his newspaper's gay-o-meter devoted to David in Victoria Newton's Bizarre column. David says it's fairly harmless and quite funny sometimes. Gordon comments how ironic it is that people think David is camp considering all the famous women he's been linked with. David smiles and asks him again if their chat is off the record, and then dodges Gordon's question by saying that just because he's linked with people doesn't mean he has ever dated them. Gordon asks him about appearing on *Parkinson* the other week, and David says it was brilliant and must have been one of the gayest *Parkinson*s ever. David then spots that Matt and Kevin have been given some sandwiches by a waiter, and catches the waiter's eye to order some poached salmon sandwiches. It's past 11 p.m. and he hasn't had anything to eat since 5.30 p.m. David's agent Conor comes over to congratulate him, and so his pleasant, brief off-the-record chat with Gordon comes to its natural end.

While David talks to Conor, Gordon asks me how I know Matt and David, and Polly from the *Mirror* joins in our discussion, explaining to

Gordon that I've been 'stalking' them for years. I've also known Polly for years. I ask Gordon where his review of the first night of *Little Britain Live* will end up in the *Sun*. Will it be in Victoria Newton's Bizarre page? I wonder. Yes, he tells me, it probably will. Most of Gordon's reporting ends up on the Bizarre page, under Victoria Newton's banner. That's how newspaper gossip columns work.

Later, when David is saying good night to me and we arrange to have breakfast next morning, he asks me if I think it was a good idea to speak to Gordon. I tell David that Gordon seems like a decent bloke, and that I'm sure it'll be fine, and that the conversation was harmless.

8

25 October 2005 – Portsmouth: day 2

The morning after the first night of the tour, Matt and David gather in the hotel restaurant for a breakfast meeting with their agents. There are major career issues to discuss. Do they want to do a fourth series? Should they just do the Christmas Special? When should the series three DVD come out? When should the tour DVD come out? Who should direct it? What should be in the DVD extras? Do they have time to work on separate film projects this year? Matt's agent Melanie asks how they're coping being away from home. David says it's fine so far, after one day, but he's frustrated that in this hotel on the outskirts of Southampton he can't get hold of the morning papers to read the reviews of their first night. Matt nods. 'It's like being in a foreign country,' he says.

'Yeah, I feel like I'm on holiday trying to keep in touch with what's going on back home. We have to phone friends in London and get them to read out the reviews to us,' says David.

They drift on to discussing other comforts that they've had to leave behind at home. 'Like teddy bears,' says Matt.

'I don't have any teddy bears.'

'Did you ever have teddy bears?'

'No,' David says firmly. 'I never had a need for a teddy.'

Matt can hardly believe it. 'You never had one as a child?' he asks. 'I used to name my teddies after my friends. Did you have like . . . a Girls' World?'

'Can we get the first-night reviews faxed to us?' asks David.

Melanie nods and says she'll ask BC to sort it out.

We discuss what to have for breakfast and Matt warns everyone: 'Careful with the chips!'

'What was wrong with the chips?' asks David.

Matt explains that he and Kevin ordered a portion of chips last night from room service because they were still hungry, and it arrived doused in salt. 'Enough salt to fill a large vial,' says Matt. He was so stunned by the salt that he told the waiter to bring the duty manager up so that he could show him, and because Matt didn't want the waiter to take the blame for the salty chips. Sure enough, the duty manager arrived promptly, and Matt removed the chips from the bowl to show him the mountain of salt left at the bottom.

'What did he say?' asks David.

'Not much!' laughs Matt. 'He couldn't really say anything. He apologised and offered to bring us a new portion of chips with less salt for free. But – and I know I'm sounding like a moaning old twat – but it was an amazing amount of salt, Dave. Honestly! It was a portion of salt with some chips on top.'

A young man comes up to the table and asks Matt and David if they mind him disturbing their breakfast so that he can take a picture of them with his mobile phone. He tells them he was in the bar last night with all his mates ('What? All of them?' asks David) and that he couldn't pluck up the courage then, but he can now. Matt asks me to take the shot so the young man can get his photo taken standing between them. This happens more or less every time they appear in public. Life must have been quite different a few years ago for famous people before the proliferation of cameraphones. Sometimes – though quite rarely – Matt and/or David might not be in the mood to have their picture taken, but if the fan is like this bloke – normal, friendly, and above all polite – then they'll usually go along with the request quite merrily. Fan demands are now probably roughly divided half and half into those who want an old-fashioned autograph and those who want a picture taken with their mobile phone. Matt says he used to be quite an avid autograph hunter, and that when his grandmother took him to the theatre they would inevitably wait by the stage door to get the stars' autographs.

If Conor and Mel have an agenda, they've got a cunningly deft way of bringing up the items on it. Mel starts off by simply asking how the tour's going so far, after one day, and after listening to Matt explain that he's coping with the technical problems only because he knows they've got a good show, and that he's worried about getting bored but at least he's got Kevin with him, then David explaining that he thinks some sketches go down better in a live situation than they might do on TV, Mel steers them gently into a discussion of what they want to do about the live DVD, coming out next autumn, and what features it should have. David's heard that some live DVDs – like U2's – have an alternative angle function, allowing the viewers to choose different ways of watching the show. Matt, who knows about these things, gets quite excited about the prospect of using this technology, and says they should also do an audio commentary. David agrees, and would also like someone to film some of the live shows in the build-up to the actual show they record professionally for the DVD (which won't happen till much later in the tour next year).

Another cameraphone-wielding fan asks to take Matt and David's picture, and this time David says, 'I'm sorry, we're just in the middle of a business meeting . . .' but Matt's already standing up to let him take the photo. So David stands up too, and smiles dutifully for the fan.

Matt and David bring up the issue of what show or shows to film for the DVD. There's been an assumption that they'll be filming some of the Hammersmith Apollo shows next September, and Matt says that it might be easier to be bold and daring with those shows because they'll be doing a residency there. Matt also mentions filming extra stuff, inserts of some kind, like a Queen DVD he's seen where in the middle of a song the DVD suddenly cuts to shots of the members of Queen on a boat. Matt says most of his live DVD references will be somehow connected to Queen. Conor says they could dress as members of Queen. David smiles and says that any filmed items like that should be kept in the DVD extras, and then they get on to the subject of the possibility of doing a film together. David says if they did a film, he would want to make it big and ambitious, and not just a little, low-budget British film. 'Dream scenario,' he says, 'would be to get someone like Terry Gilliam to direct it. Someone you'd not necessarily associate with us. I'd buy a ticket to see it.'

David also suggests maybe doing a film with the BBC, like *Tomorrow La Scala*, a small-scale but quality film that did also get a cinema release. A 90-minute film, maybe to go on at Christmas, with all original characters. Matt says he's always thought it would be funny to do something about Nelson and Napoleon. David thinks there is some kind of Nelson/Napoleon script out there.

Matt says, 'What about the Creation? We could play Adam and Eve.' He's laughing.

David wants to know if the BBC definitely wants a *Little Britain* Christmas Special. Mel says they definitely do, so David says they'll need to know about the budget, because that will affect how they write it. Matt brings up the subject of forming their own production company, maybe with Geoff Posner, to start making their own programmes rather than just have the BBC make them.

The thorny topic that crops up and keeps going round and round, in and out of discussion, is what to do about the next TV series of *Little Britain*. At one point Matt suggests maybe doing a shorter fourth series of *Little Britain* (three episodes? four?), maybe start writing it on tour and film it in the summer, or maybe the Christmas Special followed by a whole new series. David says shorter series always feel weird, and that it just seems natural to do six-part half-hour comedy series. And he adds that the BBC might not be happy with a short fourth series. Mel points out that the BBC would be ecstatic with any new *Little Britain* material whatsoever. One thing is clear: Matt isn't ready to say goodbye to *Little Britain* and its characters no matter what the reaction from public and critics is to series three. (He still remembers many of the harsh reviews of series two.) David is emotionally attached to the characters too, but he is also leaning towards branching out and doing something new. At one point he says, 'My dream scenario would be to find a classic novel of some kind that featured two strong, funny main characters that me and Matt could play, which could go out in a 90-minute special. Like Fry and Laurie achieved with Jeeves and Wooster.'

Their agents reassure Matt and David that no firm decisions have to be taken right now, and that they can wait to see what happens with series three, and how keen the BBC will be for more *Little Britain*.

On Matt and David's second night at the Portsmouth Guildhall, the National TV Awards are taking place at the Albert Hall in London. *Little*

Britain has been nominated for Most Popular Comedy. This is the event to which I'm accompanying their mums, since Matt and David can't make it themselves. In the event they win, their mums will collect the award. It's David's idea, as Matt told me earlier, and he emphasised how typical it was of David to come up with ideas of such perfect simplicity. 'I think if you somehow counted up the initial ideas for our material, you'd find that David came up with the vast majority. The final product is always a joint thing, but he's far more prolific than me when it comes to ideas.'

Diana and Kathleen are both looking very smart, similarly attired in black dresses with necklace and bracelet accessories. They're accompanied by Ralph, Matt's stepdad, and Peter, David's father – who are both in traditional dinner suits, looking a bit more shuffly and unsure of themselves as they negotiate their way among the famous. They're the first VIP guests to arrive in the special area designated for nominees only; the rest of the nominees are still negotiating the red carpet. But the *Little Britain* mums and their husbands went through the red carpet area unrecognised, even by the highly trained showbiz reporters.

The mothers have been sat together at the end of a row, with their husbands keeping each other company next to them. As far as Matt and David's chances of winning are concerned, this seems promising, because their representatives have been given easy access to the stage. Within ten minutes of taking their seats, Diana and Kathleen are surrounded by instantly recognisable faces. Davina hugs Dermot, Ant chuckles at Dec, and Paul O'Grady points at Jamie Oliver's black eye. And there's Russell T. Davies and his *Doctor Who* gang talking to the *Coronation Street* people. Billie Piper takes her seat, directly in front of David's mum, and probably doesn't quite realise that she's one of a handful of women who David, in his dreams, would quite like to become his partner. She sat on his lap at a party recently, and he told me it was one of the highlights of his life.

At 7.25 p.m. I get a text from David: 'Hope our mums are okay. Let me know if we've won. Dx.' I text him back that Billie is sitting in front of his mum, happily chatting to her. 'It's good for her to meet her future daughter-in-law,' he replies. In five minutes' time he and Matt will be hovering in the wings of the Portsmouth Guildhall waiting to go onstage, worrying about whether the sick machine is going to work in only their second performance of the tour, and maybe finding time to fret a little bit about how their mums will be coping with the job of picking up their National TV Awards for them. If they win, that is. They are firm favourites in their category though, up against *Max and Paddy's Road to Nowhere*, *The Simpsons* and *Will and Grace*, none of which get as many viewers as *Little Britain*. Matt and David, though they'd never admit it in public, are both quietly confident they'll win, and agree that their only significant rival is Peter Kay's *Max and Paddy*. The only factor going against *Max and Paddy* is that it wasn't as critically acclaimed as *Phoenix Nights*. It's still possible that the huge amount of affection in which PK is held will be a threat to Matt and David's chances. Matt told me he wouldn't mind if Peter won because he thinks he is the funniest man alive. But I think it's cut and dried. Everyone's talking about Lou and Andy right now, not Max and Paddy. Then I spot Peter Kay. I'm surprised he's there. He doesn't go to many showbiz events like this. I wonder whether maybe he knows something the rest of us don't. Has he been told that he's won? Would he really make the journey to London just to sit there looking a bit embarrassed if he doesn't win the award for which his show has been nominated?

The Most Popular Comedy category is the penultimate award of the night. This means that Matt and David's mothers have to sit there for over two hours before they find out if they're going to have to get up in front of 5,000 people in the auditorium and eight million people watching on TV and make an acceptance speech.

Mindful of the unusual task they've set for their mothers, Matt and David have at least prepared something for them to say in the event of them winning. They've kept it simple so that Kathleen and Diana don't make fools of themselves. Not that they're expecting their mothers to make fools of themselves, but they know they're asking quite a lot of them.

The mums and dads look a bit startled when rival Conservative Party leadership contenders David Cameron and David Davis appear at the top of the stage to present the award for Most Popular Drama early in the evening, and they get loudly booed. The crowd reaction to the Tory politicians seems to shock Diana and Kathleen. It's not like the BAFTAs. This crowd is made up of thousands of members of the public, rather than just hundreds of industry peers checking out the contents of their goody bags. The announcement of *Doctor Who*'s Chris Eccleston as the winner of the Most Popular Actor category is weirdly greeted by boos as well, which only get louder when Sir Trevor explains that Eccleston isn't present. Russell T. Davies picks up the award on his behalf, and ignores the crowd.

When Sir Trevor announces that the next award will be presented by Peter Kay, my doubts about the Most Popular Comedy category are eased. There's another reason for Kay to be here, not just because he's been nominated. Maybe *Little Britain* will win after all . . .

Eventually, 116 minutes into the event, Sir Trevor introduces Rik Mayall, who's presenting the Most Popular Comedy award. He reads out the nominations, 'Which don't include me, you bastard!' he says, in an approximation of his old Rik voice in *The Young Ones*. They show clips of each one (in the case of *Little Britain*, Bubbles getting burnt under the tanning machine), then Rik clears his throat in a comedy manner and seems to take an inordinate amount of time opening the envelope and eventually says, 'And the National Television Award goes to . . . *Little Britain*!' Peter Kay and his co-writer and co-star Patrick McGuinness look as if they thought they were going to win.

Sir Trevor announces: 'Matt Lucas and David Williams can't be here tonight because they are on tour, but just in case they won they sent their mothers Kathleen Williams and Diane Lobatto.' That should have been Kathleen *Walliams* and *Diana* Lobatto, Sir Trevor, but you can't get everything right. The mothers do their bit magnificently, confidently striding to the stage hand in hand under the spotlight, climbing the dozens of steps and accepting the award from Rik Mayall, who bows down before them, kisses each of them and hands over the gong.

'Hello, I'm Diana, Matt's mum,' says Diana.

'And I'm Kathleen, David's mum,' says Kathleen.

Huge cheer.

'Our sons would just like us to thank everyone who voted for them,' says Diana. Then Kathleen adds the punchline. 'Especially us, because we voted for them a hundred times for each one. Thank you very much.'

I can't work out whose grins are bigger and wider, the mums or the thousands of people in the audience, who are thrilled by this moment. I look around me and there's unbridled delight on everyone's faces. Billie looks even happier than when she went to pick up her award.

Diana and Kathleen are ushered off the stage by Rik Mayall and their moment of glory is over.

I text David and Matt to congratulate them on their win and tell them that their mums have done them proud. They'll be coming offstage about now.

Billie Piper is still grinning.

I meet the mums and dads at the entrance of the gallery next door to the Albert Hall where the official party is taking place and congratulate them on their triumphant performance. David calls me on my mobile and asks to speak to his mum so I put her on to him. She tells him they've had a lovely time, they've been very well looked after and that Rik Mayall was especially kind and considerate to them.

I want to make sure they haven't been nobbled by any tabloid hacks. Diana explains that when they went backstage after picking up the award and were ushered through the press area, a nice man made an announcement to the effect that Matt and David's representatives wouldn't be answering any questions. David's mum is off the phone and tells me, 'But one girl from the *Mirror* did start asking me questions.' Oh dear. Like what? 'Well, she was going, "Are you two friends? Do you go out together? Do you go shopping together?"' And what did you say? 'I just said I didn't know what she was talking about.'

I resolve to stay with Diana, Kathleen, Ralph and Peter for every moment of the party, because this is where the reporters are gathered, and this is where they're trying to catch even the most experienced of celebrities off guard, hoping that the haze of alcohol and fine food and glamour might ease them into a false sense of security where they say something stupid or inadvertently revealing.

It's past ten o'clock and everyone's hungry so we queue up for the luxury buffet in the middle of the room, which is densely packed with famous people, their entourages and journalists. It's so full that it takes about ten minutes to walk further than a few feet. And it's uncomfortably hot. I've never seen so many sweaty famous faces in one enclosed space that isn't really big enough to hold them.

We're at the back of a very long queue, and I calculate that it's going to be at least ten minutes before we get anywhere near to the front to get served, so I take my opportunity to visit the toilet, and briefly leave the mums and dads to their own devices.

On the way I get stopped by a PR from Channel 5 who wants me to meet a star of *CSI* they've brought over to present one of the awards. I never watch *CSI* and I'm in a bit of a hurry so I tell her I'm dying to go to the toilet and will come and say hello on my way back.

Just before I reach the toilets, I see Peter Kay's agent who kisses me hello

Kathleen and Diana at the National TV Awards, 2005

and introduces me to Patrick McGuinness, who is Paddy of *Max and Paddy* fame. He's very generous in his praise of Matt and David's mums, then whispers to me that in the middle of the event someone backstage at the Albert Hall had assured him that he and Peter were going to win the award for Most Popular Comedy. That explains the slightly odd look on their faces when the winner was announced. He won't reveal who passed on this false information but adds, 'What a fucking shit thing to do,' before passing on his congratulations to Matt and David's mums.

On my way back from the toilet I see that the queue for food has shortened considerably and I can't yet see where the mums and dads are. They must be much nearer the front than I thought would be possible in the brief time I've been away. I try to tread a path away from where the Channel 5 lady and her *CSI* man were standing, but as I try to work out where Diana, Kathleen, Ralph and Peter are in the queue, the Five PR pops up next to me. 'So let me introduce you to –' But now I'm worried because I just can't see where the *Little Britain* parents are, but I can see journalists from the *Sun*, the *Mirror* and the *Guardian* in my immediate field of vision. I apologise to the lady from Five and the man from *CSI*, telling them that I'm supposed to be looking after some people but I can't see where they are right now. The Five PR is exasperated. No one seems that bothered about meeting her *CSI* star.

And there they are, standing by a pillar nowhere near the food queue any more: Matt and David's parents. And they're busy tucking into piles of delicious-looking treats.

I tell them I'd lost them for a few minutes.

'Oh sorry, we managed to push to the front of the queue,' explains Diana.

How did you manage that?

'Well,' says Kathleen, 'no one was paying any attention. It was easy.'

2001

Getting *Little Britain* on TV in the first place was a difficult job, and it very nearly didn't even get commissioned.

Since their first Edinburgh show together, Matt and David had attracted plenty of attention from TV executives. Channel 4 offered them their own show off the back of Edinburgh, but Matt and David didn't know what they wanted to do on TV at that point, so they shied away from it altogether and concentrated on the radio shows.

They came up with small-scale, low-budget cult shows for Paramount Comedy and UKPlay like *Rock Profile* and *Mash and Peas*, and eventually BBC2 gave them a series of six 10-minute slots for a Sir Bernard Chumley series. But it came and went without much acclaim, and deep down even Matt and David knew it was rather too juvenile. And then there was the *Boyz Unlimited* experience.

So when the time came to turn *Little Britain* into a BBC TV series, they felt that it was possibly their last chance for a breakthrough.

The plan was for the show to debut on BBC3 then move to BBC2 a few months later, so the then controller of BBC2, Jane Root, had to make the final decision whether to give the go-ahead. Matt and David were summoned to a meeting at the BBC with Root and BBC Head of Comedy Jon Plowman, who executive-produced series such as *Absolutely Fabulous* and *The Office*.

Geri Halliwell and George Michael, *Rock Profile*, 2000

Matt and David sat there and it felt like the meeting was going on for a long time and that quite a lot of that time consisted of Jane Root thinking a lot and being quiet. It was as if she was going to make the decision in the meeting right there in front of them and they were watching her weighing it up in her mind. It wasn't what they were expecting at all.

Jane Root also had tickets to go to a Prom at the Albert Hall that night and her assistant kept coming in and reminding her that she only had a few minutes, and then suddenly she told them that *Big Train* [a critically acclaimed sketch show created by *Father Ted*'s Graham Linehan and Arthur Mathews] wouldn't be coming back and that if she were to commission Matt and David's series she would have to justify to the makers of *Big Train* why she wasn't recommissioning them but was commissioning *Little Britain*.

Root also questioned the wisdom of having Tom Baker narrate the series. She said she wasn't really sure about Tom Baker and asked Matt and David what they thought of him. Matt wondered whether that was some kind of test to see if they would stick to their guns. They said they were really keen on Tom Baker and they thought his contribution was great.

In return, Matt and David mentioned Anthony Head being in the cast to underline that they had a bit of a star on board, because he was in *Buffy* and *Buffy* was a big show, but Jane Root shrugged and told them that meant she couldn't play *Little Britain* next to *Manchild* [a BBC2 drama series that Tony Head was in at the time], so suddenly he became a negative.

Luckily Matt and David had Jon Plowman firmly on their side. They felt that this powerful BBC comedy veteran was putting himself on the line for them. He told Root that he believed in the show and believed in Matt and David, and he urged her to commission it. He was almost on his knees.

Eventually, Jane Root said simply, 'All right, okay then . . . do it,' and left.

Matt and David sat there dumbstruck, wondering, 'Is that it? Did we get it? Does that mean we've got a series?' They really didn't know. David kept saying to Jon, 'Are you sure?' He just hadn't expected it to happen like that. He thought Jane Root would shake their hands and say good luck and then later tell them her decision.

That night happened to be David's thirty-first birthday and he had arranged a party at Century private members' club in London, which turned into a double celebration. Matt and David were elated, albeit in a slightly confused and apprehensive manner.

They were thrilled, of course. But they realised they had to deliver the goods.

9

26 October 2005 – Portsmouth: day 3

Next night in the Portsmouth Guildhall, Matt and David have just finished the third show of the tour. The vomit machine has worked for the second night in a row, although this does mean they have to buy new microphones for every show because they get ruined by the fake vomit liquid. Tony tells me, as Matt and David take their bows, that the sketch is going to cost them £2,000 a night in replacement microphones.

There's a cramped brown room backstage with a small portable television on which ITV1's broadcast of the National Awards is showing. In a magical moment of fortunate timing, the segment of the show featuring Matt and David's mums is just starting. Rik Mayall appears on screen. I rush to the side of the stage to grab Matt and David. They're in the usual post-show kerfuffle of costume and make-up removal. So I just yell, 'They're about to show your mums on TV!' They drop everything and I usher them to the tiny room. Rik is making the announcement of the winner. Matt and David are rapt. They're watching their mums on national primetime TV, along with eight million other viewers.

David says, 'Ah, they're holding hands – how sweet!'

Matt shakes his head as if he can't believe what he is seeing. 'It's surreal, isn't it?' He mouths along the words they came up with for their mothers to say while they're saying them on TV.

David: 'There's a look of terror on their faces – blind terror.'

The mums walk offstage with Rik Mayall, and Matt and David can't stop laughing.

'That,' says Matt eventually, 'is the funniest thing I've ever seen.'

Towards the end of the first week of shows in Portsmouth and Bournemouth, a pattern is starting to emerge. David has breakfast each morning in the hotel restaurant. He'll invariably have the tabloids with him, and maybe the *Guardian*, and he'll bump into Tony or Jeremy or Paul or Sam, and Pete usually ends up breakfasting a few tables away. Matt will stay in his room and have breakfast there with Kevin. Matt and Kevin have always got stuff to watch. They record any TV programmes they're vaguely interested in on their computer, and since Matt is effectively away from primetime television most nights because he's performing the show, it doesn't take long for the backlog of recorded material to start filling up his hard drive.

The hotels they're staying in are spa-like rural retreats. Tony has chosen these places because he thinks they'll be more relaxing and luxurious than chain hotels in the town centres. But Matt and David are starting to realise the downside of this plan. They have to factor in a lengthy journey to and from the venue each day. And after the show finishes around 10 p.m. each night, and after they've signed autographs and posed for photos for fans, a long car journey through winding country lanes before they can get to their hotel and have a rest is becoming gruelling.

David goes for his swim mid-morning. He has his own additional tour of Britain's swimming pools going on alongside the *Little Britain Live* tour. Tony arranges this too. He somehow finds the quietest, least frenzied Olympic-sized public pool in each place. David usually gets a lane to himself so that he can complete his hour of lengths uninterrupted. Any kids who happen to be in the pool might duck underwater and try to catch his eye by waving at him. He'll offer them a thumbs-up in return. I watch carefully, hoping no one mistakes me for a voyeur. As the last part of his regime he swims a full length underwater, making sure I witness it, and emerges, smiling camply, as if to say, 'See what I can do!' He does the underwater length each and every time I watch him train in a pool.

When David gets back from his swim, he has lunch, sometimes with Matt, occasionally with someone else from the cast or crew, or he might go into town and eat there. After lunch he might try to find a decent clothes shop, often without luck. Matt and Kevin often check out the local cinemas to see if there's something both of them can agree on seeing.

Having this amount of spare time won't last long, however, because they've resolved to use the days to start writing next year's *Little Britain* Christmas Special, and to refine the live show.

Their days might also be interrupted by other work commitments: voiceovers for adverts or TV shows and fairly frequent press interviews. They've completed most of the monthly and weekly press for the new series. (My own interview with them in *Heat* comes out with the headline quote from Matt: 'I've never felt any gay vibes from Robbie at all.' Which wouldn't have been my choice of headline. It's the kind of quote that makes it seem as if Matt is happy to milk his friendship with Robbie for good copy, which couldn't be further from the truth. He is, in fact, reluctant to say anything on the record about Rob. When I notice a copy of the magazine in Matt's hotel room, I sheepishly ask what he thinks of the headline. He tells me not to worry, and that as soon as the word 'Robbie' tumbled from his lips he knew it would end up in the headline one way or another.)

Eating dinner before the show can get quite complicated. At the moment they're still tinkering with certain sketches, so they have to get to the venue by about six. They might not be hungry before then, certainly not enough for a big dinner, so most nights Tony makes sure there is food for them in their dressing rooms, usually chicken, salads and fresh fruit and smoothies from M&S. They still haven't sorted out a rider. Matt keeps saying he wants to go to M&S with Tony and pick out the things he likes and the things he can't eat because of allergies.

The feeling that is only now beginning to dawn on Matt and David, however, is that what they managed to achieve on that fraught first night they have got to do 140 more times over the next nine months. They were elated when they walked offstage after that first performance, after the standing ovation. Now they've got to pull off the same level of energy each night, and they might not be rewarded with a standing ovation every time. That first audience knew it was witnessing the start of something, a show that no one

In training for the Channel

else had ever seen before. It was a unique occasion for everyone involved. The audience had bought their tickets a year ago; Matt and David had been working towards that performance for months. A few days later, they are getting used to the idea that this is their routine now. A routine that revolves around having huge reserves of nervous energy between 7.30 and 9.30 p.m. each night.

At least the newspapers can always be relied upon to provide a frisson of excitement, creating a scintillating story where in truth none previously existed. A couple of days after David's off-the-record chat with Gordon, the main story in Victoria Newton's Bizarre column is an 'interview' with David. The headline is 'Bring Back My Gay-o-Meter' with a sell beneath saying, 'Walliams in plea to me.'

The article says, 'David Walliams has made a personal plea for the return of my gay-o-meter. Last week my finely tuned fairy-behaviour detector exploded after David's camp caper-too-far with Will Young on Michael Parkinson's telly chat show. But last night, speaking after the brilliant opening night of the *Little Britain* UK Tour in Portsmouth, David called for my gay gizmo to be immediately reinstated. After the show David, pictured here onstage last night with Matt Lucas, told me: "I loved your gay detector, swing-o-meter thingy. I'm not at all surprised it exploded after *Parky*. That was an hour of the campest television in history. Every time I walk out of my front door I'm aware of my gay-o-meter reading. I think it's funny."'

10

27 October 2005 – Portsmouth: day 4

David is momentarily naked together with another lithe young man in a car park in an obscure south-coast village. The tabloids are missing out on something here. A paparazzi photographer could live for a year off the proceeds of the shot I take of them with my cameraphone. Greg and David are getting changed into their wetsuits in a deserted bit of car park behind the empty beach. It's a slate-grey, chilly day. David doesn't hesitate about getting naked for a second. In fact he's enjoying it, pointing gleefully at the goose-bumps all over his bare skin.

Once he's got his black Speedos on, David seems slightly unsure of how to get into the wetsuit. Greg helps him out, and then on go the swimming cap and goggles. He puts his hands out triumphantly and points to himself as if to say, 'Look at me! Look what I'm about to do!'

Then he surveys the view ahead of him: the murky sea stretching to the horizon.

'Wow,' he says quietly. 'I'll be swimming all the way out there . . .'

Today David's got to do a couple of miles of training in this uninviting expanse of sea. It doesn't seem to have fully hit home what he's letting himself in for. Not just this morning, with this session at a harsh, chilly beach on the outskirts of Southampton, which is grim enough, but the challenge as a whole. His training regime is hundreds of lengths most days, and he explains that a lot of that will have to be in the sea in the middle of winter or in the occasional lake or reservoir – whatever's handy and nearby while he's on tour.

His fitness and swimming adviser is an eager, studiously down-to-earth ex-Olympic pentathlete called Greg Whyte. Comic Relief put David in touch with him. As they ponder how far they'll be going this morning, Greg points out that David will have to begin the cross-Channel swim next July in pitch-black darkness at about 5 a.m. He's also going to be filmed for a BBC/Sport Relief documentary. So there'll be lights and cameramen and general media scrum as he walks into the water at Dover. But once he's in, he'll essentially be on his own. Swimming for miles and miles in the darkness. How will he know where he's going? David's got no fucking idea. Greg will be swimming with him for parts of the journey, but only intermittently. The whole idea is that David swims it on his own.

And even though they're using the warmth of wetsuits today, David can't wear one when he swims the Channel. It's against the rules of the Channel Swimming Association. (One hat, one pair of goggles, one pair of trunks.) He'll just be smeared with white grease for insulation. Greg says no matter what you wear or how cold you feel, your body always ends up adjusting to the temperature of the water. David doesn't look convinced.

Apart from David and his trainer Greg, both now cutting through the water doing front crawl at what seems like a pretty speedy pace, there's only one other person swimming. An old lady in a black, one-piece swimsuit, slowly but steadily breaststroking her way through the seawater, a few metres behind David, methodically keeping pace. When he finishes his hour or so of swimming I tell him about her. He says, 'There's always an old lady, isn't there? Wherever you go, on whatever beach, you look at the sea and there's a solitary old woman, wrinkly but somehow really fit and healthy, just swimming for hours in the sea.'

I ask him what he thought about while he's swimming. 'I was singing Beatles songs to myself,' he says. 'It was fucking cold, but exhilarating. And it's a great way of escaping from what's going on right now. I had no idea that woman was swimming near us, I had no idea you were there watching us, and I didn't think about the running order of the sketches for the show once!'

'I wonder who he is,' says David, pointing at a man he's just spotted walking by the side of the road in T-shirt and jeans, as if he's just emerged from the woods. 'It's quite weird, isn't it? Why is this man on his own, the only person for miles around, on this road? I want to stop the car and ask him . . .'

We're gliding through winding, tree-lined roads on the outskirts of the New Forest. Miles go by and we barely pass a house or a shop or a pub, or a human being. Except for this mysterious figure. David doesn't stop the car. It's too late anyway, because by the time he's expressed this thought we're way past the mystery man. We turn to catch our last sight of him out of the back window. He's still fiddling with his clothes, walking unsteadily. We're never going to see him again.

David says all he has to do sometimes is encounter someone behaving in a slightly odd, unusual way and he'll want to turn them into a character for *Little Britain*. He offers the example of a woman in a bank from whom he was trying to get a bank loan once. 'It was like she enjoyed the little bit of power she had. I really needed this money, and she was tapping away at the computer, staring at the screen, not looking at me and going, "Well, let's see what the computer says, shall we?" Like she was a teacher waiting to tell me if I'd passed a test. It was humiliating. I told Matt about her and that's where Carol saying "Computer says no" comes from.'

Yesterday David had a call from his publicist. The *News of the World* had got in contact with David's bank manager because they'd heard that Carol's character was based on him.

One day David would also like to write in more depth about such characters, the people he encounters who intrigue him, maybe in a novel or in stories. 'But extracting funny characters from people we meet is what we're doing at the moment. Maybe on top of that we could also dig deeper into how they got to the state they're in. We could do something more ambitious with characters like Lou and Andy. Or we could do more of an ambitious narrative with new characters.'

Instead of a fourth series?

'Don't know. Maybe afterwards.' What isn't in any doubt, or open to any discussion or conjecture, is that whatever major TV project David has in mind to do next, it will be with Matt.

David's now got his laptop out and is going through his iTunes looking for songs to play. He's pensive. Thinking about how people become who they are has got him into thinking about how he became who he is. He puts

The Smiths on. 'The Headmaster Ritual'. 'Belligerent ghouls run Manchester schools,' croons Morrissey, 'spineless swines, cemented minds.'

David says he felt like Morrissey was singing those beautifully written words to him when he heard it. He was the model of an angst-ridden schoolboy, though he went to grammar school in Reigate rather than a Manchester comprehensive.

But he didn't enjoy his schooldays. He never felt that he fitted in. Looking back now, his young self seems almost comically anguished. It didn't seem funny at the time, though. He did at least have a soulmate, called Robin Dashwood.

'I've never ever argued with Robin,' explains David. 'Not that we've always agreed but we just have a lovely understanding. We used to go for long walks and talk. It was magical. Those were the best times of growing up. But I was never really able to communicate what I was thinking or feeling in school. Or to my parents.'

The computer screen is glowing in the darkness in the back of the car. David's singing along: being Morrissey and loving it.

He wonders how he must have seemed to his mother. He remembers being sullen and unresponsive with his parents, especially when he hit his teens. They must have wondered what they'd done to upset him. 'I could be quite wilful. Just by being sulky and quiet you could ruin the atmosphere at home. You know, during a family meal I could be silent and I'd maybe refuse to eat pudding or something, and my mum was very easily upset by that kind of thing. Whereas my dad would never really get upset.'

The teenage David could never talk about things on an emotional level to his parents. And he still doesn't. He assumes he was depressed in those days, though he never thought about it in that way while it was happening. He was probably aware that he was moody and lonely and confused and quite often bored, but he would never have known why he was feeling that way.

'Oh it wasn't easy!' He laughs all of a sudden. David regularly jokes about life not being easy after he's recounted the story of some kind of hardship, whether trivial or serious, offering theatrical pronouncements around the theme: 'No one said it would be *easy* . . . It's never *easy*, is it? . . . Why can't life just be *easier*?' And when he's swimming length after length, mile after mile, he often finds himself singing the refrain from Coldplay's The Scientist.'

'But I don't think singing that is going to help me, is it?' he smiles grimly.

Tapping along on his laptop to the rather more jaunty tune of 'Girlfriend In A Coma', David says he didn't talk to his parents about sexual matters, or relationships, partly because he was twenty before he had his first girlfriend – Katy Carmichael, who he met at university.

'That was a whole weird area I never felt I could talk to them about,' he explains. He admits he must have seemed secretive, but also he never felt a great desire on his parents' part to find out about that area of his life. He thinks they might have thought he was gay. He thinks he may have thought that about himself.

He felt like an outsider. He didn't feel he had much in common with many people, within his family and where he lived. 'I wasn't interested in sport,' he says. 'I couldn't talk to my dad about football or anything. We didn't do much bonding because there was never that much to bond about. I remember we went on a boat trip together to see the Thames Barrier and that was pretty much it.'

He explains in the most delicate way possible that his dad was maybe a typically reserved Home Counties middle-class Englishman. There wasn't much hugging or touching. It was mainly hand-shaking. David points out that what you want more than anything in life is your parents' approval. Then suddenly he tells me a story about his father. He explains that it's something his father has told him twice, not with any particular sense of what this did to him emotionally, but as soon as David heard it, he felt it was significant.

David's father was born in 1936, so he was a child during the war, when rationing was in force. One day when he was about six years old, his dad was given a rabbit. David's father quickly grew to love this rabbit and fed it and nurtured it and became quite attached to it as a pet. Then one evening he came home from school and the rabbit was strung up dead because it had been decided they were going to eat it.

'I think aged six or so that would have devastated him,' says David, 'and left him emotionally quite closed. I'm not saying in isolation that incident alone made him like that, but I think these incidents are quite forming and along with his general upbringing I think it would have had a big effect on him and made it difficult to show his emotions.'

'There Is A Light That Never Goes Out' starts up. David tells me that when his dad first started wooing Kathleen, the future Mrs Williams, her older sisters would put on the Everly Brothers' song 'Kathy's Clown'. 'That's great, isn't it?' laughs David.

David is momentarily distracted by the magical janglings of Johnny Marr's guitar.

David met Johnny Marr at the BAFTAs earlier this year. Marr was sitting with the people from *Shameless*, a few tables away from the *Little Britain* people.

As soon as the ceremony ended, David sidled over, shook Marr's hand vigorously got his autograph and told him how he was one of his idols. The expression on Marr's face was one of vibrant excitement, rather than the slightly wary look that he might get if stopped in the street by a fan on a rainy day in Manchester. Twenty minutes later David had swapped mobile phone numbers with him and was announcing, 'We're best friends now!'

'I think they're really proud of me now,' says David, going back to the subject of his parents. 'They've become very lively. They are really enjoying being the parents of someone quite famous. I think you're probably prouder of your children's achievements than you are of your own. Because in a strange way you are more to do with that . . . you created them . . . Like I think my mum is really into telling people that she's my mum . . .'

His mum is his biggest cheerleader. He tells the story of how she saw a display of the official *Little Britain* cards in the local Clinton Cards shop near where they live in Epsom. But she referred to it as an 'exhibition' of *Little Britain* products. David told his mum it probably isn't an exhibition. It's not like the V&A. Then she said, 'Well, we thought we'd go there for the afternoon, so we went to see the exhibition, and then someone came over and started looking at the cards. So we got talking and I told her who I was.' So David has this image of his mum dragging his dad down to Clinton Cards in Epsom for the afternoon for this 'exhibition', hanging out there by the display – probably for quite a long time – until eventually someone comes over and glances at them, and his mum pounces on them and says, 'That's my son!'

At the hotel after the show, Matt, Paul, Sam and Tony are having a drink and some nibbles in the bar. Matt mentions that the guys from Littler Britain, an amateur lookalike/tribute act, were at the show the previous night. 'Yeah,' says David. 'One of them said, "If you wanna have a night off from the tour, we are available." I thought, thanks, but the audience might be *slightly* disappointed.'

Matt looks through photographs of the live show on Tony's laptop to pick some out for a prospective poster campaign. He shows David the ones he thinks they should use. After making arrangements for the next day's American *Vogue* photo shoot, due to take place on the Bournemouth seafront, Matt says good night and goes off to bed.

David tells Paul that we've been having a Smiths marathon in the car. 'Have you met Morrissey?' Paul asks David. I can feel a story coming on.

'No,' says David.

'Well then, that's probably about the only celebrity I've got over you, isn't it?'

'When did you meet Morrissey?' I ask, intrigued.

'I spent one New Year's Eve with him.'

'Really?' says David. 'I don't imagine Morrissey being a big New Year's Eve type of guy.'

'You'd be surprised,' says Paul, and proceeds to tell the story of how in 1991 he went to see two members of Madness performing at a rough old pub in north London, and who should be there but Morrissey, accompanied by a 'small entourage of skinheads'. Egged on by his friend, veteran Smiths fan Paul went up to Morrissey, introduced himself and politely asked what he was doing there. To which Morrissey replied that he'd come down there to have a laugh –

'To have a laugh?' interrupts David incredulously. 'Those were his words? *To have a laugh?*'

'Words to that effect. He was there with his mates, enjoying the camaraderie. So I offered to buy him a drink, which he declined, but I was insistent and eventually he went, "Okay – I'll have a pint of stout."'

So Paul bought Morrissey a pint of stout on New Year's Eve in 1991 in a north London pub where two members of Madness were playing. We're prepared to believe that.

Then Paul takes the story up a notch . . .

Apparently they proceeded to have a nice chat about stuff like the Happy Mondays, Morrissey's favourite reggae albums and how he was fond of Madness. The boys from Madness, going under the name of The Nutty Boys, then came out and performed, climaxing with a ska version of 'Auld Lang Syne'. 'And there he was,' says Paul, talking about Morrissey, 'there he was with his party hat on, shaking people's hands, wishing them Happy New Year and dancing about to this ska version of "Auld Lang Syne" . . . How cool is that?'

David and I can't disguise our doubt. We give Paul a frank 'Oh come on!'

look and hand him the opportunity to admit that he's pulling our leg and that he's made the whole thing up. But no, he insists this is the true story of his raucous New Year's Eve in the company of Morrissey.

David explains that he has invited Johnny Marr to a forthcoming Manchester show, and Gillian and Steven from New Order are also supposed to be coming.

Tony then chips in with his own Morrissey story. David's transfixed, as am I. It turns out that Phil McIntyre, whose company Tony works for, was the promoter for the early Smiths tours and then on through the Morrissey solo years. And Tony went out on the road with Morrissey for, as he calls it, the 'Up Your Arsenal' tour.

Now this is exciting. Proper first-hand testimony of Morrissey tour action.

'I managed to get about two words out of him,' says Tony, 'and that was because I'd been called to his dressing room to sort out something that was rattling through the ceiling. He just ignored me. He was virtually cowering in the corner of his room.'

Now this sounds like Morrissey, says David, not some bloke in a party hat dancing to the Nutty Boys.

Tony continues: 'He was very very shy, and all the people around him just exacerbated it. They were intense and incredibly protective. Unnecessarily protective would be my way of putting it.'

David can imagine what it must have been like. 'Was it like "Morrissey wants this . . . Morrissey needs that. Morrissey can't be there because of this"?'

'Exactly like that,' says Tony.

Paul says, 'It's almost like they're treating him as a small baby.'

'It's a bit like Brian Wilson these days, isn't it?' says David. 'I have this vision of Brian living this incredible life where he's kind of decided to opt out of having any responsibility, and I'd quite like that, to be woken, dressed, fed, put on the stage with the lines in front of me, and you'd just have to read them and pretend to play keyboard! It'd be so easy. I'd love to be treated like that . . .'

Paul then tells a story about a friend of his who appeared on tour with a famous sketch comedy troupe and how he was just doing the minor roles, and then one of the main performers suddenly decided that he should have all this poor man's lines.

David listens avidly then says, 'You have loads of showbiz stories that are all about how awful people are.'

'The Morrissey one wasn't!' protests Paul.

'No, you're right,' says David. 'That was a lovely story.'

2002

When the *Little Britain* pilot was first shown on BBC3's launch night it was a bit of a non-event. Critics were really down on BBC3, and Matt and David got caught up in that.

They did an interview with Johnny Vaughn, who was hosting the launch of the channel, live on the night. And he asked them how the characters came about and they were talking about Sebastian and the Prime Minister and explained that Sebastian is kind of in love with the Prime Minister, and Vaughn said, 'Oh, like Smithers and Mister Burns in *The Simpsons*?'

Matt and David both thought: no, not really . . . more like Peter Mandelson and Tony Blair.

But as soon as the series proper started on BBC3, it felt like it was already turning into something of a phenomenon.

After just a few episodes had been shown, a cartoon of Vicky Pollard appeared on Richard Littlejohn's page in the *Sun*. Matt was amazed to see it, and it felt like evidence that the characters were resonating with people. On a mass scale. For David the moment when he realised he was part of something much bigger than everything they'd done before was when they went on Jonathan Ross's chat show. This was a big BBC1 programme, and they were making the audience and Jonathan laugh and they felt perfectly at home. It was all a new experience for Matt and David. They felt like they were part of the landscape for the first time.

Soon after the first series of *Little Britain* aired, Matt and David were invited to Lorraine Heggessey's house. She was the controller of BBC1 and had been really supportive of *Little Britain* coming to BBC TV. It might have helped that her kids liked it. Matt spilled wine on her carpet.

In the gap between Jane Root leaving BBC2 and her successor taking over, Heggessey staked her claim to *Little Britain* and told Matt and David she wanted to show it on BBC1. They hadn't even considered the idea.

Then Heggessey came to see a recording of series two with her family one night and it turned out to be the night where Matt and David were filming the rudest material they'd ever come up with.

They were mortified. It felt like they were being impolite in front of this woman who had been so keen on them, and who was giving her family a bit of a treat.

It didn't affect anything. In fact, they were asked if they could come up with two series a year. They politely said no. It takes them a year to write one series.

11

28 October 2005 – Bournemouth: day 5

In the cramped black van, Matt and David are trying to change into their Emily and Florence dresses. David's getting a bit exasperated because he can't put his tall wig on in the low-ceilinged space. He opens the van doors for a couple of seconds and sticks his head out into the open air. A little boy is standing outside, staring up at David with big enraptured eyes. '*Little Britain!*' he observes. David smiles and nods, and retreats into the vehicle, wig perched precariously on his head. He has to take it off again. The door's still open, and the boy spots Matt in his dress and wig.

'You should see what you look like!' says Matt to the boy, who smiles broadly. 'I'm Matt . . .'

'Yeah, I know,' says the boy.

'Yeah, I know!' Matt says in character as Andy Pipkin.

The boy laughs and says, 'Cool . . .'

'Yeah, I know,' says Andy/Matt again.

Matt asks him if he's coming to the show tonight, and the boy says he is, so Matt asks to see his ticket. 'Don't worry, I won't nick it,' he says. 'How old are you?'

'I'm eleven. Do you get people up onstage?' asks the boy.

'We do but only fatties. We get huge big fat people onstage . . . so you don't qualify. What's your name?'

The boy is called Robert, and he asks Matt if he'll be doing Vicky tonight. Matt merrily tells him that yes, he will be doing Vicky.

'And,' continues the boy, 'will you be doing er . . . er . . . the fat woman? The fat-fighter? I can't remember her name.'

Yes, Matt tells Robert, he will be doing Marjorie Dawes too.

'Cool,' says Robert. 'And are you doing that one where you're sat at the table and you say, "I think I've got a picture of him"?' He seems to be referring to a sketch in series two, episode six, in which Matt and David played two women called Rachel and Nicola who showed each other Polaroids of their male conquests' penises.

'Oh no, we're not doing that,' answers Matt. 'But we'll be doing Sebastian and the Prime Minister, and Dafydd, and Lou and Andy –'

'My mate just told me he'd seen you in town,' interrupts Robert, as if he feels the need to explain how he came to be loitering outside the van, parked next to the Bournemouth International Centre, the venue for tonight's show.

Matt introduces the boy to David.

'Oh hello,' says David. 'Great to meet you . . .'

'Can I come on board?' asks the boy, who's polite and sweet and very well mannered.

Without hesitation, David ushers him into the van. Now Robert's got his mobile phone out. 'Can I have my photo taken with you . . . lot?' he asks, and as he says so, seems to realise that 'lot' is a funny word to use of Matt and David. Then he asks David, 'Where's your wig?'

David tells him he can't put it on in the van because he's too tall.

David invites the boy to sit between him and Matt. Matt asks me to take the photo for Robert. He gives me the phone, and it's not entirely obvious where the right button is to take a photo. David sighs. 'Come *on!*' he says, in a jokey irate tone. I press the biggest button. It seems to have worked. As I hand the phone back to the boy, I notice a blurry, unfocused image of the three of them on the tiny screen. The lad just thanks Matt and David very much, and tells them he'll see them later. He's grinning and giggling as he steps out of the vehicle.

In the van now are Jeremy, his assistant Anna, here for an impromptu meeting about making some small changes to the running order, plus make-up and costume supremo Lisa, Sally the wardrobe mistress, Tony and, last to arrive, Alfie, who organises the merchandise for the tour.

Matt asks Alf how it's going.

'Two seventy-seven,' says Alf.

'Ooh great,' says Matt. 'That's better than last night, isn't it?'

'What does that mean?' asks David. 'Two hundred and seventy-seven items?'

'It means we made £2.77 a head . . . But with the free mouse-mats we're convinced we can get it up to four quid a head.'

At the moment the 'Computer Says No' mouse-mats sell at the merchandise stalls in each venue for a few pounds, but as soon as they saw them, Matt and David felt they were too flimsy to be worth any money. Alfie explains that they've worked out a way of wrapping the mouse-mats into each programme so they can become a gift you'll get if you buy the programme for £10. But only starting next week. Meanwhile, the 'Computer Says No' mouse-mats will still be on sale for a few more days.

'Is it wrong to sell the mouse-mats in the meantime?' asks Matt.

'No. Not at all. It's nice,' says Alf.

'Well, I think it will be a great giveaway,' says Matt.

David peers out of the front window of the van. He can see it's a busy Friday morning on the Bournemouth seafront, with crowds of people milling around the concessions where the pier starts.

'I think once we get to the seafront we really need to make our way quickly to the pier . . . otherwise we may never get there,' he says.

The photographer from American *Vogue* steps up into the van. 'Hey! Guys! I'm Jonathan,' he announces in a broad New York accent. He's wearing a dark green beret, matching tweed jacket and is smoking a large cigar. He clocks Matt and David in their Emily and Florence drag and says, 'Great!' They introduce themselves, and Matt explains who everyone else in the crowded van is.

Jonathan says 'Great!' after each person's name and job is announced. With that, he's off to supervise the set-up on the pier. 'Everything's gonna be great,' he shouts, as he steps back out of the van.

Tony tells Matt and David that Cosmo and Pete will be on hand in their security roles when the van arrives at the location for the shoot.

Tour merchandise

'Do we know exactly where we're going?' asks Matt. No one answers.

'I think this might just be a really bad idea,' he says.

'Too many people?' asks Matt.

David nods. 'I think I'm getting some kind of anxiety attack.'

What no one accounted for is the wind. As Matt and David decamp from the van, their wigs are almost toppled off their heads by the gusts.

Hundreds of people are standing at either side of the pier entrance. They seem to know exactly what's going on. Some official-looking men in uniforms are forming a barrier in front of the crowds. They seem to be in charge of something. Maybe the pier. Matt and David are ushered by an American guy who's organising the shoot past the officials who all nod in their direction, and towards the location at the far end of the pier. Pete and Cosmo walk just beside David and Matt respectively. Someone somewhere has done a good job of corralling these onlookers into positions where they won't be in the way of the shoot. Matt and David are clutching their wigs to their heads and grimacing as the wind blows into their faces.

Jonathan Becker greets Matt and David again as they arrive in front of his camera on its tripod. As he confers with them about the set-up for the pictures, the smoke from his cigar is billowing into Matt's face. Matt turns away sharply, gripping onto his wig. David says something but Jonathan can't hear him because of the wind and the sound of the waves crashing violently against the rocks beneath us.

'I'm a bit worried about our wigs!' David shouts.

'Oh yeah, sure. We'll wait and see if the wind dies down.' The photographer takes a puff on his cigar and blows smoke in David's face this time. 'Wow,' says Jonathan, watching the waves. 'I wanna go for a swim!'

The photographer's assistant arrives with the two-seater bicycle that Matt and David often use in sketches featuring Emily and Florence.

'There's no way we're getting on that,' says Matt.

After ten minutes, the wind seems to calm to more of a breeze, and Jonathan asks Matt and David to stand at the railings, looking out to sea. He snaps away, yelling, 'Oh great, great . . . GREAT!' getting progressively louder as Matt and David get steadily camper in their Emily and Florence guises. He's thrilled when they kiss each other on the lips.

'He was like a silent movie director from the thirties,' says Matt, removing his wig with some relief, and then, adopting an extreme accent to imitate

Jonathan the photographer, he exclaims: 'Right! Roll 'em! Okay – print it! Let's make another movie this afternoon!'

David says that if Jonathan was a character in a film you'd think he was too over-the-top to be believable.

There are now hundreds of people surrounding the entrance to the pier, beyond which the van is parked. A combination of Cos, Pete, Tony and a couple of pier officials form a kind of protective guard to escort Matt and David back. There are a few shouts of 'You're a lady!' from the fans, some wolf-whistles, and it all seems pleasantly good-natured. Matt and David are both smiling, still imagining the photographer as a character part being played by Wallace Shawn.

Just as they reach the van, a large middle-aged woman stands in front of Matt and David and says to them both, 'Sorry to bother you, but can I just shake your hands very quickly, and thank you both for making me laugh so much.'

'Of course you can,' says Matt.

'That's lovely of you to say,' says David. As we climb into the van David says no matter how irritated he might get with people taking his picture with their phones, or shouting things at him in the street, he doesn't think he'll ever tire of people coming up to him and thanking him for making them laugh. Matt says that's what this tour is all about.

David's still water arrives, with ice. Tony asks why he doesn't like ice. David explains that it's just big lumps of cold stuff that gets in the way of the drink. I offer my glass to happily receive his ice. Tony asks when the issue of American *Vogue* will come out. Next May, explains David. 'It's part of a themed section of pictures of up-and-coming UK stars, or something like that,' he says.

Matt says that it feels a bit odd to be considered up and coming in America, when they're so well established in this country. In the States *Little Britain* is shown on BBC America, and has a cult following at best.

David is given his sushi 'rainbow roll' with a salad, and Matt gets a dish with a vast pile of shredded duck on it.

'That's a big pile of duck. Does anyone want some?' He offers some to Cos, but Cos isn't hungry. He doesn't eat lunch. Just dinner, and maybe the occasional breakfast.

A slick blond man who seems to be one of the restaurant managers arrives at the table proffering his card. 'You've been invited tonight to a party downstairs at our bar and club. I'll be on the door.'

David takes the card. 'Oh that's really nice of you, thank you. We might just do that.'

The restaurant man assures them they'll have a nice area to themselves and says they can bring as many of the crew members as they like. He can rope off an area.

As he tucks in, Matt discusses how certain TV shows and actors are remembered and how others seem so easily forgotten. He mentions old Sunday-night dramas like *The Forsyte Saga*, *To Serve Them All My Days* and *The Bretts*. What, he wonders, ever happened to John Duttine who played the lead role of a teacher in *To Serve Them All My Days*? David mentions his son Joe Duttine, whom you see on TV every now and then. He says what he loved about *The Forsyte Saga* was that it was so popular that vicars complained their flock had stopped going to Sunday evening services. He points out it's unlikely anyone would bother with that complaint now.

Matt then brings up the subject of TV series that were filmed but have never been shown, like a whole series of *Minder* starring Gary Webster, and an ITV drama that Paul Nicholls made when he left *EastEnders*. And there's more than one Richard Wilson comedy vehicle that never made it to the screens. David appeared in the first episode of one Richard Wilson series, then they made a second run but never bothered showing it. Matt explains why ITV often doesn't get round to showing the series it commissions. It's because they have a policy not to pay the production company the full amount until the programme is shown.

David mentions films that get made when famous actors are in the early stages of their careers, which then come back to haunt them, like Daniel Craig, the new James Bond, who's just had to endure blurry screen-grabs of his penis appearing in the papers taken from an old independent low-budget film in which he played Francis Bacon's lover.

After lunch David goes swimming in a nearby pool, so Matt decides to go for a walk with Kevin, with a view to maybe seeing a film. Matt says he'd be happy to fill his time on this tour by staying in his hotel room with Kevin most mornings, then having lunch and maybe popping out to the local cinema in the afternoon. But a quick glance at the Odeon's eight films on offer confirms there are none they want to see they haven't already seen. Kevin suggests going for a coffee and muffins somewhere.

Matt gets stopped every few minutes by a fan or group of fans. Often they just shake his hand. Sometimes they stand there for a few seconds, confirming to themselves that it really is him off the television, and they'll maybe say something like, 'Want that one,' or 'Yeah, I know,' or '*Little Britain*'s shit.' Occasionally they ask for an autograph, especially if they have tickets for *Little Britain Live* on them that they can get him to sign. But most often, they get their cameraphones out and take a picture or stop Matt to get their picture taken with him.

On the way to finding a suitably quiet café, we walk past an art-print shop, which happens to have a painting of Matt in the window. It's the first time he's seen framed artwork of himself. The piece is a large, treated, bleached-out illustration of Matt as Dafydd, in red sleeveless top, arms folded, with an expression of gay pride on his face, against a black background with two pink masculine symbols. Within seconds of stopping to look at the print, passers-by begin to notice that Matt Lucas is pondering an artwork of himself, and a small crowd forms. The owner of the shop invites us in, and a dozen or so people wait by the front door, peering in. The owner can't quite believe her luck, and gently asks if Matt will sign the back of the print. He happily agrees but requests that any extra money she'll make from having the artwork signed should be given to Comic Relief. It's on sale for £295.

When he leaves the shop, there are now twenty or so fans gathered, asking to have their picture taken with him on their mobile phones. Matt happily obliges for four or five of them, while someone shouts, 'We love you, Matt, we LOVE you!' Matt's beginning to regret not asking Cos to accompany him on this impromptu walkabout. Kevin and I aren't much protection.

Eventually Matt extracts himself from the throng and we stride purposefully towards a café in the distance. We get sidetracked by a card shop, which has a large display of *Little Britain* greetings cards and calendars in the window. (What David's mum would call an exhibition.) Matt can't resist checking it out. It's autumn – calendar-buying season, so the walls are lined with celebrity-themed offerings. Matt thumbs through an *OK!* magazine calendar full of paparazzi shots of TV celebrities ('Why would anyone buy that?' he asks), a clearly unofficial Jude Law calendar ('Can't he do anything about that?'), a McFly one ('I met them. He was very nice. He's very nice. And cute. That one doesn't really say anything . . .') and a Cliff Richard one. Matt says he buys his mum a Cliff calendar every year for Christmas.

Matt spots a young girl checking out the *Little Britain* birthday cards. He sidles up to her.

'Want that one,' he half-whispers.

Her double-take is perfect.

It feels almost miraculous to have a whole corner of the upstairs of Costa Coffee to ourselves. A sanctuary away from cameraphones. Matt and Kevin are sharing a triple chocolate muffin, and Matt is wondering if he should be talking because his voice is getting a bit hoarse. He takes a puff on his inhaler, and sips some peppermint tea.

Kevin asks when he's had trouble with his voice before. Matt says he's had moments during all the tours he's done: the first *Sir Bernard Chumley* tour ten years ago with David, the *Shooting Stars* tour, and perhaps most painfully of all, his stint in Boy George's musical *Taboo*. I remind Matt that I came to see him in *Taboo*, when it premiered in a tiny theatre off Leicester Square.

'Do you know what?' says Matt. 'I really don't remember, but that's probably because I was so fucking stressed out.'

Matt's got mixed memories of the *Taboo* experience. He's immensely proud of his work in it, as legendary performance artist Leigh Bowery, but it was a gruelling, tense run.

'We did four shows in twenty-nine hours,' explains Matt.

The other challenging element of that period for Matt was that he was being asked more and more in interviews about being gay. *Taboo* was such a gay piece of work that it seemed fair game for Matt's sexuality to be an issue when he was promoting the show. By that point in his life and career, it never crossed him mind to conceal his gayness. But it was still something he had to get used to talking about in the media, and his family had to get used to reading about. Now he barely gives the issue a second thought. Though it is still an 'issue' for a lot of interviewers.

'Here's the thing,' he says. 'I wouldn't go out of my way to talk about being gay and having a boyfriend if I'm on a TV chat show, but if Jonathan Ross or Parky brings it up, then I'll talk about being gay all they want. I'd rather be actor or comedian Matt Lucas than gay Matt Lucas, but that doesn't mean in any way that I'm not completely happy and proud about my sexuality.'

Kevin asks Matt if he's told me the story of how his brother reacted when he first told him he was gay.

'Oh I probably haven't, have I? Well, I told him about it during an argument and he just looked at me and went, "Oh . . . *great!*" as if I'd told him that the video hadn't recorded or that I'd put the whites in with the reds and they'd come out pink. For a while I think he just didn't believe me.'

Matt credits David with helping him come out of the closet. Or rather 'kicking' him out. They first met at around the time Matt was coming to terms with being gay, in his late teens. He'd told his closest friends, but not his family. He thinks maybe he was shying away from telling them so he didn't have to deal with the actual process of meeting men and establishing sexual relationships with them.

He'd first realised he had same-sex leanings at his same-sex school. He describes it as a feeling of 'waiting to be straight'. He kept thinking, 'Okay, I like guys but maybe that's just because I'm surrounded by them . . .' He assumed that when he started meeting girls he would end up fancying them instead, or as well. But that didn't happen. So until the age of about eighteen he was rather tortured about his sexuality, and it's useful to remember that back in those days, when Margaret Thatcher was still in power and dominating our cultural and social lives, positive images of gays were rare. Matt mentions Jimmy Somerville as an example of someone who was gay but who seemed desexualised and a bit sad. Not that he's criticising him. That was how he seemed to Matt at the time. And saying someone was gay was just an insult, as of course in some ways it still is. There was nothing positive about the idea of being gay at all. So Matt felt he couldn't tell anyone about his leanings.

I ask when he had his first sexual experience, and though he's cagey, he acknowledges that he had some 'experiences' from about the age of fourteen onwards, but they were quite few and far between, and probably just the equivalent of what happens to straight teenagers when they're discovering their sexuality.

So Matt never really talked about his sexuality until he was nineteen. He remembers saying to his two or three best friends that he thought he might be bisexual, which is, he suggests, the way a lot of people deal with being gay. Eventually, he just thought, this is stupid – who are you protecting? He told them he was gay, and they were all fine with it, and everyone he told was fine with it. Another factor in helping Matt to deal with being an out, gay man was getting to know David Walliams.

First of all they went to see Jonathan Harvey's play *Beautiful Thing*

together, and Matt found its story of two teenage boys falling in love inspirational. But more than that, it was David's whole aura that helped Matt feel better about his own sexuality. 'When I first met David I kind of assumed he was gay,' explains Matt. 'Even though he had a girlfriend, he was kind of outrageous and camp and he used his ambiguous sexuality to empower himself. There was an element of "fuck you, what are you going to do about it?" to David's attitude, and it helped that he was utterly hilarious, and that he was six foot tall so he wasn't going to take any shit, and he wasn't a wispy little Dafydd type. He would do stuff when he introduced me to people for the first time, like say, "This is Matt. And he's gay!" As a joke, which would embarrass me, but also I was kind of glad he said it. I just thought: yeah I am . . .'

And if David was the catalyst for him coming out to his friends, then it was the point at which Matt got so depressed that he ended up seeing a therapist, which propelled him to tell his mum. Or as Matt puts it: 'Eventually I kind of cracked.'

Matt's weight was increasing, he was dealing with becoming famous as George Dawes on *Shooting Stars*, he was dealing with bereavement because his dad had died, he was dealing with his sexuality, and on top of all that he was smoking a lot of weed, all of which contributed to a feeling that he wasn't really able to operate. He went to a doctor because he was worried about his state of mind, and the doctor referred him to the therapist. Matt credits this therapy with changing his life for ever and setting him on a path to happiness. He sounds almost evangelical.

'I would fully recommend therapy to anyone. It was the beginning of me. I dreaded the thought of having to deal with myself and talk about myself. But it's great just to be able to talk to someone who doesn't have an agenda. To talk to someone about your doubts and uncertainties, and to help you face your fears.'

So at around that time, he told his mum he was gay. He describes her reaction as 'very shocked and surprised'. Matt was surprised that she was surprised because he thought there were lots of clues there. When I ask his mum about this later, she tells me that Matt's sexuality was just something she never thought about, or worried about. She just thought he'd get round to that aspect of his life eventually. She agrees that she was shocked, and says that she was mainly taken aback because of the thought that she might not have any grandchildren from Matt. But Matt thinks she was shocked because she was worried about how the rest of the family would react, and what her friends would think.

He says the worry for people who don't know much about the world of gayness is that they think maybe you're only telling them you're gay now because something's wrong, that you're not well, and they worry that you'll meet predatory older men, or that you'll never have a partner, and that you'll be lonely. But Matt told his mum that coming to terms with being gay was the only chance for him to be happy. To deal with it and get on with life. Far better he did that than get married, have kids and live a lie and wreck other people's lives. It also helps that he's now fully ensconced with Kevin. It's made it easier for his mum to accept it all. She does describe Kevin as 'a lovely boy'. And Matt tells her that while he may not be able to give her a big heterosexual wedding ceremony to enjoy, or maybe grandchildren, she can at least have the naches of a son who's in a major TV programme. *Naches* is a Yiddish word meaning pride and joy, usually referring to a parent's feelings.

'I may not give her babies,' he jokes, 'but I can give her BAFTAs.'

His one big regret is that he never got to tell his dad about his sexuality. But he thinks his dad may have known that he was gay. Apparently he mentioned to his sister, Matt's aunt, that Matt might be gay. Matt says he would have told him at the same time as he told his mum, and he knows his dad would have been fine with it because he could cope with anything that was thrown at him.

After he told his friends, his mum and his brother, everyone else got to know Matt was gay via the Jewish grapevine.

And after his initial reaction, when did his brother come to terms with Matt being gay?

'Oh give him another few years,' says Matt. 'He might get there.'

His stepfather Ralph (Matt's own parents were divorced) is in his mid-seventies, older than his mum, but he accepted it straight away. Matt was in the back of the family car one day and Ralph said, 'Your mother has told me the news and I want you to know that you have my full support.'

Matt giggles at the memory of his niceness.

The bottom line is that ever since he saw the therapist, he's been feeling better about himself. Accepting of himself. He says the dope-smoking may have been the cause of his period of depression. He thinks dope in some people, certainly himself, adds to a kind of depressive psychosis. Sure, he was dealing with a lot of crises in his life, but the weed exacerbated his sadness.

Maybe because of his negative association with marijuana, Matt's never done cocaine or ecstasy or acid, and that's also why he's finding it easier to be happy. When he first met Bob Mortimer in his late teens, when Vic and Bob spotted him and asked him to be part of their show, Bob told Matt that he was the angriest person he'd ever met.

'My vice and my downfall now,' says Matt, 'is food, and that's one thing I have to deal with.'

And with that Matt asks Kevin if he'd like another triple chocolate muffin.

'Do you know the exact seat the person who's got the Maltesers is supposed to be sitting in?' David asks Matt.

'No, we've never really specified it. I usually head for the end of the middle block, front row.'

'What I was going to suggest,' says Tony, 'was that I'll give, say, three people boxes of Maltesers. Is three enough?'

'Yeah, let's have three,' says David. 'I mean look, they cost nothing, and the joke is important. Let's put three out and see how we get on . . . But are they quite complicated to open, because the fun of it is seeing Matt eating them?'

'Yeah, well, I open the lid for them anyway,' says Tony, 'so he shouldn't have to struggle with the lid. And we've got normal Maltesers and these white chocolate ones.'

'I think it's good to be seen eating the brown ones onstage,' says David.

'Yeah,' agrees Matt, 'people know the brown.'

Matt then thinks for a moment, looks at Tony, who's holding a box of white Maltesers, and asks, 'Do you need the white ones then?'

'I suppose not,' says Tony. 'I'll get three tubs of brown ones from now on.'

'So those white ones are going spare?' asks Matt, and starts eating. He looks round the room and studies the off-white wallpaper and blue carpet with orange squiggles: 'This isn't a bitch or a whinge, I just wonder how someone decides to decorate a room in this way? I'd really like to know what the thought process was.'

'We could ask the vicar,' suggests Tony.

'The vicar?' asks Matt.

It turns out the Bournemouth International Centre has its own official vicar, a tradition that many old theatres still maintain, according to Tony, who's been on tours taking in most of the venues of Britain.

Matt asks what the vicar is like. Tony says he's nice, but a bit mad. He may be after a few conversions.

'Ever thought of joining Jews for Jesus?' David asks Matt.

Matt shakes his head, while sipping his mint tea. 'No, but I don't mind meeting him. He can try to convert me if he wants.'

'There's not a whole lot to do here, is there?' asks David.

Matt talks David through our day amid the crowds in Bournemouth.

David wonders who's on at the famous Winter Gardens venue. David thinks it might be Joe Pasquale, because he thinks he's seen some Pasquale posters. Matt thinks it might be Danny La Rue.

'I wonder how much Joe Pasquale charges for tickets,' ponders David. 'That's one bloke in a suit. There's probably not much difference in ticket price with what he charges to what we charge. I was looking through the brochure and our tickets are going for fifteen quid . . .'

'Really?' says Matt. 'Maybe they're subsidised . . .'

'Well, the most expensive ones are twenty-five quid. I was surprised. I thought it was a bit too cheap to be honest!'

Matt asks David about the 'interview' by Victoria Newton with him in the *Sun*'s Bizarre column. 'It's weird when they pretend you've given them an interview,' says Matt, smiling.

'Yes. It is a bit odd to be quoted talking to someone who wasn't even there,' he replies. 'And I did ask the journalist about twenty times if this was off the record. Maybe I'm stupid to be so trusting.'

Matt and David recently spent quite a lot of time with Victoria Newton's boss, Rebekah Wade. They met her and her husband Ross Kemp on the Comic Relief trip to Africa. They got to ask her how a national newspaper operates, how she makes the decisions about who and what to cover.

'Wasn't she also the editor of the *News of the World* when they ran all those stories printing paedophiles' names?' David asks.

Matt nods.

'It's weird that you don't hear anything about paedophiles at the moment.'

'You know why?' says Matt. 'They've all stopped.'

* * *

'I particularly admire the way you've turned round the idea of homophobia,' says the Reverend Stephen Jones. 'I mean, Dafydd, the only gay in the village, is just a masterstroke!'

David nods appreciatively, and asks the vicar if he's watched the programme often. He explains that he hasn't necessarily watched every episode, but he's seen enough of it to know that it's pushing back the boundaries, particularly with the gay characters, and the frequency with which Matt and David dress up as women and are prepared to camp it up. David says it's interesting how many heterosexual lads and straight couples come to the show and lap up the camper elements.

'Oh yes,' says the vicar, oozing joviality, 'they seem to love the campness. It's a celebration of campness in a way, isn't it?'

David laughs in agreement, and the vicar proffers a camera and asks if he can have his photo taken with David, and David gets Tony, who just happens to be passing by in the corridor, to take the picture.

As the grateful reverend goes to take his seat for the evening's show, David asks, 'Is it me, or was he slightly obsessed with the gayness of it all?'

Matt's talking on his mobile, expressions of disbelief tumbling out of his mouth. He can't believe it. He can't understand it. It's bewildering, but there must be something he can do. There must be somewhere he can go. There must be some website he can watch it on, or some dodgy pub somewhere that has a satellite link to Sweden or something.

He listens to his brother explaining that he doesn't think there is anything he can do.

'It just doesn't seem possible,' says Matt. 'This is Spurs against Arsenal. And it's not on TV *anywhere*?'

He puts the phone down. But he hasn't given up hope. 'I'm gonna talk to someone at the hotel. There must be some way we can watch it.'

But the match is tomorrow lunchtime, and time is running out. He's checked every website, Googled every pub in the Bournemouth, Southampton and New Forest areas, phoned all of his Arsenal-supporting friends and relatives, and so far nothing.

'Okay,' he says to me as he steps into the shower for his interval wash, 'let's liaise again tomorrow morning. I'm not going to give up. There MUST be a way we can watch this match!'

* * *

'He was good. Perfect,' says David, towelling off after his interval shower. He's in his robe, dangling his legs off the side of his chair, mock provocatively. 'Do you think he enjoyed it?' he adds, grinning.

The lad David picked out from the front row was exactly the kind of bloke he's looking for. He wants a young, confident, laddish figure, someone willing to take the extreme physical interaction with 'Des Kaye' in his stride. Earlier in the week, on the third night of the tour in Portsmouth, the volunteer turned out to be a bit shy, sweaty and visibly embarrassed. David felt slightly uncomfortable pulling his trousers down. Whereas tonight's victim, who he just managed to grapple to the floor before tugging his jeans *and* pants down, lapped up every second of the attention. Sometimes mothers in the audience offer up their pubescent sons. David has to be careful that he doesn't end up dry-humping a 15-year-old.

'If we did the show in America, I'd probably get lawsuits from everyone I molested,' he points out, 'but in Bournemouth I can somehow get away with it . . . though maybe not if they turn out to be under age. I think if I did accidentally get a 15-year-old up, it would seem wrong.'

Times have changed. He remembers what it was like when he was in his early teens and was in the Sea Scouts. This was the rather sexualised environment in which he found himself once a week from the age of eleven to about fourteen. It was run by two men for whom games meant bathtime fun, wherein David and his chums would run around while the men chased them and slapped their bottoms.

He clocks the shocked look on my face.

'Yeah, it's weird to think of it now,' says David. 'But they would do stuff like say, "Now you've got to put this wetsuit on . . . it's very tight-fitting, so you have to take your trunks off and we'll have to rub some baby oil into you in order to slip it on."'

So these guys rubbed baby oil onto your naked bodies?

David laughs. Then grimaces. 'Yes. And you wouldn't get away with that now, but back then it just struck me as a bit weird.' Getting deeper into the memories of this peculiar environment, David tells the story of the time he forgot to bring his cagoule so one of the men in charge bent him over, ordered him to take down his pants and whacked him with a sail baton – which is about three times the length of a ruler and is, David emphasises, 'really, really hard'.

'Now I would think: what right have you got to hit me – you're just a fucking Scout master!'

Then there was the time one of the leaders organised a trip to Holland. 'He hand-picked about six of us to go on a special camp.' They went to a campsite in Holland. When they got there, no one was wearing any clothes. David notes the incredulity on my face. 'Yeah ... it turned out to be a naturist camping site. So we spent the time naked, sleeping in the same tent. Now I haven't read the Scouting rules recently but I don't think they include taking the boys to naturist camp.' I ask him if his parents knew about this. Did they give their permission? 'Well, I told my mum when I got back that I'd been to a nudist camp,' he explains, 'but she didn't believe me ...'

David is wavering between finding these memories funny, and finding them slightly creepy.

'I mean, I wasn't abused. But I still think it's not quite right. There was nothing unequivocally sexual that I saw.'

But then he ponders the memory of the first night at this camp in Holland, when they sat down in a café and a naked man sat down next to them, David and his young friends, and suddenly David felt the man's hand on his leg under the table. 'I remember thinking it was quite weird but at that age you just don't say, "I'm sorry, what are you doing?" You kind of let the dirty old man feel up your leg.'

David gets the five-minute call. 'Five minutes?' he says, as if he can never quite come to terms with the fact that he's in the middle of a show and has to rouse himself for the second half. 'Shit!' His routine in these last five minutes is to put on the minimal thong, gold, sequinned ballgown and dense, furry merkin which make up his 'Anne' costume for the *Stars In Their Eyes* skit kicking off act two. He spends a large part of his professional life wearing women's clothing, and visibly enjoys it.

His fondness for drag dates back to his big theatrical break when, aged eleven, he took up acting at his 'big school' (Reigate Grammar). The school play that year was a production of *All the Kings' Men*, which David describes as 'a weird little operetta about Cavaliers and Roundheads', and initially David didn't have a big role in the show. But one day his teacher said, 'Williams! Stay behind after class,' and told him that the boy playing the part of the Queen of England had dropped out because he was embarrassed about having to wear the wig and dress. So the teacher offered the role to young David, who had no such qualms. 'Of course I went, oh okay – yes, I'll do it. So I was this queen, this proper queen. And I remember being on the stage in the dress and the wig, and though I wasn't doing much, people were laughing at my performance. I found it so exciting. I saw my mum pointing out to someone that I was her son, and I felt that I had some new power. I thought, ooh, what's this thing, what's this power? And all I was doing was acting a bit queeny onstage.' He pauses and surveys the room. 'Age eleven and already acting queeny. Already in dresses. And I've carved a hugely successful career out of it ever since.'

Standing on the stage at school, commanding the attention of the audience, gave him some taste of how it must have felt for the performers he worshipped to be doing their job. His first memory of seeing a professional show was when his mum and his sister took him to see the stage production of *Barnum*, starring Michael Crawford. 'It was magical,' he says. 'Just the idea of this big, glitzy show. And he was such a presence. Of course he couldn't resist saying, "Ooh Betty"!' David giggles at the memory. 'I think I thought that was a bit cheeky even then. But everyone laughed. I'm sure it was their favourite bit of the whole show.

'We also had this thing twice a year where your class would have to take assembly and no one ever wanted to do it – someone would read from a book, and it would be quite dull and boring. But I seized upon it to do something funny, to imitate TV characters. The first one I did was a spoof of *Game for a Laugh* and I played Rustie Lee, and I used to put custard pies in the teachers' faces, and then I did a version of *Blankety Blank* which I hosted and that was the big hit, I think, because we could make fun of the teachers with it, so I said, you know, "Mr Stather was in the staffroom dancing around and he got his blank out," so I managed to be irreverent and cheeky without being really naughty. I think it was just the right side of being rebellious. So that became the thing I was known for at school, and for about half an hour I'd become quite popular, then everyone would go back to hating me again. But it was the kind of school where you had to be good at something, whether it was football or rugby or art or something, so I quite quickly established myself as someone who wanted to be funny and would show off. I would take part in the school elections – anything that allowed me to be the centre of attention I liked. And then by the time I got to the sixth form I knew that I wanted to do drama. I think my parents were a bit worried about me doing a drama degree. I don't think they thought we were those type of people, you know: we were too normal in a way to have an actor in the family.'

Before he could ever become a proper, professional actor, David felt he had to sort out his body.

In the interval

'I was a bit fat in those days,' he explains. 'Well, I was flabby, rather than fat. Basically there was always someone fatter than me, so I wasn't ever the fat boy of the class.'

Was he happy?

'I wasn't exactly miserable. I was melancholic I think. I didn't like being made to do things I didn't want to do. Like cross-country running. I remember thinking that was just hell, and I was always one of those boys you see at the end, bringing up the rear with a miserable look on his face. I was quite serious about studying, though, and reading. We had quite dry and boring textbooks to read and I took them quite seriously.'

As for girls, David didn't encounter them at all until the sixth form. Before then, he only saw them in the distance. Then all of a sudden he was sixteen and he hadn't had any experience with girls and he was wracked with nerves just being in the same class as them.

'I got tongue-tied just having to speak in front of them. It was horrible.'

But after a while he realised that he was completely comfortable socialising with these girls in a purely platonic manner, with not a hint of sexual tension. Before long he had a circle of female friends with whom he could gossip and go shopping. These days, nearly twenty years later, he still prefers the company of women. His best friends include Denise Van Outen and Natalie Imbruglia. He feels more at home with the subjects they discuss: emotions, relationships, clothes, art, literature. He has no interest in sport, or any kind of blokeish competitiveness.

'Having said that,' he adds, fiddling with his fake crotch-fur, 'I do still get giddy and awestruck in front of a really beautiful woman. Like her.'

He means X, and grabs his phone from the dressing-room table to find a photo of her. 'Look,' he says, holding up a shot of her in a figure-hugging sheer black frock. 'The most beautiful woman I have ever seen.'

He's still staring at it when Gareth comes in to usher him off to the stage to start act two. 'Oh God,' he mumbles as he walks through the corridor towards the backstage area. 'When will I get to hold her in my arms and kiss her?' What makes the frustration of his situation with X even more excruciating is that he did have her in his arms a couple of years ago, soon after they first met. That was when they went on a few dates, and David first became besotted with her. But it didn't work out, and she got back together with her ex.

That night David and Matt join the crew for a few drinks at the bar/club downstairs from the restaurant where they had lunch. The man who said he'd be on the door is indeed on the door and sweeps Matt and David through to a seated area. For a few minutes they get to reflect with fellow crew members on an exhausting first week of the tour. But semi-drunken clubbers keep walking past and staring at them, or occasionally saying hello. And the manager of the bar is excitedly asking David what he thinks of Bournemouth.

Matt and David have each put £250 behind the bar to pay for the crew's drinks, but they can't stay longer than fifteen minutes because they're getting so much attention. They just wanted a quiet, relaxing drink.

On the way out, David shows me a text. It's from X, saying how much she's looking forward to seeing the show next week. With a kiss.

He's beaming.

Matt looks at David quizzically, wondering why he's so chuffed all of a sudden.

12

29 October 2005 – Bournemouth: day 6

At breakfast with David we go through the papers. There isn't much in the tabloids, apart from one of them listing all the ways in which Matt and David will be making money this year: the tour, the TV series, the DVD sales, the merchandise. It estimates their joint fortune as £22 million. David laughs at the idea of having £11 million, and as he lightly butters his toast he notices a small picture of himself grinning on the front page of the *Independent*.

He's in the Saturday Profile section. It's a regular weekly slot in which a journalist tries to sum up the career of a famous person and explain why they're newsworthy right now. The headline is 'Not So Little'. David skim-reads the piece, and it immediately becomes clear that it is one of those articles that repeats old stories about David and *Little Britain* that were inaccurate to begin with. There's a separate box at the bottom of the piece called A Life In Brief, which is supposed to be a potted biography of David. It's divided into five sections: Born, Education, Career, He Says and They Say. The first two are fine, but the Career bit is odd. '*Little Britain* began on

TV in 2003,' it states, correctly enough, 'with a second series a year later. There will be a third series, the pair say . . .' The third series begins in less than one week's time. The sentence finishes: '. . . then no more.' David says they haven't decided whether to do a fourth series yet.

There's a pull quote above the article which says, 'Walliams, who with Matt Lucas won Best Comedy at the National TV Awards, is probably Britain's highest-profile "metrosexual".' David raises a camp eyebrow.

The piece begins with a reference to a waste-management employee who recently sued his colleagues for making homophobic taunts in which they called him 'Sebastian' after David's gay Prime Minister's assistant, then goes on to say: 'David Walliams, though, is not gay. Probably.'

David smiles thinly. The piece then goes into the fling he had with the woman he met at an Agent Provocateur party who went on to name him in her divorce papers and got quite a lot of publicity. After a swift summary of that episode and a run-through of the amounts David has apparently earned or is due to earn from *Little Britain* and its offshoots ('All those figures are wrong,' says David), the article returns to the sex issue, referring to the 'gay-o-meter beloved of the red-tops' – or more accurately the *Sun* – before asking the oddly worded question, 'Why are we a nation apparently obsessed with his leanings?'

'Oh why? Why are they obsessed?' says David in mock pained voice.

The things that make him seem a bit gay are, according to the journalist, the fact that he's never drunk a pint of beer or supported a football team (unlike Matt who, it says here 'is both gay and an Arsenal fan') and there's an anecdote about how, before a photo shoot, David once asked David Bailey, 'Are we doing make-up?' Apparently Bailey accused David of being 'a queen' for mentioning it. David points out that he wasn't asking for make-up, just checking if there was going to be make-up, a fairly standard element of any photo shoot for a magazine.

The *Independent* article then details 'an unconfirmed list of Walliams's conquests' which 'includes Patsy Kensit, Abi Titmuss, Aimee Osbourne, Lisa Moorish, Suranne Jones, Jayne Middlemiss and Martine McCutcheon'. It does mention that the last name is 'emphatically denied' by David. 'That's because I've never met her,' he says.

There's also a quote from David talking about not being rebellious when he was young, from which the article concludes he had a happy childhood. The piece misspells the name of his best friend Robin Dashwood. They call him Robin Nashford.

But the comment that strikes David as particularly odd is: 'He has also, whisper it, written scripts for Ant and Dec.' As if that's something to be ashamed of. Everyone, David points out, loves Ant and Dec. Even *Independent* readers.

Finally, the article claims that he doesn't like it when people question if he's more than 30 per cent gay, after he said in a magazine interview with his friend Denise Van Outen that he was '70 per cent heterosexual'.

'Oh God,' he says wearily. 'I kind of regret saying that. It's not like I'd thought about it so carefully – "Oh yeah, I'm precisely 70 per cent straight" – it was just a figure that tripped off my tongue. Maybe I'm only 69 per cent.'

Maybe people were excited to see him 'admitting' that he's not 100 per cent straight?

'Maybe. As if I'm the first person to point out that people aren't necessarily 100 per cent anything. I think it's interesting that even a paper like the *Independent* can't come to terms with the idea that someone might be a bit camp and a bit gay and still have relationships with women. As if it's all so confusing.'

He pauses and smiles. 'But we will have to deal with all this in the book, won't we? My . . . sexuality . . .'

Yes, we will. Maybe we should just print the definitive list of who you've had sex with?

'Just do a chapter entitled "Who David's fucked".' He takes the paper from me and has a quick glance at the article. 'At least I look okay in the photo.'

Before we finish breakfast he mentions that his parents will be arriving any minute. 'Shit,' he says, 'I hope they didn't read that article. And if they did, I hope they don't believe any of it.'

David gets a text from Matt. It just says two words: 'Robin Nashford.'

'She didn't know who we were until we went up to collect the award,' explains Kathleen, David's mum.

'But you knew that I knew her?' says David.

'Yes, well, as soon as they sat down in front of us I thought, David knows Billie Piper, but I didn't like to interrupt her, because she did look very nervous.'

'Oh she would have been nervous,' says David.

'Well, I don't think she thought she was going to win, and I didn't just want to start chatting to her and having to explain that I was your mother. But then after we went up to collect the award, she was so lovely. She was thrilled that you'd won . . . she said, "I didn't realise it was you!" And then afterwards we spoke to Russell T. Davies and he was saying you'd make a good Doctor Who.'

'What, unprompted?' says David, excitedly.

'Oh yes. He was just saying how good you are. And he must know you like *Doctor Who*. I suggested he should have Vicky Pollard as Doctor Who's assistant.'

'I think Billie might have something to say about that!' says David's dad Peter.

'What amazed me though, about the whole thing, was how many people watch it. I got asked for my autograph yesterday,' giggles David's mother. 'In the chemist.'

'Yes, well, eight million people watched you,' says David. 'You're huge now.'

'Eighteen million people?' asks David's dad.

'No. Only eight million!' corrects Kathleen.

Kathleen's default mood is jolly. She seems to spend most of the time smiling, and coming up with funny reflections on her life, amusing tales of her daughter's stepsons, and references to David's childhood. Peter, her husband, is slightly more distracted, and less vivacious. He takes his lead from Kathleen.

David's mum asks him how his swimming is going. He explains that it's difficult sometimes to find a big and quiet enough pool where he can practice. He tells them about swimming in the sea off the coast of Southampton the other day. David's mum says she hasn't seen him swimming in the sea since he was a boy.

'The last time I remember seeing you swimming anywhere was when you nearly drowned Edgar.'

'He nearly drowned himself. I went swimming with Edgar Wright [the director of *Spaced* and *Shaun of the Dead*] in this huge, Olympic-size pool, and I just didn't realise that he wasn't that good a swimmer. He couldn't really do any strokes.'

'I think he got halfway up the pool,' remembers Kathleen, 'and then it was just too much.'

'And the next thing I knew,' says David, 'I was being tapped on my shoulder and told, "Your friend is in the first-aid room, if you'd like to go and rescue him." Like he was my son . . .'

'So when will you be swimming the Channel?' asks his dad.

David tells him it will be next summer, some time in the first week of July when all the conditions are right.

'When the tides are right, you mean? And it's not too cold?'

'And when there are no jellyfish,' his mum chimes in.

'Yeah, especially the jellyfish,' says David.

'Your sister says she's always wanted to swim the Channel too,' points out David's mum.

'She'd better get training then.'

'Yeah, I don't think it'll happen,' his mum answers.

We're in the car on the way to Beaulieu to visit the car museum there. David had first made enquiries of the hotel receptionist and she said, in her eastern European accent, 'Oh yes. They have a firewall today!'

At least that's what David thinks she said.

Pete the driver suggests she may have said 'fireworks'. It's coming up to Guy Fawkes' Night.

'Oh maybe,' says David. 'It was difficult to understand what she was saying. And she didn't seem to understand what I wanted.' He smiles ruefully. '*I* don't understand what I want!'

'No,' says his mum. 'It's been like that for a long time.'

The National Motor Museum at Beaulieu is full of beautiful cars, from vintage Porsches and Rolls-Royces to huge, record-breaking beasts like the Bluebird and the Golden Arrow. There are decades-old taxis and fire engines, and Peter Ustinov's Mercedes. David's mum explains that he's loved cars since he was a boy, when he used to look through the car magazines and memorise the cost of each vehicle. She regularly bought him model versions of famous vehicles. Now he's got a real vintage Mercedes, which he bought from Sam Taylor-Wood, though he's thinking of trading it in for an Aston Martin.

'You know we've still got all your toy cars at home,' points out Kathleen.

'Ooh, I like them . . . I'd love to have a look through them again,' says David.

'And I've got your train set. And your Action Man.'

'Oh wow. The train set's beautiful.'

'It was a special Hornby for the Queen's Silver Jubilee,' Kathleen explains to me before turning back to David. 'I've also got all your old photos. You in the mauve dress with the furry hat. Your first role in the school play. In a wedding dress.'

David smiles. 'Nothing's changed!'

'Pete's great, isn't he?' Kathleen remarks.

David nods in agreement and explains how useful it is for him and Matt to have separate drivers, so they can both go wherever they need to go, at whatever time.

'And he looks like he can handle himself.'

'Yes, but what I like about him is that he's so gentle and polite,' says David. 'Until, presumably, he's got some deranged fan in a headlock.'

'And Matt's driver seems very nice too.'

David agrees they're both great, although Cosmo does seem over-reliant on satellite navigation.

David, early cross-dressing, with his sister Julie, 1974

His mum asks him what he's doing for Christmas. David says he's thinking of going to India with Denise Van Outen.

'Hmmm . . . yeah.'

'Not too sure, are we?' laughs David, imitating her. 'Too poor, maybe?'

'It's not that. It's more that people are sometimes taken aback when they visit somewhere like that . . . It can be quite a shock.'

David says he doesn't think he'd be easily shocked now, having been to Ethiopia with Comic Relief.

'Oh sure. But I think if it was me I'd go and lie in the sun somewhere.'

'I'll do that too,' says David. He's got a whole month at Christmas when the tour breaks. 'But I'll still be around for Christmas Day with you. Then, just as you're tucking in to the yule log, I'll be leaving!'

Kathleen looks round, slightly startled. David scans the area. David and his mum realise they've no idea where his dad is.

Within a few minutes they find him among the buses, vans and trams. His head is in the bonnet of a Ford Model T van. David's dad is a retired engineer who used to work for London Transport.

David can't get that excited about really old vintage vehicles. The red Ferrari Enzo from 2004 gets his juices flowing, though. He's also quite taken with the Jaguar E-type from 1962. 'Still just an incredibly cool car.' When he sees the silver Lotus Elite from 1960 he tells his mother he'd quite like one of those.

'Now this is the classic car,' announces David's dad. 'The Ford Capri!'

David's mum explains that David's sister was once engaged to a man who drove a Ford Capri, but she luckily never married him.

A middle-aged man recognises David and shouts, 'Looking at cars?'

'Trying to!' says David jovially.

David's mum has been speaking to one of the museum guards, who told her that the Ferrari is on loan from Mark Knopfler, who lives nearby. She says how nice it is of him to let them have it. Then, after a moment's reflection, she says he might as well keep it here as in his garage.

David's worried about lunch. He thinks we should find a nice pub and book a table. 'You know these local country pubs. It's all, "Ooh no, I don't think we have a table." Everything's "no".'

'It's all for *local* people . . .' says David's mum.

'Yeah, that's somebody else's catchphrase,' David says, mock snappily.

He calls Pete and asks if he can call Tony to recommend a nearby pub and book a table, while we carry on wandering round the museum. David also wants to check out the James Bond Experience, which is housed in a small separate building right on the lawn outside the motor museum.

'I wonder if you get to become James Bond in there . . . maybe you get to shoot someone.'

I get a text message from Kevin explaining that Matt is losing his voice and that's why he hasn't called to make arrangements to watch Spurs v. Arsenal. He's going to stay in the hotel and listen to the match on the radio. The point of most concern is Matt's voice.

'He loses his voice quite a lot I think,' says David. He doesn't say anything else about it. He's looking at the toy cars for sale in the gift shop. There's one of an Aston Martin that takes his fancy.

'Are you going to buy that?' asks his mum, and for a moment it sounds like she's going to make fun of him for buying a toy car. But no. 'Let me get it for you, darling. Come on! Do you want a bigger one?'

'No, this one is nice.'

'You're going to buy that toy car for David?' asks his dad, highly amused.

'Yeah, why not?' says his mum. And she does.

David spies a copy of Lord Montagu of Beaulieu's autobiography and is amused by the title: *Wheels Within Wheels: An Unconventional Life*. The 'unconventional' bit seems to refer the aristocrat's bisexuality.

David's dad buys an official map of the area. David wonders why there are key rings with fluffy animals on them for sale. 'I love it when gift shops sell stuff totally unconnected to the attraction.'

I get a text from Matt: 'Am in room called Azalia trying to get the match!'

The sound of guns firing and helicopter blades whirring fills the room. David points at a glass case containing a nondescript blue dress and matching skirt attached to a mannequin. It's one of Miss Moneypenny's outfits. Next to it is a jet-ski from *The Spy Who Loved Me*.

David's mum says the car is nice. It's a Jaguar XKR Roadster from *Die Another Day*. David says it's okay, but it's not exactly the Aston Martin.

'I want the Aston Martin DB5. The *Goldfinger* one!' he laughs. 'It's the only reason I came. It's the whole reason for the tour.'

We pass another exhibit of an item of clothing in a glass case. It's a man's shirt. Apparently it was worn by Jaws in *Moonraker*. Even the boat that jumped high over the Florida Everglades seems unexciting here in this narrow, not particularly large room.

'It's more like the James Bond Corridor,' says David.

His mum nods in agreement.

'You'd be disappointed if you'd come all the way to Beaulieu from far away, just for the James Bond Experience, wouldn't you?'

David's water arrives with ice. He silently spoons it into my drink. David's dad asks the waitress for more bread. Everyone in the pub is being unfailingly polite and discreet, which David appreciates hugely.

His mum asks him how the renovation of his house is going. He says it's going slowly, and that it's not due to be ready until next summer, when the tour finishes. There was mention of him buying Supernova Heights in the article today in the paper about his and Matt's wealth. David takes the opportunity to point out that the piece was inaccurate about his wealth.

'Oh we don't believe that,' says his dad. 'Don't worry, son. We know it's all exaggerated.'

'It is exaggerated,' says David. 'Quite a lot. And we haven't received hardly any of the money we're due.'

'I never believe a word of it, darling,' says his mum. 'I try not to take any notice of what they print in the papers.'

'Well, *some* of it's true.'

'Maybe. But they can't even get the basic facts right. They said you were born in Chertsey!'

'Could I have the milk chocolate walnut praline please. Four of those. Some of the orange peel. Four bits of that, please.'

'In the milk or the dark?'

'The milk please. And some milk chocolate vanilla fudge, four of those, and four of the white chocolate praline, please. And four of those caraques, please – the milk ones. And four toffee turtles. Matt will like those. Is that enough toffee turtles? And some white chocolate pigs.'

David's getting a box of confectionery for Matt from an old-fashioned sweet shop in Beaulieu. While he orders toffee turtles and chocolate pigs he's keeping an eye on his mum, who's outside the shop, chatting to some passers-by.

'It looks like she's gathering people to come and meet me.'

When we leave the shop, his mum does introduce a nice family to David, and he happily greets them all, and they tell him how funny *Little Britain* is.

When we're in the car on the way back to the hotel he jokingly asks his mum whether she stopped passers-by in Beaulieu village to tell them that he was her son. She castigates him for suggesting as much.

'But I might get a badge,' she says, 'with "David Walliams's Mum" on it.'

1970s

As a kid, Matt always wanted to have a short back and sides. But his hair would never grow that way. He had rather straggly hair, a bit like his character Andy Pipkin. He used to hate going to the hairdresser's and getting itchy hairs down his back, and he used to hate having his hair washed and getting the shampoo in his eyes. But those traumas paled when he started finding clumps of hair on his pillow. Within six weeks he was completely bald.

In 1978, at the age of four, Matt was knocked down by a car. He was on holiday with his family – Mum, Dad, brother and both his grandmothers – in Portugal. One day Matt and his mum were walking down a huge main road and Matt was daydreaming and spotted his dad and the rest of his family on the other side of the street, and tried to cross over to where they were. A car came out of an alleyway, Matt walked in front of it, the car braked suddenly, but still hit him.

Matt was lying on the ground, screaming and crying. But he hadn't been that badly hurt. About five minutes later he stopped sobbing, his parents bought him an ice cream and everything seemed fine.

It wasn't until two years later that Matt's hair started falling out. If it was a reaction to the car accident, it was a very delayed one.

They tried all kinds of treatments. They tried homeopathy and acupuncture, and his dad rubbed seaweed lotion into Matt's head to try to make the hair grow, but the lotion gave his dad a terrible rash on his hands. His parents took him to hospital after hospital to try one remedy after another. And after a while – maybe about seven or eight months of this – Matt's hair did start to grow back.

But then it all fell out again. No doctor ever proved that it was a delayed reaction to the car accident, but they all assumed it was something to do with it. In fact, there was a history of baldness in the family. Matt's dad wore a wig but Matt didn't realise this for years. He would tease his dad when he was a kid and say, 'Ha ha, you wear a wig!' but it was just something silly for him to say. He never for a moment suspected he actually was wearing one. Then his dad came home from work one day with completely different hair. Soon after that, one time before Hebrew classes, Matt's dad took him aside and told him. He said, 'You mustn't tell anybody,' so of course Matt immediately went to Hebrew classes and said, 'Hey, guess what? My dad wears a wig! Brilliant, innit?' It turned out Matt's father lost his hair when he was about fourteen, so it was always possible that Matt just lost his hair prematurely like his dad, and that it was nothing to do with the car accident at all.

When he realised that his hair was never going to grow back, Matt took to wearing caps. He became a kind of celebrity at school because he was so easily identified. Then it was decided that he should try wearing a wig, so he went to a wigmaker near Baker Street. But they didn't have children's wigs in those days, certainly not ones for boys, so they gave him a ladies' wig. It was cut for him but it gave him a very big, bouffant hairstyle. Matt found the wig irritating and hot, so his Aunty Denny sewed a handkerchief into the lining to make it more comfortable.

When Matt started to wear the wig to primary school, he still looked quite odd because he didn't have eyebrows. He would also get bored wearing it and would take it off for the hell of it. When he did wear it, some of the older boys would run past and whip it off and throw it on the floor, so the wig itself became something of an annoyance.

When he went to secondary school Matt decided to ditch the wig entirely, though he still wore the cap.

Of course, Matt was still intensely conscious of his baldness. He would get

Before

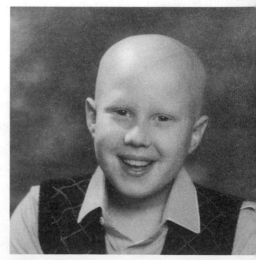

After

stared at wherever he went. But as soon as he made a name for himself as a performer in the school plays, Matt realised that his unique look had its advantages. It also meant that whenever he and his best friend Jeremy got into trouble, Matt would pull his cap over his face sheepishly, and invariably Jeremy would get the blame.

Matt wrote to Duncan Goodhew when he was seven and Goodhew wrote back and sent a few badges, one of which said 'Bald is Beautiful'. One of the first jokes Matt ever consciously told was this: 'People often ask me: how did I lose my hair? It was through shock. For instance, Duncan Goodhew fell out of a tree. Well, it was my fucking head he landed on.'

'Gargling with red sage was once suggested to me,' says Tony, 'but then I tried it and it was bloody revolting.'

'And you probably don't have any red sage on you,' suggests Kevin.

'No, I don't. Sorry,' says Tony, 'But you've got the lemons and the honey. And the other thing I'm going to suggest is doing some vocal warm-ups. Every morning when you wake up. Just to make the throat warm.'

'Yeah, I know,' says Matt.

Tony has a knack of passing on advice without sounding parental or teacherly or disapproving in any way. It's as if he lives for being useful. He also informs Matt that he's finally bought him a fridge to take to each venue.

'Thanks, Tony. I think I'll be all right. My voice is just a bit croaky,' says Matt.

Kevin asks if he'll be all right when it comes to sing Dafydd's song. Matt explains that the singing voice is the last element that goes.

Then Matt asks me if David was annoyed when I told him that Matt was losing his voice. I tell Matt he just seemed to accept it as a possibility and then put it out of his mind, probably so that he could enjoy the James Bond Experience.

Matt asks what David thought about the profile piece in the *Independent*. Matt was quite interested to read the piece because he thought he might learn something he didn't know about him. But all he learned was that they could get David's best friend's name wrong. He thinks the article is the kind of thing you'd normally read in *Daily Mail*. Not the *Independent*. But he's had his own run-ins with the 'quality' papers.

A few months ago his agent Melanie had to spend a whole day on the phone to the *Telegraph* who had got hold of a story, which they described as 'jokey', claiming that Matt was intending to charge £18,000 to appear at a benefit gig in Llanddewi-Brefi. Matt emphasises that he's never charged for a benefit in his life and never would. The *Telegraph*, nevertheless, sent a reporter to Llanddewi-Brefi to ask people what they thought of the idea of Matt charging for a benefit. They gathered suitable quotes from disgruntled people to say how disgusting it was, and they told Matt's agent they were running the story the next day.

When Mel told Matt about the piece that was about to run, he told her to tell them he'd fucking sue the living daylights out of them if they printed it. In the end the story got pulled, after Melanie and his publicist Moira had both been on the phone to the editor on and off all day, making big threats and pointing out that the story was a complete fabrication. But what rankles with Matt is that there will still be people in Llanddewi-Brefi thinking that he charged £18,000 to appear at a benefit.

Around the same time, the *Independent* printed a story that Matt and David had fallen out with Geoff Posner, the TV series producer of *Little Britain*. Matt describes the piece as complete fiction. A letter from Matt and David's people was sent to the paper, complaining about it in the strongest terms, but it was never printed, and there's never been an apology. Matt spoke to Geoff as soon as the article appeared, telling him the best way to prove it was rubbish was by carrying on working together. Now Geoff, Matt and David are in the process of starting a production company together.

'But sometimes a paper makes a mistake which is just funny.'

Last year the *Telegraph* published a family history of Matt in one of their regular celebrity family tree articles. The piece managed to get the details of Matt's parents right, but when they got to the details of his grandfather and everyone before him, things went wrong. Matt's grandmother was evacuated to Leicester in the war. She was there for six months and his father was born in that period, then two months later they moved back to London. The *Telegraph* researcher found a Harry Lucas in Leicester but it was the wrong Harry Lucas from a whole Leicester family that was nothing to do with Matt's family. Matt's family is made up of eastern European Jews. The Leicester Lucases were from solid English farming stock. So two-thirds of the article was about a different Harry Lucas. Matt delightedly read the whole thing to his brother and they were crying with laughter down the phone to each other. Matt asked Moira to tell the *Telegraph* that they'd written about completely the wrong family. But of course it's never been acknowledged that they got it wrong, and it's never been corrected.

Matt jokingly told his brother that he hopes he now doesn't get people from Leicester calling, claiming they're long-lost relatives. 'Especially,' says Matt, 'now we've got twenty-two million pounds. According to the paper.' He looks at me and Kevin and says, 'I haven't got one million quid, let alone eleven million. Have you seen my flat?'

I remind Matt that when I went to meet him and Kevin at their London flat recently, he asked me to wait outside.

'We don't let anyone in!' says Kevin.

Matt tells the story of how one of his mum's friends said to his mum, 'So now we know your son's a multi-millionaire . . .' Matt's mum just said, 'Is he?' Matt encouraged his mum to say something even more blunt. 'She should just tell her to fuck off. It's none of her business.'

Above all, it strikes Matt as a rude thing to say, and he, much like David, can't abide that kind of rudeness.

The fact that the papers have started to write about how much money Matt and David are apparently making is starting to irk them. Possibly because the implication is that they're doing it just for the money.

Matt explains, without either Kevin or myself asking him, that he and David don't even make a pound per DVD.

'Don't get me wrong, I'm not complaining. I'm not poor. But if you sell two million DVDs you don't earn twelve million quid.'

He says the paper claimed that they get paid two million pounds by the BBC for doing the TV show. Whereas in reality they don't get a tenth of that.

Kevin says that it's odd to read 'facts' in the newspapers about himself and Matt that are routinely wrong. Though sometimes they can work in his favour, like when one of the papers promoted him to the job of TV producer, when at the moment he's a researcher. Another article claimed that Matt and Kevin exchanged gold rings. In fact, they chose the least ostentatious rings they could find.

'And things that are printed wrong in one paper then get repeated constantly,' says Matt. 'It's like my dad went to prison for four years according to anyone who's read about it in the papers, but it was six months according to those of us who knew him. Because that's how long he actually went to prison for.'

It's the first time I've heard him mention his dad going to prison, and as soon as he does so, he gets up and walks round the dressing room, as if the mention of it has made him antsy. He puts the kettle on.

The fat-suit for Bubbles is hanging up on a rail. It looks disconcertingly like a big empty sack of human skin. The saggy breasts and hairy genital area are particularly disturbing. Tony has made sure Matt has lots of lemons and honey to help with his throat. He's also brought packets of M&S fruit salad, some strips of lime and coriander chicken, and smoothies.

Matt surveys the items on offer and says, 'Isn't it terrible there's all this fresh food here and I'd rather eat a McDonald's. That's why I'm such a fat cunt.'

Kevin points out that the crisps don't help, plus the fact that he pretty much eats whatever he likes. There's no admonishment in Kevin's voice. He's just pointing out the facts. I've yet to see them exchange a cross word.

Matt says, 'Yeah, I actually think I'm getting fitter as the tour goes on.'

Happy meal

Kevin agrees. 'I think you've been sweating less.'

'I've noticed the song gets a tad easier each night. I had a Slimfast for lunch and not much for breakfast.'

'There are some nice fruit smoothies here. Mango and lychee. Erm, orange, mango and apricot, or pineapple, banana and coconut.'

'Yeah,' says Matt. 'Shall we mix them all up?'

Kevin laughs. 'No. But the orange, mango and apricot sounds nice.'

'Has it got apple in it?' asks Matt. He can't go anywhere near apples. 'I'll get anaphylactical.'

'Lemons . . .' says Kevin, 'There are lots of lemons.'

We all stare at the lemons.

I ask Matt if food is his addiction. He doesn't drink much, gave up smoking a few years ago and doesn't take drugs. He says Kevin is right – he just eats whatever he likes, especially chocolate and crisps, and then the occasional Slimfast when he thinks he's just getting *too* big. Then he explains that avoiding booze and drugs is crucial to his and David's success. He's seen alcohol and drugs ruin many talented artists.

'Me and Dave were on telly a couple of years ago being interviewed by somebody who was fucking coked out of their head. I was pissed off afterwards. It was a shitty interview because of their stupid cocaine. And then we had to listen to them afterwards in the dressing room for about an hour talking shit. And this was a big star. Well, he *was* big but not so much now, probably because of that, because of drugs . . .'

Then he tells us the story of his most recent relationship before he started going out with Kevin. The fact that he's trying to be careful not to lose his voice means he has to talk quietly, almost in a whisper. As Matt tells the story, Kevin and I edge our chairs closer to him so we can hear every word.

'Before I met Kevin, I was sort of vaguely seeing this bloke who was a heavy drinker. And I remember the first time I met him, we were in a club and he was pissed as a fart. And I met him again and you know I was very attracted to him but he was really pissed again and I just said, "Look, here's my email address – get in touch if you like." Matt didn't expect to hear from him, but was pleasantly surprised when he did. There was something different about him from the normal people you meet when you're out clubbing – intelligent, a bit of an artist (though his job was working at night monitoring newspaper mentions of a particular company). They started talking on the phone a lot, and they met up again, this time in the evening before he was due on one of his late shifts. Matt left at about 11 p.m., by which time his friend had downed about five or six pints of beer. Matt remembers thinking that was maybe his way of dealing with work. And it gradually got to the point where Matt would want to leave a club when it was getting late, but this bloke would always want to stay. 'And you think: if you like me you'd want to be with me, rather than just stay out drinking,' explains Matt.

The last time Matt saw him was on a trip to the National Theatre to see Mark Ravenhill's play *Mother Molly's Clap House* ('Fucking brilliant'). They went to the bar after the show, then to a club. The usual pattern surfaced. Matt told him he wanted to go home, but he wanted to stay for just one more. Then another hour went by and finally Matt lost his patience and said he was going. 'But I warn you, if I go now and you don't come with me, that's fine but then I won't see you again.'

Matt woke up the next morning feeling sad because he really liked this bloke, then he saw there was a message on his phone: 'Matt, I really want to talk to you, I'm worried about you . . . I've made a terrible mistake, please call me, we need to talk.' The emotional plea made Matt think again. 'I thought maybe he was just having a bit of a bad night, so I rang him, and here's the thing: I said, "How are you?" He said, "Fine, fine, yeah, yeah." And he was kind of making small talk and then he says, "Sorry, what are you ringing for?" And I went, "You rang me. You said you wanted to talk to me." And he goes, "Did I?" It was like he had no memory of that at all.' Finally he told Matt that he didn't want to go out with anyone right now. And Matt thought: no, you just fucking rang me and you make me sound like I'm the fucking weird stalker when I'm just returning your call. But that was when he knew there was nothing more he could do. 'He'd have been a special bloke if not for the alcohol,' says Matt.

He pauses, takes a sip of hot lemon.

He remembers one time Bob Mortimer said to him: 'You know, Matt, you and David can have a career, because, well, you don't drink.'

His voice is sounding better. He lists all the comedians and show-business talents of the moment who don't do drugs and who never seem to get drunk – Ant and Dec, Jonathan Ross, Peter Kay, Ricky Gervais – all of them building long careers, all of them getting more popular and more admired as time goes by. Then he tells us about a few old actors he's worked with who have drink problems. One of them he describes as 'a fucking great actor' who has been stuck with mainly character roles, but who Matt thinks could have been really big. Matt remembers confronting him about his drinking, and outright asking him if he was an alcoholic. The actor said no, he was just alcohol-dependent.

'You know what though?' says Matt. 'I don't do any drugs, and I only have the occasional drink, but I can still do odd things. I went through a spate about eighteen months ago of absent-mindedly going into the women's toilets. I just wasn't thinking.'

On his way to the shower to get ready for tonight's show, Matt asks me who David was excited to get a text from last night. He'd noticed David showing me the text, and looking very happy. I tell him it was from X.

'Ooh,' says Matt. 'So he's in love with *her*?'

Yes, you could say that.

'I would have actually quite liked to sit down and have a nice chat to you, and other people on the crew. And not have my time monopolised by the manager of the bar . . .'

'I bet that happens all the time, doesn't it?' asks Kelly as she applies David's make-up.

'Sometimes. But it was a shame. It would have been quite fun if it had just been us.'

Kelly says it's only the end of the first week, and there are plenty more opportunities to socialise. David asks her if there's any gossip from last night, if anything happened after he and Matt left.

'The lads from the crew were getting quite rowdy,' she says, 'but I don't think anyone got off with anyone else if that's what you mean. But I'm sure it will happen.'

'Who do you reckon will be the first one down?'

'I don't know them well enough yet to know.'

'Hmm . . . Well, men are all dogs anyway, aren't they?'

'You mean the men on the crew?'

'No, men in general.'

Kelly laughs. 'Oh maybe, but what do you mean by that?'

'I mean men are very sexually motivated.'

'Hmm, but some women are as well,' says Kelly.

'Oh,' says David, softly, 'how wonderful.'

There's a packet of fudge for David on his dressing table, with a note attached saying, 'Thanks for the hangover,' from the crew. Next to it is a copy of the *Independent*, open at a long article by Clive James in which he bemoans the modern nature of celebrity, pointing out that some people become famous for being famous whereas the likes of Bob Dylan actually have a talent.

It gets him pondering what happened to Clive James. At one time he was on television on a weekly basis. Now you see him once a year on *Parkinson* or something, always wearing the same horrible leather jacket.

'And what happened to Clive Anderson's career? It's like you looked one day and suddenly he wasn't on television. Like Hale and Pace – wiped off the face of the earth. Do they even do anything together? Maybe they tour Australia or something. What an amazing lifestyle change to go through . . .' Gareth knocks on the dressing-room door and announces, 'Fifteen minutes!'

'Oh my God!' says David, laughing.

He asks Gareth if he had a nice time at the club last night. Gareth says it wasn't really his type of place.

'No cute boys?'

'No, none. No cock,' says Gareth. 'But I'll soon sort that out. I'll find some.'

'I think you should go for a younger boy,' says Jonathan.

'Fifteen?'

'No . . . like really young. Five or six.'

David and Jonathan Ross are talking about the Des Kaye audience participation moment.

'Well, some nights I do see mothers offering up their kids for me to take onstage. And some of these kids definitely look under ten.'

'They shouldn't even be allowed to watch the fucking show,' says Jonathan. He then explains that his son, Harvey, who's currently checking out the peculiar small opening halfway up the wall of the dressing room with 'Fire Door' written on it, is eleven. Jonathan's other children, Betty and Honey, are playing with their mother, Jane. David's mum and dad arrive. It's the first time they've seen the live show.

His mum says, 'It was absolutely fantastic!'

His dad adds, 'Well done, David. It was brilliant.'

As Erin O'Connor enters the room, David announces loudly: 'Here she is to light up the room: Britain's top supermodel!' Erin smiles and introduces David to her aunt, who is also statuesque and beautiful.

David asks me to hand round glasses of champagne. When I hand one to his father, he holds it up and proposes a toast: 'To David! To Matt and David!'

'Here's to *The League of Gentlemen*,' says Jonathan Ross.

His son Harvey is peering up at the wall. 'Why is that a fire door?' he asks. 'Who the hell can fit through that?'

David's dad mentions the press reviews of the show to Jonathan, who says they deserve all the good reviews. 'There's a lot going on up there on that stage,' he adds.

Matt and Kevin arrive in what is now a pretty crowded room.

Jane, Jonathan's wife, who's with their best friend Emily, mentions lunch tomorrow to Kevin. He and Matt and David are all going for Sunday lunch at Jonathan and Jane's new country home in Swanage. Jane tells him to bring his swimming costume so they can all have a good frolic in their pool. Tony is handing out bags of T-shirts, souvenir programmes and the like to the kids.

'I'd love to know how much merchandise you'll have sold at the end of the tour,' says Jonathan. He then asks David's parents if they've met me, 'Matt and David's official cheerleader.' David's mum says she knows me well and that we just had lunch together.

'Lunch?' says Jonathan, feigning outrage. 'Jesus. Can't you leave these people alone? What could have been quite a special day for David's mum and dad was ruined by you . . .'

David's mum tells him to leave me alone. She changes the subject by commenting on how good the show is: 'I don't think anyone's going to come away from that show thinking they haven't had their money's worth. It's very impressive in the staging.'

'It's very very slick,' adds David's dad.

'They're really putting on a good show,' says Jonathan. 'My favourite bits were David molesting that boy, and the bit with the bee and the bird in the Dennis Waterman sketch.' Jonathan asks his son what his favourite bit was.

'The beginning.'

David hands round some of the fudge. Harvey eagerly receives a handful. Jonathan tells him to say thanks, then leaves the room to go to the toilet.

'Daddy's suffering from mood swings,' says Harvey.

Jonathan and David, backstage at the Bournemouth International Centre, 2005

KFC or McDonald's is the big question. Both are handily on the route back to the hotel.

'Uncle Cosmo?' says Kevin. 'Can we stop off at KFC, or McDonald's? Or maybe both?'

Matt would like a KFC chicken burger but with McDonald's fries. He laughs at the unhealthiness of his chosen option, but points out he hasn't eaten a proper meal all day. He also feels like celebrating, because the show went down very well despite his thin voice.

'Was it my imagination,' he asks, 'or was the security guard at the front stopping anyone from standing up?'

Cos confirms that he was, despite Cos and Pete telling him to let them stand up at the end if they wanted to.

'Thought so. He prevented our standing ovation!'

Cos merrily says he can stop off at both McDonald's and KFC. But it's late, past 11 p.m., and Matt isn't convinced that McDonald's will even be open.

'KFC is definitely open,' says Kevin, 'and selling chicken burgers.'

Matt squeezes Kevin's hand and grins.

Some elements of the show change depending on where they are. When they're in Manchester, in the middle of his extended bout of 'yeah but no but yeah' in the Vicky Pollard sketch, Matt will do a special Mancunian version of Vicky, complete with Gallagheresque monkey-boy strutting. When he's doing 'Computer Says No' Carol, David will change the location she offers for a Sunseekers holiday each night, choosing a nearby unglamorous small town ('Bury . . .' Bolton . . .' 'Worthing . . .') and sure enough there'll be a small cheer from one section of the audience for the name-check of their home town. And Carol will reply, 'It's a shit-hole.'

The nature and behaviour of the audiences change too, according to geography. The southern coastal towns they've visited seem perfectly cheerful and jolly and enthusiastic, but the further north they go, the more raucous and noisy the crowds will get. Sheffield raises a din each night. At weekends, they get even more boisterous because there's more time to drink before the show, which means more people heckle.

Heckling a stand-up comedian is a fairly straightforward process: you shout something, the audience hears it and the comic fires back a riposte. But heckling a complicated, meticulously timed and put-together live sketch show is rather different. What tends to happen is that someone will shout out one of the catchphrases before Matt or David's character has had the chance to say it themselves yet, the heckler will get a little laugh from their mates but Matt and David probably won't have heard exactly what the person yelled in the first place because of the way the sound system works, because of the way the microphones are fixed to their wigs and because there aren't many gaps between lines of dialogue. They're not stand-up comedians having some kind of conversation with the audience. They are telling little stories onstage. So the heckling is an irritant. To the people onstage it just sounds like vague yelping. On any merry Saturday night's show in the north, Matt and David get used to hearing a lot of vague yelping.

Tony warned them about all this. Every step of the way he seems to be able to predict roughly what each crowd will be like. He's a guru of live touring. He seems grateful that Matt and David ask his opinions and take his advice. And they are thankful he keeps them up to date with every tiny development.

After the very first show Matt noticed audience members filming the whole thing on video cameras and taking photos on mobile phones. The latter is understandable; everyone does it everywhere they go. But the suspicion about video-tapers is that they'll be selling bootleg recordings of the show on eBay. This is the kind of thing that Matt checks up on when he gets back to his hotel room after the show. Tony explained that the venues have their own rules about putting up notices warning people not to record the show: some do, some don't. So they now make an announcement each night before the show about taking photos and making unauthorised recordings. But if someone in the middle of the auditorium wants to film the whole thing blatantly, there's not much anyone can do. It's generally too disruptive to start throwing people out mid-show.

Matt is even more offended by the new technological advancement in ticket touts. There are companies who set up dodgy websites selling tickets for shows like *Little Britain*, then when the punters show up at the venue to collect their tickets, there's no one there and no tickets. It's happening so often in the first few weeks of the tour that they've established a policy of trying to accommodate these disappointed, ripped-off fans by finding them seats at the back.

At one point Matt decided to call up one of these rogue companies. He said, 'Why are you selling tickets for *Little Britain Live* when you haven't got any?'

The woman on the phone said, 'Did you buy a ticket?'

He replied, 'No, but I want to know why you're selling tickets and then these poor people show up and you're not there and there aren't any tickets.'

'Did you buy a ticket from us?'

'No.'

'Well then, why are you calling?'

'Because you're selling tickets that don't exist.'

'Goodbye!'

Tony can usually tell who these tout victims are because they mill around near the box office looking confused and angry.

Each night a certain number of tickets are held back for guests of the cast and crew. Most of Matt and David's friends and family have arranged to see the show at some point. Robbie Williams hasn't been able to make it so far – but Matt and David understand that it's a major operation for him to go anywhere as public as a theatre venue.

Each night a local agency picks out a sweet-looking little girl to take part in two of the sketches. Many nights the child actress's mother turns out to be overbearing. One time in a south-coast town before the show I hear the mum asking for more 'gizzits'. Tony thinks she wants more free tickets but he's not sure. The young girl doesn't get to say anything and in fact is expressly forbidden from speaking; she's told just to nod in her scene next to Sam as her mum in Sunseekers. But still I come across the local newspaper in each town carrying an interview with the would-be child star, sometimes as the lead story on the front page.

Tony is the one who guides these mothers and daughters through what is needed; Tony is the one who organises so much and keeps everyone rolling along. He buys the drinks in the hotel bar after the show. He finds the seats in the hotel bar after the show. While he is acting as father, teacher, adviser and counsellor to Matt and David, his colleagues are taking on other roles.

Cos and Pete have taken to their task with gusto and devotion. They're like Matt and David's big, protective brothers. They go everywhere they are asked to go. They only eat when it's convenient for Matt and David. They play the music Matt and David want to hear in their cars. And so far they seem to be watching more or less the whole of each show from the side of the stage, helping out with the venue security if needed.

Andy the production manager tries to be the model of solid support, and generally it falls to him or Gareth the stage manager to explain what happened when anything goes wrong. They're both very good at holding their hands up and taking some of the flak. Gareth manages to do this while also providing a daily dose of old-school camp entertainment. Matt and David are starting to take a delighted interest in his eventful sex life. He seems to take as much pleasure in keeping them up to date.

As for Sally, Nicky, Kelly and Suzanne, the make-up and costume women on the tour, they know it's their job to keep Matt and David relaxed and happy in the build-up to each show and during each interval. In addition to applying make-up and helping them into their costumes, this might mean making some fresh mint tea, listening to some mild griping, trying to ignore the fact that Matt and David are naked, or even getting used to the sight of David prancing around the dressing room in his pants, improvising a dance routine to a Pet Shop Boys or Smiths song.

It all seems to be working now. There are still sketches that Matt and David are thinking of changing, or dropping, or reordering, and they make the occasional mistake each night – which the audience loves. And technically the show has settled down. David even seems to be over his initial semi-depression at the thought of having to do the same thing night after night. They've got into a groove.

Now they've just got the start of their new series to worry about, and more press, and the writing of the Christmas Special for 2006.

They are now spending much of their spare time during the day writing together in one or other of their hotel rooms. Matt readily admits that David is the one who drives their writing sessions. He is the one who insists they start at a certain time and makes sure they don't get too distracted. Matt says that if he had his way they would spend half their writing time discussing new white chocolate Kit-Kats and other limited-edition confectionery items.

One afternoon I try to observe them writing, to capture the mysterious process. David is paying tribute to Matt's skills as a performer in the Vicky Pollard sketch in which he has to enunciate lengthy, tongue-tying monologues about nut-allergic girls being so gay they can't even eat a peanut, doing a college course in *Hollyoaks* and wanting to go to the T4 Party in the Park to meet McFly but just getting fingered by Darius. Matt thinks of some new regional variations on Vicky saying 'yeah but no but', and then David announces that it's time for them to start proper work. He looks at me as if to indicate this is my cue to leave, and Matt steps in to explain that while they don't mind me watching them if I really want to, and if I think it will be useful, it will end up being a weird experience for us all, a bit like a couple being watched while they're having sex.

He's right. I stay for a little while, and I see David bringing a possible ending for a Lou and Andy sketch in the Christmas Special, and Matt enthusiastically coming up with a way the sketch might reach that point, doing the lines in the voices of both Lou and Andy, and David joining in to refine it slightly, also saying lines in both voices. It's odd to hear them voice each other's characters. As soon as one of them says a line they think will be a keeper, David types it out on his laptop.

Later, they tell me this is often how it works: that they'll come up with a funny climax, a great idea for how they want the characters to end up, and then they go backwards and work out the middle and the beginning. They think they'll be able to finish the script for the Special by the end of this section of the tour, so they're ready to film it in the summer break.

On top of all that, they've also agreed to dress up as Jordan and Peter André to recreate their wedding in a photo shoot for *Heat* magazine's Christmas issue.

Part Two

13

11 November 2005 – Manchester: day 17

'I just want someone I can sit there with in my pants and watch TV and have a nice talk to.'

Matt's going to take a lodger when he moves into his and Kevin's new house. He's just exchanged contracts and hopes to move in next January, and he says there are so many floors and rooms that it makes sense for one of his best friends to move in too, so that when Kevin's not around there's someone to keep him company. And when neither of them is around, he can look after the house.

He checks out his orange glow in the mirror, which the make-up artist is in the middle of applying, and wonders if he could do with some false teeth to complete the look.

'I think my TingTong teeth would be perfect for this,' says Matt.

David agrees and decides he should get his Judy and Maggie teeth. They call down to Tony, who's mingling with the photographer and the photographer's assistant as they set up for the shoot, and ask if he can get hold of their teeth.

Tony asks Matt how his throat is doing. Matt says that it's been fine ever since he nearly lost his voice in Bournemouth, and that seasoned theatrical thespians have told him that it's all part of the touring experience that you lose your voice and that this then makes it stronger for the rest of the tour. Tony explains that he's never been on any kind of tour ever where one of the performers hasn't lost their voice at some point. Matt says he's more worried about his skin. He tells the story of how he once had a massive spot on the end of his nose. It appeared on a Tuesday and on the Thursday he was due to go on *Who Wants To Be A Millionaire*. But it was one of the most prominent spots he'd ever had and would look ridiculous on TV. He was doing the show to raise money for charity, so he couldn't just cancel. He went to a dermatologist who helps a lot of Hollywood people and he injected the spot twice. He told Matt not to touch it even though it turned into a bleeding sore. It scabbed over almost immediately, and then it looked as though Matt had a giant black beetle at the end of his nose. Then on the morning of filming, about an hour before his car was due to arrive, he had a shower and the black beetle fell off, and all that was left was a little red mark, which could easily be covered with make-up, and he went on *Who Wants To Be A Millionaire* and no one noticed.

He has no idea what was injected into his spot.

'So we've got all of New Order coming tomorrow,' announces David, 'and Caroline Aherne. It'll be the first time she's met her ex-husband for ten years.'

'Will she mind?' asks Matt.

'I told her it might happen and she seemed fine about it. She's still very fond of him, I think.'

'And the Pet Shop Boys are coming as well?'

'Yep. The Pet Shop Boys and New Order. My two favourite bands of the eighties,' says David. 'All we need now is The Smiths to show up . . . Or at least Johnny Marr.'

'We could get the Happy Mondays. Although they probably couldn't afford tickets.'

'I do have Johnny Marr's number. Maybe I should call him and invite him. Then we'd have all of Electronic there.'

'Have you seen the *Sun* today about David Williams?' asks Matt.

'No, who's David Williams?'

Matt explains that the story is about the older actor called David Williams, whose name meant David had to change his to Walliams when he became an Equity member. 'He says, "I'm the reason David Walliams is called David Walliams" and he wants to be in the show.'

'Yes, he wrote to me,' says David. 'Oh, it would be wonderful to have someone with the same name as me doing a cameo in the show. It would mean so much to the audience!'

David's trying on his Peter André suit, which resembles something a 13-year-old would wear to his bar mitzvah.

'Do you know who I'm having lunch with next week?' asks Matt. He points to his diary on the dressing-room table in front of him. It's open at a spread for next week, and there circled on Tuesday it says, 'Lunch w/ Christopher Biggins.'

David smiles. 'Well, I've had a text from Timmy Mallett,' he says. 'He's going to come and see the show in Oxford.'

'It's like we're friends with the two people who had wacky glasses in the eighties: Biggins and Mallett.'

Matt's getting more orange by the minute. He cheekily asks the make-up woman if, when she's making him up as Jordan, she's really just applying the usual make-up routine she has for herself.

Peter André and Jordan, almost

He puts his TingTong teeth in. 'They're quite good, these teeth, for Jordan, aren't they? She can't quite smile, can she? She hasn't got much warmth.'

David wants to know if anyone's seen the trailers yet for the first night of the new series of *Little Britain*, which starts next Thursday. It's now going to be a *Little Britain* themed night, with all the continuity links for the evening's programmes read by Tom Baker and written in the style of his *Little Britain* narration. David explains that the BBC had come up with their own links, which were rough approximations of the kind of thing Tom Baker says in the *Little Britain* links, but they weren't funny enough. So he and Matt are going to sit down over the next few days and write new ones.

Matt asks me which other celebrities we've got lined up to take part in *Heat* magazine's annual Christmas Stars Dressing-up feature, and I tell him we've snapped up Shayne Ward from *The X Factor*, who's going to play Matthew Fox from *Lost*. Matt suggests we get Fern Britton and Philip Schofield to dress up as Tom Cruise and Katie Holmes. Matt's putting on the dress, which is like Jordan's pink wedding outfit. 'Or how about Craig and Anthony from *Big Brother* as Elton John and David Furnish?'

Matt signs autographs for the children in the show

David urges me not to encourage any participation from Craig and Anthony because he's sick of reading about them and seeing them in the newspapers and magazines. He suggests getting Ant and Dec to be Elton and David. 'Or,' he announces, as if he's suddenly stumbled upon the perfect idea, 'how about Elton and David as Craig and Anthony?'

Matt cracks up. 'Or Elton and David as Maxwell and Saskia!' He fiddles around with his chest and looks in the mirror, then suggests we Photoshop some bosoms onto him. He pushes up his own breasts. 'Oh, maybe there's no need. I'm more or less there, aren't I?'

David says it might better to stick with what we've got because a lot of Photoshopping would ruin the fun of it.

As Matt tries on Jordan's pink tiara, he asks David if he's seen the article in the paper about Kevin Spacey installing a chute at the Old Vic so autograph hunters can put their stuff to be signed in there. They talk again about people getting stuff autographed just to sell on eBay. Matt says he can tell the difference between a genuine fan and someone who's out to make a fast buck. Matt's been with Robbie when he's refused to sign a whole load of stuff; he tells them he'll sign one thing and that's that.

Matt and David have decided to set up an official area at each venue where they will sit behind a desk and sign autographs. Pete and Cosmo make sure the fans keep some kind of order and don't take the piss by trying to get them to sign box-loads of books or DVDs.

Matt says, 'You wouldn't expect everyone to sign autographs. Like Grace Jones. I don't think I'd expect her to sit there behind a desk meeting her fans. You want her to vanish on a magic carpet. But you'd expect Tamsin Outhwaite to sign stuff.' Then Matt catches sight of himself and David in the mirror, dressed as Jordan and Peter André on their wedding day.

'And to think they did this for real!'

Matt and David study the original photos of the wedding.

'He's trying to look happy, isn't he?' says David. 'Although his life must be so much more exciting now that he's with her . . .'

Matt lets his imagination wander. 'I think the sex with her must be like, "Right, get your penis out! Come on, stick it in! In, out . . . in, out . . ."'

'I like the way there's this thing about Jordan being different from Katie,' says David, 'as if she's got this really deep, sensitive person within her. But I bet there's no difference! I bet they're both awful!'

Some soft jazz crooning wafts out of the car radio.

David's phone buzzes. 'Oh hel*lo*!' he says excitedly.

He asks the friend on the other end if he's having a nice time, what rides he's been on, what the weather's like. He tells him that the reviews have been mostly good, but that some have been a bit critical, especially a few of the broadsheets. He gossips about Elton John's wedding, who's going to be at the stag night (Matt and David are away that night so they're going to record something to be shown on video), and how it's going to be the best day ever. And how David's going to take X, and it will be the ultimate date. Surely.

He ends the phone call with: 'Bye bye. Lots of love!' and announces, 'That was Dale Winton from Disneyworld.'

As they get out of the car and walk to Wagamama, Matt says, 'There have been one or two sniffy live reviews, haven't there?'

This is the first time Matt and David have discussed the reviews of the live show. The tabloid reviews were glowing. The broadsheet ones less so. Matt expresses surprise and disappointment at one of the reviewers who fundamentally didn't like *Little Britain* at all. 'I think it's weird to send someone to see the show if they don't like the TV show anyway,' he says. 'People want to know if it's as good as the TV show. The people who are going to come to see this show are mainly fans of the TV series and I don't think that many of them are going to be disappointed.'

'Some of the reviews are a bit extreme. One of them – I think it was the *Observer* – really laid into me and I thought: I'm not that bad!' David laughs as he mentions the *Observer* review, but Matt looks uncomfortable. Neither of them seems to like it when one is singled out over the other.

'No, that was just unfair,' says Matt. 'And inaccurate. In the end I just think people come to see the show and they like it and they feel they got their money's worth.'

'And what's your name?' asks a large, enthusiastic woman in a broad Manchester accent.

'Errm . . . David,' he says, bemused. She's holding a souvenir tour programme and she's standing in line for autographs. He nods in the direction of her programme.

'Ooh yes, you're David!' she says excitedly. 'We were trying to sell our tickets, but we couldn't get rid of them so we decided to come and see the show.' It's a confusing explanation of why someone would queue up for an autograph for half an hour without seeming to know whose autograph she's waiting for. Matt's laughing. David's pen is hovering. He doesn't quite know how to react.

The jolly Mancunian lady continues. 'Anyway I'm glad we bothered 'cos you really weren't that bad! It were quite a good show!'

David smiles and signs her programme. 'High praise indeed,' he says.

Next in line are two girls in their mid- to late twenties who seem a bit unsteady on their feet. The first of them pulls up her top and asks David to sign her tits. Her friend does the same thing. Matt puts his head in his hands.

'You'll regret it,' advises David. 'I'll sign your arm or something . . .'

But no, they want their breasts signed.

'I just don't think this pen's suitable,' says David.

Matt and David sign their arms, and their programmes, and Pete moves them on.

In the hotel bar Matt and David are telling stories. They're entertaining Michael, an Australian tour promoter who's just watched the show in Manchester and is thinking of putting it on next year in Sydney and Melbourne. *Little Britain* is shown on the ABC, the Australian equivalent of the BBC, and is a cult hit. The DVDs are selling well.

Michael says how impressed he was by the excitement level of the audience. David says that might have been because it was full of pissed-up Mancs on a Friday night.

'Really? You think that's what it was?' asks Michael earnestly.

'Oh no, I'm joking,' says David, 'though there might have been an element of that. They certainly seem rowdier the further north you go. I think they just show their appreciation more.'

Michael asks if they've ever performed to empty seats.

Matt says not on this tour. 'It is awful to see a show with loads of empty seats,' he says, and recounts a recent evening when he went to see Roger Whittaker live at the Fairfield Halls, Croydon. He was quite excited, but it turned out to be a disappointment.

'Can I ask you a question?' says David. 'How you got excited about seeing Roger Whittaker in the first place? How high can your expectations have been of a bloke who whistles?'

'He doesn't just whistle. Though he does have a number of whistling-based songs. Anyway, we got there and it's about a 1200-seat theatre, and there were only about a few hundred people there dotted around, which was in itself massively embarrassing. So he walks out and a few seconds into his opening song I thought, oh my God – he's got no voice. He must have woken up that day, found out that he'd lost his voice but didn't want to cancel the show. We should have just left but we ended up staying. Now I'm going to be in "Spotted! Matt Lucas looking grumpy at a Roger Whittaker concert".'

The Australian man asks Matt and David if they've had loads of film offers. Matt says they've been offered some small roles to do together in Hollywood films. David mentions *The Mask of Zorro 2*. They were offered the light-relief roles of two comedy CIA agents. They were busy when they were offered the parts, and turned them down.

'Then the film comes out,' says David, 'gets really bad reviews, and there's nothing about these two CIA agents, and we could have dropped everything to do those parts and for what? It would have been quite a negative thing in the end. But it is such a temptation to do a big Hollywood film.'

Matt suggests that they should tell the story of their big meeting with a notorious Hollywood movie executive.

'Oh yeah. We were summoned to meet this guy at his hotel when he was in London last year for the BAFTAs or something. So we went to see him, and he wanted us to drop everything we were doing to be in the fifth entry of this comedy franchise. And I don't think they've done the fourth one yet. He said, "No one's ever said no to me." We said, "We'll have to discuss it . . ." Then he asked us if we had any ideas for a project and we told him about doing a true story about two Victorian transvestites in London . . .'

Matt takes up the story. 'So he said, "You wanna do something about Oscar Wilde having sex with himself? Is that what you want to do? Do I wanná see Oscar Wilde having sex with himself for an hour and a half?"'

David remembers replying, 'Well, we probably wouldn't pitch it like that . . . But I thought: Oscar Wilde? Who mentioned Oscar Wilde?'

David adds that when they were in the cab driving away from the meeting they spotted their friend Graham Linehan, who directed the pilot of *Little Britain*, on his way into the hotel. He was obviously on his way to see the same Hollywood bigwig, so David leaned out of the window and shouted, 'Good luck – he's a madman!'

Michael the Australian chuckles, and announces that he's got to go to bed because he's flying to New York tomorrow morning. Matt and David thank him profusely for coming to see the show.

As he walks off to the lift, David says, 'I'm so charming, aren't I?'

'Oh you go first, David,' says Caroline.

'Can I have the roast sea bass, please? With some green beans and glazed carrots.'

'Madame?' asks the waiter.

'Ooh, I still haven't decided . . . You go, kiddo.'

I order the lemon sole.

'Has madame decided?'

'I bet I can guess what you're going to have,' says David.

'Bet you can't!'

'The steak. It's got to be steak. And chunky chips.'

'Well, no, actually I think I'll have the roast salmon,' says Caroline.

'You're just trying to be different!'

'No I'm not. I fancied some salmon. But –' she looks up at the waiter quizzically '– can I not have the horseradish crust? Or the grain mustard sauce?'

The waiter asks if madame would like another kind of crust.

'No, could I just have it without the crust and the sauce please?'

'So just the salmon? No crust? No sauce?'

'I think it might be a bit dry,' says David, trying to help out.

Caroline pauses, and glances at the menu. 'I tell you what. Can I just have the sirloin steak? Without the air-dried tomato?'

The waiter frantically scribbles on his pad. 'Any vegetables?'

'No, thanks. Well, just chips, please,' says Caroline. 'And can I have the steak very well done, please. Practically burnt.'

Caroline's brought David a present of Rufus Wainwright's new album. 'The first song is beautiful,' she says. 'I'm not that bothered by the rest of it.'

'I don't think she'd be right for you anyway,' says Caroline.

'Too common?'

'No, I don't mean that. I just don't think you'd have that much to talk about . . .'

'Well, I wouldn't know,' says David. 'I've never met her.'

'But the paper says you went out with her!'

David laughs. Yes, it does say he's been linked with Martine McCutcheon. She's always listed, along with Patsy Kensit and Abi Titmuss.

'Why no mention of you?' he asks. 'What happened to our intense sexual relationship?'

On the way up to David's room, Caroline and David argue gently about whether anyone ever knew that they went out with each other for a year. Caroline says emphatically that the papers never found out. David says they didn't know at the time, but that it has been mentioned in the papers a couple of times since then. Caroline says she's never seen it anywhere. 'It's definitely been printed,' says David. 'Like when they list the people I've gone out with, sometimes it says Caroline Aherne before Patsy Kensit and Abi Titmuss.' Caroline's sure she's never read it anywhere.

When we enter the room, Caroline's delighted by the size and glamour of it. She paces around excitedly. 'Is this a suite?' she asks. She gets no answer

David and Caroline, Manchester Apollo, 2005

because David is busy fiddling with his iPod and trying to get his speakers to work. 'David, it's gorgeous. I love it.'

The sound of The Beatles 'All You Need Is Love' fills the room. David turns it down a notch. Caroline's touring the suite.

'Cor,' she says in a tone of genuine wonderment, 'you've even got a guest bathroom! And a walk-in wardrobe!'

'I know! Why are walk-in wardrobes so lovely?'

'David, you've made it! Look at you! Like Bon Jovi. It's unbelievable, isn't it? I'm so proud of you.'

Caroline says it's so lovely here that it reminds her of New York. She loves Manhattan, feels at home there and laps up the hectic thrill of it. She also doesn't have to worry about being photographed and recognised. It's a liberating place for her to be. 'Play the Rufus Wainwright CD, David,' she says. 'Let's celebrate the fact that you've made it, and that it's like we're all in New York again together!'

'The first song is just gorgeous,' she says, singing along without even realising she is. 'Are the Pet Shop Boys coming up just for the show?' she asks.

'Yeah. It's incredible isn't it? They were my favourite band when I was growing up.' David hums along to Rufus. 'It is lovely this album, but his voice slightly tires me out.'

'Oh yeah,' nods Caroline, 'I only like the first song.'

When the first Rufus Wainwright song finishes, David takes off the CD and goes back to the music on his iPod. He looks through the pile of papers on his bed. They're all there. Every tabloid, every broadsheet and everything in between.

Caroline sits on the bed and grabs one of the papers and reads aloud: 'You are half of the most successful comedy duo of the twenty-first century.' She pauses and reads a bit more. 'You're nominated for three Comedy Awards? I didn't even know that. Brilliant.'

David giggles. 'Why don't we just read out articles about us to each other?'

Caroline's picked up the *Daily Mail*.

David asks her: 'Don't you hate the *Daily Mail* more than you hate the others?'

'I hate the *Daily Mail* more than anything in the world.'

'They're so horrible, aren't they?'

Caroline looks at me and asks, 'Will you find out all about the real David Walliams in your research for the book? I'll tell you . . .'

'I think we should discuss the sexual details of our relationship,' laughs David.

Caroline: 'Well, your sex drive is very big. You're always either thinking about it, or doing it.'

David: 'Or recovering from it.'

Caroline: 'Or thinking about it.'

David: 'Or doing it again.'

Caroline suddenly changes the subject, asking: 'Have you decided about doing a fourth series?'

David: 'No.'

Caroline: 'You're not gonna do one?'

David: 'No, we haven't decided. I'd say it's quite probable we won't. We're doing a Christmas Special . . . but I don't know.'

Caroline: 'You could do something different with the characters . . . longer sketches . . .'

David: 'Yeah, but I'd like to leave a lot of the characters behind, to be honest.'

Caroline: 'Yeah.'

David: 'But I'd also quite like to do something more with Lou and Andy. Something bigger and more ambitious. Beyond another series, the programme can't get any bigger. That doesn't mean we have to stop doing it, but once you've been on tour, done three series, sold millions of DVDs, you wonder why you should carry on. What is there to do with it?'

Caroline: 'I always think three is a good number for a series.'

David tells Caroline about his swimming. She asks if he's a good swimmer.

'You've seen me swim, haven't you?' he asks.

'I've been in a swimming pool with you,' she says, 'but you weren't doing much swimming. You were messing about. Trying to pull down my bikini bottoms.'

David laughs heartily at the memory. 'Oh that must have been lovely!'

Caroline asks David if he'll be making any moves tonight. He says he might flirt. They're both talking about a particular woman who's coming to see the show, who's gay, but who David has always found deeply sexy.

Caroline: 'You don't think she's a real lezzer, do you? Have you tried to pull her?'

David: 'Oh I do, I just won't let that stop me. I just think she's very flirtatious. Me and Robbie Williams tried to chat her up together.'

Caroline: 'You think you can turn her, don't you?'

David: 'No, but it would be nice to try. And to some extent she'd still enjoy me even though I'm not a woman . . . she'd enjoy the things I'd do to her . . .'

Caroline: 'Ooh yeah.'

David: 'I mean, I am a man but I could still do stuff to her that she'd enjoy.'

Caroline: 'Yeah, I think you're onto a winner there. There are no drawbacks for her, are there?'

David: 'Well, she doesn't keep me awake at night. But when I do see her I do think of sex.'

Caroline: 'I'm the same with Sean Bean. I just have to see him, or even hear his voice, and I feel all funny.'

David: 'Have you met him?'

Caroline: 'No, but he's got such presence.'

David: 'He's done very well for himself, hasn't he?'

Caroline: 'Who's this music?'

David: 'It's Elton John's "Are You Ready For Love?" A wonderful song.'

Caroline: It sounds like something my Patrick would sing down the pub.

David: 'Who cares what you think! Come on, let's see the Pet Shop Boys. Come ON!'

Caroline cracks up.

2001

Caroline Aherne recognised David when she saw him at the Groucho Club. She had asked to see young director Edgar Wright's showreel featuring clips of programmes he had made, and on the tape were some snippets of David from shows like *Sir Bernard's Stately Homes* and *Mash and Peas*. Caroline took a shine to him and simply went up to him one night and introduced herself.

They went out on and off for a year. She was the second person he'd ever fallen in love with.

They met around the time she was reaching the height of her fame, as she was making the second series of *The Royle Family*. David was making *Rock Profile* with Matt, but Caroline already recognised him. She's always watched a lot of TV, especially late at night. Caroline had also been in the papers for suffering from depression and trying to kill herself, and as soon as he met her, David had a feeling that he wanted to protect her and look after her. He met her a couple of times after that initial night at the Groucho, and they ended up snogging.

Unusually, no one outside their close circle of friends and family really knew about their relationship. They didn't go out of their way to keep it a secret. They just maintained a level of discretion. If Caroline was going to a big public event like the BAFTAs, they had an understanding that it would be for the best if David didn't go with her. It would have been difficult for David, who was trying to be a TV comedy talent in his own right, to be known at that point in his fledgling career as Caroline Aherne's boyfriend.

But it was different in those days. In 1999 he could sleep over at Caroline's flat regularly and there wouldn't be photographers outside. So no one ever noticed them together. When David went out for a brief period with Patsy Kensit a few years later, there would be paparazzi waiting outside her house. Of course if David and Caroline's relationship had become public knowledge, the first big round of press interviews he ever did would have been dominated by questions about what it was like going out with Caroline.

What it was like was this: it was up and down. On the one hand it was full of emotion and turmoil. But on the other, she made David laugh more than anyone in the world. She always seemed so different from him, in where she came from and what her experiences were. He saw her as a brilliant example of a huge intelligence who was, in a way, anti-intellectual. He knew from the start that she was an amazing artist but she never showed much interest in paintings or literature. And she'd only been to the theatre a few times in her life. Not that there's anything wrong with not going to the theatre, but she seemed almost opposed to it. So when a reviewer compared *The Royle Family* to Beckett or Pinter or any great playwright, as they have often done, David could be pretty sure she wouldn't know about that stuff.

For David, Caroline was someone he could never get bored of. Someone who always challenged him. Her take on everything was so sharp, so funny, and she'd get so excited about day-to-day things she'd see and hear. She'd phone David and say, 'Put on *Trisha*! Put on *Trisha*!' She loved the daftness of people. So she would watch *Trisha* and point out the silly things people said but her observations were affectionate. Full of warmth. There was no intellectual snobbery about her. Or superior class judgement. She is from that world and loves it.

She never really took any interest in how much she was being paid for something. She never even knew how much money she had. When they'd go out together, Caroline would hand over fifty or a hundred quid to homeless people. Every time.

It was the closest David's come to meeting someone and thinking: yes, you are a genius. Someone with a real artistic vision. And even though people want to see her as a tragic figure, effectively she produced a lifetime's remarkable, enduring work in about ten years. And if, after that, she had time off watching telly, then good for her. She earned it.

David loves the fact they're still really good friends. When he thinks about the kind of person he could marry and have a really enjoyable life with, he thinks of Caroline. Every day there would be something amusing and warm about her, and of course sexy too.

But their relationship was all over the place, and it came to a natural end.

David thought that if he loved Caroline enough, he could make her happy. It was really tough to find out that he couldn't.

Down in the bar we meet Neil Tennant and a director friend of his called Mike. Greetings are made. There's a lot of kissing hello. Neil apologises on behalf of Chris Lowe. 'I think Chris is in bed,' he says. I look at my watch. It's 4.30 p.m. 'It's a Lowe thing,' he says.

Neil says he hasn't seen Caroline for years and tells her she's looking well. They hug. Matt and his boyfriend arrive and sit next to Caroline.

David asks Neil if New Order are coming to the show tonight. Neil tells him that Bernard Sumner hopes to make it but is trying to find a babysitter. David says, 'I was told that all of New Order would be coming.' Neil answers, 'Well most of them are.'

'But I want the singer!' says David in a whiny tone. Then he embraces Caroline and says, 'Well, we've got the Queen of Comedy here . . .'

Caroline's thrilled to see Matt again, and tells him how excited she is that he and David are so huge. She says how popular *Little Britain* is with kids, and that everywhere she goes in Manchester she hears kids reciting the lines.

'Bob Mortimer was telling me that his son's school sent letters to all the parents telling them they shouldn't let their kids watch *Little Britain*,' says Matt.

Caroline says it's not his fault that kids love it. Then she asks him if he smokes, because she wants to light up.

'I gave up six years ago which is why I'm so fat now.'

'How did you give up?' asks Caroline.

'I ate them . . . no, I used Allen Carr's book.'

Caroline asks Matt if he's enjoying the tour, and he tells her he is, but that they've had some disturbing attention from fans in the last couple of days, such as some drunken, aggressive ones in the bar the previous night. They talk about the pros and cons of having devotees.

Matt tells a story about a fan. 'I did a thing about three or four months ago in my synagogue. They asked me if I'd go back and do a Q&A, like it was the holy homecoming of our famous son. There were about three or four hundred people there. And afterwards they set up a table on the beamer, which is like the altar where the rabbi stands, so I could sign autographs. So I was there for about an hour, and the last person who came to get an autograph was this really effeminate 15-year-old boy and my mum was kind of standing there ushering them in, and she said, "Would you like Matt to sign your ticket?" and this boy said [adopts high-camp voice] "Yes, but I can think of other places I'd like him to sign . . ." and he started to lift up his shirt. So I said, "No, no, it's okay, I can sign the ticket," and my mum's there going, "No. He'll just sign the ticket. Give him the ticket." It was like a weird dream: I was sat on the beamer of my synagogue and my mother is sitting next to me and a 15-year-old boy is lifting up his shirt for me to sign his body . . .'

Neil says, 'You wouldn't get that in the Catholic church.'

To which Caroline says: 'Well, I went to church the other day with my mum, she dragged me along, and this woman who is very holy came up to talk to me and she said [in heavy Irish accent] "Ooh how are you doing now, Caroline, I've heard you were a bit poorly and you've not been working for a while?" So I said, "No, well, I'd love to write something but nothing will come," and she said, "Well, God's given the gift to someone else."'

Everyone laughs, but David seems genuinely put out by the Irish woman's comment. 'As if God gave it to you and now he's taken it away,' he says in a tone of mild outrage, 'like it's nothing to do with you.'

David has a couple of his own 'superfan' stories. There's the woman who came to one of the Cardiff shows and sat there in the middle of the stalls through the entire performance holding up a home-made sign which had her mobile phone number on it and little flashing lights dotted around the edge. 'It was distracting,' says David. Was he tempted to call the number? 'No,' he says. 'Maybe if she'd looked like Claudia Schiffer.'

Then, in Sheffield, at the post-show autograph-signing session, there was a woman in her fifties standing in the queue with her teenage daughter, who

Not Claudia Schiffer, Cardiff Arena, 2005

looked about fifteen. She started crying. Not the young daughter, but the mother. When she got to the front of the line, she told Matt and David that she loved them, and asked for a hug. While hugging David she started putting her tongue in his ear, and whispered, 'Don't ever ever stop what you're doing . . . ever.' David told her that they'd have to stop one day. 'NO, don't ever stop,' she said. David told her that it had been lovely to meet her. And she started crying again. 'Don't cry, this is a nice thing – that you've got to meet us and hug us . . .' She was inconsolable. She walked off sobbing, holding hands with her daughter. Matt and David carried on with the signings for the rest of the fans in the queue. A few minutes later the 15-year-old daughter came back and handed David a piece of paper with a phone number written on it. 'This is from my mum,' she told him. 'She really likes you.'

The conversation flits and zigzags around. The bar area, like the suites, has a cool and effortlessly sleek atmosphere. Some of us are drinking cocktails, but Matt and David stick to fresh mint tea. They're doing a show in an hour's time. But right now it feels like they haven't got a care in the world.

Caroline asks Matt if he gets nervous before going onstage. Matt explains that he doesn't really get nervous. It's not that he's ever complacent or cocky and it's not because he doesn't care. He just quite looks forward to the moment when he arrives onstage. But oddly, sometimes he gets nervous in the middle of a sketch. Every now and then he'll almost be on autopilot and he suddenly realises it and gets jerked back into reality and it's almost like he's not aware of what he's just been doing for the last few minutes. When that happens, it's a real shock to the system and the sudden realisation of it makes him nervous.

Then she asks him if they have a Winnebago with them on tour for the catering.

Matt explains that they don't have catering, and they don't even have a rider because they haven't got round to sorting one out. 'Though I only wanted one thing on the rider,' he explains. 'Bubble wrap. But I don't think they've taken me seriously. I wonder sometimes if we should have brought a chef on tour with us.'

'It would have been expensive,' says David. 'A catering truck, someone to drive the truck . . .' Then he remembers. 'Though we are fitting in some new arena dates.'

'There's still some more money you can wheedle out of the British public!' says Caroline.

'Yeah,' says David, 'there are some people up north we haven't got twenty-five quid off.'

'Is that the dearest price for it?' asks Caroline.

'Yeah, it's not that expensive, is it?'

'No, I think it is.'

'Do you think that's too much?'

'Errm . . . no. Well, yes. I do, yeah.'

Matt laughs. 'Which of the two answers are you going with?'

'Well, I know I haven't paid for mine,' replies Caroline.

'And you still feel ripped off?' asks David.

'How much is it to see a band?' Caroline asks.

'More than that,' explains Matt. 'It's eighty quid to see a band.'

'No!'

'Yeah, eighty quid at least. For a big act. More for Eric Clapton.'

'Well, in that case,' says Caroline, 'it's a bargain. Put the price up!'

'Phil McIntyre probably will,' says Matt.

'Yeah, he's never been shy when it comes to money.'

On the other side of the table, David is asking Neil Tennant about the new Pet Shop Boys album.

'We should finish next week,' says Neil.

Caroline joins in. 'Is it just the two of you on the album?'

'Yeah, but Trevor Horn has produced it. Which is very exciting because we've always wanted to do a Trevor Horn meets Pet Shop Boys album. It's got all his tricks on it.'

Neil mentions that he and Chris have been working with Robbie Williams on some songs, not for the Pet Shop Boys album, or Robbie's next album necessarily. They just decided to write together, and Neil says how full of ideas Robbie is. Matt says of Robbie: 'He's so genial, isn't he?'

Caroline asks Neil if he did Live 8. Neil says they were the headline act in Moscow, and that he and Chris have this thing now about playing weird and wonderful venues. Interesting and spectacular venues, like Trafalgar Square.

Caroline says that she keeps laughing at the story David told her of 'what-sisname' sitting in the front row at Live 8 wearing earplugs.

'Oh yes,' says David, 'it was David Frost at Live 8 in London. Yeah, he was sitting there with earplugs.'

'Who goes to a concert wearing earplugs?' she says.

Matt admits that he did once. He went to see Badly Drawn Boy at the

Queen Elizabeth Hall and his seat was right in the front row by the speakers. A huge stack of them. It was hideous. Then he remembered he had a pair of earplugs in his overnight bag so he put them in and really enjoyed the gig.

Caroline tells her Badly Drawn Boy story. A friend of her brother's met him in the pub one night, they had a good chat, and he ended up crashing at Badly Drawn Boy's house. And in the morning he still had his bobble hat on.

David says that he met Badly Drawn Boy at a party and he refused to take his hat off. He wouldn't let David see what was underneath.

'Policemen are like that,' says Matt. 'Jamiroquai is like that.'

'He will take it off, though,' points out David.

'He just likes hats,' says Caroline.

Matt takes the opportunity to compliment Caroline on her outfit.

Caroline says, 'Oh thank you! I keep thinking I look like a fairy.'

'No, the brown and the pink look really good.'

'You know, I've been worst-dressed woman three years in a row. In *Prima* magazine. Not even a good magazine!'

'Will you go gay for the evening?' asks David.

'Er . . . yeah all right,' says Johnny Marr. His wife Angie laughs.

There's a brief debate about the relative merits of gay versus straight venues. The consensus seems to be that, here in Manchester at least, Canal Street is the place to go, offering as it does a dizzying variety of bars and clubs with varying degrees of gayness. And while we might bump into some Premiership footballers in one of the more fashionable straight clubs, the gay ones will be much more fun.

'Where we going?' asks Caroline.

'We're going gay,' says David, 'to Canal Street. Is the Queen of Comedy up for that?'

'Oh yeah,' says Caroline. 'We've got to celebrate your brilliant show. It was so amazing, David. I'm so proud of you.'

David is concerned about transport. He looks around his dressing room, where there's Caroline Aherne and three of her friends, Neil Tennant and Chris Lowe with their friend Mike and Chris's sister, and Johnny Marr and his wife Angie. All drinking glasses of champagne handed round by Tony. And somehow David wants to gather them all and make sure they liaise at a bar on Canal Street.

Right now Neil's more interested in the show he's just seen. He loved the Des Kaye sketch in particular. 'I'd like to see a Des Kaye film,' he tells David. 'I want to know the whole story of his life.'

David explains that he and Matt did come up with a life story for Des Kaye, and that he's one of their oldest characters, dating back to even before the *Little Britain* radio show.

David's making sure everyone can get to Canal Street. He says Caroline should come in his car with him and Neil and me, Chris and his sister and Mike have a cab ordered, and Johnny and Angie Marr have a car. Caroline asks what her friends should do. They say they can get a cab. It'll be fine. Caroline says maybe she should get the cab with her friends, but David wants to look after her, and he's worried they won't find the club. David puts his arm round Caroline as he shepherds everyone out of his dressing room.

Outside the theatre there are still crowds of fans milling around. 'Oh God,' frets David, as he catches sight of them, even though Pete, walking slightly ahead, won't let anyone get anywhere near them. Above all, David doesn't want to let go of Caroline. Her friends follow behind them, and just as David is about to whisk her into the car, Caroline decides to stay with the friends she's brought with her and share their cab. David looks anxious, but he lets her go. 'All right, see you there . . .' he says doubtfully.

In the car on the way to Canal Street, Neil tells David that they had a great audience tonight. David agrees and thinks it was because Mancunians on a Saturday night are up for a good time. Occasionally too up for it. Neil says that he and Matt both dealt with the slightly too raucous audience members very well.

'I hope Caroline makes it,' says David.

Five minutes later, as we're getting out of the car, we hear her voice: 'Oh my God! David! We're here!'

David's thrilled at the sight of Caroline with her friends.

'I haven't been out on Canal Street in twelve years,' she says.

A handsome young man in a slick suit is ushering us all into the club, down some stairs into a dimly lit, crowded bar area, where, in the corner, is a huge long table, surrounded by empty seats and banquettes. They've created a VIP area specially.

Johnny and Angie Marr arrive and sit next to David.

David asks Johnny where he lives. He explains that he and Angie have a place about half an hour's drive away. He's got his own all-mod-cons studio in his house. David half-jokingly asks Angie if she ever gets tired of Johnny strumming the guitar and making his music. She says no, quite the opposite, and that she's always encouraging him to play more music. She loves it. 'Wow,' says David, looking at them reverentially, 'you are the perfect couple.' Johnny puts his arm round Angie and laughs.

David then asks Johnny what projects he's got coming up, and Johnny mentions a new album. I can tell that part of David is itching to ask Johnny something about The Smiths. He's sitting next to the man whose music he loves as much if not more than anyone else's. But the other half of him wants to make sure he's talking to Johnny as his equal, as a normal, well-adjusted adult and not the 20-year-old obsessive Smiths fan within him.

'And we're still working on this idea of a box-set,' says Johnny. 'A Smiths box-set.'

'Oh?' says David, visibly trying to keep calm. 'Really? That would be amazing.'

* * *

Inspector Clouseau is fighting Kato in slow motion. David observes, while nibbling on his peanut M&Ms, that the slow motion makes it less funny.

'We talked about Lou Reed and Bob Dylan, and all the music we like.' He's reminiscing about the conversation he had a couple of hours ago with Johnny Marr. 'But I just wanted to say, "What about your music? Your music is just as important!" And I kept thinking: can I just have your autograph too!'

Clouseau and Kato hitting each other is intercut with Dreyfus trying to watch them from the floor above via a hole he's drilled into the ceiling. David says how much he likes Herbert Lom's performance. It's big and cartoony but it works within the context of a Pink Panther film.

'The thing is, I was talking to Johnny for ages, about all kinds of things, and he is so lovely. And then he kind of just casually mentioned The Smiths and releasing this box-set, and I was thinking: oh my God, Johnny Marr's talking to me about The Smiths. Please tell me everything. Now. And he told me about how he wants to put out the original version of the first Smiths album, before they totally rerecorded it. Apparently it's got different songs and sounds completely different. All those Smiths fans are going to be creaming themselves, aren't they?'

A new supergroup: Johnny Marr, Neil Tennant and David, backstage, Manchester, 2005

As an elaborate stunt involving Peter Sellers, Herbert Lom and Bert Kwouk plays out on David's laptop, he yawns, stretches his arms out theatrically and exclaims, 'Caroline Aherne. The Pet Shop Boys. Johnny Marr. All on one night. And *The Pink Panther Strikes Again* on DVD. It doesn't get much better than that, does it?'

14

18 November 2005 – Glasgow: day 23

'It has made me feel quite emotional.'

David's at his laptop. He is in the middle of an email conversation with his first love: a girl he fell for in the sixth form of Reigate Grammar. It was of course unrequited.

He was so desperate to hear from her, to find out what she is doing with her life, that he posted a note on Friends Reunited.

Within days journalists from the papers tried to get in touch with her too, much to her father's annoyance.

Then, a few days ago, he received an email from her, explaining that she lives in Vienna with an Austrian partner and three children. 'You must lead a very glamorous life,' she's written.

He wrote back:

I have just come offstage and am in my hotel room. How wonderful that you are a mum. I'm very jealous. I adore children and would love to be a dad but haven't got to that stage with anyone yet. I would love to see a picture of them, I'm sure they are very beautiful.

My life has gone a bit crazy of late. I'm delighted that the show has been a success, but sometimes it's weird. Tonight we played to 2,000 people but now I am alone in my hotel room. And I've come to realise what I thought was going to make me happy – a room full of strangers laughing and applauding – isn't enough. But I have had some amazing girlfriends in the last ten years or so and I know I will fall in love again. It's strange not having anyone to share this time of incredible success with, or maybe it's great as I can go out on dates with some absolutely amazing women, I'm not sure!

You were always so wonderful to me at school. So beautifully kind and thoughtful. You made me feel really special. You dealt with my hopeless crush on you with such maturity and sensitivity. You let me love you from a distance which at the time was all I was ready for with anyone. I thank you for that. I would have been utterly distraught if you had totally rejected me. God knows what you thought of me. Thinking about you now I realise how wonderfully full of love you were and I am sure always will be. What lucky children you have. I bet you are an amazing mother. That you liked me at all gave me an amazing sense of pride.

I can remember it all, the first time I came over to your house, the nights out, the rides to school in your brown Fiesta. I particularly remember an afternoon in that last summer at school when you came over to my house for a choc-ice and we sat on my patio and I opened the letter which said I had been offered a place at the National Youth Theatre and all seemed right in the world. I am crying as I write this. I don't know why. I was so happy.

She wrote back, thanking David for being so open with her about his feelings. She says he was a rarity: clever, polite, terribly funny, with plenty of backbone. And she admits:

I knew you had a huge crush on me and I always highly respected your feelings. If that was important for you I accept your thanks with grace. But don't thank me for being your friend, our friendship was just as important for me as it was for you, I am sure.

David replied, explaining how it was a silly idea for him to use Friends

Reunited, but that he's so pleased they got back in touch with each other. And then this:

> *There is no one special in my life at the moment, I have been in love three times I think with three amazing women, but I've never been close to marriage. I think I will get married one day though and I so want to be a dad, but at the moment I am working really hard and so tend to just go on dates. When I was younger I thought there was something really wrong with me that made me unattractive, but luckily that has lifted and I am much more confident now.*

'I don't mind bad reviews, but they're quite vitriolic these ones,' says Matt.

'Well, they were bad last year as well, weren't they?' points out Kevin.

'I think they're much worse this time,' replies Matt.

'The *Sun* liked it,' says Kevin.

'Yeah, the *Sun* and the *Telegraph* liked it. Everyone else hated it. *The Times* had an editorial about how awful it is.'

Kevin thinks it's odd that papers have started writing editorials about it. Matt agrees and says really it's just a comedy programme that people will watch if they want to have a laugh. And it doesn't matter if all the critics hate it, especially when the ratings are so good.

It's the day after the first show of series three went out on BBC1 and nearly nine and a half million people watched it, according to the overnight ratings, a huge amount for a comedy programme, the kind of figure that only shows like *EastEnders*, *Coronation Street* or *Strictly Come Dancing* usually get. *Little Britain* has got its best ever ratings on the day that it has received its worst ever reviews.

On the way to the Glasgow Clyde Auditorium, surrounded by papers on the back seat of the car, Matt says that if this was America, he and David would get some kind of sports car or private jet from their network by way of thanks. Stuart Murphy, controller of BBC3, asked Matt if he wanted something special last time *Little Britain*'s ratings gave his channel a huge boost and Matt asked for a trip in a hot-air balloon. Matt says he's still waiting for it. Kevin tells him the invitation to the hot-air balloon trip arrived in the post a few days ago. Matt is excited by the prospect.

Matt and David weren't expecting the reviews to be this negative. Having spent a year writing it, they thought they'd come up with the strongest series of *Little Britain* yet, and while they're aware that it's no longer fashionable to say that one likes *Little Britain*, because it has become such a big, mainstream cultural entity, they didn't expect this level of venom. In fact, as Matt skims over attack after attack, it starts becoming amusing just how horrible the critics have been. They've really gone out of their way to find new and creative ways to hate it.

Much of the harshest criticism has been written from a sense of moral disapproval. The broadsheet critics and commentators in particular seem to have decided that Matt and David are rampant misogynists, because they sometimes portray 'grotesque' women. *The Times* says: 'The combination of a gay man and a serial womaniser who favours white leather driving caps was never going to be at the forefront of feminist female physical representation.' The piece picks out Matt and David playing fat women Bubbles and Desiree, claiming that they are more grotesque than any other characters in the series, and therefore proof of the show's misogyny. Matt points out that there have been plenty of male grotesques in the series (Dudley, Harvey the 'bitty' breastfeeder, Lou and Andy of course) and that Bubbles, like Vicky Pollard and most of the other 'grotesque' characters in the series, is, in the end, the winner in all her sketches.

The Times reviewer goes on to say: '*Little Britain*'s obsessions are with the extreme taboos of physicality: facial hair, urine, fat, breast milk, faeces, penetration, the anus, decrepitude, arousal, ejaculation, vomit.' Well, those physical taboos certainly *appear* in the series, but its most celebrated and popular characters are Lou and Andy, Vicky Pollard, Dafydd and Sebastian the Prime Minister's aide, none of which really provide much evidence for the reviewer's theory.

When we get to the venue, David has some of the papers on his dressing-room table, open at the reviews. He says all the papers hate *Little Britain*. But nine million people watched it. He's grinning, slightly manically.

He reads the *Independent* which asks: 'Has any comedy been so desperate to offend its audience?'

Then the *Guardian*, which says, 'Familiarity has dulled many of my objections to the show, although I still can't get used to comedy blackface or jokes about senile incontinence, mental illness, etc.'

David thought the days when white comedians portraying black characters automatically meant they were being racist were long gone. He feels that misdirected and taboo sexual desire is certainly a recurring theme. But

Matt and one of the girls in the show

neither he nor Matt recognises this vicious streak that these critics perceive. 'I just don't expect people to get this angry about us,' he laughs.

'Did I ever tell you the goose curry story?' asks David.

The goose curry story involves David Baddiel, and we've got on to it now because we've been listening to Jonathan Ross's Radio 2 programme on the car stereo on the way to Edinburgh. David complains about the music. It's too eclectic. One minute you get a lovely David Bowie song, the next it's a mediocre Northern Soul effort.

Matt and David recently enjoyed Sunday lunch at Jonathan Ross's country home. Jane cooked, and did a beautiful job. Then David tells me about the worst cook he knows: David Baddiel.

'He always invites me over for Christmas and I do love his company. And one year I went round to his on Boxing Day evening for dinner, so I said to him, "What are we having to eat?" and he says, "Well, I'm not sure . . . we've got lots of leftovers from the goose we had yesterday." So I say, "All right, what shall we do with that?" "Well," he says, "I could make a goose curry." So we go to the kitchen and he's tearing off big strips of meat from the goose carcass, then he tells me he doesn't have any curry powder or anything like that. So he gets the bits of goose meat, finds some HP sauce and tomato ketchup, mixes it up and serves it with some rice and says it's goose curry. I told Jonathan about this and he teased David about it, and David got livid with me and said, "You ate it all up!" And I said, "Yeah, but I was hungry!"'

Just then David gets a call on his mobile. I can hear a male voice talking quite loudly. It sounds like Jonathan Ross. But we're listening to him on the radio.

"We're listening to you on the radio," says David. "Oh, you recorded it, did you? Naughty!" He's giggling.

Jonathan asks David about the ratings for the first episode of the new series of *Little Britain*.

David says, 'I'm really pleased. It's a landmark. Yeah, only soaps and *Strictly Come Dancing* get more viewers . . . I imagine I will never do another programme on telly that will get that many viewers. That's fine, though.' Then Jonathan says something and David asks him: 'How much do you think it's going to go down next week?'

Jonathan tells him it might not go down too much, then David asks him: 'Did you watch *Children In Need*? I watched a bit of Madonna but that was about it. It is just that Morecambe and Wise sketch with Angela Rippon stretched over five hours.'

Jonathan tells him about next week's ceremony at the palace when Jonathan will receive his OBE from the Queen.

'Have you been sent a list of rules of what you can and can't do?' asks David. 'Are you allowed to let a finger stray into her bum hole?'

David ends the conversation by telling Jonathan that he might buy a dog, 'a little gay one'. Then he adds, 'I've just told the goose curry story . . .'

When he rings off, David explains that Jonathan's got an even better story about David Baddiel. About the time he ate an undercooked buffalo steak and shat himself.

Just then David's mobile phone rings again. He answers, listens to what the caller says and tells them, 'I've no idea . . . I don't really know my neighbours. And I'm moving out soon. So I don't have any comment to make . . .'

He rings off, and explains that was the *Sunday People* on the phone, asking if he knew that the woman who lives above him in his Belsize Park flat makes her own hardcore porn videos. They're going to run this as a story in tomorrow's paper. He explains that it's true that as soon he met the woman, she did tell him that she made porn videos, but he doesn't know what it has got to do with him, and she doesn't make them in the flat itself. He says the *People* will most likely try to link him somehow to the porn woman. They will probably imply that he is *in* her porn videos.

15

19 November 2005 – Edinburgh: day 24

Van Persie shoots from 25 yards out. The ball somehow squirms through their keeper's body. The room erupts. Matt says he always thought we were going to win this match. His brother points out there are eighty minutes to go.

We're in the side room of an Edinburgh bar set aside specially so Matt and his friends and family can watch Wigan v. Arsenal on Sky Sports. All Matt had to do was enquire tentatively at the hotel if there was anywhere handy nearby we could watch the football, and within minutes this space was made available.

Matt's got his Arsenal scarf on, his brother's wearing his replica Arsenal first team shirt and his stepdad is here too. His mum and her friends have gone shopping.

Cesc Fabregas, Arsenal's young Spanish midfielder, slides a pass towards Thierry Henry in the penalty area and a flick of his left foot later it's in the net. Matt's brother punches the air. Matt says all we need now is to keep up this form over the next three or four weeks, make sure we maintain our place in the league tucked in behind Spurs and beat them when they come to Highbury in April. Then the Champions League qualifying place will be ours. After an extremely patchy start to the season, Arsenal are now beginning to capture the kind of form the fans expect. If they win today, it will be Arsenal's sixth win in seven games.

Arsenal

When Matt's dad was about fourteen he had an accident on his bike: he went over the handlebars and smashed his leg. The man who tended to his leg happened to be doctor for the Arsenal team, and as Matt's dad was recuperating, the doctor gave him Arsenal tickets. That's how his dad became an Arsenal fan. So when Matt was seven or eight his dad took him to the Arsenal every now and then but Matt wasn't that into it.

Then when he was about nine years old Matt got his first Figurine Panini football sticker album and that ensnared his interest, because he could identify the players and know their stories and suddenly it was like he knew who

Junior Gooner, aged eight

these men were, and he could follow their careers. It became more like a soap opera. When Matt was thirteen, in the 1988/89 season, he started to go regularly with his friend Darren, and he became a Junior Gunner. He'd go with his brother and his friends, who would stand in the North Bank at Highbury while Matt would go to the family enclosure in the Lower East Stand so he could get a better view. Matt would arrive 90 minutes before kick-off and stand there in his cherished prime position. Then at two minutes to three some big yob would arrive and stand right in front of him. It would cost a pound to get in, but if Matt was feeling really flush then he'd spend two pounds on a better seat, especially for the big Manchester United or Tottenham games.

From 30 yards out, Thierry sweeps a majestic free kick low into the net: 3–1 to Arsenal. 'Game over,' says Matt, and it's not even the end of the first half.

'When do you want your present?' asks David.

'Ooh, my goodness,' says Matt's mum. 'Well, maybe I'll take it now but open it after midnight . . . because it's my birthday tomorrow.'

'Yes, but tonight's the night!' announces David.

Diana laughs and repeats: 'Tonight's the night!'

'We said we'd tell people tonight,' says David boldly, 'so let's get it out in the open.' Matt is giggling on the other side of the table from his mum and David.

'Oh, we love our banter don't we, David?' says Diana.

David's looking steely-eyed. 'It's not banter. It's real,' he says. Matt is looking on with a big grin on his face, blissfully enjoying the flirting between David and his mother.

'Oh ye-ess . . . it's real,' says Diana.

'Our love is real,' smiles David.

We're sitting round a vast table in a sleek Edinburgh private members' club. It's Matt's mum's sixtieth birthday meal. She's surrounded by her closest friends and family, including Matt's brother, and her husband Ralph, and their friends Sue and Gerald.

David gives Diana a birthday card. It's an official *Little Britain* card, with his character Emily on the front. When Diana opens it, Emily's voice yells, 'I'm a lady!'

'Oh I love it!' she exclaims. 'That's hysterical. I'd never have dreamed you would have got me one of these . . .'

'Really? I thought it was quite predictable!' replies David. 'I knew you'd like it though. You'd have been disappointed with anything else, wouldn't you?'

Diana agrees that the card is perfect. She hands it to Matt, who's thoroughly tickled by it.

'A fiver for that!' says David.

Diana opens her present from David – a scented candle from Harvey Nicks. 'Mmm –' she sniffs it '– bee-autiful. David, that's so nice.'

David asks Diana if she enjoyed her starring role at the National TV Awards.

'I was absolutely staggered. Absolutely staggered about how many people watched it. All these people came up to me the next day telling me they'd seen it.'

David tells Diana that she did very well, and that he knows how nerve-wracking those events can be. He explains that he still gets nervous at that kind of ceremony. 'Really?' Do you?' asks Diana, in disbelief. He gets excited about them beforehand, and likes the idea of them, but as soon as he arrives, he finds it torturous to have to hang around and be charming to all the press people and the TV cameras. And he can't bear the wait. Diana points out that she and David's mum had to wait for ages until their turn came to go onstage and pick up Matt and David's award. David says they looked like they were born to it. They should form their own double act.

The next big event for Matt and David is the British Comedy Awards, which takes place next month, while they'll be onstage doing *Little Britain Live* in Brighton. David thinks the organisers are making arrangements to interrupt the show and present them with any awards they win live onstage. But he's not sure if they will win anything.

1980s

Matt's grandmother was a refugee from Germany and the rest of his grandparents were children of refugees. Matt's father was brought up orthodox and his mother was brought up liberal. When they got together they decided to become 'reform' Jews, as a kind of compromise. Matt's mum and stepmum and his brother all ended up working at his local synagogue, so it seemed inevitable that much of Matt's growing up would revolve round the Jewish scene.

So from the age of about six Matt went to Hebrew classes every Sunday, and he went to youth club at the synagogue each Sunday afternoon and evening, then from the age of seven he went to Cub Scouts at the synagogue. He would also go to Saturday service at the synagogue every week, and as his bar mitzvah approached he'd go to extra classes on Tuesday after school. Then from the age of twelve or thirteen until eighteen or nineteen Matt was a youth leader at the synagogue. So this Jewish community and the friends he made there were a huge part of his life. In fact, it was pretty much his complete social life.

Once or twice a week he'd be at the synagogue, not necessarily praying there, but meeting friends there, being part of that community. And he'd go away for weekends and have sleepovers at a place called Manor House which houses the Centre for Reform Judaism. These sleepovers had a strong Zionist element to them. Matt and his friends would be taught Zionist doctrine in a series of games and activities. They'd also test their Hebrew vocabulary.

As a young teenager Matt would turn up on a Friday night, sit in a circle and play games, and they'd have to sit on incredibly thin mats, and it would be either boiling hot or freezing cold. There was a constant saying of grace, and there was very little going on that wasn't somehow Zionist related. At the youth club Matt would help run the tuck shop or he'd DJ and play table tennis and snooker and he'd do drama. And he loved it all.

There was a show in 1985 called the *Youth Review* to celebrate fifty years at his synagogue and Matt starred in it, performing to several hundred people. He was in the show with the Cubs performing a song: 'If I was not a good Cub Scout I know what I would be,' and at one point he was dressed as a big milkman going 'milko . . . milko . . .'

That was Matt's life – as much as anything – being in the synagogue. Yet he never really became a devout practising Jew. For Matt, his Jewishness gave him a community, a group of friends, activities to keep him busy, but the one thing it never really gave him was any sense of religious devotion.

Our food starts arriving, and Matt's brother has ordered something vegetarian from the menu. David asks him why he doesn't eat meat. Matt's brother says he only eats kosher meat, so more often than not in restaurants he ends up going vegetarian. David was a vegetarian until about three years ago, when he decided he couldn't do without Parma ham and the occasional juicy sausage, but he tries to stick to free-range or organic meat and poultry.

David's intrigued to find out from Matt's mum how Matt ended up with his specific eating habits. Diana said he got into burgers and chicken and chips when he was a teenager and stuck with them. Even now he won't eat fish or eggs or cheese. His brother explains that Matt has never seen what the function of cheese and fish is. He just always preferred something more solid: meat. Matt's brother says he's pretty much the same.

Diana says Matt's favourite food is still her chicken soup. She asks David what his favourite meal is. He loves comfort food like shepherd's pie but if he could choose one meal to eat it would be a nice piece of sea bass. Diana says Matt loves shepherd's pie.

David initiates a discussion with my Glaswegian friend Cameron about whether Scots are an oppressed minority. Cameron thinks some Scots feel that way, but he doesn't. Matt's brother says he doesn't see much evidence of the cultural oppression of Scots. David thinks they might be oppressed but not in the same way that black people are. He thinks there's an increasing number of people now who like to think of themselves as victims, because that enables them to place themselves on the moral high ground. For example, the Jews have historically been victimised, but now it seems like the Palestinians are the real victims, at least in Israel and the Occupied Territories. David likes to provoke debate and try to get to the nub of an issue. He's brought up the oppression of Scots with a Scot, and now he's moving on seamlessly to the victimisation of Jews with a whole Jewish family and me.

Matt's brother listens and nods and then says it's interesting to walk through Israel and witness the wariness between the Jews and the Arabs. He says it can't be denied that the Arabs who live in Israel do have a hard time of it. David wants to know what he means by that. Do they live in poverty? Matt's brother says it's not like the kind of poverty we see in parts of Africa. He says they'd probably have phones in their homes, and basic facilities, but maybe not a car, and essentially they do live like second-class citizens. He says when you walk down the street as a Jew in Israel and you see a Palestinian they will often give you a nasty look. 'Like two people forced against their will to live in the same space,' explains Matt's brother, as he orders mango sorbet for dessert. 'It's quite surreal. Unlike anything I've experienced here. But it's a relatively new country and one day they'll iron these problems out.'

David asks if Palestinians and Jews live side by side. Matt's brother says there are some communities that live very close – the equivalent of Sutton and Cheam.

'Okay, here's a question for you,' says David. 'Do you think some Palestinians resort to suicide bombing because of their desperate political situation or because they are religious extremists?'

'I think they resort to it because of their political situation but the mental process that contributes to them becoming a suicide bomber is heavily religious. That's how they're sucked into it.'

Matt's brother seems to be the polar opposite of Matt. He's a slim, almost slight figure, with a neat crop of silvery blond hair. At first sight, he seems deadly serious, studious even. But I'd seen him watching Arsenal earlier in the day and he was getting hugely excited each time Arsenal came near to scoring. As he explains that he's not sure if the Palestinian/Israeli conflict will ever be resolved, a waitress emerges to give his mother a tiny birthday cake with one candle on it.

David and Matt's mother Diana, Edinburgh, 2005

We all sing happy birthday, and Diana thanks everyone but says she doesn't want to make a speech.

'What do you mean?' says Matt. 'You stood up in front of all those people at the Albert Hall and now you've got nothing to say?'

'She'll only do it if she gets an award!' says David.

Diana cackles at the theory, then thanks everyone for coming and says what a privilege it has been to celebrate her sixtieth birthday in such wonderful company.

Matt's brother says it looks like a nice piece of cake, emphasising the word cake in the style of Marjorie Dawes. Diana repeats the phrase 'nice piece of cake', impersonating her son's character.

David says it would be nice to go for a walk round Edinburgh tomorrow. I tell him that Cameron has suggested going up Arthur's Seat. 'Oh I see,' says David. 'Well, that sounds very nice but it's not where my interests lie these days.'

Our friend Daniel has arrived at the restaurant and is suggesting going to the local gay club CC Bloom's after Matt's mum's meal is finished.

David looks at Matt's mum and announces: 'Soon we can start dancing and carousing, and then we can start getting off with each other.'

'Ye-esss,' says Diana, smiling.

'It's one minute past twelve, so let's welcome the newest OAP in the country,' says Matt's brother.

'Shall we sing one more verse of "Happy Birthday"?' asks Diana's husband Ralph.

David says it sounded so awful the first time we sang it that we should all think very seriously before we embark upon a reprise. As we leave the restaurant Matt's brother asks which club we're going to. David says it's a gay club over the road. Matt's brother says, 'Oh okay,' and strides off after the rest of his family. David winks at me and says, 'Come on, it might be full of kosher cock.'

The floor is sticky. 'Ray Of Light' by Madonna screams from the sound system. A large woman in a black shiny boob tube gyrates drunkenly in front of us, seemingly for David's entertainment.

Then the cameraphones come out. David tries to smile for each of the young gays who are taking his photo. We squeeze through the throng from one side of the bar to the other, encircling the packed dance floor. The dancing gays salute David, or wave or just elbow each other and point. The mood of the place is jolly, down-to-earth and not especially sexual. It's unashamedly tacky. We stand on the far side of the club surveying the writhing dancers. Suddenly a small circle of admirers gathers round. 'Yer fookin' brilliant, man,' says a slight, teen-looking blond boy. His friends agree vehemently. David thanks them. They gather for a group photo. David obliges.

'It's fun and everything,' grimaces David as another gaggle surrounds him for a photo shoot, 'but I think I might have to leave now.' There comes a point when a certain number of people crowding round him and clamouring for his attention becomes too much. Everyone in the room seems to want something from him, even if it's just the slightest acknowledgement of their existence or else an indication of how happy and funny he is. In real life. But right this second he's not sure he can give them what they want. Or live up to their expectations.

I look at my watch. We've lasted twelve minutes in CC Bloom's. It's time for David to go to bed.

2000

London's gay scene was a completely new world to Matt, but he feared the consequences of being spotted at one of the bars or clubs. He was frightened of word getting back to his family, through someone who recognised him or through the press, that he was gay. He was out to almost all of his friends and colleagues in his late teens, but he still hadn't told his family. When, in his mid-twenties, he finally came out to them, he felt able at last to pursue a more liberated lifestyle and – who knows – perhaps meet someone special.

Most Saturday nights Matt and his friends would go to Old Compton Street in Soho and do a quick tour of the bars before ending up in Heaven, the most famous gay club in Europe, where a dazzling array of men would gather to drink, dance, take drugs and flirt with each other. Matt regards this period as a second adolescence. He felt he had a lot to learn and quickly. Relatively inexperienced, he was discovering the feelings and emotions that most straight people encounter, act upon and hopefully resolve in their mid-teens. Here was Matt, ten years late, a grown man, now being confronted by the stomach-churning pain of rejection when someone you like doesn't feel the same, the embarrassment of dodging the unsolicited attentions of someone who doesn't float your boat, the mixed signals, waiting for that text message, trying to work out whether the guy who just smiled at you was being friendly or making a move, deciding how long to wait before calling someone back, trying to figure out whether the guy who asked him out but then cancelled the date really had come down with the flu or had now moved on . . . On top of that were the insecurities of being overweight, bald and, just to add to the confusion, sort of famous in a culty, post-*Shooting Stars* way. Matt was initially reserved – his onscreen flamboyance equalled by his real-life lack of confidence. To Matt's constant surprise, however, as he learned to *appear* more confident, or at least less desperate, despite his reservations about his appearance, people started to come up to him and ask him out. As one of his conquests once confided in him, 'You may not be the perfect ten but you've got something.'

But even if Matt fancied someone like mad, he wanted to get to know the bloke first. He had to *like* the person before sleeping with him. But what would invariably happen is that these men would get Matt's number and that was it. He wouldn't hear from them again. Maybe he had been too nervous, maybe the other person was drunk or on something else that made them over-affectionate, maybe they had caught the eye of someone more attractive instead, maybe they lost their bottle or maybe they didn't fancy him in the first place and were just getting off on chatting up a 'celebrity' – who knows?

Gradually, though, Matt started to see some action. There was an intense four-month fling with someone who was physically Matt's type but with whom ultimately he had very little in common, and a three-week dalliance with a swoonsome but ultimately insane soap actor. There was a tall, handsome musician who wooed Matt with gifts and hung about outside the theatre where *Taboo* was on and then disappeared back to his boyfriend (whom Matt had known nothing about); the tortured fashion student Matt had secretly admired from afar for years; the stunning, melancholy nineteen-year-old model Matt stupidly fell for, who didn't return his calls, causing Matt a miserable few weeks, compounded by the fact that the model's face appeared in every frame above the escalator at Oxford Circus and then, as he exited the station, having made sure to close his eyes and avoid the glare, immediately pouted at him from an enormous poster in the window of Top Man, before somewhat less gloriously turning up naked, full-frontal, in the back of a free gay mag a few months later. Then there was the alcoholic artist (who showed Matt his portfolio, full of paraphernalia from his own one-night stands – phone num-

bers, pubic hair, *condoms*); the short, boyish teen in the tall stilettos; the frag-
ile but beautiful deaf guy in a home-made Union Jack T-shirt he met on the
night of the Queen's Jubilee; the bitchy, name-dropping brother of a TV presenter; the blokey Welsh Black Sabbath fan; the Essex boy who drunkenly
screamed, 'Look! Do you wanna relationship or not?' on the first date; the
cheery Brummie hairdresser – all highlights and St Tropez, and the funny,
straight cocky Danny Dyer-like stockmarket boy who started chatting to Matt
one night in Heaven but who was definitely straight, who baffled himself by
swooping in on Matt for a kiss but was definitely straight, and who burst in on
an unsuspecting Matt in a toilet cubicle even though he was straight . . .

Suffice to say that over the two or three years he was out on the scene Matt
had his fair share of adventures, had his heart broken numerous times, and
perhaps inadvertently wounded a few others. But as much as Matt enjoyed
the frisson, the electricity, the 'who knows what may happen' of walking into
that club a single man (somewhat let down by the fact that, due to the heat in
Heaven – an underground, windowless den – his glasses would steam up on
entry, making him feel a tad seedy), Matt was starting to think that what would
be really nice, what he was starting to *crave*, was a proper, actual boyfriend.

16

20 November 2005 – Edinburgh: day 25

James looks like James Martin the TV cook. But this James is a spiritualist medium who specialises in 'mediumship, psychometry, relationships clairvoyance, and medicine cards'. David picked him out because of the relationships clairvoyance element of his skills. David wants to know what might become of his fledgling relationship with X. He hasn't heard from her for a few days, and is fretting slightly. Not that he believes for one moment that any kind of medium can provide him with genuine insights into his life. But he is tickled by the idea of finding out what one of them might have to say. And he's intrigued to find out how they work.

So we're upstairs in a church on the Royal Mile, where a handful of mediums of different types are gathered, sitting behind tables advertising their techniques.

David sits opposite James, who shuffles some cards, but all the while stares at David intently. He speaks in a low, intense Scottish burr.

'Well, life is a bit of a rollercoaster for you, David, isn't it? There are a lot of ups and downs. There's a certain amount of sadness and a certain amount of regret, and I certainly feel you're needing direction in your life in this present time. There's a certain amount of confusion in you and stress. In time it'll sort itself out but you need to make decisions.'

David nods.

'There are two children I can see but they won't tell me any of your business. Who's John, David? Someone from your past?'

David shakes his head. He doesn't know anyone called John.

'Can we think of a John who's passed away?' asks James.

'I can't think of one,' replies David honestly.

'That's fine. Let's hold on to that one,' James says, then changes the subject. 'You've got two choices right now in life. One that's going round in your head. I'd like to say you're going to have to make changes in your life right now. There's someone in your life who's drinking too much alcohol. I'd like to say you've been hurt in the past. I'm not gonna say that that's gonna repeat itself.'

'You're not gonna say that?' says David, trying to understand what he's talking about.

'No, I'm not. I'm gonna say you're quite a deep person, but I do think you hold back sometimes. You hold back on what you feel. And I think this should change. There's gonna be a lot of travelling for you, with your work. And there's gonna be a nice opportunity for you. Don't think it'll be all doom and gloom 'cos it's not. But there's a chance for a relationship. Have you just had some dealings with property, David?'

'I've just bought a new house.'

'Ah yes, well that's validated by my reading. I see a farm maybe. And a courtyard. I see a retreat for you maybe. Is there an opportunity to do with music around you right now? A small thing or a large thing?'

'Musically? Possibly . . . maybe.'

'Well, take it. There's also talk here of possibly going to America. Are you having trouble with your sleep right now?'

'Yes.'

'Well there are a lot of negative thoughts going round. And I'd like to say be more positive. And I'd like to say please close the door on the past. Do you understand that, my friend?'

'Yeah. I suppose.'

'So I certainly feel there's been a certain amount of sadness in your past, but you need to let it go. And I don't think you should take any medication.'

'No medication?'

'No. Not for your sadness. I think you should exercise and walk, go for walks, instead of medication. Is there some anxiety within you, David?'

'Maybe, yes.'

'I don't see that as being a problem for you for ever. I see a lot of strength in you to overcome your anxieties.'

'Okay.'

'What I want to do is take you forward. It's telling me to take you away from something. I don't know if you're an actor or performer or something, but I see there's an invite coming to do something else. Something new. A new opportunity. I want to push you to it. I want to say you must be your own man. Very good financially as well.'

'Oh that's good.'

'And this opportunity will be music to your ears. If I say something financial is in the balance right now, do you understand that?'

'Erm. Kind of.'

'Well, I want to say that this will be resolved in a way that is good for you, my friend. This person I see is saying "about time" . . . Er, David, can I speak to you about . . .?' He tails off. '. . . I tell you maybe he's trying to give you validation. Maybe hypnosis has helped. Or maybe it can still help? I'm not saying you can use it to sleep. I see a beautiful new bed. Have you bought a new bed?'

'No, but I've bought a new house so there will be a new bed.'

'Ah well, I see a beautiful large bed. At one time you had a few opportunities and you dug out the right path and went in the right direction. And there's gonna be a lot more opportunities but they haven't shown themselves yet. And have you had trouble with a car?'

'Well, I'm selling my car because I had some trouble with it.'

'Good. Sell it. It's trouble. And they're showing me a Porsche. Might you buy a Porsche?'

'I hadn't planned on it, no.'

'Well, I see a Porsche. I'm being shown a Porsche. There seem to be a certain amount of illusions you must deal with right now. Do you understand that, my friend? Illusions. They're telling me what to say and they're saying illusions. I'm seeing someone buried across the water. A grandfather who was maybe serving in the war?'

'I had a grandfather who served in the war but he's buried here I think.'

'Okay, well, ask about that. A quick yes or no, David, do you have a sister?'
'Yes.'

'Okay, well I'd like to talk about her just now. I feel there's been a rough time in her life. And I'd like to say she's gonna get over this and she's gonna see what life is all about. She's had a dark, dark time, but I see her coming out of it. They're holding a candle for her, as if to say they'll be around to help her.'

'When she was very young or when she was an adult?'

'Well, I would go to a time when she wouldn't have wanted to hear that. But now they're providing a certain amount of love and protection for her. You understand that? And you can help her and talk to her, and that is a gift. She still wants you to share in her care. There's also talk about her house.'

'Yes, she's doing up an old house.'

'Is she having heating problems in her house?'

'Maybe. It's a very old house.'

'Well, it'll be fine. She'll be fine. I also have a gut feeling about someone being dishonest with you. Do you have that feeling?'

'Maybe.'

'Well, you're right. I see someone putting a face on or a mask on, or maybe there are two of them. Two people with masks on who are talking about you behind your back. One of them might have a drinking problem. Be very careful, David. It's as if they're drawing you in. You're like a ship in the night without a lighthouse to guide you and you might hit the rocks. They're being very dishonest. But you do know what's going on deep down. It's as if your nose has already smelled them.'

The medium pauses for breath and looks straight at David. He says, 'David, is there a very beautiful female in your life right now?'

'She's not quite in my life.'

'She will be!'

'I hope so.'

'She's very beautiful. Her heart is in the right place, but she's very strong. Don't let her dominate you. Has she been on the phone today? Has she been in touch today?'

'Not yet today.'

'She will be.'

'Have you got any questions?'

'Errm . . . Do you see marriage and children?'

'I'd ask a different question: happiness comes first, my friend. Happiness comes under that. I see happiness. And I see letting go of the past. I see someone from early on and he's trying to give you a good validation here. He's saying, "No more silly thoughts." Do you understand that, my friend? He says, "No more silly thoughts."'

'Yes.'

'No more silly thoughts,' says David. 'Well, that's a bit vague.'

David conjectures as to whether James the medium really thinks he has special powers, or whether he's just learned the skill of seeming like you're predicting facts about someone's life, making profound insights into their life.

'A lot of it was very vague stuff,' he explains. 'And sometimes when he said something specific, it was wrong. Someone called John. A grandfather buried overseas. Then he goes, "You've had a sadness in your past?" Well, yes, I have. But that's not that unusual, is it? Then he said, "Do you have a sister?" And I was thinking, what if I said no, would he then have said, "Brother? Ah okay!" Then he said one or two things that were *so* specific. Something about getting the plumbing checked in my sister's house.'

Yet when David asked him outright whether he could see marriage and kids in David's future, he wouldn't really commit either way.

A studenty-looking girl comes up to David while we're standing outside the church, and asks him to sign her copy of *The Runaway Jury* by John Grisham. She doesn't have any other bits of paper. 'Shall I pretend to have written it as well?' asks David.

11.58 p.m. Text from David: 'The medium was wrong. She never called.'

1980s – Banstead, Surrey

David was secretive. His parents and sister learned to accept that about him. The front door would open and he would say, 'I'm going out.' His mum would ask, 'Where are you going?' David would say, 'Out.' She would ask, 'Who are you going with?' He would answer, 'No one you know.' And that would be that. He rarely brought friends home. He didn't seem to have any girlfriends. In his late teens his family did begin to suspect that he might be gay. But his mum wasn't going to let that possibility affect her relationship with him, or how she treated him. His sister Julie wondered about his sexuality too, but assumed he would have told her if he was gay. At the same time she teased him about not having a girlfriend. But then, she teased him about being podgy and spotty too. Julie would even, on occasion, squeeze teenage David's spots for him, whether he liked it or not.

In his mid-teens David looked very different. He was overweight and ungainly. But because he was big and tall, his schoolmasters wanted him to focus on rugby, which was the school's compulsory sport. One of the Welsh games teachers told him, 'What are you doing poncing around on the stage when you ought to be propping up the front row of the scrum?' David hated all team sports with a passion.

He started to lose weight when he realised he wanted to be onstage and meet girls. He lost three stone one summer, when he knew he would be going to the National Youth Theatre and he knew he would be mingling with girls in the sixth form. To lose the weight he simply stopped eating things that made him fat and did some exercise. But this swift transformation from geeky overweight boy to lithe, more confident performer was typical of David's single-mindedness. When he decided to do something, or take a particular path, he would follow it through with utter determination.

Similarly he was always prepared to push things as far as he could.

When he was sixteen he won a schools public-speaking competition and chose as his subject: This House Believes That The Argos Catalogue Is The Work Of The Anti-Christ. In his school assemblies he was always trying to be as risqué and cheeky as possible.

And once he became a performer, and drew laughs with his campness, he would milk his image as the school's affected thespian. He was nicknamed Cuthbert because he was regarded as posh, even though his family background was unpretentiously lower middle class. So he embraced the name and used it for his first comedy character, aged 12, called Cuthbert Hogsbottom. Later, when he was in the Cadets, they used to call him Daphne as a way of suggesting he was gay. So he camped it up even more. David thinks it's true what the comedian Ben Miller once told him: comedy is a way of controlling people's laughter *at* you so you turn it into them laughing *with* you.

He would always make sure he looked smart, and was buying beautifully embroidered shirts even at the age of fourteen or fifteen.

As he got older, and he became more confident of his outlandish image, so the dichotomy between David and his rather mundane school and suburban background became wider. At least he had his best friend Robin with whom he could share all his frustrations.

17

2 December 2005 – Bristol: day 35

Matt looks at the photo byline at the top of the page and assumes it's a lesbian. I try to convince him the writer is very much a man. A large young gay man who writes a column for the *Independent*. This column is titled, 'Why I Hate *Little Britain*,' and those words are also splashed provocatively in huge type across the top of the front page.

The piece kicks off with a list of three *Little Britain* sketches the writer seems to have taken most offence to, although oddly one of them, in which a man got up out of a wheelchair 'and was so mentally disabled he just walked into a wall', doesn't actually exist. The general tenor of the article is that *Little Britain*'s targets are the weak and disadvantaged in society, that it is sadistic and cruel, unlike the journalist's examples of current TV comedy gold such as '*Nighty Night*, Ricky Gervais and Chris Morris'. But the sentence in the professional controversialist's column that will astound everyone who knows Matt and who happens to have read it, is this one (in the middle of a discussion of the portrayal of Dafydd):

'I know Matt Lucas is gay (although he is still so conflicted about his sexuality he almost never discusses it publicly).'

The columnist clearly didn't see Matt merrily discussing his sexuality in front of about seven million viewers on *Parkinson*. (Months after this anti-*Little Britain* diatribe, the same writer, in a column about Stella McCartney, attacks journalists who gratuitously rip a famous person's reputation apart, writing: 'it seems that as soon as somebody is considered A Celebrity they become a blank space onto which we can project the most hateful motives without a shred of evidence.' And when the same journalist also later writes a column entitled "Pinter does not deserve the Nobel Prize", David realises he shouldn't ever have paid any attention to the writer at all.)

Matt shrugs. 'The idea that I'm conflicted about my sexuality is just so offensive. Where did he get that from? I suppose it's just someone trying to make his name, isn't it?'

The journalist's peculiar verdict on Dafydd is: 'the only gay in the village . . . is based on one endlessly repeated comic premise: there is no prejudice against gay people in Britain any more, but shrieking gay misery-queens like Dafydd are so obsessed with being victims they obsessively see prejudice where there is none'.

'No prejudice against gay people in Britain any more?' laughs Matt, witheringly. 'So *that's* what we're saying.'

Cos is starting to worry that we're not on the correct route to the Drama Department. Matt doesn't recognise this road. He feels mildly embarrassed because he did go to university here, but he just doesn't remember the way. Cos stops and asks a bloke who looks like a student. But the man shakes his head and says he thinks we're going in the right direction but he's not entirely sure. We've got half an hour to get there.

Matt gets to the bit in his article where the columnist claims that Vicky Pollard is a 'walking, smoking Richard Littlejohn column, a compendium of every prejudice ever spewed towards single parents'.

Matt points out that more than anything, she's an observation of the way certain people speak, of the peculiar phrases they come out with. Apparently, we're not allowed to make fun of working-class people any more. The *Independent* piece says, 'We look back on Jim Davidson blacking up as a head-scratching, imbecile black man with horror. But why is a public schoolboy dressing up as a head-scratching, imbecile single mother any better?'

Matt says he knows the guy is deliberately exaggerating to make his point, but yes, there is a difference between Jim Davidson making fun of blacks and Matt and David creating the character of Vicky Pollard.

'Anyway,' says Matt, 'the thing about Vicky is: she's a winner. She's strong. She's always in charge of the situation. She turns everything that happens in her life to her own advantage.' He sits and studies the article for a few seconds. 'Oh fuck it, we're just trying to make people laugh. Vicky does make people laugh, doesn't she?'

Not according to this columnist, who says, 'Perhaps a tiny sliver of this would be forgivable if the show was actually funny, but it is as entertaining as a burning orphanage.'

Even the millions of fans who do find the programme funny are, according to this column, 'people without a sense of humour'. So it's not okay to make comedy out of working-class single mothers, but it is okay to assume that the eight million people laughing at *Little Britain* are without a sense of humour, as, presumably, are the hundreds of thousands of people laughing at Matt and David's characters on this tour.

'Ooh, this looks vaguely familiar,' says Matt, staring out of the window. 'You know what the problem is? I kind of stopped paying attention after a while, when I lived here. Because I was already doing my comedy, going to the university just became such an inconvenience. I just found it so hard to pay attention at lectures. And I clearly paid no attention to where anything was. I remember just sitting there and everything drifting by me at the tutorials. And we had about thirty-five hours of classes per week. Everyone assumed we did no work, but it was pretty intense. And they took a register every class!'

Cos stops again, and asks a young couple. They seem to think the Drama Department is further up this hill. Yep, they seem fairly certain.

So we keep going up the hill.

Matt's finished with the article. 'Fuck,' he laments, 'he really really hates us. It's odd to read someone ranting about you like that. But I suppose I'm getting used to it.'

He's masochistically leafing through the pile of papers in the back of the car, most of which contain negative reviews of *Little Britain*. He thinks if they had avoided putting Mrs Emery pissing in the first episode then maybe the critics would have given the series an easier time. Then, as if he realises he's starting to sound sorry for himself and decides to snap out of it, he adds: 'But fuck it, those sketches got the biggest laughs when we played them out to the studio audience . . .'

He tells me about a cartoon in *Private Eye* which depicted kids wearing *Little Britain* T-shirts and an adult saying, 'Kids say the unfunniest things,' which brought home to him how *Little Britain* is now almost a byword for pervasive, mainstream comedy, in much the same way that the cultural commentators suddenly decide the likes of Dido or Coldplay or James Blunt represent safe pop music. 'We've become this uncool thing.'

He thinks it's the same for anyone who gets really big in Britain. 'Like the Spice Girls . . . or Robbie Williams. I mean, journalists don't have a good word to say about Robbie but it doesn't change how you think about him. He's still wonderful.'

Matt looks up from the papers and out of the window to check where we are and if we're anywhere near our destination. 'I think it will be unjust if the story became how terrible *Little Britain* has become, because I think this is the best series yet.'

Cos sees a tall man in jeans and a T-shirt, and winds down the window. 'Excuse me, mate, are we on the right road for the Drama Department?'

The man says we're practically outside it.

'And maybe,' ponders Matt, 'maybe we should just crack on and do something else. We're getting away with it now, but I'm not sure if we can carry on with it much longer . . .'

After a few seconds' contemplation, as almost always happens when Matt spends any time thinking about a subject that irritates or annoys or frustrates him in any way, he ends on a note of defiance. 'Fuck it. We'll be fine . . .'

As Cos slows the BMW down, Matt recognises the building up ahead: it's the Drama Department. 'Well done, Cos. We made it! Shame on me for not remembering. Everything looks kind of vaguely familiar.'

Matt checks his face out in the mirror. 'Shit! I'm covered in spots. My face is a wreck!'

Martin White shows us into a big office of the Drama Department and sits Matt and David down behind a huge table. He's a slim, grey-haired, very well-spoken man who talks in deliberate, slow, precise sentences.

Matt and David are here to answer questions about their career in front of an audience of current Bristol University drama students in an event organised by Martin, their old drama principal. They had a character in the *Little Britain* radio series called Martin White who was a drama principal,

Prague, 1997

and now in the sketches set at university when David says, 'Martin, it's *Linda*,' that's a tribute to Martin White too. Linda is named after Linda Fitzsimmons, a classic old-school feminist tutor from their university days. Martin explains that he will introduce the event, and he will be asking Matt and David the questions, at least to start with, after which the students will get their chance.

Martin says, 'I assume there's nothing much that's off limits?'

Matt says he can ask them anything. David nods in agreement.

'Oh good,' replies Martin. 'I know, David, you were quite keen there's no recording or filming. That it is purely a private event. And I have made sure that is the case.' He makes it sound like a formal announcement.

'I wish I could say the same for our live shows,' says Matt. 'The entire audience seems to be filming it some nights.'

Martin asks David if he remembers the productions he was in during his time in the Drama Department. David says he was only in one or two recognisable shows – including *A Midsummer Night's Dream* in which he played Bottom – because most of the time he was doing 'devised' pieces.

'I sometimes wonder why we spent so much time doing stupid perfor-mance art things,' says David, 'because really performance art is more about art than acting.'

Martin admits the students still like doing their own 'devised' pieces a lot of the time.

'I wonder what they'll be like,' ponders David. 'I wonder if they'll hate *Little Britain*. They might all think it's homophobic, reactionary rubbish.'

Martin leads the way into the auditorium, where about a hundred Bristol University drama students greet Matt and David like they're returning heroes.

David surveys the room and whispers, 'Look at them. So bright and eager and beautiful.'

Martin is very much in charge. He's not going to take any shit from the students. He ushers Matt and David into their seats next to him on the stage and slickly introduces them to the audience by making the point that not so long ago Matt and David would have been sitting where the students sit now, eagerly devouring any information that came their way. Martin explains that he'll kick things off with some questions of his own, but then the students should feel free to ask whatever they like.

'But hands up, please,' interrupts Matt, grinning. 'I don't want to see chaos.'

David as Bottom in *A Midsummer Night's Dream* at Bristol University, 1989

1990s – Bristol

When David went to university he saw it as an amazing opportunity to reinvent himself. It was a chance to escape from the image he had at school, where he got used to routinely being called gay by his fellow students. He was also confused about sex and his sexuality. He fancied the girls he'd eventually met when they arrived in the sixth form, but he'd also had sexual experiences with other boys, and it all felt very far away from actually having proper sex and forming real romantic attachments to people. He was socially awkward and would go to youth clubs and not really know what to do.

He had also begun to feel trapped at home. A moody young man in the routine world of middle-class suburbia. David's attitude as a surly late teenager was crystallised one time when he was listening to a suitably out-there KLF remix of a Pet Shop Boys song in his bedroom, and his mum came in and asked, 'What on earth are you listening to?' and David said, 'It's the avant garde! You wouldn't understand!'

When he arrived at Bristol, he felt as if a new version of himself was about to be unleashed. It took time, though. Initially he was stuck in grim college digs and had to share a tiny room with a complete stranger, which he hated. His shyness around women caused many moments of awkwardness. In drama classes, David dreaded the moment when the pupils had to get to know one another and break down any barriers between them by embracing and then rolling over each other on the floor.

Luckily he met Katy Carmichael. She was one of the beautiful people. She was already appearing regularly on television in the series *Bread*, which everyone was very impressed with. Once he'd met Katy, David felt he'd got in with the cool people, a clique of self-consciously clever and talented types. The avant garde.

There was David, Katy, who eventually became David's first proper girlfriend, Myfanwy Moore, who would end up producing *Little Britain*, Callum Greene who now lives in New York and works with Sofia Coppola, and Jason Bradbury who's now a TV presenter. And Myfanwy went out with Dominik Diamond who was in the year above, and Simon Pegg, a friend of theirs in the same year as Dominik. Simon was adored by everyone, especially the girls. He would perform comedic pieces in the Studio Space: love poems to animals and suchlike. He was funny and cute and lovable.

No one seemed to find David lovable. Unlovable maybe . . .

Simon Pegg's sweet routines were an exception. Bristol was generally a self-consciously serious environment. In classes and meetings the students would spout the same po-faced and politically correct platitudes. There was an almost Stalinist atmosphere among David's peers in the Drama Department. It felt like you had to subscribe to a set of values. David had to keep his fondness for *Carry On* films secret, for example, lest someone accuse him of gross sexism. Anyone admitting to finding something amusing about the sight of Barbara Windsor losing her bra in *Carry On Camping* would be considered to be advocating pornography. If anyone had admitted they voted Conservative, they would probably have been stoned to death.

People often went away at the end of term and came back in the new year with a new sexuality and were proud of it. Katy would refer to the kind of people they'd see going to lectures but who never did anything or said anything interesting as 'the insipids'. They enjoyed being quite harsh.

David fell in love with Katy about two years before he actually went out with her. He didn't have sex with any girls at university, and was beginning to think that it would never happen. He was confused, and he still thought he might be gay but he wasn't sure. What he did know, as soon as he became good friends with her, was that he was in love with Katy. To David, Katy was the most glamorous figure. She was sexy, charismatic, and already a proper, professional actress on TV.

But Katy didn't fall in love with David. She didn't know what to make of him at first. He was camp yet chivalrous with the ladies, popular with their peers but also solitary. But as they became friends, she grew to appreciate him more and more. He was loyal, gentle, kind yet also devastatingly funny. They would hold hands all the time, his huge hands engulfing her tiny ones. For years they were like brother and sister, although Katy joked that he was like her funny uncle. They would hug each other a lot, and have long sessions staying up all night talking about everything and anything. They became inseparable. She would visit him in his room at Manor Hall for peppermint tea and flapjacks, sit on his rug and listen to Liza Minnelli, Cole Porter and the Pet Shop Boys. He had an immaculate music, book and film collection. Katy was impressed by his incredibly neat handwriting. It was almost as if he was from a different era. There was nothing student or chaotic about him. He was fastidiously well presented and determined about everything: from eating good vegetarian food to getting his essays in on time. And he had a darkness, too, that people would often misinterpret. Katy admired that complexity.

David and his first love, Katy Carmichael, 1995

But she didn't have romantic feelings towards David. Yet.

Then one night, just before the end of their time at university, they ended up kissing.

For David it was an historic moment. She changed his world because until that point he hadn't got drunk or sat up all night or had sex with a woman. Katy woke David up to all that. She was a much freer and more open person.

Sexually, David had been paralysed by women. At school he only came into contact with girls in the sixth form, and because he thought he might be gay and because he put women on a pedestal and was petrified of what might happen should he actually come into contact with one, he only pursued un-attainable women. By falling for girls he knew would reject him, David erred on the side of safety. With Katy it was different.

On the last night of university David had a dizzyingly intimate evening with Katy. Late at night he washed her feet in the bath and they then walked through the streets of Bristol together at three in the morning. It felt like the whole world was open to them. David was intoxicated. He didn't ever want it to end. David thought he would be with her for ever. And she is still, to this day, the person he's had the longest relationship with – four years.

During his time at university and then beyond, David wanted to be noticed, but he didn't yet have the proper justification. Katy used to encourage the show-off side of his personality. She liked to dress him up. They frequently performed together at university, and most of the time he'd want to be as naked as possible in their performance art shows. One time Katy, dressed in a corset with a sprayed silver face and metal wig, dragged David in a patent-leather codpiece round on a lead, singing, 'Je cherche a millionaire' badly for a Futurist cabaret performance. He had pound signs drawn on his naked bot-tom, a false moustache and a whip in his mouth. He was up for anything: the more grotesque and subversive the better, and he didn't care what anyone thought. He defied categorisation. One time they were going to a fancy dress party, and David put on a schoolboy outfit and Katy wore a wedding dress, and when they got to the party David realised it wasn't fancy dress at all. Katy knew all along, and just wanted to have some fun. There was also a sailor's outfit she liked David to wear, and she encouraged him to cross-dress too.

She seemed to enjoy the idea and sight of David wearing women's clothes, and David quite liked it as well.

During those three years at Bristol, Katy realised he was becoming increas-ingly flamboyant and charismatic in his dress sense and personality.

In 1991 they went to New York, and spent most of their trip dressed and wigged up as Andy Warhol and Edie Sedgwick. They ran around making Super 8 films of each other at the Chelsea Hotel and on the subway, and at the top of the World Trade Center.

While they were going out, David was always impeccably romantic. He bought her cards and flowers; cooked her meals in his one-bed flat in Belsize Park. Every Saturday night they went clubbing. They'd have dinner then she would sit on his knee while he fixed her false eyelashes and she would do his eyeliner before they went to the big gay dance night called the Love Muscle at the Fridge in Brixton. It became a weekly ritual. One time he wore a Barbie outfit: a pink mini-kilt from Top Shop, a skin-tight T-shirt, white knee-length socks, a pink Barbie watch and hairclip with pink sequins around his eyes. Katy wore a nylon charity-shop wedding dress with a veil and six-foot train, which he carried around the club all night like a page boy.

Yet along with the flamboyance, David was also highly disciplined about his work. He and Matt would meet up every day at one or the other's place and they would write from 10 a.m. until 5 p.m. And even though much of their work around that time ended up being rejected, David always felt they would make it in the end.

But his relationship with Katy was volatile and intense. He was possessive and fiercely protective of her.

They split up when Katy went away to do a play. They did a lot of splitting up and getting back together, but eventually Katy met someone else while she was performing in that play and she's still with him.

David was desolate. He felt helpless seeing her with someone else. Like there was nothing he could do . . .

All he could do, in fact, was write to her, keep in touch and try to stay friends. She's still a hugely important person in David's life. Still the woman who woke him up to the possibilities of life. The one who helped him realise that he could have a passionate love affair with a woman. The one who helped banish the fear and confusion that David had felt about women since he was a boy. Now he knew he could fall in love with a woman and that was what he wanted. That was how he was going to find fulfilment.

'Do you think that fame has changed you and made you more arrogant?'

'Well there we are,' says David, slightly taken aback that this is the first question from one of the students, and it's from a rather pretty female student too. 'Let's start at the bottom and work our way up.' He laughs.

Matt says, 'Someone once said fame changes the people around you more than it changes you, and I think on this tour I've noticed that life has changed. People treat us like we're special. They're excited to see us. Stuff gets arranged around us – do you know what I mean? So maybe we have to just make sure that while we're getting treated like we're special, we don't start believing it too much ourselves. While obviously enjoying it!'

'I think people away from London are much more honest with you,' points out David, 'and they get much more excited to meet you. Where I live in London, people like to maintain a certain attitude of cool. But when we're shopping in Boots in Newcastle, people come up to us and thank us for what we've done and tell us not to stop, and that's just lovely.'

'I like to think I'm just as arrogant now as I've always been,' adds Matt, to general laughter.

'I tell you what's nice about the fame: it does help make you more confident in your creative ability. You know, this level of success is greater than we ever expected to have, with the awards we've won and the ratings that *Little Britain* gets, and it does give you that extra feeling that we can do this, we can be successful comedians and performers. So that's changed us maybe. But as for being arrogant . . . No, I hope not. So *shut up!*'

A fashionable young man asks the next question: 'What do you think about the way characters like Sebastian and Dafydd have done for the way gay people are viewed in Britain?'

'Well,' ponders David, answering very carefully, 'I hope that we have done a good thing, and brought a lot of questions about sexuality and the discussion of sex into the mainstream, because this is a show that got nine and a half million viewers last week. When I was young there weren't characters who identified themselves as gay on TV. You had camp characters like Dick Emery but they never identified themselves as having sex with other men. So we're quite proud of, for example in the Dafydd sketches, bringing discussions of the gay sexual acts into primetime TV. I imagine there are nine-year-old boys out there watching our show and they might ask their mothers, "What is fisting?" and I think that's wonderful!'

The audience erupts into laughter.

Matt asks the bloke who asked the question what he thinks of their portrayal of gay characters. The student says he thinks the gay characters have been amazingly positive in bringing gayness to the masses.

Graduation day, Bristol University, 1992

Martin chips in by asking how Matt and David are dealing with the criticisms of the show in general, and the newly harsh attacks on their work.

David admits he's surprised that their series has been slated the way it has, but that's just the nature of criticism when it comes to the third series of a show like *Little Britain*. To say nice things about it would be rather boring now.

Martin continues on the subject of criticism and says the show is now getting attacked for being somehow politically and culturally reactionary. Matt explains that of course the last thing that he and David ever set out to do is create stereotypes or underline people's prejudices. David points out that first and foremost what they're creating is a comedy programme, and trying to make people laugh. He mentions the example of the Mrs Emery incontinent pissing sketches, and says the interesting thing for him about them is that it feels taboo to admit that the sight of someone pissing uncontrollably in an inappropriate location is funny. He says that it is also tragic at the same time, and, like so much of life, comedy and tragedy can exist and occur simultaneously. They're not trying to be horrible about incontinent people. 'We're depicting a moment that in life would be both funny and sad, if we're going to be honest about it.'

Matt adds that he sometimes gets the feeling that critics resent the fact that he and David are white, middle-class men, implying that they shouldn't be allowed to create characters that are working-class single mums because they're not from that world. But if the observation rings true and is funny, then why should it matter who is making the observation, and what their background is?

David notes that they do also have upper-class characters. And that he would hope that critics can judge the work without even thinking about the background of the people who've created it. He says it always happens though, and that when Martin Amis brings a new novel out, the critics will harp on about his privileged upbringing, rather than discuss the merits of his writing.

Matt says he hates to use the word, but so much of that kind of criticism is to do with the idea of *Little Britain* becoming a 'phenomenon'. Maybe the critics aren't comfortable with so many people reciting the catchphrases and wearing the T-shirts. Maybe all of that is why the critics seem to hate *Little Britain* so much. It's barely even about the reality of the half-hour sketch shows that go out every Thursday on BBC1, it's about this thing: this phenomenon.

* * *

'You can't find the dolls because everywhere's sold out . . .' explains Alfie. 'We're pleading with them to give us more dolls to sell. That's the beauty of the website.'

Alfie runs the *Little Britain* merchandise site with a passion. Matt and David are sharing a dressing room at the Bristol Hippodrome, and Alfie is having an impromptu meeting with them about merchandising opportunities. He makes every possible way of expanding the range sound incredibly exciting.

The merchandising of *Little Britain* started like this – Matt and David always assumed they would have a stall at each venue on tour selling T-shirts and suchlike. But what precipitated all the official merchandise that came out before the tour even started was that two large retail chains got in touch with Matt and David to let them know that unofficial, essentially bootleg items were about to be sold in their shops and that there was nothing Matt and David could do about it, apart from sanctioning their own proper, licensed gear. Which is how they ended up agreeing to sell the array of official *Little Britain* merchandise that Alfie puts on the website.

'I think we're going to be beating every other site out of the water. We're second now. We're beating Peter Kay's site and now we've got Marillion in our sights. I think we should be taking something like ten million pounds a year.'

'Ten *mil*-lion,' repeats David, in disbelief. 'Not bad, I suppose.'

Alfie mentions how grateful Janet Street-Porter was to receive her goody bag the other night. All the VIP guests who come to the show get a *Little Britain* carrier bag filled with *Little Britain* merchandise. According to Janet Street-Porter, this is a rare treat. She goes to all kinds of shows and events, and is hardly ever given any kind of souvenir. She was thrilled. Matt says it was very nice of her to say so.

Kevin arrives and gives Matt a bag of satsumas. Matt hugs him. Kevin asks how the Bristol University event went. Matt says he really enjoyed it, and that the students seemed pleased to see them and asked lots of good questions.

David says it was a nice event. Although he didn't see many attractive girls there. 'So it was a waste of time!' he jokes. 'I mean, I did this talk, and you'd think at least one of the pretty ones could have come to talk to me afterwards.'

David's promised Martin from the university that he'll get two free tickets for tonight's show, for him and his teenage son. He's enjoying the process of doing his old college tutor this favour. A reversal of roles from when Martin was the man in charge of the Drama Department. David's loving this moment of holding sway, yet being magnanimous about it at the same time.

Kevin asks David if he's recovered from the thrill of meeting Madonna last night. David says it hasn't quite sunk in.

Matt and David were helping to turn on the Christmas lights at Stella McCartney's shop on Bond Street. They dressed up as Lou and Andy and did a little routine for the media. And of course Stella's best friend Madonna was helping out too. David says it was odd to perform their little bit in front of Madonna and then attempt to have a nice, laid-back chat with her afterwards.

The first thing David told Madonna was that he'd enjoyed watching the interview she gave to Dermot O'Leary on Channel 4 the night before. She told him she hadn't seen it yet, and asked if it was any good. David said it was fine, but that there was one peculiar moment when Dermot sang 'Danny Boy' to Madonna. 'They left that bit in?' asked Madonna incredulously. David confirmed they did, and that it was slightly odd. He said you don't get that kind of thing on *Parkinson*, and suggested that the last time he interviewed her Parky pretty much ended up letting Madonna take over. She replied that he lulls you into a false sense of security because it feels like you're just having a nice chat and then he'll ask a really difficult question. David slyly dropped in the fact that he and Matt have also been on *Parkinson*, to emphasise that it's normal and natural for him to be talking to her. Then suddenly David just abandoned all sense of propriety and simply told Madonna that he'd been to every tour she's ever done and bought every album she's ever made. 'You've been to all the tours?' she asked. 'Did you see the last one?' David told her that, yes, he saw the last one, and that he loved it, especially 'Die Another Day' with its spectacular visual scheme. He then asked Madonna if she was aware that gay magazine *Boyz* refers to her as 'Our glorious leader'. At that point, just as Madonna was registering surprise at this revelation and explaining that she didn't know, a friend of David's came up to him to say hello, and that was it: the moment was over. The chat with Madonna was done. And then it sunk in: he'd just fawned over her. Almost in a panic, David told Stella McCartney he'd just met Madonna and gushed. 'Oh don't worry,' said Stella, 'she loves gushing.'

David says Madonna was exactly how he hoped she would be. She was nice, but not too nice. She was still special. He didn't want her to be self-effacing or modest. He wanted her to be Madonna.

'Yeah, Madonna was fun', says Matt and he then points out that later that night, at their show in Oxford, they had another celebrity encounter. Timmy Mallett came to see them. 'I never thought I'd meet Madonna and Timmy Mallett in the same day.'

2001

One Saturday night, in Heaven, of course, Matt caught the eye of a guy across the room who was quite nice-looking, in a boy-next-door way, but who differed from the rest in that he had an open, welcoming look about him. Matt offered to buy him a drink. Turned out he recognised Matt, knew his work from *Shooting Stars* but was actually more of a fan of the shows that Matt and David had made for the Paramount Comedy Channel five years earlier. The longer they chatted, the more they seemed to have in common. The bloke was a big football fan, and although he didn't support Arsenal, he still had an in-depth knowledge of Matt's team. They talked about their jobs, their lives, their taste in comedy, their love of TV. It was one of those times when you meet someone and just connect. As he talked to this guy, and it grew later and later, Matt stopped drinking – stopped needing to – and caught sight of the rest of the room, thronging with sweaty, drunk, drug-fucked people, and it felt like this man and Matt were the stars of the show and all these people around them were the extras.

This guy felt different, he had substance and, unlike almost all of Matt's previous conquests, was older than him. But Matt's new friend didn't live in London and was going back up north the following night. In the meantime he would be staying at a friend's flat. Matt gave him his phone number, and in the confusing haze of the end of the night, they were separated. Matt managed to find him again, they quickly said goodbye, but Matt was suddenly too embarrassed and shy to get his number. When he got home at 4 a.m., Matt thought he might have found the one for him.

It seemed like he'd met a special person. Someone he could connect with, someone who didn't insist on having sex more or less there and then. They hadn't even kissed. Matt hadn't offered his number because he'd had one of those moments where you suddenly think: I'm not good enough for this guy –

look at me. But now, in the car on the way home, Matt started to think: this guy had just come out of a long-term relationship with someone twenty years older than him, so he probably wasn't that concerned with looks. He was probably looking for something deeper than that. He assumed he wouldn't be like the others who played the game of waiting a day or two before they got in touch. Or maybe didn't even get in touch at all. No, Matt knew this one would text him by the next morning. He knew he would be in this man's life now.

The man never rang back.

Matt told me about the story in as much detail as I have just recounted for two reasons. I'll get to the second reason later, but first of all, Matt tells this story because he feels it typifies the sort of experience lots of young men go through on the gay scene. Hopes raised, hopes dashed. Despite the fact that two men met and really hit it off, the chances of a successful gay relationship founded on the club scene are still small. There is so much baggage, so many difficulties involved in two men getting together and making a go of it. Despite the veneer of respectability the gay scene has achieved in the UK mainstream in the past few years, the increased visibility in the media, the abolition of Clause 28 banning the 'promotion' of homosexuality in schools (whatever that is), the legalisation of an equal age of consent, the law allowing civil partnerships – things improving all over – Matt still believes that dysfunction lies at the heart of most of the young men he has encountered.

There is still a stigma about being gay, there are still families and friends who react badly to the news, memories of being bullied at school, or worse sexually abused, of being different at precisely the age when you crave fitting in, and then, still, as an adult, work colleagues who snigger, neighbours who gossip, and so gay people, however hard they try, still have a weighty social disadvantage to contend with. This often manifests itself emotionally. 'We want commitment and security but often don't allow ourselves to have it, as if we somehow don't deserve it,' Matt says. 'Another factor that is completely forgotten is that when you walk into a gay bar and you see other men, that's it. That may be all you have in common. Your sexuality. Not ethnicity or geography or class or religion or a hobby or your profession or your age or anything – just sexuality. Which, when you think about it, is a pretty spurious reason for being in a room with someone.'

Basically, says Matt, wondering why you haven't met the man of your dreams in a gay club yet is like wondering why you haven't become best friends with the geezer who sits next to you at football each week – you're supporting the same team but that's probably about it.

Matt was initially surprised not to hear from the guy he met that night in Heaven, and then gradually became really upset about it, let down. He was also confused. It sounds silly to think that it occupied his mind for a good few months, but it did, even though he tried to forget it. He carried on going to clubs and meeting people, dating, but he couldn't help but compare each guy with the man he met that night. Eventually, almost a whole year later, in a sudden, idle moment, almost when he thought he had moved on, a lonely Matt decided to try to track him down on the internet. He visited a chatroom located in the man's home town and posted all he could remember about the guy as well as some coded references to himself that only the man would recognise. Amazingly, thanks to a friend of the man, who saw the posting and recognised the description, within three hours Matt and the man were chatting away on the phone.

2002

Two weeks later. The man Matt had spent months thinking about and had managed to find again was planning to visit London on business. He suggested he and Matt meet. Matt couldn't wait. He'd long since given up on the idea of a relationship with the man but he was determined to find out why he hadn't got in touch.

England were playing Argentina in the 2002 World Cup and, remembering that the guy liked football, Matt proposed they watch the match together in a bar over a couple of beers. They did. England, to everyone's surprise, knocked Argentina out of the cup. But that was the only spark Matt felt. In the light of day everything Matt had celebrated about the guy – his ordinariness, his lack of pretence – felt like a negative. They spent a pleasant but unremarkable afternoon together. The guy explained, when Matt asked him, that he simply hadn't felt the same way about Matt as Matt had obviously felt about him, but that he realised that Matt might have liked him and had therefore decided not to 'lead him on'. What he didn't count on was Matt tracking him down.

Matt felt like an idiot. What was it that convinced him that this man was The One? He realised afterwards that he'd fixated on the one person who seemed to make sense amid the giddy madness of Heaven. Based on just those few hours of conversation, he had created an ideal vision of this perfect man. He didn't really know him, and so the more perfect he had been able to make his image. He mythologised the guy. So in the end it wasn't about the guy at all – this was about Matt, and his desire, his need to find someone special to spend his life with.

Now the mystery of why he'd never called back was solved. He was just a normal bloke, and not the one for Matt at all. Matt felt, above all else, relieved. A weight had been lifted. Time to move on and to stop trying to find that special someone in the loud, smoke-filled clubs. Admitting defeat, he resigned himself, as many gay men do, to a life of flings and one-night stands. Vapid, short-lived pleasures.

And then he met a man with a ginger beard. Not his type at all. His name was Kevin.

Matt and David are fiddling around with the show all the time. Two sketches (an Indian restaurant routine which showcased Matt doing a series of quickfire impressions and catchphrases, and Matt's character Viv using her signature word 'gorgeous' to describe stained-glass saints in a church) have now been dropped entirely, and they've started writing together for a few hours each day, reworking a few of the live show bits they think can be improved (Dudley and TingTong's introductory sketch, which has now been seen on TV, and the Emily and Florence scene). At one point David confesses that the show doesn't really come alive for him until the great moment of release when he gets to play Carol yelling 'For fuck's sake!' to Paul's doddery old man stumbling slowly towards his seat in Sunseekers. And that's five sketches in.

The audiences seem quite happy with those opening five sketches.

Some nights each character will be cheered enthusiastically as soon as they appear. Other times the audience will just cheer for their favourites: Lou and Andy, Emily and Florence, and of course Vicky Pollard; always Vicky Pollard. David's theatrically Scottish hotelier Ray McCooney – unseen since the first series – gets a big welcome-back response most nights; and a roar of approval in Edinburgh and Glasgow.'

Every now and then audience members will come to the show dressed as their favourite characters. Amateur Emilys and Florences are a pretty regular sight; one time there are two young boys in beautifully accurate versions of Lou and Andy. And some of the fans even bring banners, usually with a variation on a catchphrase written on it. Sometimes with 'David, be my boyfriend' in marker pen.

When Matt or David notice a pre-teen in the audience – and there are plenty of them – it's a disconcerting moment. How do the parents explain the fisting and rimming references?

At least you can rely on the north. The two shows in Blackpool went like a dream, and the Opera House is such an evocative old theatre that they've decided they want to film the live DVD there next spring.

As Matt and David try to discern patterns in their audiences' behaviour while the tour winds on, they are also attempting to impose more shape and structure onto their own day-to-day routine. Most weekdays they write together in between breakfast and lunch and David's swimming. So they always feel busy. Weekends they encourage friends and family to visit. Both sets of parents have seen the show a couple of times now.

At first I was surprised by the frequency of visits from the families. People with 'normal' jobs rarely have their parents visit their workplace to see them in action. Of course, Matt and David's work is far more exciting, and there is a show to see. But there's more to it than that. Their friends and family members are visiting them several times on this tour, and that's because it seems only natural for Matt and David to get as much regular support as they can from those closest to them. It's why Kevin is here almost all the time with Matt. Why David loves it when his best mates stay with him in his hotel room (he makes sure the hotel supplies an extra bed). It's more than just Matt and David making sure they have people to keep them company – it's both of them creating their own close-knit support systems.

They're not living in traditional nuclear families doing regular jobs with fixed hours; instead, their existences are dislocated and irregular. And being on tour is making life even further removed from normality. They're away from their homes, moving from place to place, hotel to hotel, glimpsing wildly different parts of Britain. They're missing London, where everything seems available and within easy reach. When I've been away from the tour for a few days I make sure I return in time for the weekend and get the train to see them on a Friday morning. Often I get an anxious text from David reminding me to bring him a copy of the day's London *Evening Standard ES* magazine. One time I forgot and he seemed devastated. Since then, if I fail to get one in London before boarding, I often find myself stalking the aisles of the train looking for a discarded copy. And why is he so desperate for *ES* magazine? He tells me it's because it is always full of beautiful, eligible women. Which is true. But I also think it's because he misses all his favourite things about London. About home.

All the habitual elements of their lives are being disrupted by this tour. They're even having trouble keeping up with *The X Factor* (although Matt makes sure he records it every week). Matt can't get to see Arsenal. Even if David wanted to date someone (and he surely does), it would be difficult. His life, he says regularly, is on hold. He's also pointed out that when he and Matt first worked together and made their early forays into radio and TV, it was David who was in long-term relationships, while Matt was invariably single. Now that they're successful, the positions have been reversed. Matt's life at least has an underlying stability. Perhaps that's why David's parents are even more frequent visitors than Matt's.

They are also both palpably embracing the stability and support that they're getting from the people around them on tour. The cast and crew. Running jokes, post-show drinks at the hotel bar with Paul and Sam, karaoke sessions, old rock-tour war stories from Tony, tales of Gareth's sex life – it's all helping to give them a feeling of security while they're in this disorientating state.

They're even starting to use all the criticism they're receiving to entertain each other and everyone around them. I caught David joyfully explaining to a friend how the papers have even seized upon the decline in ratings from the humungous level of the first episode to the merely great figures of subsequent weeks as further evidence of the apparent inexorable decline of *Little Britain* – even though this is still by far the most popular series yet, and still the highest-rated comedy currently on TV. Matt and David's moments together are dotted with wry references to everyone hating them. They compare notes on the most outrageous criticisms they can find. At one point David excitedly finds someone on the internet writing, in all seriousness, 'Am I the only one that thinks *Little Britain* series three isn't funny?' Even better, he finds a reply further down the page: 'No, you're not the only one to think *Little Britain* isn't funny. I'm ashamed to belong to the same race as those who voted *Little Britain* as Best Comedy.' Matt giggles gleefully when he hears this.

Here's the peculiar contradiction Matt and David are faced with: they're being bombarded by more and fiercer attacks on their work than they've ever received before at the very time when they're reaching the height of their popularity, and when they're performing night after night to (mostly) ecstatic crowds.

In the end all the relentless criticism is put into perspective in an unlikely little moment. While we were absent-mindedly whiling away the journey from Newcastle to Liverpool in the back of David's car by thinking of all the media attacks on *Little Britain*, David received a call on his mobile. He mouthed to me that it was from Elton John. I edged closer to him to listen.

'Hi, David? It's Elton.'

'Oh hello!'

'I just wanted to say – don't worry about the bad reviews. I'm so fucking angry with all these critics. Just ignore them.'

'Oh thank you for that.'

'I mean it. Just ignore them. The series is great. This is so fucking typical of this country. As soon as you become successful they start criticising. I've been through it myself. Just ignore it.'

'I will. Thanks so much.'

'Well, that's what I called to say. Ignore them. Bye, David!'

So now David's trying to ignore the critics.

But there is a looming event that's been at the back of David and Matt's minds for the past few weeks: the British Comedy Awards, which take place live on TV right in the middle of their show in Brighton. They've been nominated for three awards: Best TV Comedy, Best Actor and a special writers' award, named in honour of Ronnie Barker. The organisers of the awards have made arrangements to send a camera crew to the Brighton Centre on the night, so the presumption is that Matt and David have won at least one of these awards. But all they know is that at some point during their live show, Matt and David will be interrupted by someone who will call the proceedings to a temporary halt in order to present them with an award. They've no idea at what point in the performance this might happen, although they've been led to believe that on the night itself, the producers will let them know roughly when they intend to intervene for the big moment. It's also possible they could win more than one award and have more than one interruption. And the Comedy Awards are notorious for overrunning. So the chances of the planned interruption occurring at the intended moment are minimal. Matt just hopes he won't be stopped mid-song. David would rather not try to receive the award while he's playing Sebastian totally naked and trying to put his penis between his legs. In front of seven million viewers.

18

14 December 2005 – Brighton: day 45

6.35 p.m.

'I nearly bought a painting today,' says Matt. 'But I ended up buying a postcard of the painting instead.'

He shows the postcard to David, who lets out a noncommittal grunt.

The painting is of the Brighton seafront by the pier.

'It's a big, smart painting,' explains Matt. 'You don't get the impact of it there. It's beautiful if you look at it up close. But it costs twelve grand.'

He's got a postcard of another example of the artist's work, of a deckchair on the beach. David says he doesn't really like that one. Matt nods and says the big one is the one he would love to buy. Maybe he'll go back there tomorrow and get it.

David's also been trying to buy a prized object. A Tardis. He was hoping to bid for the model of the Tardis actually used on *Doctor Who*, which was up for sale at Christie's, but he couldn't get to the auction because he was recording *Top Gear*.

Matt asks David how his interview with Jeremy Clarkson went. David says it was okay, but Clarkson seemed nervous and wasn't as in control of the situation as David had expected. David tried to engage him in a conversation about cars, but Clarkson wasn't having any of it. Matt laughs.

'Which award have we won tonight – do you know?' asks Matt.

'I think we've won two, because they're coming to us twice. One of them is the Ronnie Barker Writer of the Year Award. Which one is Denise giving us? Do we know?'

'I don't know, no,' says Matt.

All Matt and David have been told is that at some point during tonight's show, Denise Van Outen will interrupt the performance, walk onstage and present a Comedy Award live to Matt and David, and the whole thing will go out to six or seven million viewers.

Matt asks: 'So for Best Comedy we're up against *Extras* and *Catherine Tate*? Only three nominations?'

Yes, there are three nominations in each category.

'And in Actor there's us, Ricky Gervais and Chris Langham? It seems a bit unfair on Paul Whitehouse.'

'Yes,' agrees David. 'He must be thinking: "What the hell do I have to do to get a nomination?" He plays hundreds of characters in *Help*, doesn't he?'

'I've been kvetching all day about the speeches, and what we should say. All I can think for the Writers' Award is that we don't need to say anything that funny because we can make it all about the honour of receiving the inaugural Ronnie Barker award. And I think we might be receiving it from either Ronnie Corbett or Ronnie Barker's widow . . .'

'Yeah, I don't know when we're getting that award. There doesn't seem to be any provision for giving us that one. That's if it's true that we've won two.'

'That will really stick in the critics' throats, won't it?' observes Matt. 'Us winning an award for writing. They won't like the fact that we've won that at all . . . But it's hard to think of something funny to say because if you're there on the night, you're much more in the spirit of things, aren't you? You know what the atmosphere of the room is.'

'I think the funny thing about it will be that Denise is interrupting our show. And we can just stay in character.'

'That's true, especially if she arrives just when you're naked in the Sebastian sketch. Although that would give away the ending of the sketch.'

There's a variety of ready-made salads and chicken noodle dishes on the table of the Brighton Centre dressing room. David picks at one of the salads absent-mindedly and explains that he's too nervous to eat. 'It's odd not knowing what's going to happen. It's bad enough we're doing our own show in front of three thousand people, but we've also got the Comedy Awards to worry about.'

Matt says he can still manage to eat. 'I'm good like that . . . But have you heard about this Channel 5 documentary?'

'Oh God, yeah, the documentary!' says David, as if he's remembered that he has another thing to worry about.

It turns out an independent production company is making an unofficial TV biography of Matt and David, part of a series about the lives and careers of 'showbiz marriages', which will also include Tom Cruise and Katie Holmes and Ant and Dec. Matt and David have had a steady stream of their friends calling them to let them know they've been asked to take part in the show, and have of course turned them down. But now they want to know who *has* agreed to take part. Matt assumes that some of the people they worked with years ago might appear. Maybe David's old comedy partner Jason Bradbury, and Dominik Diamond. Apart from those, Matt can't fathom who would get involved. 'I'd really like to know though.'

David says it will probably be just a cheap and shoddy clip-job, but that it's still slightly disturbing to know this whole programme is being made behind their backs. 'You do wonder what they'll try to unearth.'

Gareth arrives. 'Hello, that's your half-hour call.'

Matt thanks him, and asks how he did last night in Blackpool. Gareth says it was a good night, and he picked up a cute boy in the queue waiting to go into the club. Matt asks how cute. Gareth shows him a picture he took of the lad on his mobile phone, taken while the boy was lying in bed next to him naked. 'Jesus,' exclaims Matt, impressed, 'he's stunning. He's like a blond Adonis.'

'Yeah, not bad,' says Gareth. 'He was really sweet too.'

'Did you get his number?'

'Yeah, but I'll never see him again.'

Matt laughs. 'Any more pictures?'

'Yes,' says Gareth, 'but they're very rude.'

Matt says maybe he should keep them to himself then, for the sake of decorum.

'Also,' says Gareth, moving on to professional concerns, 'I wanted to ask: after you get your award, is the plan to go back to where you were in the sketch?'

'Yes,' says Matt, 'we'll see what happens, but after we get the award we'll have to pick up and finish the sketch.'

'Okay. Is there anything you need in here?' asks Gareth.

'I did ask for a small boy,' says Matt. Gareth says he'll see what he can do.

Matt points out how Gareth's invariably successful attempts to pick up gorgeous young men on his nights out on tour prove that in the gay world it's all about confidence. Not that Gareth's hideous or anything, but neither is he, by his own bluntly honest assessment, a particularly 'hot' young man. But he is funny and engaging and above all bold. He knows what he wants and he goes out to get it. And he frequently finds it.

Just as we're discussing the peculiarities of gay male cruising, Matt's mum Diana turns up. She's wielding some DVDs and books for Matt and David to sign. And she's got a copy of the *Jewish Chronicle* on her, which has got an advert in it for the World of Kosher restaurant in a London street that's called Little Britain, featuring a photo of Matt as Dafydd with his head replaced by a cartoon turkey and a speech bubble coming out of his mouth, saying, 'I'm the only turkey in the village!' There's also a photo of Matt and David as Emily and Florence with a speech bubble saying, 'We are lady lady turkeys, yes we are laaadddies!'

'Look at that! Cheeky fuckers!' says Matt, perusing the ad.

'Yes, it is cheeky. Is there something you can do about that? Legally?' asks Matt's mum.

'I wouldn't imagine it would be worthwhile to sue a kosher food restaurant,' says David. 'I don't think it would get us anywhere.'

Diana takes a grape from Matt and David's plate. David tells her to leave the grapes alone. He's counted them and he knows exactly how many there are. Diana laughs and says sorry. "This is much nicer than the dressing room you had in Edinburgh, isn't it?' she says.

Matt explains that the dressing rooms vary from being very nice to quite horrible. This one is somewhere in between: large (though Matt and David are sharing it) but rather functionally municipal.

Matt's leafing through the day's papers, checking out the previews of the Comedy Awards. The *Independent* says it's a battle of the so-so comedies, *Extras* versus *Little Britain*. Matt lets out a yelp of wry laughter. David cackles mirthlessly and says to the faceless journalist: 'Well, *you* make a comedy programme then. It's not that easy.'

North London – 1980s

Matt's closest friend Jeremy's parents divorced when he was two, so he knew about the concept from an early age. But that still didn't dull the immense shock of discovering that his own parents were splitting up.

Matt can't remember his parents ever arguing much at all. Maybe that's what added to his feeling of surprise. There was no way he could ever have guessed it was about to happen. There was never much of a build-up.

One day their parents simply sat Matt and his brother down and turned the television off and told them that they'd decided to separate. His dad, John, had already been sleeping apart from his mum for a while. He would quietly slip downstairs after everyone else had gone to bed.

The first thing Matt said was: 'Is it my fault?' Of course his mum and dad tried to reassure him and his brother that it wasn't anything to do with them. Much later on Matt did find out the reasons for his mum and dad drifting apart, and it had nothing to do with him or his brother. The marriage had run its course.

Matt and his mum and his brother stayed in their family home after the divorce but it didn't feel the same to Matt once his dad had moved out. It felt like a sad place. And his dad had to go and look for somewhere new to live, checking out these really small, poky places to buy because he didn't have much money.

And then one Saturday morning John had gone round to look after Matt and his brother – because he used to see the boys at weekends – and he told them there was someone coming round to look at the house because it was on the market . . . and then he rather warily told them that actually it was a lady friend of his called Andie, someone he had met once or twice, and he asked Matt and his brother to be nice to her. He didn't say it was someone he was going out with, but it was quite clear what the situation was. She was the first woman he'd met and started seeing after the divorce from Matt's mother. They'd met at a singles' group that Matt's father had attended, and she simply smiled at him and that was that. They became friends because she seemed like a nice, happy person – although she had just lost her husband to a terrible illness.

So suddenly Matt had a new stepbrother, Darren, and stepsister, Barbra. His dad and his dad's new partner Andie didn't get married for a few years but it was obvious they were going to be together. When Matt first met his stepbrother Darren, he said, 'Oh no . . .' because he was one of the kids from Matt's synagogue who had been teasing him in Hebrew classes about having no hair.

But they became good mates, even though Darren is a Tottenham fan. Matt's mother dated for years but it wasn't till around the time that he lost his father that she eventually settled down again. Matt always felt he should carry on living with his mum, but his brother went to live with their dad for a while. For a few years, Matt found that difficult to deal with. But he and his brother got over it.

7.37 p.m.
The two-man camera crew stands by the side of the stage, while the first half of the show gets under way. With them is their producer, who's deep in conversation with Tony. They're hoping to go with the award presentation some time during the Sebastian sketch, but nothing at all can happen until 9 p.m. when the Comedy Awards show starts in London. Denise Van Outen is presenting the award, but she's off having dinner somewhere in Brighton because she knows she won't get to do her bit until well into the second act. After that they'll have a better idea of how the timing is going. If the show in London is running late, then anything could happen. 'At least,' says the producer, '*this* is a well-oiled machine.' He means *Little Britain Live*.

'Well, it is what it is,' says Tony, modestly.

'It's going to be like a game of chess,' says the producer. 'It'll be a minor miracle if it works.'

The TV producer offers to run through the rest of his plans with Tony. After the presentation of the award by Denise, Matt and David's show carries on as usual, but then, when the performance is finished, there are two more Comedy Awards requirements. They'll need to grab Matt and David from their dressing room about ten minutes after the show has finished for the presentation of the Ronnie Barker award.

'I'll need to get them upstairs where we'll set up the cameras.'

'You tell me two minutes before you need them,' says Tony.

'Okay. I'll need to do two things with them. There's no vision up there so they'll just hear things from London.'

'So it's going to be Ronnie Corbett speaking to them from London?' says Tony. 'And he'll explain what the Ronnie Barker award is about?'

'Yes, Ronnie will talk to them and Jonathan will talk to them.'

'And I presume it will be a slightly sombre moment?'

'It will have come off something slightly sentimental but then it will lighten up. And Jonathan will seal the whole thing off and say goodbye to the boys. The second thing that happens is Jenny Eclair will talk to them for an ITV2 interview for the show afterwards.'

'Okay. ITV2,' says Tony, wondering whether they'll want to do an ITV2 interview. 'Do you mind what they wear? At the moment they've got some dressing gowns to get into once the show finishes.'

'Lovely, that sounds perfect. It might be an idea for us to synchronise watches.'

8.21 p.m.

'They seem quiet. Very quiet . . .' says David. 'It's quite an impersonal space.'

Matt walks in. 'It's quiet out there, isn't it?'

David nods. Performing at the Brighton Centre is proving to be a chilly experience.

'It's the quietest I've heard so far on this tour. Is it because of the design of the auditorium? Maybe it doesn't feel like a communal event to them. It's a bit disconcerting though.'

'Well, they've got some big treats to come in the second half, so maybe they'll get more enthusiastic. But there's no atmosphere so far, is there?'

Gareth comes to tell them that it was a very quick first half. Forty-three minutes. It's usually upwards of forty-five.

David says that's because there was no laughter. He asks if that means they'll be starting the second half earlier. Because they need to synchronise it with the Comedy Awards. Gareth says that's all being taken care of, and that they'll start the second half at five minutes to nine.

Matt's getting antsy. 'It's just so hard to think what the mood at the awards is because we're so divorced from it.'

David thinks they should just worry about what happens onstage. 'We should create our own moment here because there's nothing we can do about what's happening down there.'

'Yeah . . . I just don't like not knowing what we should say.'

Tony says he's been told there could be some script changes or some running-order changes to the Comedy Awards. 'Oh, and Matt – Bob Mortimer's here.'

'Oh great. Shame he's watching the show with such a quiet audience.'

Tony explains that Bob was saying in the first half that the audience here is always unresponsive. Matt wonders why that is. If maybe they're slightly spoiled or something.

Andy the production manager says the audience here is always hard to please.

'Well, whatever it is,' says Matt, 'they ain't fucking laughing.'

9.03 p.m.
The Comedy Awards producer tells Tony that the show in London has started two minutes late.

Tony can only look at his watch and mutter: 'Oh. Good start.'

Denise Van Outen has arrived backstage and is looking at her clipboard intently. The two-man crew set up their lights and camera.

Tony goes off to check out how the TV show is going. He comes back seven minutes later and says, 'They're hardly cracking through it.'

As the Sebastian/Prime Minister sketch begins, the soundman fixes a microphone to Denise's frock. She's still surveying her script.

'Is it called the British Television Comedy Awards?' asks Denise. The producer tells her it's just the British Comedy Awards.

Matt's mic seems to be cutting out. He's saying, 'Are you ready, Sebastian?' But David doesn't seem to be able to hear him.

Tony says there's no way she's going to get onstage before the end of the Sebastian sketch. Matt and David will be wondering what the hell is going on, and when – if ever – they're going to get their award.

The only sketch left is the Dafydd encore. Once they get into Dafydd's song, it will be difficult for Denise to find an easy way to interrupt. Tony's shaking his head. He doesn't think Matt and David are going to appreciate the song being interrupted. The producer's listening intently to his earpiece. His hand is on Denise's shoulder. Everyone seems to be in a state of suspended animation.

Onstage, Matt starts to sing the song. He gets one line into it, when Denise gets the tap.

She strides on, mic in hand and says, 'Ladies and gentlemen, I'm ever so sorry . . .' She invites David to join her and Matt downstage. 'As you may

know, in London it's the British Comedy Awards live, and I have great pleasure in announcing that the winners of the Best TV Comedy are Matt Lucas
and David Walliams for *Little Britain –*'

Half the audience decides to cheer and get to their feet, swept up by the
excitement of it all.

David kicks off an impromptu acceptance speech, thanking Declan
Lowney, the director of the TV series, the producer Geoff Posner . . . (In
fact, Declan directed the third and current series. The director of the second
series, for which they've won this award, is Matt Lipsey. When Geoff mentions this point to Matt and David later, they're mortified and make sure
they call Matt Lipsey to apologise.)

Matt just says he can't hear anything and then thanks everyone who
voted for them. Denise says Jonathan's got something to say to them, and
over the loudspeakers they just about hear Jonathan tell them that Chico is
in the audience in London. Matt looks nonplussed and confused. David
does too, but says, 'Is it Chico time already?' to much laughter. Jonathan
thanks them and congratulates them. That seems to be it. So David jokes
that Denise should 'fuck off now' and let them finish their show. She laughs
and apologises for interrupting, and leaves the stage. Matt puts their per-
spex Comedy Award on the fake pub table and resumes the sketch from just
before the start of the song.

The audience cheers again. They've certainly livened up now.

10.06 p.m.
David is frowning. He slipped over before the encore because the stage was
wet.

Matt looks pale, shell-shocked.

'Sorry I was so distracted during Michael and Sebastian,' says Matt, 'just
not knowing what was going on . . .'

'I know. It was horrible,' agrees David, 'and the sound wasn't right, was it?
I couldn't hear anything. And I fucking slipped on the stage.'

'It was a fucking tough show, wasn't it?' adds Matt.

'Well, it was tough because they didn't come on in the show where
they said they would. It was confusing. And then when I ran round for
the curtain call I fell over. I just can't be falling over in the middle of the
show.'

Gareth apologises for the wet stage and says it was something to do with the dry ice. David tells him he can't worry about the fact he might fall flat on his arse in front of two thousand people.

While David has a shower, Tony arrives to talk Matt through the next pieces they have to do for the Comedy Awards. He explains the Ronnie Barker award presentation will be done upstairs in a room where the Comedy Awards people have set up a backdrop and speaker system so that Matt and David will be able to hear Jonathan and Ronnie Corbett. Tony says they should be prepared for it to be quite a sombre moment.

Matt plonks the Comedy Award they've just won on the dressing-room table among the bottles of mineral water, grapes, bananas and satsumas.

David emerges from the shower muttering: 'I just kept thinking when's it going happen?'

Tony says the TV people need to mic Matt and David up in about ten minutes' time. So they've just got enough time to meet and greet their guests, including Matt's mum and Bob Mortimer. But now David can't find his pants.

Sally the wardrobe mistress is searching the dressing room. No luck.

'I really do need my pants,' frets David. Sally can only apologise. She doesn't know where they are.

He wraps his robe around himself anyway, and goes to greet the guests.

10.22 p.m.
'You've taken our jobs away from us, David!' says Diana. 'It should be up to us mums to pick up your awards for you!'

David smiles. 'Well, you had your one chance. And you blew it.'

'Ohhh,' exclaims Matt's mum. 'Didn't you think we were brilliant?'

'Wee-ell. You were very good,' says David. 'But I think we can only play that card once, sadly. Much as I'd love you to become our permanent representatives at all awards events.'

Matt's mum cackles at the thought of it.

Tony tells Matt that there'll be another five minutes or so before they're due for the Ronnie Barker award. Bob Mortimer tells Matt that he should be very proud of the show. Matt's beaming. It's obvious that Bob is a bit of a mentor to Matt. Matt asks him how the making of *Tittybangbang* is going. It's a new sketch show being made for BBC3 by Vic and Bob's production company. Bob says it's going well, but the BBC keep telling them they need to make it more like *Little Britain*. Matt says he can only apologise.

Bob has given Matt a pile of about twenty Swiss chocolate bars, a present from him and his partner. Bob and Matt share a profound love of chocolate and have whiled away many pleasant hours discussing it. Though to Matt's slight bewilderment, Bob has never liked white chocolate.

Matt's mum notices the gift and says, 'Matt, you don't *need* any more chocolate!'

'I always need more chocolate,' he replies.

10.31 p.m.

'Oh dear,' says David, checking out the room where they're about to be interviewed on ITV2 and then receive their Ronnie Barker award. 'I don't think we should have those posters up.'

Someone has thoughtfully put up a handful of *Little Britain Live* flyers on the wall behind the chairs where Matt and David are supposed to sit. But it just looks like they're taking the opportunity to gratuitously advertise *Little Britain Live* in the middle of the Comedy Awards.

Matt agrees that it looks a bit tacky, especially when this is supposed to be quite a sombre moment in which they're going to have the honour of receiving the inaugural Ronnie Barker award. They insist on having them taken down.

The Comedy Awards producer sits Matt and David down on a pale blue sofa, next to which is a wooden table with a bucket of champagne on it and two champagne flutes, presumably to symbolise the celebratory glamour of the moment. Matt and David are told that they should look down the lens of the camera in front of them as they talk to Jenny Eclair for the after-show party TV coverage.

Action.

'Hello, Jenny Eclairs,' says Matt.

'Hello, Jenny . . .' says David. Silence. 'Are you there?' More silence.

The producer apologises and explains they won't actually hear Jenny and that he just wants them to say that they're here in Brighton and they hope Jenny is having a good time at the after-show party.

'So what are we saying?' asks David, falteringly. 'I don't . . . I don't understand what we're doing.'

The producer explains it's just a bit in which they can say hello to the ITV2 viewers. They're not going to be interviewed by Jenny Eclair at all. David says that wasn't what they agreed to do, and says he doesn't think it makes much sense. Matt agrees and says he doesn't feel comfortable with it. David says they would have done it if it had been the straightforward interview they thought it was going to be, but just saying hello to someone who isn't even there just feels odd. 'We're not that desperate to get on TV,' he says. Matt laughs.

The producer apologises for the confusion and says they should forget about the whole ITV2 thing, and just do the Ronnie Barker award bit, which is due to take place live in about six or seven minutes' time.

Matt's mum is watching from the back of the room and says it's a shame because she liked Matt's 'Jenny Eclairs' joke.

10.49 p.m.
Matt looks paler than usual. David's visibly jittery. They've won their awards, conducted their TV appearances, met and greeted their guests, but the overarching feeling of the night is that they couldn't hear anyone laughing during their show. They're playing here again tomorrow night, and they're coming back to Brighton next year on the second leg of the tour for seven more dates.

'I'd quite like to buy out the rest of the dates we're supposed to be doing here,' announces Matt. 'Do you know what I mean? I just feel like we weren't getting anything back.'

David says that maybe tomorrow night will be better. 'Maybe,' admits Matt.

Matt's mum arrives back in the dressing room. 'Absolutely brilliant!' she announces. 'You did so well . . . the pair of you.'

19

18 December 2005 – Cardiff: day 48

'That girl in *Swimming Pool*...' says David, as his water arrives, with three chunks of ice in it, 'is unutterably gorgeous.' He's talking about Ludivine Sagnier, whom he watched on Sky last night in his hotel room, after recovering from another disappointingly quiet show in Brighton (which was attended by Ronnie Corbett and his wife Anne, who told David that she thought the show's sound was wonderful). It's a bit far from the sex, drugs and rock-and-roll touring lifestyle.

Nearly two months in, he's hardly had any nights out at all. And when he has been out, it's mainly been to gay bars and clubs in Manchester and Edinburgh. David prefers going to gay bars, because there's never any hostility and it's always like going to a party.

We're in an Italian restaurant having lunch. Out of the window we can see Cardiff city centre, thronging with Christmas shoppers. We've chosen the most private table in the room, but it's such a family-friendly place that a steady stream of children come up to David asking for his autograph.

'Did I tell you what happened on *Top Gear*?' David asks. When he arrived at the studio, the researcher asked David if he minded that Clarkson might touch on the gay-o-meter in the *Sun*, so David agreed. 'Then Jeremy Clarkson's first question to me was: "So are you gay?" I went, "Well, who's asking?" And he said, "I am!" So I said, "Well, I definitely wouldn't have sex with you."'

Clarkson then made fun of the way David was apparently washing his car in a camp manner in a picture printed in the *Sun*. David asked how he's supposed to wash his car. Clarkson told him he would look more manly if he used a bucket. 'Do I look like the kind of man who'd own a bucket?' asked David.

David explains that luckily the programme is going out on BBC2 between Christmas and New Year, so hopefully no one will see it. He agreed to take part in the show because they arranged for him to borrow an Aston Martin DB9 for the weekend.

Of course the reason Jeremy Clarkson asked if David is gay, and the reason the *Sun* has its gay-o-meter, is that David doesn't come across as being entirely heterosexual. He has revelled in campness ever since he was a teenager.

He slightly regrets that time he told Denise Van Outen in a magazine interview that he is about 70 per cent straight, not so much the explicit confirmation that he's a bit gay, more the bald simplicity of the statistic. What he meant was that everyone has a bit of gayness in them, in his opinion, and he certainly does. "At least I'm man enough to admit it," he says.

And there's more to that part of him than being able to acknowledge that men can be sexually attractive too. Most of David's friends know he was confused about his sexuality. Then Katy came along at university, and he realised he could have a fulfilling relationship with a woman and that that was what he wanted, and what he still wants. But, he says, 'If I fell in love with a man now, I wouldn't hold his gender against him. Can I have the bill?' The last sentence is said to the waiter, not me.

The waiter nods, and then two kids come up to David, one of them wielding a *Little Britain* script book and a felt-tip pen. 'Well, you've got the book. I can't argue with that,' says David, and signs it, adding: 'Make sure it doesn't smudge.'

With waiters and autograph-hunting fans seemingly out of the way, David talks about how he thought he might be gay at one time. His interests seemed quite gay, and most pertinently of all, he was really scared of women.

The waiter approaches to see if everything is okay.

'Do you do a fresh mint tea?'

The waiter nods. David sips from his water. The ice cubes have melted into it now.

I ask David if Katy was worried by his sexual confusion.

'Perhaps,' he explains, 'But I was always honest with her. And it wasn't anything to worry about in the relationship because she knew I loved her and would always be faithful to her. Maybe deep down it might be a fear for some women, but I don't think it needs to be because if you love that person then you love that person. If not, you'd just as easily go off with another woman as a man.'

Yet he does know that the idea that a man might be capable of liaising sexually with another man is still a tough one for many people to deal with.

'I just think the gay male sexual act fills people with anxiety, in a way that lesbian sex doesn't for instance,' he says. 'I think there's a general cultural anxiety about gay male sex . . . which is why there are so many jokes about it.'

He also thinks people don't like to deal with bisexuality. People don't like to accept that sexuality is fluid and can change.

'For example, what happens when you're in prison?' he says, a situation in which so many men apparently start having sex with other men. 'Now is that because you suddenly accept that you have needs and you have to rely on men to satisfy them?' he asks. 'People are wrong to polarise things.'

He says he finds it amusing that people can't understand that a sexually ambiguous man like himself can have relationships with beautiful, desirable women. As if they find it suspicious, as if he's trying to 'prove' that he's not gay. As if he could be bothered to behave in such a contrived way.

The way David sees it is that for years he couldn't conceive of being attractive or fully formed enough as a man to be of any interest to beautiful women.

'I will tell you one time that helped define things for me, or at least gave me some kind of reassurance that I wasn't being untrue to myself. It was when we were at the Montreal Comedy Festival and I was talking to Graham Norton about the issue of sexuality, and he said in the end it's not really about sex and who you have sex with, because you can more or less enjoy physical sex with anybody, but it's about who you want to wrap your arms round at the end of the day. And for me, that's women . . . Ever since I fell in love with Katy, I have wanted to be loved by and love women.'

Yes, but maybe even that feeling can be fluid . . .

'Yes, I remember Eddie Izzard once saying to me, excitedly: "Well, I'm Britain's first out transvestite comedian . . . so why don't you become Britain's first out bisexual comic?" And I just thought, no thanks. I can't think of anything worse, walking around with a label attached to you. I still just want to be me. However confusing I might be for some people.'

David knows that people will always want to try to classify him, to put a label on him. But he doesn't want to compromise his own ideas about who he is. One of the many special things about Katy was that she didn't need him to simplify his identity for her. She loved him for who he was – in all his camp, occasionally cross-dressing, splendour.

A lad who looks about nine years old suddenly pops up at our table as David finishes his mint tea, holding a ticket for tonight's show at the Cardiff Arena.

'Do you know my name?' asks David.

The boy looks momentarily bewildered. 'You're from *Little Britain*!' he announces.

'Yes,' says David laughing, 'but do you know who I am?'

'You're David,' says the boy, as David starts to sign the ticket, '. . . or Matt?'

As the lad trundles off happily David says, 'Oh God. I don't know who I am.'

The default radio station in the car is Radio 2. This suits both Pete the driver and David, although David points out that 90 per cent of the time the music is rubbish, though every now and then Jonathan Ross will play Bowie or Dermot O'Leary will play The Smiths, as he is right now. 'The Boy With The Thorn In His Side'. That and 'Please Please Please Let Me Get What I Want' are the songs David says most define him. David says he often ends up in the car travelling from one venue to the next at around midnight when Janice Long comes on. And it's a bit like listening to the sound of a lonely woman having a nervous breakdown.

'If there's anybody out there,' he says, impersonating her soft, feminine Liverpudlian tones, reminiscent of Linda from the *Little Britain* university sketches, 'let me know if there's anything you hate at the moment. What do you really *hate*?'

David has the feeling that it's just him and maybe a rapist somewhere listening to Janice after midnight on Radio 2.

Matt dreamed he gave birth to a baby last night. And it looked just like him. He woke up feeling broody. David asks him if it was a painful birth.

'No, it was easy,' explains Matt. 'It just came out like having a crap. And the pregnancy only lasted six months.'

'That's because you're famous,' says David.

'Of course!' laughs Matt.

Matt wonders if his broody pregnancy dream was something to do with the stress of the Brighton dates, with their lack of atmosphere and audible response from the audience.

'I would seriously like to know how much it would cost for us to buy out the remaining Brighton dates. Just make sure we don't have to do them.'

David looks up momentarily when Matt says this, but doesn't seem to take it seriously as a proposition. And he adds that the last night's show was better than the one before. Matt says he could hardly tell any difference.

Adding to his general sense of frustration, he describes having gone back to the gallery where he saw the painting he really liked in order to buy it for the admittedly vast sum of £12,000, but it had been sold.

'That'll teach me not to just act on my impulse. I never see any paintings I immediately fall in love with. I saw this one, was a bit scared off by the price, even though I can afford it, and I've lost out on it.'

David says there's nothing worse than setting your sights on something and missing out on it. He hopes Matt finds another painting he likes as much.

'Thanks, David,' says Matt. 'I hope so too.'

1996

Matt used to watch comedy shows on TV with his dad. *The Two Ronnies. Morecambe and Wise. Only Fools and Horses.* And that was all he ever wanted. His dad bought *Monty Python* as soon as they came out on video and watched them with Matt on their VCR. They were one of the first families in the street to have a VCR, which they rented.

Matt's dad had been ill for a few weeks, and had lost a lot of weight. Matt was away on tour doing *Shooting Stars* with Vic and Bob at the time and hadn't realised how ill his dad was until he saw him one Sunday night and he needed two sticks to walk and looked incredibly thin. But his dad called him up the next day and sounded hopeful. He'd just set up a new business and was in optimistic mood. He told Matt that he had felt ill, but had been to a doctor who told him it was a virus and now he was on the mend. Then on the Wednesday, Matt got a phone call from his stepbrother Darren to tell him his dad had died. He was fifty-two.

He felt like his whole world had caved in. He was in shock. It was the saddest moment of his life. The biggest thing in his life. One of the manifestations of the shock was that for a few days afterwards he would look at other people's faces and not be able to piece them together to make a coherent whole.

It's not something he ever got over. He never saw it coming. And he never saw how much it would affect him, and the rest of the family. For a year after his dad's death, Matt couldn't really laugh or smile. He still has problems picturing his dad. He still has problems talking about him. And he still thinks about him every day.

Matt went to see his and Kevin's new house on Tuesday; it was the first time he'd been to see it since he bought it. He just stood there for one moment, with his brother next to him, and he said, 'God, I just wish Dad was here to see this . . .'

Matt has been shopping with Kevin in Cardiff city centre. They went to M&S, where Matt pulled his cap as low over his face as he could and wrapped himself up in his coat, but he got spotted and in the end had hordes of fans surrounding him. He still managed to find a nice hat and scarf, although Kev said he looked like John McCririck. 'Which makes Kevin my Booby,' says Matt.

Kevin grimaces.

'You don't mind me calling you the Booby, do you?'

'You called me that all the way through *Celebrity Big Brother* anyway.'

Gareth comes in to give Matt and David the fifteen-minute call. But before he slips out there's some probing to be done about his social life.

'Well, what happened?' asks David.

'Oh it was quite boring . . .' says Gareth.

'What, no cock and bum fun at all?'

'Oh, I had a bit of that . . . What happened was: there was very little in the club, it was really quiet, so I left and walked through the car park and immediately saw this lad who looked quite nice, so I nodded to him and he nodded to me and I said, "Come here . . . where are you going then?" And he said, "I'm going home," so I said, "Well, my hotel is just over there, would you like to come with?" and he said, "All right then," and that was that. Instant pick-up! So he came back to the hotel for the night.'

'And then what happened?' asks David.

'What do you think?' says Gareth.

'Did you fuck him?' asks Matt.

'No, I didn't fuck him.'

'Why not?'

'Oh, I just wanked him, and sucked him . . .'

'Well, that's all right.'

'But I woke up this morning,' explains Gareth, 'and he wasn't there. Vanished. So I had that instant panic of "Fuck, where's my wallet" . . . But no, it was all there . . . Which was good, because he had a trustworthy face.'

'Well, it was when you wiped your cum off it,' suggests David.

'Yeah, but the funny thing was,' says Gareth, not batting an eyelid, 'he left his pants.'

'Well, I often leave mine as a memento,' laughs David.

'Did you get his number?' asks Matt.

'No, but I gave him mine.'

'Do you want to hear from him again?'

'No. Not bothered; he was good for a night.'

'Well, that *is* a romantic story,' says David. 'Especially with the pants.'

'Actually that is one of your *more* romantic stories,' says Matt.

Gareth laughs, and says he's happy to provide as many tawdry tales as he can. Matt says he's having fun and should continue to have fun if he's enjoying it.

2003

There was a period when *Little Britain* was becoming a phenomenon, and Matt and David were becoming increasingly famous, when David acquired a reputation in the press for being a 'ladies' man' and a 'serial dater' and having a 'roving eye'.

The reasons for this were fairly straightforward. It was partly coincidental that in the long build-up to Matt and David achieving mainstream success, David had three long-term girlfriends. The last of those, a young actress, split up with David before he made the first series of *Little Britain*. But ever since success really arrived, David hasn't been able to find a woman he feels is the one he wants to settle down with. And he has been trying to find that woman.

To the tabloids, of course, it felt like they had a new single man to write about, who was handily meeting a series of famous women. And of course he was rather camp and comedically flamboyant, which only added to the intrigue.

In reality, David did meet some beautiful famous women with whom he hit it off and went on a number of dates, including Patsy Kensit, Abi Titmuss and Lisa Moorish. But he also met some unknown women, and dated them too. He wasn't behaving in a way much different to how thousands of single men in their early thirties behave. Except he was now in the public eye, and some of the women he was meeting were, unsurprisingly, in roughly the same field of work as him.

Perhaps the woman David came closest to establishing a long-term relationship with during this period was Patsy Kensit.

Matt introduced Patsy to David. He'd known her for a while, and one day she mentioned to Matt that she rather fancied David, so he told him, and David naturally jumped at the chance of meeting her.

It didn't take long for him to become very fond of Patsy, and her children. As he grows older, David meets more women who have kids or have been divorced. While he loves kids, and clearly enjoys bonding with them, he has also found it hard to know sometimes what his role should be with them. After all, it's not his place to tell them off but he does try to be loving and friendly and playful with them. Quite rightly, though, a mother is always going to love her kids more than any man who comes into their life. But even knowing that, David would have quite happily coped with the complications of seeing a woman with kids.

In the end, Patsy got a long-term job in Yorkshire working on *Emmerdale*, and she decided that, what with being a mother as well, she couldn't sustain a relationship with David. So just at the time when David was getting his head round the idea that they would be together for a long time, Patsy split up with him. On Valentine's Day.

The next day David went to a fashion show and bumped into a woman he'd met a couple of times previously and had immediately found irresistibly attractive. She said, 'Hi, David!' and he was so taken aback by the sight of her up close, by her sheer beauty, that he physically reeled and took a couple of steps backwards. He tried to chat with her like a normal human being but he was shy and nervous.

A couple of weeks later he went on his first date with her. They had a few nights out together, but she didn't want to take it further. Unfortunately, David couldn't stop thinking about her. She is X. He found her really warm and funny and was instantly smitten by her. He was also more attracted to her than any other woman he had ever met.

When it came to Abi Titmuss, there was some unpleasant snobbery surrounding their relationship. She was regarded by the papers as being a lower form of celebrity. But David found her incredibly sexy, and good fun. And after he met her and had some good times with her, there was no way he was going to judge her by her media reputation. If he met a busty glamour model who appeared on reality TV programmes but got on really well with her and was attracted to her, then he would happily go out with her. And hang the consequences. A part of him might even enjoy the consequences.

One aspect of Abi's personality did surprise him. When they first became friends, she was being stalked by a stranger, to the extent that she became afraid of going back to her own home. So David put her up at his flat and looked after her and she was hugely grateful. Far from the brassy glamour model, she was vulnerable, and David wanted to take care of her.

But such was the nature of Abi's life, as a woman whose fame and earnings rested so squarely on the proliferation of photos of her, that it was difficult for David, as a famous person in his own right, to be with her for very long. The relationship came to an end when Abi asked David to take part in an arranged paparazzi photo shoot with her, a request he turned down.

What perhaps links the women David has gone out with, or ended up in longer relationships with, including the actress, the last woman he truly loved and who left him most hurt and pained and distressed, is that he enjoyed the process of falling for them.

He liked them to have all the power. He loved being hopelessly in love. He wanted to be smitten. It always left him feeling vulnerable but maybe he liked that feeling too.

'I bet he really thinks he's it, doesn't he?' says girl A, in a deep Welsh accent. She's wearing a sheer black top, somewhat akin to a bra.

'You can tell he does,' agrees girl B, who's more demurely dressed in a white vest. 'We should introduce him to Candy.' Candy isn't her real name – it seems best to change their names.

What's so special about Candy? I wonder.

Candy, it turns out, only goes out with rugby players. Sometimes footballers, but here in Cardiff, rugby players are on a slightly higher rung of fame.

But David's off the TV.

'Yeah, she'd like him. He's even better than a rugby player,' says girl B.

It turns out that this bar, Tiger Tiger, is the place in Cardiff where the local sports personalities and their girlfriends hang out. Or, as girl B puts it, this is where you come to pick up rugby players. It was chilly and wet outside when we arrived. A line of miserable-looking young people in soggy casualwear stood waiting for the nod from the bouncer that it was their turn to gain entry. But in here now it could be a Spanish bar in the middle of summer. The boys are in tight T-shirts; the girls in skimpy tops and minuscule skirts.

Girl B announces that she's more interested in David's friend Matthew Rhys, who comes from Cardiff. He's cuter, apparently. She asks me what Matthew does. Is he a rugby player? No, he's not, I tell her, but I don't want to tell her what he really does because I'm not sure he needs her to know that he's a successful actor. So I lamely tell her she'll have to find that out for herself. This just makes her even keener on him. Girl A, meanwhile, tells Rhys Thomas, who's in town to see the show and is sitting next to me with his girlfriend Lucy (one of the stars of the BBC3 comedy *Tittybangbang*), who is suffering from hiccups, that she thinks I'm more interesting than David. She says this in a very loud voice. Rhys laughs and says I'm equally as interesting as David, and then asks if she thinks he's as interesting as either of us. She ponders the question and says he is as interesting as I am and that we're both more interesting than David, who has, by now, been accosted by Candy.

I only know the woman sitting next to him at the end of the banquette is Candy because her friend, or acquaintance, girl B, pokes me to tell me that it's Candy. 'There you go,' she says, nodding in David and Candy's direction. 'I hope her boyfriend isn't here.'

Oh dear. Boyfriend. Is he a rugby player? I ask. Kind of, is the peculiar answer.

Rhys is now deeply embroiled in conversation with girl A, who wants to express in every way she can muster how unimpressed she is by David. There's an odd tone to her pronouncements now. An almost obsessive need to assert that we are all just as good as, if not better than, the most famous person in the room. She says it's just typical that he'd be talking to Candy.

Rhys whispers to me that Candy is, obviously and undoubtedly, the sexiest of these Cardiff ladies who have gathered on this 'VIP' banquette. (It's been so designated by a helpful barman/bouncer who escorted us – David, Rhys, Lucy, Matthew and me – to this top-floor area, which he promised would be slightly less crowded than every other part of the bar.) Rhys then adds that he's finding himself unable to talk to girl A or B without feeling embarrassed.

Just as girl A has seemingly run out of different ways to express her disdain for David and his fame and everything else she can think of, she walks over to join in the conversation with Candy. She clearly knows Candy, and had no compunction interrupting their chat.

Girl B looks to the heavens.

Lucy's still got hiccups.

David decides to rope Matthew into his three-way chat with Candy and girl A. This way it doesn't look quite as though all the attractive women in the room are swarming round David, even though they are. Matthew bravely joins in.

Rhys asks girl B if this is the kind of scene that occurs regularly in Tiger Tiger on a Saturday night. 'Oh yeah,' she says, 'though I don't know where all the rugby players are tonight. Usually there'd be loads of 'em here already. Maybe they're playing away today.'

And does she know most of these rugby players personally?

'Oh yeah, we see 'em in here in the VIP area most weeks and chat 'em up. And sometimes spend the night with 'em. You two,' she says, indicating Rhys and me, 'you two seem nice. Nicer than the others.'

We don't quite know which others she's referring to, but I surmise she means we are, by our patently obvious discomfort and nervy social ineptitude, coming across as being rather likeably unimpressive, in comparison to David and Matthew, who seem more at home with all the attention they're getting. Of course, Rhys is a fine performer and comedian and actor too, but he's with his girlfriend, and has no reason even to bother trying to be smooth and seductive.

I notice that Candy and girl A have left David and Matthew. Rhys leans over to ask Matthew what's become of them. They've gone to the toilet, apparently. David checks that we're all right and happy and enjoying ourselves. Rhys says he's having a great time watching David getting all the attention. David smiles and says he has no idea what he's doing.

At that moment yet another girl arrives at David's side to speak to him. This one is showing off more of her admittedly impressive physique than any of the others and is flicking her flowing dark hair all over the place.

Girl B comes close to Rhys and myself to tell us conspiratorially that the new girl in David's zone is always here too, and that she's a top catch.

Rhys and I nod vigorously.

Girl A and Candy are back, and now all three decide they want to talk to David at the same time. David is starting to look embarrassed, although a part of him will be enjoying the attention. Within a few minutes he says maybe we should head back to the hotel.

Rhys and I enthusiastically agree to depart, but Rhys says we can always get a cab if David wants to use his car. The implication being that if David wants to go off with one (or more) of the girls he's been talking to this evening, then we won't get in the way.

'That won't be necessary,' says David simply.

Matthew decides to stay, because some of his Cardiff friends are on their way to meet him.

On the way out of Tiger Tiger, David is stopped at the bottom of the staircase by another girl, even more scantily clad than any of the others, who whispers something in his ear, and passes him a piece of paper.

In the car, Rhys asks his girlfriend how her hiccups are doing.

She thinks they've gone.

He says that's good.

She agrees, and explains that she once had hiccups for hours.

Rhys wonders if you can die from hiccups.

David says you can die from it, and in fact most people who get them do die.

'Rhys . . . Rhys . . . ask me where the party is!'

'Where's the party?'

'In my pants,' says Matt. 'I've always wanted to say that.'

Matt's recorded it all on his video/TV combi. All three hours of it. We're gathered in his hotel room expectantly. All of us, except for David, who's gone to his room after an exhausting Saturday evening performing the show and then socialising at the Tiger Tiger club. He enjoyed the experience for a while. Some of the women were attractive, and there was a certain glamour to the situation. David enjoyed the attention, but he wasn't inter-ested in any of the women and in the end he just felt like going to bed. But Rhys and his girlfriend Lucy are here, avid for the recording.

'I hope it's all come out,' Matt says. 'It may not be great quality, but I just pray it's all recorded.'

Russell T. Davies says he shouldn't worry, because we can always go to his apartment across Cardiff Bay where he's Sky-plussed the whole thing any-way. He points out we can actually see his flat from the balcony of Matt's room. Matt says that someone he knows threw his television set off the bal-cony of this very room, that this person always throws his TV off the balcony whenever he stays at this hotel. Not through any sense of anger, just out of habit.

'Apparently Dido throws televisions *into* hotel rooms,' says Paul Putner. 'Or drives the car into the swimming pool car park.'

Matt stands in front of his TV and video combi.

Russell says that's what he likes to see: a man with a telly.

Rhys asks Matt if he's using old-fashioned video-cassettes. 'Yes. Basically this is a new thing called a video. Well, it's a television combined with a video recorder. I bought it for *I'm A Celebrity Get Me Out of Here*. £79.99 from Argos.'

Matt suggests they whiz through the whole show because it's already quite late – past midnight – even though they don't know the result. Russell wants to know who everyone would like to win. Everyone shouts out 'Shayne'. Someone shouts 'Journey Shite'.

Russell says he wishes they still did *Pop Idol* over here in the UK as well as *The X Factor*.

Kevin asks us all if we'd like something to eat or drink, and orders a whole load of treats from room service.

Journey South appear on the screen to sing 'Don't Let The Sun Go Down On Me' and Russell says, 'They're not gonna win, are they?' Matt presses the fast-forward button.

Lucy asks if they're brothers. Matt says no, but their names are Len Journey and Ken South. Rhys says when he was little he couldn't understand how two people handily called Little and Large could meet each other and form a double act. Russell says Journey South are, at least, very well groomed.

Matt's friend Pedro, who's over visiting from his home in San Francisco, has no idea who any of these people are. Matt apologises if it gets boring for him. Pedro arrived today during the interval of the show at the Cardiff Arena, and I've yet to see him take off his white woolly beanie hat.

1999 – London

Matt met Pedro in late 1999. He was one of the first people Matt got to know when he started going out to gay clubs. He was unaffected, intelligent, a big Arsenal fan, and he lived near Matt. So they used to go clubbing together, and out of all the many people Matt saw at nightclubs, Pedro was one of the few he would socialise with outside of that world. What impressed Matt was his smartness, matched with his modesty. He never boasted. In his early twenties, Pedro devised an interface to use on mobile phones and was constantly being poached and headhunted by mobile phone companies. But Pedro gave all that up, including huge wages, to live with his boyfriend and study in America.

Everyone at Heaven fancied Pedro because he was so blokey. If Pedro wasn't there, Matt would phone him and say, 'Right – a Darren, a Steve and two Bens have asked after you.' The most beautiful boys wanted to chat him up. But he met this one bloke – a broad, brash American, totally the opposite of Pedro – and it was instant, genuine love at first sight. And they've been together for five years.

Pedro always wore hats. He used to wear baseball caps in particular. Matt could never get him to take off his hat.

Andy the binman comes on and belts out 'When A Man Loves A Woman'. Matt explains that when *The X Factor* started he thought Andy was going to win but as time has gone on . . .

'He's got blander?' suggests Russell. Matt nods.

When Shayne appears, Matt asks if anyone saw the headline in today's *Mail*: 'Rags to riches – Nerves tonight for Shayne, Son of a Rapist'!

Russell lets out his trademark huge roar of a laugh. Lucy observes that Shayne must win. Rhys says that in the videotape they're showing, which has been filmed in his family house, his kitchen looks awful, so the rags-to-riches tale must be true. Lucy says if his dad looks anything like Shayne, she wonders why he would ever need to rape anyone. Russell's laugh gets even louder. Warming to her theme, Lucy says that's what you'd want in a rapist: someone who looks like Shayne. Her boyfriend Rhys says he's glad she said that and not him.

Matt tells us all that Rhys once created one of the funniest things he's ever seen. He first met Rhys when he was a runner and then a script editor on *Shooting Stars* and he made a videotape of the final scene of *The Omen* put to the theme tune of *Minder*.

Rhys says it amuses him that Dennis Waterman claims he doesn't watch *Little Britain*. Russell thinks it's amazing that Waterman and Rula Lenska ever became an item and stayed an item for so long. Matt says it's a shame you don't see Lenska on TV any more. Rhys points out she was in *Footballers' Wives: Extra Time* on ITV2.

Journey South are singing 'Happy Christmas War Is Over' with their acoustic guitars, and Rhys wonders if they'll have kiddies singing with them. Two seconds later about thirty children wander on to the stage.

Paul asks, in horror, if that will be released as a Christmas single. Russell explains that no, they've all recorded versions of the same song, a new song, and whoever wins will get their version released next week, in time for it to become the Christmas number one. Russell pauses for a few seconds and admits how he's frightening himself with his knowledge of the inner workings of *The X Factor*.

As Simon Cowell tells Andy that his performance was wonderful, beautifully sung, Matt wonders if any of the judges will say anything horrible about any of the acts during the final. Russell says he hopes they will, otherwise it'll be a bit dull.

A few minutes later Shayne sings 'When A Child Is Born' and Simon tells him that it was the worst song so far, but that he turned a duff song into something quite good.

Matt says he liked it, especially the big key change in the middle.

Journey South perform 'Let It Be', and Rhys says he's sorry but he thinks they're going to win. Matt says the awful thing about them winning will be that they'll cry.

The camera cuts to the studio audience and a shot of Trevor McDonald swaying to 'Let It Be'. A cheer echoes round the room. Lucy asks which of Journey South is the oldest. Matt says the one on the left is the father of the one on the right.

Rhys is looking through the DVDs on Matt's hotel room table. '*I, Claudius*?'

Matt says he and Kevin have been watching it throughout the tour and that it's the most rewarding thing he's seen for ages. And Don Brennan from *Coronation Street* is in it. 'Isn't Christopher Biggins in it too?' asks Rhys. Matt says he is, and that he's a really good actor.

Shayne sings 'Somewhere Over The Rainbow'. Simon Cowell says that wasn't the best performance of the night. It was the best performance of the whole series. Matt points out that still makes it the best performance of the night. Russell lets out a huge cackle. Russell's laugh is fabulously entertaining and as huge as the man himself. And he must be about six foot six.

Shayne is crying on the TV. Matt rewinds the tape to see him crying again. 'That is quite sweet,' he says.

Kevin fast-forwards the tape to the moment when the third-placed act is announced. When Kate Thornton reveals Journey South are out, we all gasp. Russell lets out a huge bellow, and then says he almost feels sorry for them. Paul says, 'What a relief!' Matt thinks both the final two acts – Shayne and Andy – will have successful careers, whichever of them wins. Kate Thornton then throws over to Andi Peters, who's in the factory where the CD single recorded by the winning act is about to hit the presses. Matt asks Kevin to fast-forward the tape.

Andy performs the song that's going to be the single, then Shayne sings the same song. Matt points out that whoever wins will probably sing the song again at the end of the show, so Kevin skips to the end of Shayne's performance, during which Matt wonders what's happened to David Sneddon from *Fame Academy*.

Kate Thornton announces that ten million people have voted. Matt says Kevin should have stopped after five million calls. Then he asks Russell if he ever votes on these programmes. Russell says he gave up after the glory days of Will and Gareth, then Russell's boyfriend Andrew reminds him that they've often voted to evict people from *Big Brother*. 'Oh yes,' confirms Russell. 'I voted that Maxwell out. I fucking hated Maxwell and Saskia . . .'

Finally, Kate Thornton announces the winner: Shayne. Yelps of delight all round. Matt declares him a worthy winner. Russell concurs, and says he could be around for a few years.

As the tape finishes and we all say our goodbyes, it's 2.25 a.m. This is the latest Matt's stayed up during the whole tour so far, and it's been a perfect way to spend an evening, he says.

20

19 December 2005 – Cardiff: day 50

David asked for every Sunday newspaper, except the *Sport*, to be delivered to his room. There are none outside his door when we leave for breakfast, but Matt's room next to him has a huge pile of papers outside it. He says Matt won't be up for hours yet, and grabs four or five of the papers and asks me to remind him to replace them so Matt will be none the wiser.

At breakfast, the first story he reads in the papers is a classic tabloid kiss-and-tell about Robbie Williams.

He thinks Robbie's become almost immune to these stories. It must hurt if a woman with whom he's had some kind of proper relationship sells her story to a tabloid, but he expects a fling to end up in the papers. It's part of the deal.

David orders a full Welsh breakfast with poached eggs, no black pudding and some baked beans.

He stumbles across another tale of someone sleeping with a celebrity in one of the papers: 'Elton lost his virginity with me . . .'

'So it's a 34-year-old kiss-and-tell,' laughs David. 'That's brilliant.' Elton's civil partnership ceremony is taking place next week, so they'll be desperately scrabbling around for any story that will connect him to marriage and being gay.

David is in a state of high anticipation about Elton's wedding. Not only is he attending this historic, ultra-glamorous event, but he's also taking X and using the opportunity to make it as special a day as he can.

Now he's got to the sections of the papers with previews of Christmas TV, including the final episode of this series of *Little Britain*, and *The South Bank Show Special*. The *Sunday Times* is snotty about the latter. David sighs. 'We really can't open a paper without being slagged off,' he observes, with a sense of amused resignation. 'We don't know why or what we've done. All we're doing is trying to make people laugh, and now it's like we've done a bad thing and people hate us. It's like we're actually *evil* or something.'

The waiter, possibly alerted by David's anguish, asks if everything is okay.

'Yes,' says David, 'it was lovely. Can I have it all again, please?'

'You've already forgotten to do what I asked!' David whispers at me. 'We need to replace Matt's papers.'

Through a combination of picking up some replacement copies and tidying up the ones he's been reading, David does manage to reassemble the pile outside Matt's hotel room door.

'Christmas Day . . . *South Bank Show Special* . . . Melvyn Bragg's latest flirtation with the lowbrow . . . Their self-importance bears no relation to their worth . . . Awkward lunch with Barry Humphries. . .'

Matt's reading the *Sunday Times* TV guide.

'I thought our lunch with Barry Humphries was great!'

Matt then points out that on the next page there's a positive preview of the Christmas Eve episode of *Little Britain*. Shouldn't there be some consistency?

I don't think it works like that.

'No. Never mind, eh?' says Matt says. 'But sometimes it makes me wonder if we got it wrong somewhere along the line.'

Cosmo argues that the live shows get a fantastic response.

'Yeah, except Brighton!' Matt laughs. 'But you're right, Cos. I think of last night and the reaction of people. And it doesn't really tally.'

Cos says the papers never get the details right. He tells a story about how he worked on a Whitney Houston tour, during which the press reported that Bobby Brown hit her. Cos says he was there during the whole of this particular occasion and he didn't see anything between Whitney and Bobby. He saw the story in the paper a few days later and thought, 'Hold on – when did this happen?'

Matt agrees with Cos. He thinks about his life for a few seconds and comes to the conclusion that it really doesn't matter that much if every newspaper critic in the country sees it as their duty to condemn *Little Britain*. Matt and David have nearly finished this leg of the tour. Most nights they've had a euphoric response from the audience. They're playing to 11,000 people in Manchester in a few days' time. Then he and Kevin are off to Elton John's wedding. After that they're going on holiday to LA for Christmas, staying with Robbie Williams for some of the time.

'We're flying with Virgin Upper,' explains Matt, 'which is really business class but you pay fifteen hundred quid for it. I flew economy for years, then one time I bought premium economy and I got upgraded and the problem is once you've been in Upper you just don't want to go back. They know they've got you. That's why they upgrade you. So what seems at first like an act of kindness is more like giving you your first hit of heroin . . . so now I'm addicted to Upper.'

Matt's got a shoe dilemma. He's wearing his new brown corduroy suit which has been made specially for him but he's forgotten to bring any proper shoes. Can he wear trainers with the suit? Will the cameras even pick up on his shoes?

Yes, they will, according to Geoff Posner, who's producing today's special programme.

'I'm furious with myself because I haven't got any shoes,' says Matt to Aaron, the costume guy.

'Would you wear Marks & Spencer shoes?' asks Aaron.

'Of course . . .'

Aaron offers to pop into Cardiff city centre to get Matt some smart shoes from M&S.

'Are you sure?' asks Matt, not wanting to put Aaron out. 'I could do it barefoot like John and Yoko. Can I have cufflinks, too, if you're going to M&S?'

Matt looks at himself in the mirror. He likes his new suit, but says that he has no dress sense at all. When he was having this and another suit made, he asked what he should get, and the suitmaker gave him some advice and Matt took the advice. In the past, Matt has deliberately stuck to a simple, preppie look and worn lots of blue. Because he's always been overweight, he never liked shopping for clothes. Now he needs to wear suits fairly often so it's lucky that he can afford to get them made for him. 'I could come on in a T-shirt and jeans, but I think if David's going to look natty then I'd be letting him down if I looked scruffy.'

Rob Brydon arrives and waves at Matt as he walks into the dressing room. He's on his mobile, and laughing. He must be talking to David.

Rob is hosting the show today for BBC3, and will be interviewing Matt and David, as well as asking them the questions that will help ease their way through the three live 'commentaries' they have to record for the special *Little Britain* night going out on BBC3 on Boxing Day. The commentaries are like the audio extra you'd get on a DVD, but in this case Matt and David will be performing them in front of a studio audience. And once they've done those, they'll also be answering questions from the audience. Matt thinks it's all very complicated and he doesn't know how it will work. If it will work. But he's trusting Geoff will make sure it all runs smoothly.

Rob greets Matt and asks how he's doing.

Matt says he's exhausted but it's the kind of exhaustion you get used to. Though he's looking forward to the break in five days' time.

David arrives after his swim, and Geoff gathers all of them into a grim BBC Wales green room where some fresh fruit and cursory nibbles are available. Lunch will be served, Geoff assures them.

David asks Matt how he enjoyed *The X Factor*.

Matt says it was good but it went on and on . . . 'We were up till quite late. Did you hear us?'

Before David can answer, Geoff decides he has to explain how the show is going to work: 'The pattern of the show is that Rob makes a short introduction and then you guys have a chat with Rob.'

David asks if Rob is going to set out the stall of the show, and explain what will happen. Geoff says absolutely he will, and he'll remind people that they can use their red buttons on their remote controls to access the live commentary. Then, explains Geoff, there's a clip of Rob in *Little Britain* in the sketch where he has an erection. Rob raises an eyebrow.

David asks if Rob will take charge of the commentary section: 'Otherwise you end up just describing things that are on screen. I'd rather you drove it and asked us as many things as possible.'

'Oh sure,' reassures Rob. 'I'll be driving, David.'

Geoff explains that in the second half they'll bring on Ruth Jones to talk about playing Myfanwy the barmaid. Rob will ask her about playing a lesbian. 'Was she lesbian from the beginning?' asks Geoff. Matt says she was, kind of, in the radio show, and then they made her lesbianism more explicit in the TV show.

Geoff says they'll then go into episode two from the second series and explain how the episodes are a bit different between BBC3 and BBC1. The BBC1 versions are censored. They've picked out the bit where the old lady says, 'What that boy needs is a big fat cock up his arse.'

David doesn't think that Ruth is in that episode. Matt confirms she's not.

'Isn't it slightly odd to have her come in and do a commentary on an episode she's not actually in?' asks David.

Geoff says, 'Well, we will show clips when she arrives on set.'

'Maybe we can just mention that she's not actually in the episode,' suggests David.

'We can ask her, "What would you have done if you had been in this sketch?"' says Rob. Then he turns to David and points out that Matt and David will have to explain why they've chosen these three specific episodes to talk about.

Geoff says that finally they'll go to an audience question-and-answer session.

Matt asks what the questions are like. Geoff says they're variable. 'There's one about if Doctor Who split up from Rose, which *Little Britain* character could be his new companion.'

David sighs. Matt laughs.

'How many questions are there?' asks Matt.

'About half a dozen,' says Geoff. 'They aren't great . . .'

'Oh well,' says David, then, turning to Rob: 'Will you go out into the audience and do all your funny stuff?'

'Of course!'

2002 – Greece

David and Rob Brydon became best friends when they worked on a TV film for the BBC called *Cruise of the Gods*. It was a comedy set on a cruise boat, but in the middle of filming off the Greek coast the boat crashed. So the cast and crew had to move to a smaller vessel and everyone had to share sleeping quarters. David and Rob ended up sharing a room, which meant sharing a bed. So an intimacy developed between them. It was also a period of sadness and turmoil in David's life, and Rob was caring towards David. They started sharing the details of each other's lives.

They also developed characters they would slip into whenever they were together. The characters were an old married couple who had fallen out of love with each other. David would taunt Rob and say: 'You weren't like this when we were on the boat . . .' and Rob would call David on the phone and launch into: 'You don't realise how much you've hurt me . . .'

Rarely has a conversation taken place between them since they first shared a bed on that boat that hasn't revolved around their faux marital bickerings. To the frequent bemusement of observers . . .

Matt's shoes have arrived from Cardiff M&S, thanks to Aaron. And Anthony Head has arrived too, to discuss his role as the Prime Minister in *Little Britain* as part of the live commentary session. Rob Brydon and David are checking out each other's suits in the dressing-room mirror.

'It's Richard James bespoke,' says Rob, 'or hand-made, as I like to think of it. I've never been happier with a suit.'

But as Rob watches David fixing his tie, he realises they're both wearing dark blue, with white shirts. He thinks they're going to look like Il Divo, or worse, G4. 'I'm like the little tenor,' comments Rob. 'Stop looking at yourself, David!' he admonishes.

'I look like I'm going to get married,' says David.

'That'll never happen,' shoots back Rob. For a split second David looks genuinely stung. 'I wonder whether I should wear a tie,' continues Rob. 'I might just look like a shorter version of David.'

David suddenly bursts out in mock indignation: 'If you don't want to wear one, don't! Wear what you want. Just stop going on about it!'

Anthony Head smiles, fondly looking at the two of them bickering, and asks, 'What exactly is this show about?'

'It's about ME!' laughs David. 'Sorry, I thought you might have been told what it's about.'

'Not really.'

David explains that it's like a live DVD commentary, and Rob is hosting 'and hopefully you'll be joining in . . .'

David and Rob Brydon as Desiree and Roman, *Little Britain* **series 3, 2005**

Tony says he'll try his best. He runs his hand through his lush, long hair and wants to know how David is doing, how the tour is going. David explains that he's exhausted, mainly because of the swimming. Tony asks him if he's been practising swimming for a part. David smiles and says it's not for a part. It's a serious thing.

'Are you joking?' asks Tony.

'No, I'm not joking,' says David, 'and when you find out why I'm doing it you'll be embarrassed that you quizzed me like this and you'll want to write a letter of apology.'

Tony laughs and says, 'See you in there, luvvie.'

It's the first time I've heard an actor use the word luvvie without a hint of irony.

The set is decorated with huge, larger-than-life-size cut-outs of Matt and David. Matt thinks it's slightly freaky to be surrounded by giant representations of himself. David says he might steal them and decorate his new house with them; maybe create a special floor filled with them . . .

A few minutes later David is apologising to Geoff for getting over anxious. He's just a bit exhausted with it all. He's performed fifty shows. Swum thousands of lengths. Worked most of those show days on something or other, whether it be writing 2006's Christmas Special with Matt, or doing photo shoots, or being interviewed.

There's one more big challenge before Christmas: their first arena show, in Manchester, to an audience of 11,000. Then they can enjoy their Christmas break. And Elton's wedding . . .

21

20 December 2005 – Manchester: day 51

'I'm trying to think of it as just another gig in Manchester,' says David tentatively, while pacing around backstage. 'It's not like we can change the jokes or anything, just because it's five times as many people.'

David thinks of the previous big gigs they've done. The Albert Hall . . . Live 8. But neither of those were their own show. They were part of the bill. This is all down to them. It's their responsibility to entertain 11,000 people. Or as David puts it, not to embarrass themselves in front of 11,000 people. 'It is a bit daunting . . . this is double the previous largest number of people we've performed to.'

But he's supposed to be thinking of it as just another gig.

Matt's not even bothering trying to do that. He peeks behind the curtain and checks out the auditorium. 'Fuck . . .' He grimaces. 'It looks so much bigger. So many more people.'

David doesn't dare look.

'I wonder if they'll just all watch the screens rather than the stage,' says Matt. 'It'll be fine if they do, I suppose.'

They make their way back to their dressing room, which is itself a vast, cold space. They've already exchanged Christmas presents. David's got a top-of-the-range video camera from Matt and Kevin. David gave Matt a pale brown leather Prada travel bag. He thought of the idea when he saw Matt walking down the street with his rucksack.

Paul Putner has been surveying the auditorium. He says with the screens and everything it looks like the Blonde Ambition tour. Matt says it's the Bald Ambition tour.

'It's amazing to think we haven't even broken the back of this tour yet,' says Paul.

Kevin says he feels exhausted and he doesn't even have to do anything.

Matt says his voice is tired, and when he sits down and thinks about it, he's tired of the show too. Last week in the middle of the Dennis Waterman sketch he had a blank. He looked at David in his silly Dennis costume and for a moment wondered what the hell they were doing, the two of them, in wigs and make-up onstage in front of a few thousand people. It scared him, and afterwards made him realise how good it was that there was a break coming up. 'I'm glad we're not doing six more shows straight after this, let's put it that way.'

As he says this, he's slumped on his back on a sofa in the middle of the dressing room. Kevin gently rubs his stomach.

Paul says Marjorie Dawes will be interesting tonight because Matt will have to try to find someone fat to take onto the stage from 11,000 people.

'You know, the weird things is,' reflects Matt, 'I haven't really given it much thought. I just know I go down stage left and that's about it. I have no idea what's going to happen when I go into the audience.'

Paul the promoter arrives, yelling, 'Woah! It's fucking impressive out there!'

'Well, it's big!' says David.

'It is that!' shouts Paul. 'Seven and half thousand . . .'

'I thought it was supposed to be eleven thousand,' says David.

'Oh it will be. I mean we've got seven and a half thousand in already.'

'Well, the rest better bloody get here soon,' says David, laughing.

'Listen,' says Paul, suddenly adopting a tone of high seriousness. 'Have fun out there, David. Have fun. Enjoy it.'

Sally, who does the costumes, notices a big bruise on David's arm. She asks how it happened. David thinks it was when he slipped on the stage in Brighton. 'I did complain,' he says. 'I didn't want to be difficult, but the stage was wet . . . I better not fall over in front of eleven thousand.'

David goes to the toilet for about ten minutes and, when he emerges, points out that performing in front of 11,000 people is a great cure for constipation.

Matt asks if anyone's got a sick bucket. He says he hasn't felt nervous for weeks. Months even. But now – well, this is different. This is a whole new thing.

'Did it look like I wasn't enjoying it?' asks Matt.

Kevin and I tell him he looked fine.

But Matt explains he couldn't hear the audience laughing. He could hear a big echo a lot of the time, and his microphone cut out some of the time. It didn't feel like much of an atmosphere. All in all, it wasn't very enjoyable. Kevin says it was a different kind of atmosphere – lots of shouting and a bit of drunkenness, but lots of laughter too. Most of the 11,000 people are enjoying it.

Matt says he could hear some women shouting 'Matty!' in the middle of sketches. There's not much you say in response to that.

A slightly downbeat Paul Simon song is playing on Matt's iPod so he asks me to change it.

I click through the songs in his iTunes. Matt has unique taste in music. His favourite band, the band whose music obsesses him, the band he's seen live more than any other is . . . The Proclaimers. Not The Beatles or The Smiths or Bob Dylan or Madonna but The Proclaimers. He's aware that this is regarded by most music fans as an unusual choice. But he's not persisting in his love of them to be different, he's just proudly and unashamedly in love with their music. He's even written the sleeve notes to their *Best of* album. He's also very fond of the Pet Shop Boys, Robbie Williams and Ben Folds, all of whom I skip through on his iPod. He recently met Ben Folds, who asked him to appear in one of his videos. Matt found him a delight.

I've found a song I know Matt will love to hear. 'You're My Best Friend' by Queen. Queen is the band that first grabbed him and never let him go. They became a crucial element of his mind's landscape as soon as he heard them. In his early teens his mother used to work for an optician in Watford, and she would take him there for day trips. Matt would occupy his afternoons rummaging around the market stalls looking for second-hand albums. He bought a Queen one for a pound, loved it, and each week he'd go back to the same stall with his pound and buy another one, until he had all the Queen albums that were available. '*Sheer Heart Attack* was my favourite,' he says. 'The one that's got "Killer Queen" on it. But I was just crazy about Queen, and everything to do with them.' He tells me what happened when Freddie Mercury died. He was seventeen. 'I was absolutely devastated,' he says. 'As if he was my friend. One of my best friends. I got into a proper depression. So I decided to go to his house to pay my respects, dressed in black. And I left a note on his door saying, "There Can Be Only One . . ." which was the strapline to *Highlander*, which Queen did the music for.'

'We just wanted to say thanks so much for all your hard work,' says Matt, talking to the entire cast and crew who have been gathered backstage just before the start of the second half. 'We really appreciate everything you do . . . from getting the show in and out of each venue to dealing with us . . .' The crew laugh in unison.

'Yeah,' chips in David. 'We really are grateful for everything you do and we know it's not an easy show to work on, and that we're not easy either –' more laughter '– but the show just wouldn't be a success without all of you. So we hope you all have a really good break and a fantastic Christmas. And see you in the New Year.'

Applause.

Act two begins with David as Anne doing *Stars In Their Eyes*. A drunken woman somewhere in the middle of the front stalls shouts out 'Dave!' Then she shouts it repeatedly, perhaps every ten seconds, about fifty times in total. Her mates join in, with some general but incoherent shouting. A woman in the row in front of them asks them to stop, and gets a pint of beer thrown over her. She flees to the toilet in tears. An impressively huge security man moves towards the drunken gaggle of women. They try to protest, but he removes them within a few seconds, with ruthless efficiency.

'I enjoyed it a little more the second half. But somehow you feel a little bit more responsible when there are so many people there. You shouldn't necessarily, but you do. And there was a group of drunk people quite near the front . . . they were a bit distracting.'

Kevin explains that they were eventually thrown out when one of them threw a pint over some poor woman.

'Really?' says Matt, shocked. 'That's disgusting. Was she all right? I could hear them shouting things like "Maaaatyyyyy!" Really funny.'

'I thought they were either drunk or mentally ill,' comments David.

Kevin says the woman who had the beer dumped over her was in tears.

Matt suggests we find her and give her a T-shirt. Kevin and I attempt to track the victim down but by now the entire auditorium is empty. Eleven thousand people have gone home.

When we arrive back in the dressing room, David is just getting into his pants. He asks if the direction of the screens was good, and whether there were any close-ups of his bottom.

I assure him that the audience will certainly now have full knowledge of every contour of David's backside.

'Having the screens helps,' points out Matt. 'It's quite addictive to watch the screens. Maybe we should have them for more of the venues.'

Tour supremo Phil McIntyre arrives. 'Hey!' he yells. 'What was that like? You got a standing ovation!'

'Did we?' asks David. 'I saw a few people standing . . .'

'Oh, there were more than a few.'

'Maybe they were putting on their coats,' says David.

'Definitely.'

'I think the screens are great,' says Matt, 'because the people who are nearer the front who can normally see can still see, but the people behind them have a more enhanced experience . . . It took me a while to get used to it. When we first came on I think I was being quite big, but then I calmed down a bit and did it normally.'

Phil points out that the great thing about the screens is that you can be as small as you want to be because the whole audience can see the expressions on the performers' faces. Phil adds that the sound was great, which takes David by surprise. He was hearing a lot of echo from the stage, which he didn't realise was going to happen. 'I don't think you can have your best best gig in a place like that,' he says, 'but I think we delivered . . .'

'I saw another comedian play here,' announces Phil, 'who shall remain nameless.'

'Eddie Izzard?' says Paul.

'No, I'm not saying . . .'

'Bob Carolgees and Spit the Dog?' says David.

'Close!' Phil laughs. 'Anyway, he got about a tenth of the response that you guys did . . .'

Matt wonders whether their audience was the same number of people that Newman and Baddiel played to. Phil explains that it was double their audience. They only did 5,600. They started in the round, and they blanked off half the seats. They only had tickets sold on three sides of the arena and they only sold every other row of seats. 'But good luck to 'em,' says Phil, ''cause they did a really good job of publicising it.'

David laughs and says Phil is the fount of live comedy knowledge, and thanks him and Paul very much for coming. Phil says they wanted to be here in case it didn't work, in case the arena environment somehow proved unsuitable for this show.

'And if I was you I'd be celebrating,' says Phil forcefully, 'because that is an achievement. That is a big step . . . to play to that number of people, and to get a standing ovation.'

Paul joins in: 'It's a triumphant night . . . a historic night for comedy!'

'Yeah, you should be congratulating yourselves . . .' says Phil, really picking up steam now, 'the sketches delivered so well . . . the costumes and performances . . . it worked so well. The whole thing.'

'I was pleased the make-up still looked good on the big screens,' says Matt.

'The wigs looked great. Well worth the money!' adds Phil.

Matt smiles. 'That's why we wanted to spend all that money on the wigs . . .'

'Well, now we're glad you did!' says Paul, and laughs raucously.

Paul Putner walks into the room, towelling himself off, and gets a big round of applause and cheers.

The other Paul says: 'Eleven thousand people laughing about you rimming Shakin' Stevens . . . how did that feel?'

Paul laughs.

David mentions the echo again, and says that it sounded weird from the stage. Phil asks him when he first noticed the echo. Right from the beginning, David tells him.

'Hmm . . . have a word with Ian,' Phil says to Paul. 'See if there's anything we can do about the echo . . .'

'Have him shot,' says David, deadpan.

David's talking about how great it feels to have Phil and Paul on your side. He says that before they started the tour he didn't really have much of an idea what they actually did, what their jobs were, as the promoters of the tour, and now all he knows is that they do a pretty impressive job – whatever it is.

We're caught in the traffic coming out of the show.

David's in a good mood now. He and Matt have proved they can play their show to an arena-sized audience. Now they've got a month's break before the second leg of the tour. And tomorrow is Elton John and David Furnish's wedding, with X.

'I'm meeting up with her at 5 p.m., a few hours before it's supposed to start. And hopefully I've made sure it will be a special day for her.'

He has bought her a heart-shaped, diamond-encrusted pendant necklace. This is David's Christmas present to X. He's hoping she gets the not entirely subtle symbolism. But he doesn't know what will happen. He doesn't know if she'll go along with the romance of the whole day. He hopes she'll be swept up by it.

I ask him what he'll be wearing. He says he's going for a traditional look. Traditional, but hopefully immaculate. His jacket has got a shawl collar, a bit like the one Morrissey wears in *The First in the Gang To Die* video. He's half fretting wildly about what might happen with her, and half just looking forward to the whole event.

It's got him thinking about weddings in general. He says that there are elements of the traditional marriage ceremony he loves. 'The phrase "With my body I thee worship" ... pure poetry ... It's a wonderful way of describing sex.'

He says that he would get David McAlmont to sing at his wedding, and maybe Shola Ama. And he would want to get married like James Bond in *On Her Majesty's Secret Service*. He'd like to drive off in an Aston Martin decked with flowers. That's the plan. Without the bit that follows when Bond's wife gets shot five minutes after they get married.

'Oh God,' he says, going back into anxious mode. 'I hope she's not freaked out by it all. I hope there's not too much pressure on her . . . Maybe I'll just end up copping off with David Furnish.'

Shania Twain's 'You're Still The One' comes on his computer's iTunes. He says it's such a beautiful song. The only song of hers he likes. But it's perfect. If Bob Dylan had written and sung it, everyone would admit it's brilliant.

Pete asks David what he'll be doing for Christmas. David explains that he'll be going on holiday to Egypt on Boxing Day for a week or so, and then he's hooking up with Denise Van Outen for a trip to the Maldives.

Before that, he'll be with his family in Banstead for the full Christmas Day family experience. He'll be going with his parents and his sister to his Aunt Viv and Uncle Les's in the evening. And he knows exactly what will happen: he's very aware that it's slightly strange when someone is on TV and you bring that person into a family environment. He is at pains to point out that he's not special just because he's famous, and of course everyone is, in their way, special, but he also knows that his mum is very proud. She has a totally natural and understandable tendency to throw the spotlight on him all the time. He thinks at some point she'll ask David to talk everyone through the fact that he's just played to 11,000 people, and he does think it's lovely that she's so excited by it all, and he admits that he does like the attention, but he also worries when it's at the expense of others. He also knows that she'll wants everyone to gather round and watch *The South Bank Show Special* on Christmas night. He assumes the family will be interested in it, but even then it might be a challenge to stay up and watch it at eleven o'clock at night. But they probably will.

Pete laughs his hearty, northern laugh and says he might force 'the wife' to watch *The South Bank Show* too.

As Morrissey sings 'Trouble Loves Me', the car pulls up at David's flat.

'Thanks very much, Pete,' David says warmly. 'It's been very painless. All I wanted to have to worry about for the past few months was doing the show, and that is all I've had to worry about, mainly thanks to you.'

They shake hands.

'See you in a month,' says David, 'and have a great Christmas.'

The Manchester show turned out to be a fitting climax to the year. Not just the calendar year, but the months of planning and work that have gone into producing the show. It felt like all the elements of the production were working in sync by the time the Manchester Arena date arrived. So much so that, after fifty performances, everyone was locked comfortably into the routine of the show. Having to do it for an audience of 11,000 people roused everyone. It was back to the tension and excitement of that first rocky night in Portsmouth. In the end it was a celebration of how far everyone had come. A huge family celebration.

Now they all know they can present this show to that number of people. They've learned how to do week after week of a big, live comedy production. And they've learned how to do it in an arena. The days of wondering if the vomit machine was going to work seem a very long time ago.

Of course glitches and cock-ups still happen. It would be boring if they didn't. The moments when the show goes wrong are the times when it feels special. As long as the audience isn't utterly bewildered. Matt and David know every ebb and flow of their performance, so there are certain key times each night when they can screw up a line, forget a word here or there and that will be the excuse to veer merrily off-script. The longer they end up ad-libbing and freewheeling, the more the audience laps it up, and the more fun Matt and David have.

In the same way, they lap up the audience-participation bits. When David pulls up a young lad from the audience and when Matt finds a fatty in the crowd, they're suddenly let off the leash. Not too far off, but enough to provide another escape into unpredictability each night.

Quite what the routine of the tour would have done to Matt and David's minds without these improvised moments each night doesn't bear thinking about. When the tour was about to start, both of them blithely predicted they would go mad within weeks of doing the same show each night. They've had their moments, but as I watched them finish the show in Manchester and set off for their Christmas and New Year break, they seemed entirely happy. They couldn't wait to get out of there, but they'd maintained their sanity. Helped in no small part by Tony, Gareth, Ian, the wardrobe and make-up women, Paul, Sam. And especially Cos and Pete. All of them, the entire cast and crew, are essentially operating as Matt and David's support team. They're all working to keep Matt and David happy. (While making the show function at the same time, of course.) And it's not because they're the stars. It's more that everyone knows this tour is the culmination of Matt and David's vision. Conversely, Matt and David have come to rely on them. Their team.

David can't wait to relax, read his books, be with his friends and family, and go off to Egypt and the Maldives. But he also told me he won't know what to do with himself when he gets home. He'll suddenly have to prepare his own meals, do his own shopping, make his own decisions. Luckily he's got Elton's wedding to take his mind off this whole new world of uncertainty. Both he and Matt told their drivers how much they'd miss having them around.

It seems entirely natural that Matt and Kevin have taken to referring to Cosmo as 'Uncle Cos'.

Part Three

David and Denise in the Maldives

22

Christmas 2005 – Windsor

There was a huge traffic jam as all the VIPs tried to arrive on time. An endless parade of limos and chauffeur-driven cars, surrounded by dozens of paparazzi and camera crews from TV news stations. They had to sit there in the back of their cars, trying to stay calm and look normal and happy and not too irritated while flashbulbs exploded in their faces and cameramen shone blinding white lights through their windows.

But once they managed to arrive, it lived up to all expectations.

As soon as he walked into the room, David saw Michael Parkinson, and went to say hello to him. Standing nearby was a heavily bearded Michael Caine, who said to Parkinson, 'Can you introduce me to David?' Parkinson did the honours and Michael Caine proceeded to tell David that he and his wife Shakira were big fans of *Little Britain*. David asked, 'Are you growing your beard for a part?' and Caine said, 'Oh let's not talk about me, let's talk about you.'

David was thrilled that Michael Caine even knew who he was.

There were other surprises. David didn't expect to end up chatting for quite a while to the glamorous wife of a Premiership footballer. She had a heavy continental European accent, a bit like Bubbles-lite. Within seconds of speaking to her, she told him, 'I'm so *bored*!' In answer to more or less anything David asked, she replied, 'I'm so bored!' He immediately thought she could be the germ of a new *Little Britain* character.

Matt and Kevin would never have expected to spend so much time with Dhani Harrison, and to be so enchanted by him. Matt had met him before, at Stella McCartney's Christmas Lights event. But after talking to him this time round, he has decided Dhani is the coolest man on earth.

It was also as if every person Matt and David had ever done on *Rock Profile* was gathered in one place.

They sat with their guests for the night, Kevin in Matt's case of course, and David's date X, and on their table were Lee Hall, who wrote *Billy Elliot*, and Peter Kay and his wife Susan. Peter was on brilliantly funny form. He made Matt laugh like a drain. David couldn't imagine sharing a table with anyone funnier.

And while it was nice to see old friends like Graham Norton, Stephen Gately and the Pet Shop Boys, Matt was especially excited to meet 'the great' Elvis Costello, who seemed genuinely impressed when Matt listed his favourite albums of his, making sure to pick all the obscure ones, like his album with Anne Sophie Von Otter, and work with composer Richard Harvey and a fairly obscure track called 'Couldn't Call It Unexpected No. 4', which Elvis said was his own favourite thing he'd ever done.

George Michael was also there, despite recent public disagreements with Elton, and he commiserated with Matt, saying that he had a similar experience with the same *Independent* columnist.

Oddly, Matt didn't actually get to speak to David Furnish all night.

David spoke to Prince Andrew for a while. He was perfectly engaging, but when David tried to press him on whether the royal family watched *Little Britain*, he became rather more coy. It would, of course, have been totally indiscreet and against protocol for the prince to have admitted that his mum watches it, but David still got the feeling that she might have sneaked a peek.

But for David, the most magical element of the whole event was just being there with her, X. She seemed to appreciate all the efforts David had made to turn it into as special a day as possible. She cried a little when he gave her the diamond heart necklace, and didn't want to accept it until David insisted.

Back in the hotel room she asked David, 'Why have you been so kind and generous to me? No one has ever been this generous to me.'

David looked out of the window for a moment and then said what he wanted to say for years: 'It's because I'm in love with you . . .'

She didn't answer. But she looked rather sad, and then hugged him.

In the end, that was it. David started to think that maybe there wouldn't be a future for him and her. But he still left room in his mind to think that if he carried on being the best man he could then maybe he could still win her over. Just sitting there with her at the end of the night taking out her hairclips for her felt like one of the most erotic experiences of his life.

Matt exchanged Christmas presents with Kevin the next night. And Kevin had a surprise for Matt. It turned out that the Philip Dunn painting that Matt had seen in the gallery in Brighton a few weeks ago and had fallen in love with and gone back the next day to buy, only to find that it had been sold, had been bought by Kevin. For Matt. And he'd kept it secret all this time. Until Christmas. Matt was gobsmacked.

He flew off to Miami with Kevin a very happy man.

David spent a very pleasant Christmas with his parents, and contrary to his expectations, they didn't all have to watch *The South Bank Show Special* together on Christmas night at his aunt's house. Instead they watched it at his parents', on Boxing Day morning in their pyjamas, and it was rather good fun.

BOXING DAY EVENING
Text from David: 'I think I really am in love with her . . .'

29 DECEMBER 2005
The *Sun*'s Bizarre column has pictures of David with lots of bags full of last-minute Christmas shopping. He's asked me to keep him informed of any mentions of him in the papers while he's away, so I text him to tell him about these harmless shots.

He texts back: 'Just seen the pyramids and the sphinx. Stunning. And met Jefferson Hack at the airport so have hung with him a bit. Do I look fat in the pictures?'

He looks fine in the pictures.

Another text: 'I keep on replaying the night of the wedding in my head. I am so smitten.'

NEW YEAR'S EVE, 2005

10.14 a.m.: text from David in Egypt. 'Have you seen today's *Sun*? Apparently there is a picture of me in a wetsuit. I would like to know what they wrote.'

I rush to buy the paper. His cross-Channel swim is supposed to be a secret. There's due to be an announcement about it in a few months' time, when official media partners will be involved and when the BBC have started filming their Sport Relief documentary about the whole thing. Luckily the *Sun* doesn't seem to know why David was in his wetsuit swimming in a lake. They've just got the photos. The article says he's been 'training'. But not for anything in particular. I text David the good news.

His reply: 'Good. Thank God for that.'

NEW YEAR'S DAY, 2006

David is on the front of the *Sunday Mirror*. The headline is 'TV David wanted me to be his Lay-dee'. The sell is 'Exclusive: *Little Brit* star and lap-dancer'. It takes up half the front page. The article is about one of the women who spoke to David when we were in the Tiger Tiger bar in Cardiff. I remember them chatting for about a minute. Yet she's got her story on the front page of the *Mirror*. It's a would-be kiss-and-tell, but as she herself admits, she didn't actually have any kind of sexual liaison with him. She just gave him her number. She's got her story on the front page by claiming that she turned him down. Above the story are the words, 'Showbiz exclusive: The only girl in the village to say No to randy David.' It's a story about a famous person not having sex with a lap-dancer.

Later, on the phone from Egypt, David is intrigued to know how much a woman gets for selling her story about not having sex with a celebrity to a national newspaper. I remark that tabloid-journalist friends of mine often describe how some young women deliberately target clubs where they know they'll find famous men they can try to seduce with a view to getting a story out of it.

I call a contact of mine who knows people at the *Mirror*. The lap-dancer got a couple of thousand pounds. Not much for a kiss-and-tell. Because there was nothing to tell.

8 JANUARY 2006

David is on holiday now with Denise Van Outen.

'We've arrived in the Maldives,' he says by text. 'You'll be pleased to know we are staying in separate villas so there will be no nooky. Saw a bit of Celeb BB. Astonishingly good. Do keep me up to date. Dx.'

10 JANUARY 2006

There are photos in all the tabloids of David and Denise sunbathing on the beach. David can be seen reading Alan Bennett's book *Writing Home*. Denise is reading *Paula, Michael and Bob*, about Paula Yates, Michael Hutchence and Bob Geldof. David looks rather pale and pasty. He'd only just arrived and taken his first opportunity to sit on the sun-lounger when the photographer struck. Denise is looking bronzed and glowing in the photos.

David texts me and asks if he looks fat.

I text back one word: Lithe.

15 JANUARY 2006

David's very excited about *Celebrity Big Brother*, especially now he's heard that Sir Jimmy Savile has entered the house. I have to break the news that Savile is only in there for one day. He tells me something else exciting is happening over in the Maldives. Denise has set him up on a blindish date with a famous and sexy female pop singer. Denise is fed up with him talking about X. Not only has she had to endure David wittering on incessantly about his love for X, but she also had to convince him not to send a letter he had written to X, expressing his deepest feelings for her. So in turn for getting David to agree not to send the letter, she tells him she'll set up a date with this very beautiful pop star. That sounds like a good idea. Take his mind off 'her'.

'Yes,' he says, 'but I love her.'

He and Denise have also made a vow: if neither of them has found a life partner within the next two years, they'll marry each other. David has visions of dragging Denise tearfully down the aisle.

17 JANUARY 2006

X has been away working in Los Angeles, and David tells me he wants her to do well, but not that well, as he wants her to come back to England and live with him.

Then: 'She is so beautiful sometimes I find it hard to look at her.'

So is he still going on the date with the pop singer?

'I am meeting up with her. I remain in love with X, but I haven't heard from her for weeks. I don't think she is into the idea of going out with me at all. Oh life is painful.'

19 JANUARY 2006

Towards the end of David's first day back from holiday, David gets a call from 'her' in LA. They talk for an hour. At the end of it he feels very happy.

Then he explains: 'She said she has worn the necklace a lot.'

That's a good sign. She's been thinking about you . . .

'Not as much as I've been thinking about her.'

He explains that X is staying out in LA for a while to see if she can get more work. He doesn't know when he will be able to see her again, but he does now think there's hope again. She told him she wasn't seeing anyone over there. This is important news.

'That's about as serious as we got. We just talked about other stuff for an hour, but it was still lovely.'

David's going to send her some flowers for her birthday on Monday, and a pair of Chloé shoes.

'I hope she likes them,' he says. 'That's all people like us have got, isn't it? Hope. We've got to cling to it.'

22 JANUARY 2006

David's been on his date with the pop singer. Denise came along too, as David was a bit scared to go on his own. He had a nice time, though nothing happened between them.

Would you like to see her again?

'Not really. My heart was elsewhere.'

Part Four

23

23 January 2006 – Bloomsbury Theatre, London

'With such a silly little joke, there's really no point doing it unless everyone gets it immediately . . .'

It's a Typhoo/Thai food pun. Matt as TingTong brings David as Dudley some Typhoo. He was expecting some Thai food.

David suggests they need a really big box of Typhoo teabags with the logo as big as possible. People at the back of the theatres need to see it. Tony says they can get one of those big family boxes of Typhoo. David is still not convinced it will be clear enough. 'We need to see what it looks like first. We might need to get a prop.'

Stage manager Gareth dispatches his assistant to get a box of tea from the nearest shop.

There's also the issue of what music will play while Matt gets ready for TingTong's traditional Thai massage. Jeremy the director suggests they find some stock pan-pipe music. David suggests they get David Arnold to come up with something, but he doesn't know about this sketch yet. Jeremy points out they need the music in two days' time when the tour starts up again in Newcastle.

This is the first time Matt and David have seen each other since their Christmas and New Year break. They're here to rehearse this new sketch they have written for the show. They've decided to come up with a new TingTong bit – set in a hospital where TingTong is coming to visit Dudley whose leg is in plaster – because the one they've been doing on tour is the same as a sketch people would have seen on TV when the third series started in November. They feel they should provide something fresh, something no one will have seen before.

Also at the rehearsal space in a studio beneath the Bloomsbury Theatre in central London are the director Jeremy, Paul and Sam the supporting cast, Tony the tour manager and stage manager Gareth and his assistant.

Everyone seems in good spirits, although Matt says he may have to make a few phone calls because his laptop computer's hard disk was accidentally wiped clean last night when he was downloading something. He's remarkably calm about it, convinced that his technical man will be able to restore everything. David's happy, though he will have to wait all day until he finds out X's reaction to the birthday presents he sent her. She's in LA, eight hours behind. That's at least a whole day of fretting he's resigned himself to.

Matt goes through his Thai dance routine, which includes lots of strange vaguely eastern-sounding bleeps and squawks, and climaxes with a rendition of 'Let's Do The Timewarp Again'.

Everyone in the room is laughing at Matt's performance.

Jeremy asks, 'Is there any way we could shorten the dance?'

Matt says, 'Oh yeah, for sure. We could even cut the whole thing. Do we need it?'

David says they should keep it, because the audience has been responding very well to the Thai dancing in the TingTong sketch they've been doing already on the tour, and because 'It's a great bit of performance'.

Matt smiles, visibly appreciative.

Jeremy agrees that it's a fantastic performance but in this new sketch he thinks they may have something even funnier coming up.

'Let's try it,' says Jeremy.

Matt performs the dance routine again, and then continues the sketch, offering David as Dudley a traditional Thai massage. This involves Matt putting his hand under David's blanket and miming wanking him off. Matt's vigorous hand movements are met with laughter from everyone in the room, including himself. David just smiles knowingly.

'That's some good wanking,' says Jeremy.

So disconcerting is the sight of Matt wanking off David, albeit through the art of mime, that Paul Putner forgets his cue to come in and interrupt Matt. Matt just carries on wanking off David. David looks confused. Jeremy halts the sketch, and there follows a discussion about how long Matt should be pretending to masturbate David.

'You're doing it very well,' says David.

'Shall I do it for real?' asks Matt.

'Yeah, but I'm not sure if I can come for real.'

'Oh go on!'

'Maybe I'll come on special occasions – every Friday and Saturday night . . . Or maybe I'll come in London. I can come in London.'

Jeremy smiles.

Later that night David gets a call from X in LA.

'I am in heaven,' he says afterwards.

24

24 January 2006 – Hammersmith Apollo

I'm holding the home-made book that Tony has given me. It's a spiral-bound diary of the rest of the tour, given to every member of the cast and crew, a page a day, with details of each venue, each hotel and so on. 'Shit,' says David, 'that tour book looks twice as thick as the last one . . .'

'How many pages is it?' asks Matt.

I flick through to the end: 120 pages.

'Does that include our days off?' asks David.

Yes, it does, I tell them, and try to count them up. But most of it is actual shows . . . ninety-five of them I think.

'We've still got one day off most weeks,' says Matt, sounding like he's trying to convince himself that it'll be fine. 'But in a few weeks' time we won't know ourselves.'

David says, 'At least we've got some stretches in nice places. Four or five nights in Bristol and Manchester.'

'Yeah, and a lot of those cities have Wagamamas. I know where every Wagamama is in the country now. I think of places as Wagamama places or not. Name me a city and I'll tell you if it's a Wagamama city . . .'

'Newcastle?'

'No, and it said on the web there was one in Newcastle. But there wasn't. Manchester's got two, Bristol, Nottingham, Dublin, Birmingham and Glasgow. I think that's it. Those are the Wagamama cities. We always have Wagamama's, don't we, Dave?'

David nods, but he's got other things on his mind: 'They've got Selfridges *and* Harvey Nichols in Manchester. That's everything taken care of. Selfridges and Harvey Nichols in one city. I'll be fine there.'

Everyone's back from holiday, gathered at the Hammersmith Apollo for a full technical run-through, including the choreographer who's going to check up on the current state of the Dafydd dance routine. Jeremy the director describes the day as a chance to get everyone refreshed and ready for the resumption of the tour the next day.

Matt, David, Sam and Paul are going through the dance. Sam Spencer Lane, the choreographer, is watching them intently.

I sit in the stalls with Jeremy and Gareth.

Unprompted, Jeremy whispers to me: 'Aren't they wonderful?' He's studying the concentration on Matt and David's faces as they go through the steps of a dance they've already performed fifty-two times to sell-out audiences on tour. 'They're so professional,' continues Jeremy, 'much more so than regular theatre actors. They'd never be doing this. They'd never have this much commitment.'

Will Jeremy be going back to see some more of the tour dates?

'Oh yeah. I love it. And they still take my notes. They're halfway through the tour, and after the show they sign eighty autographs, fight their way through all the well-wishers, say, "Sorry, we've got to see our director," and they sit there and they listen and they make notes. Remarkable.' He pauses. 'You saw how they were talking their way through the TingTong sketch yesterday, turning it over. Just great. Matt will be a director one day. He could be a director now. He understands exactly how the stage works, where everyone should be and where they should all go. I've mentioned his name to a few people as someone who could do really well for a show. Not just bringing his celebrity status but also because he'd make it a really good show.'

Gareth has been listening intently. He says to Jeremy, 'It seems amazing to think back to the week in Twickenham now, doesn't it?'

'Oh God, yes. It was a nightmare week. Nothing was ready, we couldn't do anything in the right order, everyone was confused and nervous.'

'You said I'd gone to the dark side,' says Gareth.

'You *had* gone over to the dark side. You were in a very dark place.'

'Yeah . . . it's because I had to stage-manage and do the assistant stage manager's job as well. It was a nightmare.'

'It was tough,' says Jeremy. 'It was a horrible place in Twickenham. Horrible. Everyone was miserable. I was directing a theatrical show and we were really in a big, nasty rock venue.'

Matt and David have finished their dance rehearsal. The choreographer is happy. They're happy. Jeremy says the secret of Matt and David's success is that they always want to learn. They've done this dance hundreds of times, but they're intent on finding ways of making it better. There's a kind of parental pride on Jeremy's face.

25

11 February 2006 – Manchester: day 61

'Okay,' says Matt. 'You'll have to turn off your recorder though.'

We're in his hotel room and Matt's got something secret to play me. He made it with Robbie Williams when he and Kevin were staying with him over Christmas at his house in Los Angeles. Chris Heath, who wrote Robbie's book *Feel*, was there in LA helping out with lyrics for some songs Robbie and his writing partner Stephen Duffy were working on, and there was one particular song which Rob and Stephen were getting frustrated with, because they loved the melody and the music they had come up with but they didn't particularly like the words. So Rob asked Matt to join them in his bedroom to work on this song, and sure enough Matt came up with an idea for the words. He suggested telling the song's story from the point of view of a man who suffers from obsessive compulsive disorder and really wants to go out on a date but his condition is so severe he can't even leave the house. The subject of the song would be having a dialogue with himself in his head. Rob loved the idea, and said they should try to hone it into something, and asked Matt to sing on the song. To help dramatise the idea of this man having voices in his head. Rob sang his part, and Matt got to watch Robbie Williams vocalise his words. But when it came to Matt's turn to sing, he was so nervous he waited till Robbie went off to play football and recorded his vocals alone.

No one else knows about the song. Certainly not the paper that months ago reported erroneously that David was writing songs with Rob. Maybe nothing will come of it. Matt doesn't know if it will ever be released, but he tentatively cues it up on his Powerbook and plays me the MP3. Once I've turned my recorder off.

When a friend plays you something they've created, it's always a bracing moment because you have to steel yourself in case you don't really like it and you have to feign enthusiasm for the sake of decorum and friendship. When it's Matt Lucas playing you a song he's written and recorded with Robbie Williams, all of those concerns are hugely magnified. So as I listen to the song my first response is relief. It is instantly catchy, with intriguing words (which seem to be about staying in with your partner on a Saturday night) and a classy, Pet Shop Boys feel to it, and Robbie and Matt's vocals on it are really strong. It was recorded in about a day and it sounds to my untrained ear much slicker and more finished than a demo. When it finishes I enthuse about it, because that seems the only honest reaction. There's no point holding back. It sounds like a really good song.

Matt looks utterly chuffed with it.

David offers round some chocolate bars to all of us in his dressing room.

'Have you not got a caterer?' asks Chris Lowe. 'That's the only reason to go on tour – catering. You think Madonna goes on tour without a caterer?'

'Well no, I don't imagine *Madonna* does,' replies David.

'We saw Peter Kay earlier. He's just like he is on telly, isn't he?' says Chris.

David agrees Peter Kay is every bit as funny as he is on TV. He explains that famous people he doesn't know sometimes come to see the show. It's part of the whole generally accepted system that celebrities can usually get tickets to see shows. (A celebrity's 'people' will just call up the people of the people performing the show and politely ask for tickets, and the performers will invariably give them the tickets, which will, as a matter of course, include backstage passes and entry to any after-show drinks; this works for stage plays, rock concerts, comedy gigs and pretty much any kind of live show.) Steve Cram came to see the show a few weeks ago, for example, and

David says it was nice to meet him but he didn't really know what to say to him. It was a test of his social skills. Then he asks Chris: 'So you've done Madonna's remix?'

'Yeah, it was fun. Oh, and Neil is giving an award at the Brits to Madonna.'

'Why aren't you going?' asks David.

'I don't like awards.'

'I think you should go.'

'No, I don't want to.'

David dons his merkin for the first sketch of act two.

Dainton, the legendary Pet Shop Boys' personal assistant/security man and friend, laughs and says he wants to go and stroke it. David tells him to feel free. Dainton motions towards the furry genital wig but just holds back from touching it. David looks delighted by the sight of this huge man (Dainton's nickname is 'the Bear') oh-so tentatively approaching his little merkin, as if it somehow might be dangerous.

The discussion inevitably turns to where we'll be going after the show. David went to a straight bar called the Living Room the previous night so is quite keen on going to Canal Street tonight. He canvases opinion, points out that the Living Room is '*very* straight'.

'Last time we were here,' says Chris, 'you were blowing kisses at Neil. It looked a bit dodgy. What were you doing with him in the interval?'

'Nothing,' replies David. 'Would you have liked me to do something with him?'

Chris guffaws loudly, then takes a moment to survey everyone's footwear. He points out that we might not get into the Living Room bar because we're wearing trainers.

'Of course you'll get in,' says David. 'You're Chris Lowe. From the Pet Shop Boys.'

'I dunno,' says Chris. 'You never know up here.'

'I'd rather go to Canal Street then,' announces David.

David's plans for the evening suddenly surface onstage during the Dennis Waterman sketch in act two, when Matt as Dennis's agent gives David as Dennis a letter.

Matt: It's from Rula.

David: Rula Lenska?

Matt: Yes, Rula your ex-wife. Rula from *Celebrity Big Brother* . . .

David: Yeah, I know her. Rula Lenska from *Celebrity Big Brother* . . .

Matt: Yes, and *Rock Follies*.

David: I don't think anyone's heard of *Rock Follies* except you. Are you fond of musicals in general by any chance?

Matt: I am. How did you guess that, Dennis?

David: Just a hunch. I bet you'll also be going out to Canal Street later!

Matt: [laughing] Well, I might do. But in fact it'll probably be you going to Canal Street later, won't it?

David: True! I think I am going to Canal Street actually . . .

The audience roars with a sense of local pride.

Before David can head off for his night out in Manchester, there is the regular post-show signing session to attend to. One of the mini-throng is a middle-aged man who seems to be blind and is accompanied by his son who looks about twenty. The son says his dad is a local author and would like to give a copy of his novel to Matt and David. They politely accept it. David looks at it quizzically and hands it to Matt. It's about death.

Then a woman reaches the front of the queue and tells David, 'This is going to be a challenge. I have an unusual name. I'll spell it out.' David is poised with his marker pen hovering expectantly over the lady's programme. 'It's Olivia. My name's Olivia. Spelled O-L-I-V-I-A.' David looks up at her. 'Yes,' he says, 'I think can manage that.'

Matt can't stop himself from giggling.

* * *

One of the bouncers on the door glances at our feet and shouts, 'Trainers!' seemingly at no one in particular. He doesn't seem to have recognised David or Chris, but his colleague next to him who has a clipboard tells him to forget about the trainers. 'It's *Little Britain*,' he says.

David, who is wearing the trainers, is swept up the stairs and into the venue and we all follow on after him.

It was decided in the end that we would go straight tonight, at least to begin with, and are starting at the Living Room. Tony has phoned the bar already and politely asked if they could try to find a private corner of their establishment where David and his friends won't be too bothered. It's an unusual and pleasant sensation to be shown to an empty seat as soon as you arrive somewhere. There aren't quite enough seats for all of us, however.

Backstage at the Birmingham Arena, 2006

Within seconds, Dainton has procured more chairs so we can all sit down, and by arranging a circle of seats around David has created our own ad-hoc VIP area. As soon as we're all seated, women begin to circle David.

After twenty minutes or so, David's conversation with these various women ends and he says, 'Come on, let's go gay,' so we decide to move on to somewhere less slick, less straight. Somewhere gay.

Pete drives us towards Canal Street. David tells Chris that he's been listening to the new Pet Shop Boys album and likes the fact that it sounds so varied. He asks Chris if Trevor Horn produced the whole album. 'Yes,' says Chris, 'it's the first time he's produced a whole album for us. He's done a great job.' 'What did he do before?' asks David. '"Left To My Own Devices?"'

'And "It's Alright",' says Chris.

'"Left To My Own Devices" has so much in it, doesn't it? It's like your "Bohemian Rhapsody".'

'Yeah, without the sales.'

'But I mean there are so many amazing sounds in it.'

'Are there made-up words in it?' asks Mike.

'Neil makes up all the words,' says Chris, laughing. Then he tells us that he watched a really good programme last night on the making of Pink Floyd's *Dark Side of the Moon*.

'Are there made-up words in *Dark Side of the Moon*?' asks David.

'No. I dunno. I was just saying . . .'

'Oh, I see. Well, did all of them take part?'

'All of them! It was amazing.'

'Dave, did you meet them when you did Live 8?' asks Mike. I like the fact that he's taken to calling David 'Dave'. The only person I ever hear call him that is Matt, and that's on a fairly occasional basis.

'I met the drummer,' says David. 'He said, "Well, I'd rather be mowing my lawn today."'

Chris says he heard Pink Floyd sounded amazing on Live 8. We discuss the history of Pink Floyd. The line-up changes, how crap the film of *The Wall* was. Chris says he still needs to get some money out of a cash machine. David says he could just put it on his card, but Chris says he likes to have cash with him. David remembers a time he was with Chris in the Groucho Club and Chris wanted Neil to pay for the drinks 'because you've got more money then I have'. Chris says it wasn't that Neil earned more money than he did, because he didn't, it was more that he'd been burned a few times when he put his card behind the bar and ended up with bar bills of hundreds of pounds. 'That's why I pay with cash these days,' he says.

We go to a vast gay club. It has three floors, all of which have a determinedly down-to-earth feel. There seems to be a fairly equal mix of women and men, a large smattering of non-white faces, and even though there are plenty of lithe young men with their tops off, there isn't much of a sexual atmosphere. We head for the top floor, where the nice young man who seems to run the place shows us to a far corner with an array of empty seats specially for us. Every few minutes someone comes up to David and says hello or takes his picture with their mobile phone. When a particularly large and feisty gaggle of young blokes surround David, all of them wanting a shot of him with them on their phones, Dainton intervenes and gently corrals them away and back onto the dance floor. But David is taking it all in his stride, more so than he normally would. He seems to be unashamedly enjoying the attention, and the obvious fact that, in between concentrating on their dance moves to slick R&B tunes, most of the clubbers' eyes are trained on him.

A few metres up Canal Street we reach somewhere that's got a much glitzier feel to it. The huge bouncers are all big uniformed men, and in between them slim young guys with earpieces pace around checking out every patron who's about to enter. It seems to be quite a strict system. One of them squeals at the sight of David and shows us into the club.

This place is hot and steamy; full of muscle boys gyrating suggestively. There are no women to be seen. David elicits excited exclamations from every one of these boys he passes. In the other two clubs, most of the crowd seemed to notice him, but some of them were indifferent. Here it seems like every single hot young thing is also a fan of *Little Britain* and none of them can quite believe their luck that they're in the club that one of its stars has decided to visit on his night in Manchester. Dozens of cameraphones are being waved in the air. A half-naked teenager puts his arm round David and a semi-circle of other young guys forms to take their picture.

'Where's Matt?' one of them asks.

'He's at the hotel,' says David.

'Which hotel?'

'I'm not telling you . . .' says David, laughing.

As more and more of the clubbers notice David, they exclaim, 'Oh. My.

God.' Rarely must have those three words been exclaimed so often in such quick succession by so many different people. And even though David has only had a couple of drinks all night, and certainly hasn't taken any other kind of drug, he seems to be loving it all.

Now three huge, half-naked blokes have surrounded David and are all taking photos at the same time.

He hasn't turned down one request for a picture or autograph all night. He's embracing it. He's having fun with it.

On the way back from the club, David tells a story that Jonathan Ross told him recently about George Clooney. Jonathan was at a charity dinner at the Cannes Film Festival, and Clooney was a guest, so everyone there was thrilled to see him: this Hollywood megastar, an ultra-famous object of desire who gets photographed wherever he goes. And as he arrived at the dinner and tried to make his way to his table, he was stopped by everyone. Every single person in the room wanted to meet him, shake his hand, get a shot of him on their phone or just say hello. And George Clooney couldn't even get to his table to eat his dinner because he made sure he greeted all of them. He managed to be gracious and nice and charming and funny to everyone. Jonathan sat there in awe at this man who had achieved the perfect pitch of stardom. Tonight David tried to give pleasure to everyone who wanted to meet him, to give them what they wanted and be some kind of ambassador. He was trying to live up to their expectations of David Walliams from *Little Britain*. It helps that most people are really nice, and they're greeting him as if he's something special, even though he doesn't necessarily feel special.

Ben Elton is simply a very nice man. He's just gone to the toilet, and while he's briefly away from the bar, David takes the opportunity to pay tribute to him. He doesn't seem to have any bitterness or cynicism about him, despite the fact that he's been pilloried by the press for the past ten years at least. It's interesting for David to see how a performer, especially a comedian, has learned to deal with endless criticism.

Phil McIntyre is here too, in the bar of the hotel; Ben is another of his clients. Ben's also currently on tour and Phil explains that tonight in Manchester three of his company's shows have been staged simultaneously: *Little Britain*, Ben Elton and the Rod Stewart musical *Tonight's the Night*, for which Ben Elton wrote the script. In fact, Phil has been given an elaborate award by Clear Channel, who own all three venues, to commemorate this unique achievement. It's perched on the table and is about two feet tall. Phil then explains that he himself asked Clear Channel to give him the award. 'That makes sense,' says David.

Ben returns from the toilet and tells us he has been socialising with the young cast of *Tonight's the Night*, who are standing around on the other side of the bar, and all of whom look like they were born to star in musical theatre, although Ben tells us that only one of the male cast members is gay. It turns out that one of these non-gay cast members is taking Phil's attractive young daughter out for a night on the town. David and Ben joke that Phil will have the lad 'seen to' should anything untoward happen to his daughter.

'Don't worry,' says David. 'She can always have an abortion.'

'WOAH!' says Ben, who can't believe David just said that.

Phil looks at him in disbelief and just says, 'Steady . . .'

'Have I gone too far?' says David.

Phil laughs, to general relief.

To change the subject, David asks Ben how his show went, and Ben says it was one of the good ones, and he jokes that, unsurprisingly, a lot of his material is now about having kids and being a parent. He says that stuff makes for good material and that it went down well.

Just as David and Ben are discussing the finer points of doing live comedy, a member of The Strokes walks by, recognises David and says, 'Dude!' in a loud but lovely New York accent.

'Hello you!' says David. It's Albert, the one with curly dark hair. He's all smiles and bouncing energy. David and Matt met The Strokes when they appeared together on Jonathan Ross's chat show last year. Albert tells David that he's become a big fan of *Little Britain* since they first met, and that they watch DVDs of the show on their tour bus.

'It's great, man . . .' says Albert. He offers to buy us all drinks. While he goes to the bar, David and Ben discuss how thrilling it is to have Albert from The Strokes buying them a drink and talking to them, with his head-to-toe all-black clothes and effortless sense of rock-star cool. When he returns from the bar he's in an even more enthused state. He points wildly at Ben Elton.

'Dude!' he says excitedly. 'I just got told who you are. Man, is it true? You're the dude who wrote *Blackadder*?'

Ben Elton, slightly bewildered, tells him it's true. It was indeed him who wrote *Blackadder*, with Richard Curtis.

'Man, I fucking love *Blackadder*. That show is genius, dude,' Albert says, grinning broadly. 'Hey,' he adds, 'I'm with two fucking Brit comedy geniuses!'

David laughs and says, 'We're with a fucking member of the coolest band on the planet!'

David asks Albert if it's as much fun being in The Strokes as he hopes and imagines it is. Albert says it pretty much is and tells a story about a sexual escapade in Norway, at which point another member of The Strokes arrives. It's Fabrizio, who goes out with Drew Barrymore. If Albert is charismatically sexy and cool, Fab, as we're asked to call him, oozes erotic rock-and-roll chic. He's stick-thin, with stunning cheekbones. He, too, tells David that he loves *Little Britain*, and waxes lyrical about *Blackadder* when he's told who Ben Elton is. Albert explains that he just told the Norway story.

'Ah cool,' says Fab. 'Can I say I just never have sex. In fact, I've never had sex . . .'

David looks him up and down, surveying his lithe body. 'Look at you,' he says. 'What a beauty!'

Fabrizio smiles wryly and says nothing.

'What's your waist size?' asks David.

'Twenty-eight inches,' says Fabrizio without missing a beat. 'Maybe twenty-nine.'

'Oh, I think twenty-eight,' says David. 'There's nothing of you! How do you stay so slim? Do you not eat?'

Albert interjects. 'No, he eats loads.'

'And all of it shit,' adds Fab.

Ben wants to know what Fab will look like in ten years' time.

'I'll be a fat bastard,' says Fab.

'But a beautiful one,' says David.

It's nearly 4 a.m. Fab and Albert encourage Ben to talk more about *Blackadder*, which Ben willingly, modestly does, pointing out that he hasn't watched any of it for years.

'You should, man,' says Albert. 'It's fuckin' funny shit.'

David asks for poached eggs on some brown toast.

'So,' says David, 'The Strokes are astonishingly cool, aren't they?'

He analyses how they look and sound perfect, exactly how you'd imagine they would be, yet they don't seem contrived or pretentious.

'While Ben Elton is brilliantly uncool,' says David. 'Just a very nice man . . . I think it's interesting for him to have got all those terrible reviews for *We Will Rock You* and *Tonight's The Night*. But he doesn't seem bothered by it. And why should he care? He wrote *Blackadder*. One of the best sitcoms of all time.'

A few days' later, there's a story about David in the *Sun*'s Bizarre column. Victoria Newton claims that at the *Elle* Style Awards he desperately tried to chat up Elle MacPherson only to be rebuffed because she didn't know who he was. The rather terrible headline is 'Belittle Britain For David'. The article begins with this interesting justification: 'David Walliams loves to mock others in an ever-increasingly cruel way on *Little Britain*. So it was with great joy that I witnessed David suffer his own embarrassing misfortune at Monday night's *Elle* Style Awards.' So it looks as though it has now become a general critical assumption, based presumably on the reviews of series three, that *Little Britain* is cruel. Of course, the *Sun* did print a glowingly positive review of the first night of the live tour, having been granted special access. So the idea behind Newton's opening gambit seems to be to justify her own nastiness on the grounds that David is nasty himself, or at least his comedy is. The piece continues: 'He tried to charm (or some might say smarm) Elle MacPherson – but fell spectacularly flat on his face. Despite his theatrical introductions, it was obvious that a bemused Elle had absolutely no idea who he was – and she wrote him off as just another oddball male admirer. Cocky David dramatically lunged over to Elle at the posh pre-awards dinner. He said: "Good evening, darling. Are you a fan?" Elle looked totally baffled. David ploughed on: "Of *Little Britain*, darling. For I am he."' This sounds like an attempt to mimic the kind of thing that David might jokingly say, but it doesn't quite ring true. I've never heard him say 'darling' like that, even in exaggerated camp mode. It all sounds too contrived.

David is annoyed and bewildered by the piece. He says the truth is that his friend Patrick Cox, the shoe designer, asked him if he wanted to meet Elle MacPherson. David said yes, of course, that would be nice. Patrick introduced them to one another, explaining that David was one half of *Little Britain*. David calmly, politely and totally without agenda asked her if she'd seen it, and it turned out she hadn't. They made some more polite party talk. She seemed very nice. And that was it. The whole conversation lasted about five minutes.

David says he'd never say something like 'Of *Little Britain*, darling. For I am he.' Even in jest.

He guesses that someone at the party must have seen him talking to Elle MacPherson and decided to make that into a juicy morsel of gossip. 'I do feel like never talking to the *Sun* ever again,' he says. 'But in reality you just can't make that decision. It's annoying because we've just agreed to do a sponsorship thing with them for the Channel swim for Sports Relief. I would have been happy to do it with the *Mirror* but it doesn't sell anywhere near as many copies as the *Sun*, and I want to raise as much money as possible.'

Then he asks if I've seen David Attenborough's *Planet Earth*.

'Part of me would love to be something like a marine biologist,' he says. 'What a noble life that would be.'

Matt says the remarkable thing about David is his single-mindedness and determination. Once he decides he wants to do something, that is it: he will commit to it with utter dedication. Sometimes people can take this element of his personality the wrong way, because he can fight his corner so vehemently, but Matt says it's a big part of what makes David tick – this strength of will. He saw it when he first got to know him and realised that David would always stick to his flamboyantly camp persona, no matter how mystifying some people found it. One time they were walking through the streets of Edinburgh and David was wearing a Jean Paul Gaultier skirt that Katy had bought him for his birthday. Some hard-looking Scottish lads said to him 'Hey! Why are you wearing a skirt?' To which David replied, 'Because I've got some imagination!' and walked on.

We're having tea in his hotel room and Matt is talking in particular about the swim. David is practising right now in a pool somewhere. Matt says on the one hand he can't even comprehend the enormity of the task, and doesn't think he's told David just how in awe of the whole idea he is. And yet at the same time it is a typical David endeavour. Typical of how driven he can be. He gives all kinds of examples, from David being the one who always makes sure they meet on time for their writing sessions and keeps them on track to meet deadlines and get everything done, to his thoroughness in making sure they think of the best people to bring on board in all their projects and analysing all their different options. To the way he rarely corpses during their performances, as if that would be a tad indulgent. Not that David is some kind of machine. Far from it. This sense of resolve also emerges in his dealings with women. I mention to Matt how David's friend Robin Dashwood told me how David pursued the most beautiful girl in school and bombarded her with gifts and flowers to try to woo her. And no one else would do; he fixated on the one girl. The girl he's recently been e-mailing and who now has three children and is living in Vienna.

Matt didn't realise until recently which woman David is obsessed with, but he recognises the signs of his resolve. And hopes it doesn't end up too sadly.

At least swimming the Channel is something that is entirely in his hands.

26

10 March 2006 – Brighton: day 84

'Now my dad says he wants to swim the first mile of the Channel with me.' David is changing into his show costume and is momentarily in his pants. He's looking noticeably more defined and slimmer around the stomach.

'It's sweet but I don't think he realises quite how horrible it's going to be. Five in the morning; freezing cold water; dark. I think it would be quite a shock to the system for a seventy-year-old man.'

Matt and David are in Brighton for the first time since the shows before Christmas that Matt in particular disliked so much, when he thought the audiences were cold and unresponsive. He's in a fairly chipper mood now, though. It was his birthday a few days ago. David got him a framed photo of Lou and Andy with Paul McCartney taken at Live 8. And an orange juicer. His mum made him six bowls of chicken soup ready to put in his freezer, which, Matt says, was a particularly good present. He also got various books, scented candles, DVDs and a model of the child-catcher from *Chitty Chitty Bang Bang*.

Tony comes in and announces that Courtney Love might be coming to see the show. Her people have asked for tickets, and asked what she should wear. 'Clothes?' says David.

Dale Winton is also coming to tonight's show, and David's mum, dad and sister are on their way too. 'Dale and Courtney,' says David. 'That's a pretty good line-up, isn't it?'

'And didn't we hear Martine McCutcheon's in town?' adds Matt.

'Apparently.'

'And didn't you used to go out with her?'

'Yeah. I've never met her but I did used to go out with her . . .'

In the interval, Dale Winton and David's family are mingling in the green room next to Matt and David's changing room.

David, in his robe, pops in to say hello, asking if everyone has a good seat and if they're enjoying it. Dale says tears of laughter have been running down his face.

'David, you're very naughty with that boy onstage at the end.'

'I thought of you the whole time,' says David. 'I thought you'd like that.'

'Oh I loved it. It was brilliant.'

David's mum asks if Dale would have liked to go up onstage and let David manhandle him. Dale says, 'Oh of course! Being touched up by David – it would be fabulous!'

David reminds us that he wouldn't be able to do that bit of the show in America because the boys he fondled would sue.

'But what did the boy say when you finished with him, David? When you came offstage?' asks Dale. 'Because he wasn't gay, was he?'

David says, 'He's gay now.' And with a twirl of his robe he goes off to change for act two.

Dale is, like Matt, a big Arsenal fan, but he didn't make it to the European Champions' League match last night against Real Madrid because he had 'a mental showbiz night' instead. He went out with Cilla Black to the Ivy. 'Shirley Bassey was at the next table so she came and said hello. And there was a very strange combination at the next table –' for some reason Dale adopts a stage whisper '– Trudie Styler and Courtney Love.' I tell him that Courtney Love is supposed to be coming to see the show tonight. 'Really?' he says. 'That's amazing. Well, I did speak to her last night. I know Trudie so she introduced us to Courtney. She seemed very nice.'

There's no sign of Courtney yet though.

Back in the dressing room, David asks, 'How's the mood in the green room? Angry?'

He wants to know how his mum and dad and Dale are getting on. I tell him that Dale has been regaling them with stories of taking Cilla to the Ivy and dropping her off at Tramp before he went home to bed.

'Yeah,' says David. 'Cilla's not as old as you think. Because if you think about it, she was sixteen when she first became famous. I mean, she is in her sixties, but she's not yet seventy, is she?'

Matt says there's someone in the box filming the whole show with a video camera. 'It's just so fucking rude. And distracting,' he says. 'If I was doing my own show I would refuse to carry on. I'd say get the video camera and the footage and tell the audience that as well. But that's why I'm not a solo artist! I just can't be relied upon!'

On the plus side, Matt says he thinks the audience is slightly louder than they were the last time they were here.

'I'm really trying my absolute hardest,' says David, 'because Dale Winton is here.'

Tony comes in and explains that Courtney Love is on her way, but that she didn't leave London until 7 p.m.

'Hmm,' says David. 'She might see some of the second half.'

At 9.05 p.m. Courtney Love arrives. She's wearing a spectacular white lacy dress, and takes her seat accompanied by a pale, slim man dressed in black. I go behind the stage to tell David, while Matt's up front doing the Marjorie Dawes sketch. Courtney's here, I tell him. 'I've just heard,' says David, 'just in time for the end of the show!'

In the Dafydd sketch Matt changes the line from 'I wanted to be a martyr to the cause, like a modern-day Graham Norton' to 'a modern-day Dale Winton'. It gets a big cheer from the area of the audience sitting in Dale's vicinity. Tears are indeed streaming down Dale's face.

'We met last night at the Ivy, darling.' It somehow sounds right for Dale to use the word 'darling'. 'I was opposite you at dinner.'

Courtney explains that her friend, who's sitting at the back of the room with his feet up resting on the table, smoking and texting, is from *V*, a New York fashion magazine. Courtney points in his direction just as he's bending down to fish something out of his bag and revealing his bare pale buttocks. He's wearing a thong.

Dale Winton and David's family and Courtney Love and her companion are in the green room, waiting to congratulate David on the show. Dale introduces me to Courtney, and I offer her some champagne. She declines but would like some water. She tells me she's been drink- and drugs-free for eight months.

David and Matt arrive and everyone in the green room cheers.

Matt introduces himself to Courtney. She explains that she loved the show, loves *Little Britain*, but particularly loves *Rock Profile*. She says that she'd seen Matt do his version of Shirley Bassey on *Rock Profile* and how weird it was to meet her last night at the Ivy. She says Shirley looked amazing, and that *Rock Profile* got her through rehab. Matt asks how she came to see it. Did she get the DVD? She tells the story of how some British friends recommended it to her and she bought the UK region 2 DVD, luckily had a DVD player that 'swings both ways' and watched it throughout her time at the clinic. Matt asks what she's been up to in London. She explains that she had a macrobiotic breakfast at Trudie Styler's, went for a meeting about a top-secret stage project, went to a Dirty Pretty Things gig, and visited her friend Woody Harrelson, currently starring on the West End stage. Woody told her to stay off the 'pharmaceuticals'.

'He always says that to me,' she says. '"Stay off the pharmaceuticals, Courtney!" I love Woody. And I'm only on mood-stabilisers.'

David tells Dale that they changed the line about Graham Norton to Dale Winton specially for him.

'Well, I hope I went down better than Graham Norton,' says Dale, who then takes the opportunity to introduce David to Courtney.

'So you know Lisa Moorish well?' says David.

'Yeah, I love Moorish,' says Courtney. 'What do you smell like?'

'Like a sweaty person who's been onstage for two hours,' he says.

'Oh is it you, Matt? Are you wearing something nice?'

'Maybe,' says Matt. 'Paco Rabanne or something . . . I love your dress.'

'Oh thank you. It's Chloé. Don't ask where the earrings come from. They're a bit common!' She's wearing long, ornate silvery earrings.

'But that's good,' comments Matt. 'Where are they from?'

'Top Shop! But the shoes are from Harvey Nichols.'

'And have you seen *Little Britain* before?' asks Matt.

'Oh yeah. Of course! But *Rock Profile* is my favourite.'

Dale takes the opportunity to say his goodbyes: 'Bye, Courtney – twice in one week! Who'd have thought it!'

'I know,' says Courtney, 'and with Shirley Bassey too . . .'

David says he's very jealous they met Shirley Bassey, and asks Dale where she lives. 'In Monte Carlo . . .'

After he has gone, Courtney asks what kind of shows Dale hosts. David explains he does Saturday-night entertainment shows like the National Lottery. David's dad is standing behind him and is asking me about Courtney. I explain that David is explaining to Courtney Love who Dale Winton is. David then introduces his sister Julie and his mother Kathleen to Courtney Love. While all this is going on, everyone gets their picture taken with Courtney. She explains that she's had paparazzi following her all day, and some guy from the *Star* has been calling her on her mobile phone. But she graciously poses for everyone's photos here.

'That's an invasion of privacy,' says David. 'And the *Star* would just make it up anyway, so I don't know why he's even bothering to call you.'

David asks what Courtney's plans are tomorrow, and she explains that she's going for the macrobiotic breakfast with Trudie Styler again. 'She's just the perfect person.'

Courtney explains that she's also been chanting and practising Nichiren Shoshu Buddhism. She says every time she chants, something good happens in her life.

She asks David what he does to keep his mind and body fit. He tells her about the Channel swim.

'That's amazing! I feel overdressed,' she says all of a sudden.

'No,' says David, 'you're the most stylishly dressed person we've had come to the show.'

Then they go back to the subject of their mutual friend Lisa Moorish, who David dated briefly a while ago. 'She's great, and she's a great mom to those kids,' says Courtney, meaning the children she had with Liam Gallagher and Pete Doherty respectively.

David laughs. 'After those two I must have been a breath of fresh air.' Then he adds: 'But I really liked her kids. It's difficult when you go out with someone who's got kids and you get attached to them.' David says he's got to go because he's driving back to London.

Courtney tells him she also saw him in *Cock and Bull*, a film in which he has a brief cameo. The main part is played by Steve Coogan, of course, with whom Courtney Love was reported to have had some kind of dalliance. Coogan briefly becomes the elephant in the room. But David swiftly says, 'It's very nice of you to mention that, but I'm only in it for a few seconds.'

'Well, I remember you in it,' says Courtney.

Matt introduces Paul Putner to Courtney and she says, 'Oh I know you. You played Robbie Williams in *Rock Profile*.' It turns out she's also watched the *Making of* bits on the DVD, and Matt and David's audio commentaries. She really, really loves *Rock Profile*.

Matt says he hasn't seen that stuff for years. 'And I'm not being disingenuous. I just don't watch our old stuff much. We should get you some British comedy DVDs. Do you know *Peep Show*? You'd love it.'

'We could have breakfast tomorrow, Matt. You wanna have breakfast?'

'Oh sure. Where are you staying?'

'At the Dorchester. Come have breakfast. It'll be great.'

'I can't. I thought you were staying in Brighton. I'm staying here overnight. Sorry . . . David's going back to London though.'

Courtney calls over to David, who's saying goodbye to his parents. 'David, you wanna have breakfast with me tomorrow morning at the Dorchester?'

David, Courtney Love and Matt, Brighton Centre, 2005

He's taken aback. 'Ermm . . . that's a very kind offer. Go on then, yeah.'

'Are you sure?' says Courtney.

'I was only pausing because I have to do some filming at the BBC . . . but fuck it, that would be lovely. But what about Trudie Styler and her macrobiotic treats?'

'Well, this is a chance to have a full, proper breakfast with you. Fuck the macrobiotics. We'll have a real breakfast. Nine a.m. at the Dorchester. It'll be awesome. It's a shame Matt can't make it.'

David's dad chips in: 'Can he bring his dad with him?'

Courtney says, 'Sure, whatever!'

'Right,' says David's dad, 'I'll be there at eight thirty!'

David smiles. 'Be very wary,' he says pointing to his father, 'he may make a lunge.'

David calls to tell me he's had breakfast with Courtney Love and that she was lovely, charming and most of all disarmingly honest. In fact, he seems to have become her confidante. Within a day of knowing her. But he was very careful not to be in any way flirtatious.

A few days later there's an article about David and Courtney in the *Sunday Mirror* gossip column: 'Lay-Dees man David Walliams may have bitten off more than he can chew with his latest romantic target . . . wild woman of rock Courtney Love. They met when the American singer went to see his *Little Britain Live* tour in Brighton – and the comedian is now said to be infatuated. Renowned womaniser Walliams, 34, is desperate to travel to see her in LA – and he is likely to succeed in his bid to woo Courtney, 41.'

The piece continues: 'A source said: "Courtney loves *Little Britain* and was thrilled to meet the guys. They got on really well and they were all laughing and joking after a few drinks together. She seemed especially taken with David. They swapped numbers and went their separate ways, but he has been trying to get in touch with her ever since."'

The source added: 'When David sets his sights on someone, he doesn't give up. He has been trying to get in touch with her ever since their meeting. But he may have finally met his match with Courtney. She eats men for breakfast.'

As soon as David entered into a conversation with Courtney Love it was inevitable that it would be reported in the papers like this. But as for actually having breakfast with her in front of other people in a hotel restaurant – well, that's just asking for trouble, isn't it? The truth is that if Matt hadn't have been staying in Brighton the night Courtney came to see the show, it would have been him having breakfast with her; or possibly all three of them together, and there would have been no story.

Meanwhile, tour promoter Paul Roberts has been adding yet more dates. He calls them Operation Regional Mop-up – when they go back to the big cities where they've played a handful of shows before and make sure they sweep up any fans who might not have been able to buy tickets for the first tranche of shows.

This means thousands more people seeing the show, and hundreds more fans lining up each night after the performances to meet Matt and David. And a few more peculiar experiences, like they've just had in Liverpool, when a woman came up to ask them to sign her programme. David asked who they should sign it to; the lady said 'to Debs'. Matt and David signed it to Debs. Then they were told by the woman that Debs couldn't be there that night. Oh, why is that? asked David politely. Because Debs is dead, was the answer. I'm very sorry, said David. And with that the woman thanked them and disappeared.

27

11 March 2006 – East London: day 85

David's not feeling well. He's been up all night coping with extreme food poisoning.

'Both ends,' he says. But he still seems in chipper mood, maybe because he's in the presence of Sam Taylor-Wood, who is one of his two ideal women in the world (the other being Stella McCartney). He explained to me the other night on a drive back to his hotel that sometimes he meets a woman, always an unattainable woman, and immediately thinks: how will I ever find someone as perfect as this? It happened with Sam and Stella. Their beauty, creativity, effortless charm mixed with earthy honesty and their sense of fun. That's what he loves about them. Of course, both women are very happily partnered up. Everything David has said about Sam seems true, as she gently persuades Matt and David to do everything she needs them to do. She's calm, warm and full of intriguing, indiscreet yet fond stories about very famous and beautiful people. David chips in with his own choice anecdotes. Including the story of how Caroline Aherne once said to her brother, 'Imagine you met a beautiful woman and she had a gorgeous, perfect body. But no head. How long do you reckon you could go out with her for?' And he thought about it for a few seconds and replied: 'About a week.' The story, told in David's pitch-perfect Caroline impression, reduces everyone in the room to fits of giggles.

Matt is in good form too, explaining about his various allergies as the catered food arrives. He is slightly worried about the day's football, though. He needs to know how Spurs are doing against Chelsea. He wants Spurs to lose so Arsenal have a chance of overtaking them and grabbing fourth place, the Champions League-qualifying place in the Premiership. So while Sam Taylor-Wood shoots Matt and David in suits and bowler hats with umbrellas, I've got my digital radio pinned to my ear attempting to keep track of the Spurs game.

Chelsea score. I shout out the news to Matt. He yells, 'Great!' Sam shoots him.

David asks Sam about all the incredible people she's photographed, who was easy to work with, who was difficult.

She tells the story of directing the video for Elton John's 'I Want Love'. She had to film nine or ten takes of Robert Downey Jr miming to the entire song, and eventually managed to get the understated feel she was looking for by gaffer-taping his hands together.

When Sam's heavily pregnant assistant walks in, Sam notes that there are a lot of hormones swirling around the room today, because she is pregnant too, as is another of her colleagues. 'I'm a hormonal cow!' is how Sam puts it. David says he wouldn't be surprised if someone else got pregnant before the day was over.

'Nice here, innit?' says Matt. Sam's studio in east London is exactly like all those scenes of artists' studios you see in films – a vast loft full of effortlessly beautiful furniture, and huge prints on the walls of some of her most spectacular photos.

Matt asks David if he's eaten anything yet. David says he hasn't.

'You should have some toast,' says Matt with concern. 'Dry toast.'

David says he'll try to force down a lunch of some kind.

Matt asks if there's any score update. He explains that he had to keep in touch with the Arsenal score against Real Madrid during the show on Wednesday night. Every time he finished a sketch and was changing backstage, he made sure someone would be on hand to tell him if any goals had been scored. In the end no goals were scored at all. Which was great for

Matt and David with Sam's dog, by Sam Taylor-Wood

Arsenal. Now Matt, like most Arsenal fans, wants the dream scenario to happen: we win the Champions League and thus rob Spurs of their right to qualify anyway. Matt says he heard that Alan Davies has it in his contract that he can't film on an Arsenal day. But he doesn't know if it is true.

While her assistants are getting some new clothes and props organised, Sam shows David and Matt the new *Simpsons* live action title sequence on her laptop. They're suitably impressed, but Matt wants to show David something else on the internet. He's heard that there's an interview with Arabella Weir in *The Times* this morning in which she slags off *Little Britain*.

'*No!*' says David. 'Arabella Weir is slagging us off now?' He's tickled by the very idea of it. Arabella 'Does My Bum look Big In This?' Weir.

Matt finds the article. It's true. She says, 'I get depressed by television, I don't think any of it is good. If women were controlling and commissioning television in equal numbers to men, we wouldn't get shows like *Little Britain* – we are the only country in the world to think that men dressed as grotesque caricatures of women is hilarious.'

David reads it and laughs again.

'I know,' says Matt, giggling too. 'Arabella Weir!'

David says he likes the idea of the whole of *Little Britain* being grotesque caricatures of women. Every single sketch.

Sam asks Matt and David how the tour is going. Matt says it's generally great, but he had a complete tosser last night onstage in the Marjorie sketch. He couldn't find a proper fatty, so he picked an enthusiastic red-haired student who was waving his arms around, and when Matt invited him up, he immediately started to play up and try to take over the sketch and make fun of Matt/Marjorie, saying things like, 'No, *you're* fat – look at you.' Matt ended up making fun of his red hair and saying, 'I am a woman alone up here and very vulnerable . . .' He was trying to turn it round and regain control of the situation, but this kid was horrible, and Matt couldn't quite tell if the audience was on his side or not. 'It wasn't pleasant at all,' he says.

David says it crossed the line and became uncomfortable to watch, and that when someone is intent on causing trouble, there's not much you can do as a performer to stop it. That's the gamble they take every night by inviting people from the audience to join them onstage.

But, Matt says, they're learning how to deal with these situations, and he thinks if it happened again he might respond better, or at least not let it get to him. 'Are we about halfway through now?' Matt asks David.

'Aren't we about seven weeks in to this leg?'

'No, I mean about halfway through the whole tour?' says Matt. 'Have we done one hundred yet?'

'Oh, I don't know,' says David. 'I don't want to start chalking them off. I don't want to be like the Count of Monte Cristo and start counting off how long I've been in prison.'

28

15 March 2006 – Manchester: day 89

'Yes, I molested Will Young onstage last night,' David tells me.

He recorded a podcast interview with Will in Manchester in the afternoon. He said he was coming to the show that night, and he asked if there was any way he could come onstage and do something with Matt and David. Maybe at the end or something. So David and Matt sat in their dressing room discussing if there was any way to incorporate Will into the show. They thought about the Dafydd sketch, which does reference Will Young, but couldn't work out the best moment to bring him on. They thought of just letting him come onstage at the end, but that didn't seem to make much sense.

It was Tony who suggested David could use Will as his victim in the Des Kaye sketch.

'It was a good idea,' admits David. 'But I worried that using a gay man in that sketch doesn't work so well. It's funnier for me to invade a straight person's body.'

Nevertheless David went down into the audience and saw Will Young 'looking a bit grungey in his hat' and invited him onstage. Surprisingly, not many in the audience recognised Will immediately, because once he was onstage he was a bit sheepish and hunched over with embarrassment. David didn't hold back though. He wrestled Will to the floor, 'and luckily his trousers were quite easy to pull down'.

Then once he had him on the ground, he pulled his pants down as well. So the audience was treated to a rare sighting of Will Young's bottom.

'And while I was dry-humping him I said, "It doesn't matter . . . don't worry – your career's over anyway." He seemed to really enjoy it. Then as we were rushing offstage he whispered to me, "I'll get you back one day."'

In fact, he got David back within minutes by coming onstage to take a bow after the encore and pulling David's trousers down.

'It was fun, but not much for me to worry about. Everyone in the audience has seen me naked so it was just another little moment of exposure. I don't feel there's any part of my body that's private any more. Everyone keeps telling me they can see my penis between my legs every night in the Sebastian sketch.' The audience had recognised Will Young by then.

But the evening's excitement didn't end there. In the hotel bar afterwards, David and Matt met Prince Naseem Hamed. David's knowledge of sport is tenuous, but somehow he formed an immediate bond with Nas. Within minutes of meeting him, David was telling Hamed, 'I'm gonna whup your ass,' and engaging in a spot of shadow-boxing with him. 'I wouldn't have done that with Mike Tyson,' he says.

His explanation is that Prince Nas immediately seemed so vibrant and cheery and enthusiastic, infectiously so, that David knew he could spar with him verbally, calling him 'boy' and making mild fun of him and the boxer's tough, street persona. Nas was so taken with David that he invited him for some proper sparring at his gym in Sheffield when the *Little Britain* tour arrives there. David loves the idea but is also scared.

'He's a proper boxer. He could hit me quite hard.'

David also loves the idea that Nas is pretty much the ruling king of Sheffield. He told Matt and David that if they wanted anything or wanted to go anywhere or get into anything while they're in Sheffield, Nas can sort it out for them.

'Will Young and Prince Naseem Hamed in one day,' says David. 'It doesn't get much better than that.' I remind him that he said the same thing last week in Brighton about Dale Winton and Courtney Love. And when he was in Manchester with Caroline Aherne, the Pet Shop Boys and Johnny Marr. And then with The Strokes and Ben Elton.

'I know,' he says. 'It doesn't get much better than all those either.'

The next day Prince Nas came to see the show, and on the way called Matt from his mobile to check if there were any rude bits in the show. So Matt had to go through the various rude moments with Nas, and wondered whether he might just turn his car round and not bother. But in the end Naseem did turn up with his wife, and endured the occasional saucy, cheekiness of the sketches.

Matt says the thing about Naseem Hamed which surprised him was his vulnerability. Sure, he seems to own Sheffield, and he's a boxer and hugely successful, but he was also sweet and vulnerable, and worried about the rudeness. Which Matt wasn't expecting.

29

1 April 2006 – Bristol: day 103

'I've actually only got a small chance of getting there,' explains David. 'Twice as many people have climbed Everest than have swum the Channel. And 90 per cent who attempt it don't make it. So it's quite likely I won't make it. And if I don't I'd rather not become a byword for failure, like Paula Radcliffe. Greg, my trainer, was telling me she would have been close to death when she had to pull out of that marathon in Athens because she was so dehydrated, and no one takes that into account. God knows what they'll make of me if I don't make it . . .'

Maybe people will make more of an allowance because he's not a professional athlete. Yes, that's true, he agrees, but he still thinks he might end up as the punchline to a lot of jokes. Especially if there's not a lot of news that week.

But on the other hand, this is the biggest challenge of his life, and so much greater a physical task than anything he's ever forced himself to do. And he *does* have to force himself. When he's training in the sea, he has to tell himself that he can't just get out and give up. At first it's so cold and rough and miserable in the sea that his first instinct is to stop. He doesn't *have* to do it. But he tells himself: 'Come on, be a man. You said you would do this, so you must do it.' And he's quite enjoying that. The dialogue with himself. There aren't many times in your life when you challenge yourself to that extent.

At the same time the BBC is trying to make an entertaining TV show about this. They want him to do various things that aren't part of the training, like swim in David Beckham's pool, when he should be swimming in the sea. And they would like him to have his parents on the boat following him, but his dad is seventy and his mum gets seasick, so a twenty-hour boat trip across the Channel might not be the best thing for them. He doesn't want to have to worry about them on the boat while he's trying to swim the Channel.

We're walking round Bristol, near where David used to live as a student. He's slightly freaked out. Partly because there are only three months to go until he has to swim the Channel, and it's too late to back out of it now, and there's a BBC film crew following him around for Comic Relief. Partly because Matt pointed out that they've just performed their hundredth show of the tour, yet they've got about forty more shows to do until the summer break. Partly because he's here in Bristol where he blossomed as a performer. But mostly because he has just been speaking to X on the phone, and while it was a perfectly pleasant conversation, it's becoming increasingly clear that she isn't interested in pursuing any kind of relationship.

And tomorrow he doesn't even have a day off because he and Matt are filming the Pet Shop Boys video.

'I'm trying not to get down about the X situation, but you know what doesn't help is that she's quite a vague person. And while she's being vague, that makes me want to work her out even more. I don't know . . .'

Two girls in their early twenties stop David and ask me to take a photo on their phone of him. They're on their way to a hen party.

'We love you by the way,' one of them says as I take the picture.

We walk past the building where David lived.

'I had this small room, which was comfortable but spartan, with a fireplace. It felt like I was entering a great academic institution. And that I was going to be living in enjoyable poverty.'

It was exactly how his romantic young mind imagined a university digs should be. I ask if he had any Saturday jobs of any kind.

'No!' He laughs. 'I spent all my spare time doing drama. I preferred being poor to doing a boring Saturday job.'

We find a café in the square where David used to while away many Saturday afternoons, and as David enjoys a fresh peppermint tea and a slice of cake, Matt calls. He wants to know if we've heard any more about the Channel 5 documentary coming up that purports to lift the lid on Matt and David's lives and career. According to Matt's agent, it is due to be transmitted in a few weeks' time.

David's face darkens. Something else to fret about. Matt wants to know if I might be able to get hold of a copy of it. I'll certainly try, but I have a feeling that Channel 5 and the production company won't be too keen on letting the person who is writing a book with Matt and David see their unofficial documentary.

David says he feels like getting their lawyers to put an injunction on it, or at least to try. Matt says he'll get their agents to look into it, and talk to the lawyers.

'I know it's just going to be a silly little thing,' comments David, 'but if I start to think about it, I do feel a bit sick . . .'

I wonder if there is anything specific he's worried about, any particular aspect of his life he doesn't want to be covered in this programme.

'No. Just the whole idea of people delving into your life is horrible.'

1980s – London

David and Robin Dashwood bonded over the Pet Shop Boys. When they discovered they both had all the Pet Shop Boys records that had ever been released and that they were both fascinated by everything to do with Neil Tennant and Chris Lowe, they knew they would become best friends. They would spend hours walking and talking about their favourite Pet Shop Boys songs. They would go to Pet Shop Boys concerts together. And they would hungrily read every article about them and every interview.

As their friendship developed, David and Robin also used to go on trips to London together. While their schoolmates and peers were going down the pub, or going to parties and clubs, or hanging round in groups on street corners with their bikes, David and Robin would get the train to central London and go and see a film, or visit the theatre, or maybe even just walk around and talk.

One day, while they were looking round the shops in Covent Garden, they spotted their hero: Neil Tennant. So they followed him. For two hours. Instead of plucking up the courage to go up to him and ask for his autograph or just have a chat, they decided to stalk him for a while and study him from a safe distance. Eventually, when they saw that he was trying to hail a taxi and realised he was about to leave the area and go on his way, David and Robin actually introduced themselves to him. Robin said, 'We just need to say that we love you!' Neil thanked him very much. David then said, 'You're a living god!' and Neil thanked him. And got in his cab.

David and Robin spent the rest of the afternoon going over and over in their minds every word they had said to Neil Tennant. And wondering if they had got it all wrong.

David and Matt as the Pet Shop Boys for *Rock Profile*, 1999

30

2 April 2006 – Alexandra Palace, London: day 104

Matt asks his mum what she thinks of this idea that Neil Tennant has had for an alternative World Cup song. To the tune of 'Go West' they would sing 'You're shit and you know you are . . .' with all the *Little Britain* characters singing the song to a Pet Shop Boys backing.

'What do you think, Mum? Would people be offended if we sang, "You're shit and you know you are"?'

'Yes, that would be a shame,' says Diana.

'Well, that's that then!' says David.

Matt's mum Diana has given me a lift in her car to the Alexandra Palace set where Matt and David are starring in the video for the new Pet Shop Boys single 'I'm With Stupid'. She treated me to a lovely lunch at her house, over which we discussed Matt's childhood, his rise to fame and everything interesting she could think to tell me about his life so far. She even let me look through his school reports. But the highlight of the morning was when she showed me a videotape of Matt practising his Hebrew recitation for his bar mitzvah, in which the 13-year-old Matt cracks up in hysterics while trying to remember his lines. It was also strangely reminiscent of what happens most nights on this tour.

This is also a chance for Diana to pay Matt a surprise visit, and he's loving it already, especially as he gets to watch his mum interacting with Chris Lowe and Neil Tennant.

Chris Heath is here too. He is writing the text for a forthcoming Pet Shop Boys art book. So we're both recording everything that Matt and David and Neil Tennant and Chris Lowe say. And we're recording each other. And two camera crews are filming everything. And there are two stills photographers snapping away constantly. At one point, without realising the ludicrousness of the situation, David politely but firmly asks one of the cameramen to stop filming Matt chatting to his mum because it's a private moment.

As Matt and David are called on set, three little kids ask for their autographs. 'We've got to go on set, I'm afraid,' Matt tells them. 'We'll try to do it later. Or I'll do it via the power of the mind!'

'I'm With Stupid' video shoot, London 2006

'And what's the idea of it?' asks Diana, meaning the concept of the video.

'We're not sure, to be honest,' admits Matt.

Matt's mum says she has dressed up specially and put some make-up on because she knew she was going to be seeing David. 'I like to look my best for you.'

'Oh yes,' says David seductively. 'You know what I like. I like them quite tarty!' and bursts into hysterics. As does Matt's mum.

'I found your school reports as well.'

'Oh no!'

'But it helped jog my memory.'

'What did they say? Too fat? Lazy, but very good at colouring in?'

'No! You know what was interesting was that they all said you wrote very well and with great humour. Very interesting to see that. What vision they had!'

The director tells Matt and David that this section takes place at the end of the video, in which Matt and David's characters address the real Pet Shop Boys.

David thinks that because it's a reveal of Neil and Chris being tied up, Matt and David's characters should ask them something innocuous but say it in a slightly menacing way.

'We're sort of two fans putting on a show recreating their videos onstage.'

'Ooh, really?'

'Well, it's quite strange,' says Matt, then, changing the subject: 'Are you out tonight then?'

'No, I don't think so. Why, is that a hint? Are you trying to get rid of me?'

'Oh no, not at all. Stay as long as you want.'

'Well, we're staying in tonight anyway, aren't we, Diana?' interjects David. 'We'll just have an early one, shall we?'

'Are we? If you'd like to, David.'

'Yes, we can watch a DVD. *The Bridges of Madison County* maybe? Bottle of wine . . .'

'Ooh, sounds lovely.'

'Okay, we've just got to go and do our bits . . .' says Matt.

In the trailer, Chris Lowe asks Matt's mum if she's been following the *Little Britain* tour up and down the country. She says she has seen it a few times, but hasn't exactly been following them everywhere.

'No,' says Matt, 'Pete and Kathy are beating you at the moment. They've been six times!'

'Oh really? Oh no . . .'

'Well, I'm not upset, I'm just saying you're losing at the moment.'

'We have seen it three times,' says Diana.

'Yeah, and Pete and Kath have seen it six.'

'I've seen it twice!' says Chris, cackling.

'I think when you have children you have to bring them up, not just when they're kids, but you have to keep on with that role all the way through. I'm not sure if you're meeting that responsibility.'

'Oh sorry, Matt! We'll come again if you want,' says Diana.

'I'm joking, Mum. All I'm saying is that David's parents have been more often than you.'

'We've been to Edinburgh, Brighton and Sheffield.'

'Well, that's quite up and down. Quite all over the place,' says Chris.

'It's just a shame, that's all,' says Matt, mock indignant. 'Pete and Kathleen came two nights in a row.'

'I don't believe you!' says Diana, checking her diary. 'We could come on the fifteenth.'

Meanwhile, there's some confusion about shoes. Matt isn't sure if he's wearing the right ones. He thinks David might be wearing the ones he wore in a scene they filmed earlier today.

'Have they got your names on?' asks Chris.

David says they haven't, but they should check with the wardrobe person which pair of shoes is which.

Diana asks how long Matt and David have been here. David explains they've been here since 10 a.m., which Chris says is quite a late start for a video shoot. Neil Tennant points out that you should never arrive for a video shoot before 11 a.m. because you just spend the whole time sitting around waiting for something to happen.

Frank, the stylist for the video, arrives in the trailer, and David immediately wants to know who he deals with at Dior. 'Can you get a bespoke suit without going to France?'

Frank explains that it's difficult.

'Life is so difficult,' says David. Neil giggles.

David asks if he knows which the right shoes are for the orange outfits that they're wearing for the next scene. Frank's not sure.

Neil asks Diana if she's here specially to watch their video being made. She explains that she's really only here because she was giving me a lift and took the opportunity to pop in and see Matt. She didn't even know what Matt was doing today. Matt says he tries to keep his movements secret from his mum, and explains to Neil and Chris that I was meeting with Matt's mum for this book, which will be similar to Chris Heath's books on them. Chris Heath, sitting silently in the trailer making the occasional note, just smiles.

'Yes,' says David, 'and Chris is going to write a book about Boyd writing a book about us. And Boyd is writing a book about Chris!'

Matt tells Neil and Chris that his mum is going to see Il Divo soon.

'Yeuch, do you like them?' asks Chris, disapprovingly.

'Oh yeah! They're great!'

'Oh God, I hate them.'

'And she likes G4, and . . . Hayley Westenra . . .'

'She's fan-*tas*-tic. Fabulous voice.'

'And you like KT Tunstall . . . and James Blunt . . .'

'Oh *yes*.'

'He's the butt of a lot of jokes at the moment,' says Chris.

'Yes, but why is that?' asks David. 'When did that start to happen? I don't understand it.'

Chris says Jimmy Carr made a cruel joke about him at the Richard and Judy book awards when he said that at least John Peel didn't ever have to hear James Blunt.

Matt thinks there are a number of factors that have contributed to him becoming a figure of fun: first of all, his surname rather unfortunately rhymes with something rude.

Diana says, 'Oh really? That would have an effect?'

'Do you know which word he means?' asks David. 'What word does Blunt rhyme with, Diana?'

Diana smiles inscrutably.

'Come on, I'd love to hear you say it!' says David, excitably.

Suddenly she says 'Punt!' very loudly.

'What?' says Matt, stunned. He thinks she just said 'cunt'.

'I said punt!'

'Oh sorry . . . Jesus, I thought you said that word . . .'

Matt continues his theories about Blunt. It's to do with him being middle class. Neil suggests that 'You're Beautiful' is such an overpowering song.

'It's a *fab*-ulous song!' says Diana.

'And isn't there swearing in the song?' asks David.

'Yes,' says Diana, 'and I have got to say that the word is unnecessary . . .'

'What swear word is on it?' asks Chris.

'Tell them, Diana,' says David, goading her.

'Well, he says "fucking high" . . .'

'MUM!' Matt feigns high shock.

Chris is in hysterics.

Neil says he has never ever heard his mum say 'fuck'.

Matt says that can't go in the book.

Chris says it's a bit of a cop-out to edit out the word from the single version. Matt's mum says it was just unnecessary to put it in at all.

Matt asks if the Pet Shop Boys have ever had to make any edits to their songs for TV or radio. Neil says he's never put any swear words in his songs. David asks Diana what she thinks of Philip Larkin putting swear words in his poems.

'Well, this is it again,' she answers. 'It gets everywhere!'

David and Neil get into a discussion of Larkin poetry. David says he finds it amusing that he was so right wing. Neil questions if he really was right wing, because British academia at that time was so left wing, that maybe Larkin was being satirical or deliberately provocative by expressing right-wing views. Neil says when he went to North London Polytechnic if you admitted to voting Labour you were considered a Nazi.

David says that he saw some people demonstrating against Condoleeza Rice on TV yesterday and they interviewed one of them on the news and she said, 'Well, the first thing we have to do is get rid of capitalism!'

Chris cackles madly at this. Neil says he could imagine himself saying that in the mid- to late seventies.

Matt says that reminds him of a great Tony Blackburn story. He was hosting a radio show once and had more time left at the end of it than he realised so he decided to devote the final seven minutes to a phone-in on how to solve the troubles of Northern Ireland.

Matt and David get the call to film the next scene. David still wants to know if he's wearing the right shoes. The wardrobe woman thinks they seem fine.

'Because Matt thinks I'm wearing his shoes . . .'

Matt says maybe he's going mad, but he thought he was wearing those shoes earlier in the day.

On his way to the set, David explains that he loves quizzing Neil Tennant on anything that comes into his head because he has such an interesting take on everything.

Diana takes her opportunity to go home, and says goodbye to everyone. Matt says he still can't believe she swore.

'Oh *don't* say that!' she says, mortified.

'It's getting to the stage now where I can't go to a live public event of any kind because I'll just get annoyed by people talking,' says Chris Lowe.

Back in the trailer, Matt has just told how he was in the middle of singing Dafydd's song a few days ago, noticed someone in the front row recording it on their video camera, and in the middle of the song shouted, 'Oi! Turn it off!'

Chris says he went to the *Sinatra* show at the Palladium and had to tell two Japanese girls to shut up.

Matt says his mum loved that show, and he quite wants to see it.

Chris opens a chocolate bar and says Cadbury's fruit and nut bars have got smaller over the years.

Matt asks David if he'd like to see the *Sinatra* show, and he says he would if he had a lot of spare time on his hands. He says he hasn't got anything against it in principle, but he'd quite like to see the footage.

'That's the only reason to see it,' says Chris.

Matt brings up the subject of the Cirque Du Soleil, who will be doing a new show soon, which pays tribute to The Beatles. Neil says he doesn't like anything about the Cirque Du Soleil: their aesthetic, their music . . . 'And the comedy,' chips in Chris. 'Isn't it supposed to be funny?' he says.

All those shows: Blue Man Group, Stomp . . . 'People banging bloody dustbin lids,' says Chris. 'I've got no time for dustbin lids. "Aren't we clever to have made musical instruments out of bits of scrap metal?" I hate that!' He leaves for a wardrobe consultation.

Matt's looking through the newspaper, and he tells the story of how he was looking for the April fool's joke in the tabloids yesterday and joked to Kevin that he'd found it, and showed him the story of a violent sex crime.

Neil looks suitably shocked, then laughs and says, 'You're supposed to be the nice one, Matt!'

It is a reference to the perception a lot of people have looking on from afar that, of the two of them, Matt is the jolly, sweet, kindly one, whereas David is darker, moodier, perhaps edgier.

In fact, it is more complicated than that. They both have a strong interest in the dangerous and the taboo. They are both tickled by the idea of saying and doing things that are over the edge of what is considered normal and respectable. Ever since they performed their first and spectacularly rude live shows in Edinburgh, they've both taken a certain delight in shocking people and seeing how far they can go. On TV, in many ways they have to rein in their darker instincts, especially now they are on BBC1. But in private, when they're with each other or with friends, they know that the further they go, the funnier it will be. Part of the joy of being with them away from audiences and cameras is seeing how naughty their humour can get. So Matt finding the most horrible, sick and disgusting story in the paper to use in his April fool's joke to Kevin is no great surprise because he knew it was the funniest way to go.

'But I do think it's really weird when old people get sexually attacked,' says Matt.

'David's sniggering quietly,' says Neil.

'Well, it's difficult to know what to say about it, isn't it?' explains David. 'I mean, are we saying that we can imagine it more easily when younger people get sexually attacked?'

Chris comes back into the trailer. Matt tells him they're discussing old people being raped.

'Oh God,' exclaims Chris. 'I bet David brought that subject up!'

Neil cracks up.

'No, it was Matt, actually,' protests David.

Chris says whoever started it, they probably shouldn't bring the subject up the next time they go on *Parkinson*.

David launches into an impersonation of Parky discussing such sick and twisted issues, which sends Neil and Chris into paroxysms of laughter.

Then David, skimming through a Sunday paper, announces: 'Oh at last some good news: Rose West is marrying her glam rock lover!'

'What?' says Neil. He thinks David is making it up. But it's true, at least according to the paper: Rose West is engaged to some guy who tours with Slade.

Matt mentions Primrose Shipman and comments on how odd it is that the wives of mass murderers are called Primrose and Rose.

David says it must be so horrible to be the relative of a famous murderer, like the mother of one of the Jamie Bulger killers.

Matt asks if anyone has read the story that one of the Bulger killers is a 23-year-old gay man who now legally has to tell any would-be boyfriend of his what he did when he was a kid.

Neil says, 'No, really? Well, that's a play at the Donmar Warehouse!'

'Or even the Royal Court!' says Matt.

Chris suddenly notices David's trainers. 'Are they Louis Vuitton?' David confirms they are. Neil says, 'Oooh!' Chris says he didn't even know Louis Vuitton did trainers. David remembers a time when he was with David Furnish and Furnish told David that his Louis Vuitton trainers were now impossible to find. David says it felt so good to have something that David Furnish didn't have and that he really wanted. 'Apart from my bum, of course!'

Matt gives me a lift in the car that's taking him home from Alexandra Palace.

He talks about how much he likes Neil and Chris, how he wouldn't have given up his one day off in the week for many other people, and how lovely it is to sit there with them, bouncing off each other.

Like Matt and David, the Pet Shop Boys were friends first, and a double act second. And they still are friends. They socialise together, they enjoy each other's company, they make each other laugh. Sometimes they bicker. After twenty years together, they're utterly at home with each other. They're a natural fit. Matt and David have been together professionally roughly half that time, but Matt can easily see them staying together for at least another ten years. He says people reading this book might think it's odd that he and David travel around in separate cars and go and do their separate thing much of the time. But equally, they eat together when the timing is right, and they're writing together most days before each show. And while they don't explicitly talk about it or plan it out, they have come to an implicit, perhaps subconscious, understanding of how best to get on, how to stay friends.

31

6 May 2006 – Birmingham: day 132

'I was impressed with him: he seemed clever and knowledgeable. I think he could do a lot for us.'

David is talking on the phone to his agent about Simon Fuller. Matt and David had a meeting with Fuller yesterday, about various options open to them in their career.

On the way up to his hotel room, David asks his agent if there's any way he and Matt are going to be able to see the Channel 5 documentary before it airs.

Legally, it doesn't seem like there is anything they can do to force the channel to let them see a copy, and the production company keeps saying the programme isn't finished yet.

'It's just that there are things in my life that are incredibly . . . personal,' explains David, 'and I don't want them to be discussed by other people on a television programme.'

But how many people know about those things? David shrugs and says he's not sure – some.

'You know, there are things I haven't told you,' he says, 'really painful things that I wouldn't be able to go into detail about.'

It feels like he wants to talk about these matters soon. He says he will. He's still learning about how to come to terms with them himself.

The Channel 5 programme is gnawing at the back of his mind because of the uncertainty of what it contains. He says maybe one day he'll be able to not worry about this kind of thing.

He's fretting a little bit about tomorrow's BAFTAs, but after attending them for the past two years, he does at least think that he and Matt know how the whole evening will go, how to handle the red carpet and the commotion. The one thing they don't know how to handle yet is the feeling of losing. He thinks they will find out all about that tomorrow.

Anthony Head would like something less skimpy to wear. He and Ruth Jones, who plays Myfanwy, are here in Birmingham to rehearse for the DVD shoot on Monday and Tuesday, when the regular live shows in Blackpool will be enhanced by these special guest appearances from the regular *Little Britain* TV co-stars.

In the climactic Dafydd song, when the entire cast joins in for a big gay dance, everyone has a luridly homosexual outfit to wear. David's in his PVC shorts, Matt is wearing a bright red thong. So the costume department has come up with a revealing, brightly coloured and shiny get-up for Tony. But he's not having any of it.

'That,' he says, pointing to the minimalist shorts, 'is not going to happen. I'm in my fifties, for God's sake!'

Matt, who's standing next to him onstage as they try to get the dance steps in sync, reassures him he doesn't have to wear anything he feels uncomfortable in.

'Good!' laughs Tony. 'Because I'm not fucking getting my bare chest out!'

'How about a vest-type thing?' suggests David.

'Yes, I need a vest. At least a vest,' confirms Tony.

'Vest for Tony Head!' yells David. He then jokes with Tony that he should follow his example and go totally naked onstage. Tony says, 'Fuck that.'

David whispers to me that X came to see the show in Southend a while ago, and told him she saw his penis accidentally pop through when he squeezes it between his legs for the climax of the Sebastian sketch. 'I'm not sure I want her to see it in that state,' he says.

Rehearsing with Anthony Head, Birmingham, 2006

As Matt, Geoff and Tony discuss the logistics of Tony's gay dance outfit, one of the costume people arrives clutching a large lump of what looks like foam. She's showing it to Geoff Posner, who is directing this slightly revised version of the stage show. He says it looks okay, but they may need it to be furrier.

Matt notices the prop-in-progress and asks what it is. Geoff tells him it's a prototype turd. In the Women's Institute vomiting sketch that ends act one, there's a line about the children's fancy dress competition being won by a young girl dressed as a turd. They always planned on having a child come onstage in a giant turd outfit but couldn't get permission from the authorities in time for the start of the tour, so they scrapped the idea. There are very strict rules about what you are allowed to get children to do onstage. For the forthcoming Blackpool shows, however, they want to reinstate the turd costume, so here is the fledgling effort at designing it.

But Matt thought they already had a turd costume designed ages ago, before the tour started. He remembers seeing a big, brown, furry turd costume. Yes, admits the wardrobe woman, they did have one but they threw it away when it was decided they couldn't go through with using it on the tour.

'Oh,' says Matt, slightly shocked. 'I wonder how much that cost!'

7 MAY 2006 – GROSVENOR HOUSE, LONDON

'Hey, when he arrives, why don't you tell David that I'm not here yet,' suggests Matt to me mischievously, 'that'll get him worried . . .'

Kevin laughs and says that would be naughty. Matt goes to change into his dinner suit in the toilet of the hotel bar. He's been whisked here by courier bike from Highbury. Today was the last ever Arsenal game there. They beat Wigan 4–2, so Matt is in a good mood, though he is sad he's been to see a game at Highbury for the final time. Last night he was upset, thinking about his trips there as a kid with his dad. If you're a devoted football fan like Matt, you measure your life by your memories of matches. In particular, he can reflect on how he began to deal with the death of his dad by working out how he was feeling at certain key moments at Highbury.

But then today became a celebration. Not only of the end of an era at Highbury but also of Arsenal at the very last moment managing to climb one place above Spurs in the league to claim the final European Champions League qualifying position. And Thierry Henry scored a hat trick. Sadly,

Matt had to miss the closing ceremony because he knew he had to get here. David arrives. He looks nervous. He asks if Matt is here. He's too tense to have any kind of practical joke played on him.

Matt emerges from the toilet.

'Hello, how are you?' says David.

'Great, thanks. Did Boyd tell you I was here? I wanted him to tell you I wasn't here yet just to get you worried . . .'

David laughs. 'I'm already shitting myself. We've got about a hundred interviews to do on the red carpet . . . I didn't need to start worrying about you getting here from Arsenal.'

Matt apologises for even coming up with the idea, and we get in the car to take the 200-yard journey to the Grosvenor House Hotel.

David points out that it's going to be different from the previous times they have been to the BAFTAs – because they're not going to win.

Well, I suggest, you never know . . .

'No,' says Matt firmly, 'we can't possibly win. It would be incredible. I think Catherine Tate will win. She deserves it. She keeps missing out and it's outrageous really.'

David agrees and hopes that Catherine Tate will win. They're up against Tate, the Paul Whitehouse/Chris Langham series *Help* and *Creature Comforts*. David says it would be weird if they won this year, with all the criticism they've received for the third series. Matt says that is true, but he is still proud of the series, and still thinks that if the BAFTA jury watched the final episode (which is the one they submitted for judging), they would definitely consider it worthy of a BAFTA. He doesn't want to sound arrogant but he thinks that last episode is the best they've ever done.

But both Matt and David have the unshakeable feeling that, within the industry at least, it's not their time any more. The moment has passed. This is surely Catherine Tate's year.

David whispers to me that I should try to find the press room when we arrive so I can tell him who has won their category.

As soon as the car doors open, screams rain down from the crowd lining the red carpet. 'David, we love you!' 'Vicky Pollard!' '*Little Britain!*'

Kevin and I sidle to the edge of the carpet and look on as Matt and David work their way methodically through the camera crews, the TV reporters, the paparazzi, giving interviews, posing for photographs, smiling and laughing.

At the BAFTAs with Catherine Tate, 2006

David spots Nadia from *Big Brother* and asks her to pose with him and Matt for a photo. He knows the papers will love that peculiar combination. They only turn one person down. They don't want to be interviewed by Channel 5, because they're responsible for this imminent unofficial documentary.

After bumping into Jonathan Ross, his wife Jane and their friend Emily, Matt and David come face to face with Noel Edmonds, who introduces his three beautiful daughters to them and tells them they're all big fans of *Little Britain*. Noel's daughters nod enthusiastically.

I fail to find the press room. David has to endure a tense wait until he finds out that *Little Britain* has, indeed, failed to win.

But Catherine Tate doesn't win either. The Best Comedy Programme award goes to *Help*. Both Matt and David seem genuinely more disappointed on Catherine Tate's behalf, and commiserate with her. Catherine doesn't try to hide her disillusionment. And when she fails to win the two other awards that she's up for, Matt says he feels angry for her.

It has been a long, gruelling evening with only Jonathan Ross making any kind of funny, entertaining speech, so Matt and David leave the BAFTAs towards the end of the three hour ceremony, well before dinner is served. They're feeling irritated and sad, but mainly because Catherine Tate didn't win a single award.

32

9 May 2006 – Blackpool: day 135

'That was exhilarating, wasn't it?' says David as Lou.

'Boring!' mutters Matt as Andy.

They're sitting in Blackpool's biggest rollercoaster filming a special sketch for the live DVD. They have just gone round the huge climbs and dips and 360-degree loops of the Big One for the second time. David says it's not as bad as the Space Mountain in Disneyworld where he went with Jonathan Ross and family and just felt sick. Matt remembers a Coney Island ride he and Kevin went on that seemed bigger than this, but he's mostly worried about losing his wig as he goes upside down.

Geoff Posner indicates a break in filming, so Matt and David take the opportunity to have a word with Matt's agent Mel about the Channel 5 documentary, which is due to go out in three days' time. They still haven't seen it, or come close to seeing it.

David asks Mel why Channel 5 won't let anyone see it. She says it could be all kinds of reasons, but the production company say they were really late getting it finished. She doesn't think it will have anything particularly newsworthy in it.

'So you're saying that no one in the country has an advance copy of it?' he asks.

'According to Channel 5 they don't.'

Matt names a couple of TV executives they've worked with who now work for Five and Paramount and wonders if they can get them a copy. Mel says she's tried those routes, and while they've gone through the rough contents of the programme with her, they won't let them see it. She also points out that they have warned the production company and Five in the strongest terms that if there is anything even questionable in the programme they will sue the arse off them. David says that's all very well but he'd rather they did something about the programme *before* it goes out.

'I know, I know, David,' says Mel, 'but legally we haven't got a leg to stand on . . .'

'I just think we should still be doing everything we can to get hold of the programme.'

Mel says that I might be their best bet, in my role as a TV previewer. I tell them I'll see if any of my contacts has been sent a copy. Matt suggests they

Blackpool, 2006

may not have sent it out because they know they will get better previews if journalists *don't* see the programme.

Geoff calls Matt and David back to the rollercoaster for another take. I call a few TV journalist contacts. None of them has been sent a copy of the documentary.

'Did Lee Evans film his DVD at an arena?' asks David.

'Yes he did,' says Matt from 2 Entertain, the company that distributes the *Little Britain* DVDs.

'And didn't that do really well? Wasn't it like one of the biggest-selling DVDs of the year or something?'

'Yes, it did about three-quarters of a million by Christmas.'

'But didn't we do a million of our second series DVD?'

'Yes, with the box-set as well. Lee's one was the biggest-selling live DVD.'

'And what did *Extras* do?'

'*Extras* did about 350,000 . . . something like that. Quite modest really.'

'When did we sell most of our second series DVD?'

'The first week was fantastic. Sold more then than the series one DVD. About 140,000. And it held up really well up to Christmas. The major difference was that series one kept going and going and going beyond Christmas.'

'Well, I think the difference was that series one was the first thing that people could buy, and it went from BBC3 to BBC2, so people were still discovering it.'

David wants to know what the biggest-selling live comedy DVD ever is. Matt says it's *Peter Kay Live in Bolton*, which sold 1.4 million. He explains that they expect the *Little Britain Live* DVD will significantly outsell the series three DVD. The live DVDs of *Bottom* and Steve Coogan sold a lot more than the releases of their TV series.

David asks what the lowest-selling DVD ever is.

It turns out the lowest-selling comedy DVD is the BBC2 show *Up in Town*, which starred Joanna Lumley.

'And how many did it sell?'

'It sold zero copies in the first week . . .'

'Oh my God,' gasps David.

'Shit!' recoils Matt.

'And since then?' asks David.

'About ninety . . .'

The people making the behind-the-scenes footage for the DVD want to know what the arrangements are for filming the show tonight and at the hotel later. David says there are also camera crews from the BBC due to film him for Sports Relief, plus the stills photographer from the video company. The DVD producer would like to get some footage of Matt and David leaving their hotel to get to the venue.

David suggests maybe the DVD people could film tomorrow, but he's not sure what they're doing: he'll be swimming in the morning, and then writing with Matt in the afternoon . . . 'and after that I'll be masturbating . . . they can film that if they want'.

'That'll be a real DVD extra,' says Matt, 'but it'll have to be an R18.'

Matt from 2 Entertain asks if his swimming is being filmed by someone else. 'Probably,' says David, 'but you can film them filming me . . .'

The 2 Entertain people are intrigued and amazed by the Sport Relief swim. They fire questions at David: how long will it take? Where will he start from? What happens if he doesn't finish? Is he doing it on his own?

'I'm doing it too,' chimes in Matt. 'I just don't talk about it.'

David explains that after the first few hours his pacemaker and trainer Greg can get in and swim with him every other hour for an hour.

'Won't you get wet, though?' asks Matt.

'I'll try not to.'

'And what's the longest swim you'll do before that?' he asks.

'About eight hours, which I'll be doing in Croatia, next month.'

'And with the sun's rays on the surface,' says Matt. 'Won't you get burned?'

'Well, I'll put a lot of sun lotion on, but it'll wash off . . . so I'm not sure what will happen.'

David asks if Matt is going to be there on the boat of his friends and supporters. Matt explains that he'll be filming *The Wind in the Willows* in Romania in the week David is supposed to be swimming the Channel, but he will try to fly back for it as soon as they decide which day he will actually be doing it.

David thinks he will have to stay in Dover that week, waiting to get the go-ahead from the authorities that the weather and currents are all right. They will make the decision at 7.30 p.m. the night before. But Greg thinks it's not a good idea to stay there. David is worried if he doesn't stay there then he'll be caught out having dinner in London somewhere quaffing a Bloody Mary when he gets the call.

'I just want it to be early in that week,' he says. 'If I have to wait around for days I'm going to get really anxious. I'll hate it.'

Ah, we've found it. The Starbucks. We have been searching for somewhere to sit and have a hot drink for at least half an hour. If this was London, we'd have stumbled upon one within five minutes.

David reflects on how rarely he has been able to do this on the tour so far: sit and relax and watch the world go by. He didn't think it would be like this, doing so much every day. Most of the time they have been working in one way or another in the lead-up to the show in the evening. David has been doing his swimming, they have both been writing, whether it be new sketches for the live tour or the Christmas TV special, they've done photo shoots, promotional interviews, voiceovers. Or filming new sketches on the Blackpool rollercoaster. And they've also ended up meeting children with terminal illnesses a few times each week before the show, and visiting children's hospices. All in all there have only been a handful of days when they weren't really busy, when they got to relax a bit. In one way David is pleased that he and Matt have had so much to do, because he has never had the chance to get bored. But as he tucks into his marshmallow lolly covered in hundreds and thousands, he admits he is utterly exhausted.

Just as David begins to explain that what is starting to annoy him about his swim is people feeling angst-ridden and stressed about it *on his behalf*, Anthony Head pops into view, on a similar odyssey to find a relaxing place to pass the time before tonight's show.

'Oh thank God for this . . .' he says, gesticulating at the Starbucks outside which we're sitting.

Tony grabs a chair and joins us, and as soon as he does so, a group of children swarm over to get his and David's autographs. Tony says this reminds him of his signing days, when he takes two days to sign about a thousand autographs for a flat fee. David never knew such events existed. Tony explains there are different types of conventions. There are ones where he gets to answer questions from the audience, which are the most enjoyable, and there are those that are just mass signing sessions. Now, having just appeared in an episode of *Doctor Who*, he can appear at *Doctor Who* conventions as well as *Buffy* ones. It's a whole new world, he says.

David wants to know if they ever ask him questions about *Little Britain* at these events. Yes, he says, they always ask the same question: how do you keep a straight face? Now he just answers that he doesn't. And that the editor judiciously cuts out his laughter. David says the real answer to that question is that you're concentrating on what you're doing and filming yet another take and so it's just not funny any more.

Tony laughs. Journalists, he says, always want to know what it was like to be French-kissed by David as Sebastian. To which he answers that it was a total surprise and that he suddenly found he had David's tongue in his mouth.

David suggests he could re-create that moment later tonight onstage.

Tony is already nervous enough about the Dafydd dance routine and wearing that skimpy outfit. David tries to ease his fears by pointing out they're only performing it in front of a couple of thousand people. The rest of the week, up until Sunday's final show in Sheffield, is made up of arena shows.

David explains Paul Roberts's Operation Regional Mop-Up exercise to Tony, revelling in pronouncing the words 'Operation Regional Mop-Up' in an approximation of Paul's no-nonsense northern accent. 'Mad, isn't it?' he adds, in his own accent. He also says he knows in the future that he will be glad he has done this tour.

Tony says quite right, and that it has been perfect timing. And that the media's criticisms of *Little Britain*, telling them that it's over, are ridiculous. It's far from over, he suggests.

'Never say never,' says David. 'Even if we only finish this tour, do the Christmas Special and then move on to something else, we could still come back to it in years to come. We could come up with new characters. Revisit old ones . . .'

This is the first time I've heard David verbalise the future of *Little Britain* so clearly.

'Oh, and they rang me up to do some programme about you . . .' says Ted Robbins, who's going to be doing the warm-up for the audience tonight for the filming of the DVD.

'Here we go,' says Matt. 'Yeah, it's a Channel 5 programme. They've asked anyone who had ever worked with us to go on it. But no one who really knows us is going to be on it.'

'I told them to get stuffed,' says Ted.

'Thank you. We really appreciate that,' says Matt. 'We don't know if it's going to be a hatchet job or what, but we've heard there's one guy contributing to it – Gary Reich – who worked with us for about one day once. So God knows what insights he's going to have . . .'

Ted says there are so many of these programmes these days: unofficial biographies. He also proceeds to tell a series of fantastically rude stories about Little and Large, Cannon and Ball, and Bernard Manning.

Matt and David love Ted. He represents the old school of proper British comedians. But unlike some members of that old school, Ted is also a lovely bloke. He has been doing Matt and David's warm-ups before the studio recordings of *Little Britain* for years, and has appeared with them in *Rock Profile*. Before he goes to get his make-up done, he tells one final, splendidly self-deprecating story about how he got a call from his agent regarding the new series of *Bullseye*, explaining that they were going to have a celebrity on the show every week. But it turned out they wanted Ted to be a back-up in case one of the celebrities dropped out. So he was being asked to be a back-up celebrity on the new revival of *Bullseye* on Challenge TV. He turned them down.

'I've been asked by someone to donate some tickets to a charity called Hope For Palestine . . .' says David tentatively. 'I told them it would probably be a "no" because you are Jewish and . . .'

'Oh well,' says Matt, 'I personally wouldn't have a problem with it. But er . . . it's a weird one, isn't it? I just want peace. But it would be a big story in the Jewish press if I donated some tickets to a Hope For Palestine charity. So I don't know what to do. I mean if I said to you, shall we donate something to a Pro-Israel charity?'

'There aren't any, are there?'

'Yes there are.'

'What – Israeli charities?'

'Yeah, there are charities like Jewish Care and stuff.'

'But that's different to a Pro-Israel charity.'

'Yeah . . . well, let me think about it. I mean, I have to be careful, but in principle it seems fine.'

Matt goes on to explain that he hates oppression and violence of any kind, and that while there are suicide bombers in the Occupied Territories, that doesn't excuse violence from the other side, from 'his' side.

David reminds him about the kind of thing Matt's friend Philip Salon was saying about Israel and Palestine at the GQ Awards.

'Oh yeah,' says Matt, 'but that's just Philip. He's obsessed with Israel. He's going to give all his money to Israel when he dies. But he's still an amazing person, and a great friend. I've learned so much over the years from Philip. A lot of people have. I mean, Boy George learned a lot from Philip. The way he talks is very much how Philip talks, the kind of clothes he wears and his style in general. A lot of it is from Philip. He was there right at the start of that scene . . . he was so influential.'

'But does he hate Palestinians?' says David, laughing.

'Well . . . I don't know about that. I think he just really really really loves Israel.'

They let the issue die down.

They've only had one real argument so far during this tour.

It was after they came offstage in Oxford recently. At the end of the first half David as Judy has to kiss Matt as Maggie on the lips.

Matt said to David, 'You hadn't shaved.'

David said, 'Sorry?'

'Please could you shave because you're causing me pain.'

'Well, I don't shave every day because it irritates my skin.'

'But you're causing me a lot of pain.'

'I'm causing you pain?'

'Yeah. Pain.'

'Not just discomfort?'

'No, pain.'

After 126 shows, that was their biggest row.

A few weeks after that, as they're approaching the last handful of dates, David remembers seeing *Imagine*, the John Lennon documentary, where Lennon sings 'How Do You Sleep', and ends up singing "How do you sleep, you cunt?". 'And you think, hold on, how did you get to the point where you hate each other? Weren't you best friends once? I can't imagine it ever getting to that point with us.'

Matt agrees. 'I think usually whoever's slightly more passionate about something wins. Maybe about once a week something goes wrong onstage and in the interval we might have a disagreement and clarify what's going on.' And it's sorted out by the time act two begins.

There have been two occasions when Matt felt totally helpless onstage: once in Brighton when Marjorie Dawes couldn't find a fatty and he ended up with the really unpleasant student who tried to get the better of him. The other time was a few weeks ago when, just as the Dudley and TingTong sketch was starting, Matt looked at David with his silly teeth and David looked at Matt with his teeth and there was a glint in each other's eyes and they just dissolved into tears of laughter. They had to stop and apologise to the audience and Matt stood there thinking, 'Am I going to just carry on laughing for the whole sketch?' In that moment he realised that he had reached that state of tiredness and lethargy and nervousness that makes you laugh uncontrollably. In the end Matt had to go offstage and talk to himself, tell himself to sort it out. He stood there saying to himself: 'Don't be a prick because people have come to see this and paid good money.'

As the final few shows go by, Matt and David have been in reflective mood.

Perhaps the fundamental lesson they've learned on this tour is that even a bad night is a good night. Matt says it's a bit like sex in that respect. They have realised that even when the audience is quiet or when there's something not quite right in the air, which occasionally happens, the show is still a good show so people come away from it happy; they've still had a great time.

David thinks their real achievement is having created something that's part of the cultural landscape. 'Like I stood there onstage one night and listened to the cheers when Matt came on as Dafydd and I thought, this is interesting because one day this didn't exist. Dafydd didn't exist. And now he does, and now he's known to so many people and they love him and they want to hear him say he's the only gay in the village. He's part of their landscape now.'

The unexpected joy of the whole tour? They've had people coming up to them wherever they go and thanking them for what they do, for making them laugh.

David says he gets very touched when they're signing autographs after the show and people – it's often men in their fifties and sixties – look him in the eye and say, 'Thank you so much for the laughs you've given us,' and they talk to Matt and David like they've done something profound. That kind of affirmation works wonders when you have to read reviews saying, 'Please can this be the last series!'

They have been thinking about where to go next, what to do after this year's Christmas Special, which they're writing now. They can see themselves doing a Lou and Andy one-off story one day. They've also discussed doing some kind of kids' version of the characters, perhaps with Aardman

Animations doing claymation cartoon likenesses of Lou and Andy. There's this new possibility of a film financed by Simon Fuller, though Working Title would also be interested in doing a film project with Matt and David.

But the kind of long-term vision they both seem most sure of is a new kind of BBC1 show. They feel they could come up with their own prime-time series: a studio-based sketch show, but something looser and more flexible, with a little bit of a *Two Ronnies* flavour, plus something of a *French and Saunders* feel. It might be called *The Matt and David Show* or *Lucas and*

Ruth Jones, Matt, Tony Head and David, backstage in Birmingham, 2006

Walliams, but they wouldn't necessarily sit there on stools or behind a desk introducing the show as themselves. They might create characters loosely based on their personas. It could be a loose format, incorporating ideas like Vicky Pollard having a chat-show segment, and maybe they could go back to doing characters based on current celebrities more in the *Rock Profile* mode. It could be a topical, reactive show. They could spoof films and TV shows, something they have always banned themselves from doing in *Little Britain*. Whatever it ends up being, they both seem excited by the prospect of making a mainstream comedy show for the BBC. And now they've established their own production company with Geoff Posner, they would be able to make it too.

Matt wonders if whatever they do will be slagged off now. David thinks that may be the case, but also that nothing is permanent. Opinion ebbs and flows.

'*Little Britain* is weird because it's become such a cultural event that it's got an in-built self-destruct button,' notes David.

Matt reminds us that you can still get some pretty good *Little Britain* slippers. But the script books are already half price, or even less. His mum called him the other day. She said, 'Matt, I'm in WH Smith's. The script books are one ninety-nine. Do you want me to buy a load?'

The show in Blackpool goes as well as could possibly be hoped. Right from Ted Robbins's warm-up onwards, the audience seemed completely up for it, climaxing with a standing ovation. Ruth Jones and Tony Head had a great time in their special guest roles. Tony was happy in his gay dance outfit, which had a waistcoat cunningly thrown in. So as we drive to Manchester, David is in a good mood. He's happy because the official recording for posterity of the *Little Britain Live* show has gone so well.

When we get to the hotel in Manchester, over hot chocolate and cookies we have our most intimate conversation so far.

As I sit there listening to him, I start to realise that David has had a much more troubled life than I thought. He tells me about the painful experiences in his childhood that came back to haunt him later in life and how it caused him so much distress that he seriously became ill. How he ended up not sleeping properly for over a year. How he got very thin. How he ended up being admitted to a psychiatric hospital.

He didn't realise it at the time but he was in a state of depression. The insomnia was the most obvious manifestation of it. He simply stopped being able to sleep. And it happened to be a crucial, intense period in his professional life, as he and Matt were finishing the writing of the first series of *Little Britain* and were getting ready to film it. They both knew it was a turning point in their career, and they also felt that *Little Britain* was going to be a huge advance in quality from the material they had written before. Yet at that very same moment, on the cusp of creating the show that would make them household names, David was wracked with misery.

At night when he tried to find some solace in sleep, he couldn't. He wouldn't be able to get to sleep and on the rare occasions when he did, he would wake up from nightmares in a cold sweat. His friends gave him all kinds of advice – put this under your pillow, take that medicine, say these words, don't watch too much TV late at night. But nothing worked. And sure enough, after nearly twelve months of not sleeping he was starting to go a bit mad. He was anxious, exhausted; even delusional. He was losing weight rapidly. It was starting to look increasingly likely they would have to cancel the shoot. David was desperate for that not to happen. He prided himself on always being professional.

He had to book himself into a hospital. It was the saving of him. The treatment he received was a careful combination of very good psychotherapy, in which they touched upon distressing events that had happened in his childhood that helped explain the way his mind worked, and also highly effective antidepressants, which helped him to cope with his unhappiness. The one without the other might not have worked – the counselling minus the drugs or vice versa. But the treatment as a whole helped him understand for the first time that his depression was an illness, and that he wasn't a bad person.

This bleak period forced David to confront the painful events in his past that had led him to fear women and be confused about his sexuality. He was also very lucky to have such good friends like Rob Brydon, who came to pick him up from hospital, and David Baddiel and Morwenna Banks, who put him up at their house.

I remember Matt explaining how important therapy had been to him, when he needed help dealing with the death of his dad, his ballooning weight, his sexuality, his burgeoning fame and his fondness for spliffs, all bearing down on him at roughly the same time.

Matt prefaced the story of his difficult times with a wry apology that it might seem like he was corresponding to the cliché of the comedian with

David, aged four

the troubled past. And that you could probably say the same for David. I wasn't quite sure what he meant at the time. I know now.

33

13 May 2006 – Nottingham: day 139

Matt and David have performed 138 dates. There are only two more to go in this huge leg of the tour. They're just crossing the finishing line. This is their fourth night at the Nottingham Arena. And it turns out to be one night too far. A tough, troublesome last-minute hurdle.

Matt works out that they have probably played to over fifty thousand people in Nottingham already. This show adds six and a half thousand to that. It's also FA Cup Final day, so a large proportion of the audience seems to be drunk. They've been fairly raucous but manageable throughout the show. Then Matt goes down into the audience to find someone for Marjorie Dawes to bring onstage, as he has done 138 times before, but he just can't find anyone.

Suddenly, from behind his back, a girl comes walking towards him. He turns round and sees her swaggering and staggering. She has stood up to tell him that she wants to get up onstage with Marjorie Dawes. She's clutching a big glass of beer. Matt asks her to put it down, clearly fearful that she might at some point spill it on him. So he agrees to get her onstage. It seems like the only option.

But as soon as she climbs the stairs and arrives on the stage it becomes clear that she is utterly drunk. She starts to wander around rather absent-mindedly. Matt gets her to stand still for just about long enough to do the Marjorie Dawes routine, which does climax with Marjorie ridiculously shouting fat insults at her victim. The idea is that it is so ridiculous and over the top that no one should be offended, and it has worked that way 99 per cent of the time so far.

But as Marjorie calls this woman a fatty-fatty boom-boom, she starts crying. In a theatre-style venue few of the audience would have noticed. But because this is an arena, the show is being viewed on huge screens, so the whole audience can see Matt making this incredibly drunk girl cry. They start to boo him. But he carries on and finishes the sketch, boos ringing in his ears.

Afterwards, Matt says it was gruelling, but oddly he quite liked it. In a way, it felt liberating to have one audience out of the 139 they have performed to turn against them. It brought out their healthy belligerence. He thinks it's good to be alerted to the fact that things can go wrong.

'You shouldn't ever think as a comedian that you will never, ever die.'

2002 . . . Kevin

Matt had hooked up with his friend Tom to go to Popstars, a 'mixed' nightclub that takes place on Fridays at the Scala near King's Cross station. The two often went to clubs together. Popstars had been situated in a number of locations across north London, but now it was in the Scala it was big and impersonal. The cloakroom queues stretched round the club, killing the atmosphere. Unlike Heaven, which was more plastic and yet somehow more enjoyable, Popstars was defiantly indie and full of beery Friday-night attitude. Matt found it very cold and was almost always left feeling alone and depressed. Looking back he cannot understand why he consistently returned to the place. Tom had arranged to meet James, whom he had already hooked up with a couple of times after the pair had met on Gaydar, the dating website. Matt had a tough time on Gaydar. Like all of his friends, he had a profile, but unlike his friends, he daren't put up a photo of himself. When he did go online and start chatting to someone, he was out of luck. As soon as he'd make a connection and send a photo to the person of a man who looked astonishingly like George Dawes, they'd invariably assume he was taking the piss and leave the chatroom.

That night in Popstars, Tom had brought Matt along and James had brought his friend Kevin. Left on the sidelines while their friends smooched, the pair got to talking. Unlike some, Kevin didn't make a big fuss about Matt being on the telly, which was refreshing. Kevin was normal.

So here's the second reason Matt told us that long story about the guy he met in Heaven whom he thought might be The One and who turned out not to be . . . Matt used to see a therapist. He was going through bereavement, the complications of fame and coming out all at the same time and felt he needed to talk to someone, to help him make sense of it all, without an agenda. When he recounted the tale about the guy he met in Heaven and the pair considered various reasons why the guy had not called Matt back, the therapist suggested that Matt had not given the guy the actual signal that he liked him. Matt argued that he didn't have the confidence to initiate a kiss with him, partly because he didn't want to face the possibility of rejection, at least not yet, and partly because he didn't want to embarrass the guy if he didn't feel the same way. The therapist explained to Matt that there were plenty of other ways of showing that you like someone. The therapist told Matt that he could have given the guy a lift back in his taxi that night, from Heaven. That would have been a *gallant* thing to do anyway, and would have shown that he liked him too, without being too forward.

Matt remembered this conversation, that night in Popstars, when Kevin explained that he lived twenty-five miles away and had to get the last train home. It was barely midnight – very early in clubland – and Matt breezed out of the club with Kevin and the pair walked to King's Cross station. The train was delayed by half an hour, announced the PA system. 'You go,' said Kevin. 'I'll be fine.' But there's nothing gallant about abandoning someone at midnight at a railway station to sit among the drunks and junkies. They waited together, and chatted and laughed, and when the train came Matt saw Kevin safely onto it, and watched Kevin as he stood waving, and smiling *that* smile, as the train rode off into the distance. Matt was smiling too, and with good reason. In his hand, he had a piece of paper with Kevin's number on it.

Rule number one is you're not supposed to ring someone the next day, but Matt did. And the pair met up the day after that, and met up again and again. It turned out that they were just compatible. They liked the same TV shows, the same food, the same music. Kevin was creative too. He showed Matt some of his writing. Matt thought it was brilliant. And Kevin, like Matt, was highly capable of being very silly. He made Matt laugh like a drain. And he was almost as messy as him. It was only a matter of time before the pair moved in together.

Matt and Kevin feel destined to be together. Matt and David have shared *Little Britain*, have been firm friends for sixteen years and close collaborators for twelve, but for over four years Matt has also been lucky enough to have Kevin McGee to share his life with. In January 2005 the pair exchanged plain silver rings as a sign of their commitment to each other. In May 2006, Matt – having read in the papers several times, somewhat to his surprise, that he and Kevin were planning a civil partnership – decided that perhaps it was time to pop the question after all. To his delight, Kevin said yes.

34

14 May 2006 – Sheffield: day 140

David asks his mum and dad if they watched the Channel 5 programme. His mum tells him they did, reluctantly. They weren't going to watch it at first, and then they thought it would be silly to ignore it. He asks what they thought of it and his mum says she quite enjoyed seeing some of the old clips of Matt and David, especially the footage of David doing a turn at university with Jason Bradbury. David's dad is amazed they got hold of those clips. David assumes that Jason must have given them to the production company, along with their graduation day photo, which he feels a bit sad about.

'Yes, and I didn't like the set-up of the programme,' says Kathleen, 'all the stuff about you and Matt being engaged, and then married . . .'

'That was a bit strange,' agrees David.

'It was all a bit contrived,' says Kathleen. 'And tacky. And then at the end when someone said something about you having your own demons but that you also had to carry Matt's around too, I didn't know what that was about.'

'Nor do I!' laughs David. 'But the person who said that really didn't know us.'

'Who was that?'

'Just some guy we worked with very briefly.'

His mum says she found what Dominik Diamond was saying quite odd too; that he was almost suggesting that he was funnier than David but that David had made it and he hadn't.

'Yes, you know what I thought was the weirdest thing about it? They made themselves like bit players in my story. It makes out that all Dominik has achieved is being at university with me, and kind of knowing me. Why would he want to put himself in that position?'

'And it almost came over that Jason was your first comedy partner but you were only at university with him; you didn't do anything professional with him . . . Then they had that doctor on saying that you shouldn't be making fun of urinary problems,' says Kathleen, laughing.

'Oh yes,' adds David's dad. 'They showed the clip of the weeing lady.'

'As if the public doesn't find the whole idea of urinary problems funny anyway,' says David.

'I think it's peculiar that poor old Vicky Pollard gets blamed for all the teenage pregnancies in this country,' says Kathleen.

David agrees. He says how weird it is to think that they came up with this character who is a representation of the ways that certain young women behave and speak, and now people are aping the character, and now commentators are saying the country has been ruined by Vicky Pollard.

'Well no,' says David indignantly, 'it was an observation!'

His mum claims you just have to drive past the local school and you'll see a lot of kids trying to be like Vicky Pollard; and if you walk past them on the street they really do talk the way Matt does when he performs the character. David tells the story of how they were filming a Vicky Pollard sketch for the last series on an estate and he heard this girl saying, 'Things are gonna get well hectic!' He mentioned it to Matt and they decided to have Vicky saying that phrase in the sketch.

David's parents are glowing because they have just returned from a holiday to Rome, which was David's seventieth birthday present to his dad. They had a wonderful time, flying first class and staying in a beautiful old hotel, but now his mum in particular is anxious. Her daughter Julie is about to give birth to her first child, and her son David is about to undertake a perilous swim across the English Channel. She's been having dreams and nightmares about both. She says that once these things take hold of her mind, she can't let them go. She's fretting that Julie's baby will be really big. David was well over nine pounds when he was born, and was very long. David's dad says his mum worries if she hasn't got anything to worry about. She denies she's quite that bad.

Matt arrives for lunch and greets David's parents. 'Hello, other mother!' he says, kissing David's mum.

We sit down to have lunch, and Matt also wants to know what David's parents thought of the Channel 5 programme.

Kathleen gets straight in there and describes it as shoddy. David's dad nods in agreement but says there was some interesting footage.

Matt explains that it was one of the oddest experiences of his recent life. He watched it on his computer on the way back from a show, and sat there shouting at the screen. It was a version of his life being portrayed on TV that he just didn't recognise.

'There was a guy in it called David Spicer I met once about twelve years ago,' he explains, 'and this bloke called Gary Reich we worked with on an animation show called *Sick and Twisted* for Channel 4. We worked with him for a day in 1999, didn't we, David?'

David confirms that the programme was full of people he didn't know.

'This guy Gary came to my house for forty minutes to record me for a radio show. It's so strange to have him talking with such authority. Then there was a guy I was at school with who I hadn't seen for about fifteen years and who wasn't a very nice bloke. Then there was this guy called Alex whose older brother was someone I knew and I went to his house once when I was twelve. He was described as an old friend of mine. That was *really* tenuous.' David says the whole programme felt like it had been made about twelve years ago.

Matt sat there watching the old clips of himself and David doing really early performances and felt relieved that they had got a lot better and funnier.

'They would have had to get a lot better,' says David.

'It was like a weird dream to have all these people on it who have nothing to do with us,' adds Matt.

In the end, though, Matt thinks it could have been a lot more distressing. David agrees.

To add to the weirdness of the experience of watching this fictional version of himself on the documentary, Matt got back to his hotel and logged on to his laptop to find that a friend had emailed him a link to a Matt Lucas homepage on MySpace. It was someone pretending to be Matt, welcoming fans to join him on the site as his friends. David says he had a very similar bogus MySpace page created in his 'honour' a few weeks ago and had to get it removed. He points out that whoever is pretending to be Matt could use the webpage for nefarious reasons: to 'groom' young fans and suchlike.

Matt says the most annoying aspect of the fake him on MySpace was that it claimed Matt liked to relax by watching *Little Britain*, which made him seem narcissistic.

He lay there at the end of the evening trying to go to sleep and grappling with two faux, virtual versions of himself: the 'documentary' one and the MySpace one. Two other Matt Lucases, neither of which he recognised.

David's mum says she thinks both Matt and David are dealing with their success and fame very well.

'Well,' says David, 'we're learning. Anyway, you're famous as well. How are you dealing with it?'

'Well, I only shop in Waitrose now.'

David's dad joins in the fun. 'She gets free meals at restaurants now just by mentioning your name.'

Kathleen then explains that people do treat her differently. Acquaintances of hers come up to her and mention things they've read about her son. Like what? David wants to know. She gives an example of when some woman mentioned she'd read that David had just bought this big new house and that it cost millions of pounds. David laughs and says she should have told her to mind her own business. His mum said she more or less did. Matt says he gets annoyed when his mother's neighbours start asking her stuff about him and his money and his new house.

Kathleen then starts talking about how young some of the kids in the audience have been when she's seen the show. The last time she came to see it with her daughter they saw all these eight- and nine-year-olds.

David says he thinks all the really rude bits of the show go over their heads.

'Funnily enough,' says Kathleen, 'I was saying that I didn't understand some things you say. Some of it goes over *my* head.'

'Like what?' asks David.

'Well, like the pearl necklace thing had to be explained to me . . .'

Matt and David crack up, then Matt puts his head in his hands.

'Oh God,' says David. 'Who explained it to you?'

'Well, I happened to say that some things went over my head, so Julie explained it to me.'

'And what words did she use?'

'NO!' says Matt. 'We don't need to know, do we?'

David cackles.

Kathleen blushes. 'I can't remember, David. Well, there we are . . . maybe I've had a sheltered upbringing.'

'A healthy upbringing,' comments Matt.

David is holding a plastic bag full of tins of cake and sundry baked treats, all made by his mother and brought here for him to share with the cast and crew. He offers some slices of brownie and cake round to the costume and make-up girls, then says, 'The thing that's been a bit of a misery is having the same Marks & Spencer microwave meals every day . . .'

Matt nods. 'I originally assumed with this size of crew that there'd be a caterer and we'd pick up food from a table in a room before the show, but we were told the cost was prohibitive and that the crew gets their own take-away anyway . . . but I dunno, we can maybe do that next time. Would you like to have catering, David? Or is that an extravagance?'

'We could have a masseuse, and a private chef.'

'. . . and a Filipino boy,' adds Matt. 'A friend of mine has got a private chef at home, and it's brilliant. He heard me going on once about chicken soup and matzoh balls and the next time I was at his house the chef had made some chicken soup and matzoh balls. It was amazing.'

'We could get our mums to cater,' suggests David. Kathleen's cake is going down very well.

Just then, David's parents arrive in the dressing room to wish them luck for the show: the last show of this run.

'Ooh, here she is!' announces David, ushering his mum into the room. 'And here *he* is!' he adds, doing the same for his dad. Within seconds, David's dad is explaining to Tony the tour manager how he has plotted a route back from Sheffield to Banstead tomorrow. David's mother points out firmly that it is she who does the driving.

'I'm very impressed that your mum does all the driving,' says Matt.

'Oh yes. My dad is the map-reader.'

'Are women allowed to drive?' asks Matt.

'More and more, yes,' says David.

'Oh good. I do think they should be. It's just a bit of a political hot pota-to, isn't it? Like gay marriage.'

Matt explains that they would have had Prince Naseem here tonight as their guest, after enjoying such a great night with him in Manchester a few months ago. But now he's in prison serving his sixteen-month sentence for reckless driving.

Matt and David are ready to prepare for their 140th show of the tour. The soundman arrives with the microphones. The make-up girls apply the pow-der. The costume people are on hand with the right vest and the correct tracksuit bottoms.

David says the mere idea of doing this size of tour again makes him feel a bit sick. Not that he hasn't enjoyed it. 'One hundred and forty dates. You know this is the biggest comedy tour ever? It's official. Phil McIntyre says so. Over 750,000 people will have seen it.'

Matt hopes that in a few years' time they can do another tour. 'But we'll never do one as big as this. Because we'll never be this big again.'

David says he's trying not to think about the fact that they are going back on tour in a few months. Seventy-five more shows.

'I'm relieved this leg of the tour is finishing today,' admits Matt. 'I'm ready for it. I'm ready for the break. There was a period about eight weeks ago where for a week I had an internal crisis because I felt trapped in the middle of the tour. I really didn't feel right. But I kept it to myself. Doing the shows themselves cured me of it. And do you know what the funny thing is? One friend of mine who'd done a huge tour like this told me that Dave and I would never speak to each other ever again. But we've got on really well, haven't we?'

He thinks that while they are quite different people, with many different interests, this tour has been something they have been able to share.

David smiles. 'There's a part of me that would like us both to die now,' he says suddenly. 'Me and Matt. Because if we died now then people would say, "Oh I loved that show they did. It was great. And we're sad they died," but if we carry on we might do something shit, then people will go, "They're rub-bish now!" And I'm not sure if I want to go through all that.'

'Yeah,' says Matt wistfully. 'I know what you mean.' He then tells us how he spoke to Kevin today and explained that something will happen to him over the next few weeks: 'I might be very up, I might be very down, I might be very energetic. I don't know what it will be like. But something will happen.'

Gareth puts his head round the door. 'Beginners!'

Matt says he has to go to the toilet. 'Yes, it's true,' he says. 'Even I do actually have to use the toilet sometimes . . .'

On the way from the dressing room to the stage of the Sheffield Arena, David tells me that X spoke to him on the phone yesterday.

As soon as she started the conversation David could tell she was nervous about something. And then she told him that she really likes him, values his friendship, but she finally made it clear that, as she put it, she can never, ever, ever see him as being anything more than a friend.

David tried to carry on the phone call in a chatty, almost matter-of-fact way, as if that would help lessen the devastating blow of hearing that she couldn't ever be his partner. 'Never, ever, ever . . .' Until those words came out of her mouth, David explains, he was still clinging to the possibility that by being more successful, more interesting, more giving, more generous, more amusing, he might still one day be able to win her over.

As he was pondering the unequivocal finality of the conversation with X, David phoned his best friend Rob Brydon, who always finds a way to joke about whatever pain David is going through, and it always helps David feel better. Sure enough, Rob says, 'You should have just said to her: "Well, what are you trying to say here, reading between the lines? Never ever ever? What does that *really* mean?"'

'The thing is,' David whispers to me, 'I just want to be happy now as well. I've had this period of success without anyone to share it with. Wouldn't it be great to have a wife and kids with me to enjoy all this? . . . I know that fulfilment won't just come from this. Me and Matt have had three babies together with our three series, but now I want real babies. And not necessarily with Matt.'

Matt sweeps up behind us and asks David if he's okay. David smiles. 'Yes,' he says, 'one more to go.'

They sneak a peek at the giant video screen at the side of the stage, which is showing close-ups of goofy members of the audience. Thousands of people are laughing already.

Matt mentions to David how much fun the lunch was today with his mum and dad. And he wonders if David's mum really knows what a pearl necklace is. David sniggers. 'My sister told her, apparently. I just want to know what she said . . .'

'Well, Mum,' says Matt, embarking upon an impersonation of a slightly proper, middle-class woman in an attempt to sound roughly like David's sister, 'you know when . . . er . . .'

'. . . when Dad spunks up . . .' says David, picking up the impression and running with it, 'and says "face or tits" and he sort of misses both . . . well, it ends up on your neck, doesn't it?'

'And you sort of slightly enjoy that sense of humiliation and degradation confirming your role as the woman and his as the man . . .' says Matt. 'Well . . That. Is. A. Pearl. Necklace!' Matt is guffawing now, almost uncontrollably. And David is laughing with him.

But it's time for the show.

Epilogue

The Swim – 3 July 2006

David has received a handwritten letter from Tony Blair wishing him good luck with his Channel swim.

Among the phone messages from his friends the night before, David Baddiel tells him: 'If you find yourself in any problem please get out of the water. I look forward to giving you all the money. Frank Skinner sends his love.'

Denise Van Outen says: 'Oh my God. I wish you all the best. You're gonna be in my thoughts and prayers. And you're gonna be an absolute nightmare by Wednesday, with everyone congratulating you. On top of the BAFTAs and everything.'

Rob Brydon leaves a message interrupted by comedic sobs: 'I don't want you to do it; I'm afraid for you; it'll be horrible. But seriously, wow! If you do this it'll be quite an achievement. If you fail – quite humiliating. Think of me when you're faltering, and Belgium seems a long way away . . .'

Ronnie Corbett: 'We'll be thinking about you while you're doing your ordeal. Good luck with it.'

But it's not all good news. He's also started receiving hand-delivered

David on the beach at Swanage with his dad, 1974

correspondence at his house from the woman who has been sending him lengthy hardcore letters, describing in rhyming couplets the sexual things she wants to do to him. One is a two-page poem describing in painful detail how she would like to engage in a series of sexual acts around his bottom ('I'd put my fingers up your warm, dark hole . . . And you'd squeak with delight as I buried like a mole . . .'). In the end, he's had to inform the police, simply because she now knows where he lives and does seem to be worryingly obsessive.

Just something else to think about while he gets his mind and body ready for the swim.

4 JULY, 4.10 a.m.
'Are you ready for it?' he asks me.

Am I ready to sit in a boat watching him swim the twenty-one miles of the Channel? Yep. I think so. Is he ready?

'No!' he laughs. 'Mad, innit?'

Breakfast is a bowl of porridge with brown sugar, bananas and honey. And some more sugar. Greg has the same. It feels like only the two of them really understand what David has let himself in for, what the next twelve to sixteen hours will entail. David has followed Greg's training and dietary advice to the letter for the last twelve months. Every day he has swum exactly the number of lengths set by Greg; he has swum in lakes and rivers, and flown to Croatia to swim for eight hours in the same kind of conditions he will face today; he has eaten every meal making sure it fits into the diet, which has meant putting on weight for the last two weeks to make sure he has enough body fat to insulate himself from the threat of hypothermia. He weighed 14 stone two weeks ago, but now he's 15 and a half. 'I was so slim!' he wails jokily. Greg himself, who doesn't have an ounce of fat on his body, couldn't even attempt this length of swim in the chilly English sea. It would be too dangerous. But he will be getting into the Channel every few hours for a spurt of swimming to help David along and to keep his pace steady.

David has been in Dover for three days waiting for the call from his tech team telling him the conditions are right. Last night he got the call.

'It's only swimming though . . .' he says.

His mum suggests it's quite a big swim, reminds us all that it could take sixteen hours, and offers me a sea-sickness tablet. And some sunblock. She and Peter are well prepared.

Matt calls from Romania to wish him luck. 'I'll probably get out after five minutes,' laughs David. 'The money's raised, so who gives a shit?' David's dad guffaws. His mum smiles wryly. Matt says he'll call me every couple of hours, whenever he has a break in filming, to check how he's doing.

Twilight in Folkestone harbour. A gentle breeze ruffles the surface of the water. Seagulls are circling and singing. An entourage has gathered around David: press officers from Sport Relief, local officials, Mike from the Channel Swimming Association, reporters from 'media partners' the *Sun* and Radio 1, Kevin from Comic Relief, and the crew from the official BBC documentary chronicling the swim. It feels like a family gathering. David looks round and smiles at everyone and says, 'Thank you all for coming.'

There are a few unofficial onlookers too: a cameraman from the local BBC News, a few local newspaper journalists. But David doesn't care. He's talking to Mike Read from the Channel Swimming Association who will be adjudicating the swim and making sure all the rules and regulations are followed. Mike tells him he has to have a drug test. 'David, I have to ask you,' says Mike, 'Have you taken any drugs?' David replies simply: 'No'. 'Thank you.' And that was the extent of Mike Read's drug test. The actual start time and departure point of the swim has been kept secret from everyone apart from the handful of people who are here to follow and support him. The Sport Relief team is fretting; they want David to be left alone, to feel happy and comfortable and for no one to get in his way as he prepares for the journey ahead. He'll be leaving from Shakespeare Beach in Dover, a couple of miles from here, but it's difficult to get to on foot, so his boat will be taking him there. Katie from Sport Relief wants all his supporters to leave swiftly as soon as David's boat departs for Shakespeare Beach so that the unofficial press don't have time to follow us and won't know where to go.

'You'll be fine,' exclaims Mike Read, who has swum the Channel thirty-three times and is thus known as King of the Channel. 'Just put one arm in front of the other!'

David climbs onto his boat. He's not sure who he will be able to bid farewell to once he gets to Shakespeare Beach.

'Say goodbye to the little ones!' he yells to me.

We're watching David swimming. He's approaching the Dover shore. David's dad points out how odd it is that he has to swim this little journey from his vessel to the beach, just so he can then walk back into the sea and

5.30 a.m. Shakespeare's Beach, 4th July 2006

officially start the swim. Just a few hundred feet to get himself ready for the twenty-one miles or so.

He emerges grinning. His entire body, tanned a vibrant brown after weeks of preparatory sea swimming under the summer sun, is now covered in smears of creamy off-white lanolin. He takes his goggles off to greet his parents. 'I've just done it!' he says.

David's dad is slightly out of breath after the long walk down dozens of steps to get to Shakespeare Beach. David's mum is quiet.

The unofficial reporters and crew are hovering close by. Katie is trying to form a one-woman shield to keep them away from David. Above all else she wants him to be unimpeded. She wants a safe and tidy start to the event. At this stage it's all about keeping David in a good frame of mind.

'Okay,' says David deliberately, 'well . . . this is it.'

He shakes his dad's hand. 'You've been a very good father,' and then kisses his mum on the cheek, 'And you've been a wonderful mother.' He waves at the rest of us. 'It's been nice knowing you!'

And with that he marches off into the sea. At 5.31 a.m. he starts swimming. David's mum is teary-eyed.

'He's in good hands,' says Kevin Cahill.

'I know he is,' says his mum. 'It's just . . .' She tails off.

Six minutes later we're squinting at the sea as we watch David disappear into the distance.

There's a mild wind blowing, but the surface of the sea feels calm. As soon as our boat catches up with him, and we see him steadily making his way across the water, it seems like he's taking the whole challenge in his stride.

'Look, he's doing great,' notes Phil McIntyre.

'Looks fucking good,' nods Alfie. A little section of the tour family is here, to keep boosting and supporting him just like they did when he was about to step out onto the stage in front of 11,000 people in the Manchester Arena. His mum and dad study him with obvious pride. This is the same sleek, steady freestyling stroke I watched him do that first time he trained in the sea off the coast of Southampton nine months ago. Except he seems to be going faster. Greg, on his tech support boat, which is sailing inches away from him, blows his whistle. David stops to tread water. He lifts his goggles, squints and recognises us waving at him. His parents and I all wave to him rather tentatively. We're not quite sure if we're supposed to interrupt him;

break his concentration. Laura from Radio 1 shouts, 'Three hundred and ninety-one thousand!' at him – the amount of money he's raised so far. Phil yells, 'Where's your mate Matt? What's he doing?' David smiles and shouts back, 'It's my promoter! Will this help ticket sales?'

Phil and Alfie are in hysterics. Greg and his assistant dangle a long pole around David's head. There's a cup hooked onto the end of it with some carb-heavy jelly in it. David laps it up, and then gets a cup full of mouth-wash held out for him. He needs it to help deal with the constant flood of salt-water into his mouth. And that's it. His feeding break is over. He waves at us, puts his goggles back on and resumes the stroke, as deliberate as it was before.

Our boat feels like it's rocking slightly. Two and a half hours into the journey, with the breeze picking up, David's mum starts to look uncertain. She's grimacing. Alfie asks if she's all right. Pete is at the other end of the boat, enjoying Phil's roguish banter. Alfie tells her you're supposed to keep your eye on the horizon if you're feeling sick.

Mid-Channel

'I'm not feeling all that well,' admits Kathleen. She's taken her seasickness pills, but she's pale and jittery. Alfie yells down to Pete to tell him his wife is a bit poorly. Alfie rubs her back. 'You all right, love?' asks Pete.

'No,' she says, 'but Alfie's looking after me.'

Phil advises her to move to the centre of the vessel. She'll be steadier there. 'And keep looking at the horizon,' he adds.

'Yes, so they say,' replies Kathleen. 'I'm trying, but it doesn't seem to be helping.'

Strapping young John, who's manning the boat with his father Phil, arrives by Kathleen's side with a large blue bucket. Ten seconds later she's using it. She'll be needing it intermittently throughout the rest of the journey across the Channel. And during the trip back to Dover.

From our vantage point it looks like David is doing brilliantly. The sun is gleaming off his browned back as he glides through the water. And past the jellyfish and pools of sewage. But when he stops momentarily after eight hours, he looks pained. He treads water and starts stretching. He's cramping up. This is the crucial period in which many Channel swimmers find their bodies seize up and can't take any more strain. The thousands of strokes take their toll. Greg is shouting at him, encouraging him, goading him on. David takes up the stroke again. Steady as he goes.

'His back's getting browner and browner. This is gonna be one hell of a tan,' observes Phil, staring through his binoculars.

The camera crew on our boat want to get a shot of David's dad watching him swim, while the producer asks him how he's feeling. Pete finds it difficult to turn back to the camera to answer the questions while also watching his son. Fact is, none of us can take our eyes off David. He's mesmerising us. Word comes through that David is slowing down a tad. If he doesn't speed up in the next few minutes and make sure he can get to France within an hour or so, the tide will change and sweep him up into its current and take him miles away from the bit of coast directly in front of him. Or, as Phil puts it, 'He's gotta get a move on and finish or else he'll be taken round the corner!'

If he does get taken round the corner, it'll add hours onto the swim. We're worried those extra hours and extra miles would break his resolve. Or more likely, break his body.

Greg jumps into the sea and starts swimming next to David. He's driving him on; moving him faster.

'Fuck-in' 'ell!' yells Phil. 'He's going like the wind!'

'He does seem to be going faster,' nods Pete.

He's going to beat the tide. He can see the coast.

Matt calls me and asks how he's doing. I try to explain the tidal situation, but I'm not sure if I understand it myself. Essentially he'll either finish in about an hour, or else if it goes badly, in about four hours. Matt says he wishes he could be here, cheering him on. He asks if David can hear us on the boat. I tell him he can, and Matt sounds reassured. The idea that he would be feeling alone in this final, crucial stretch is a lot to bear. But in fact he's clearly aware of the three boats around him, and the helicopters and planes that circle overhead – all there for him.

'Love?' shouts Pete. 'Kathy love! He's about to arrive!'

David's mum can just about raise herself and crane her neck in time to see her son swim those last few metres. She smiles. Pete shakes his head. 'This is unbelievable,' he says. David is emerging from the water. A crowd has gathered to line the cliff above him. It's 5 p.m. exactly. He's done it. Cheers, whistles, whoops of joy. And it has taken him ten and a half hours. Nine months ago Greg told him it might take sixteen.

While we're watching with open-mouthed awe as David stumbles onto his feet in France, I call Matt. But David seems very unsteady. Greg shouts that he needs to clear the water and climb onto one of the rocks to make sure he has officially arrived. Otherwise he won't have swum the Channel. We're not sure if David can hear. We're not sure if his exhausted muscles can keep him upright and shift his body onto the rock.

Matt answers the phone. 'Did you say ten and a half?'

'Yes. Ten and a half.'

'Ten and a half hours?'

'Yes. That's right . . .'

'No. I can't believe it. I thought it was supposed to take fifteen or sixteen?'

'Yep. But he's done it in ten and a half,' I tell him. 'No one can believe it. *He* can't believe it.'

I'm watching David clamber unsteadily onto a huge rock on the coast of France. He looks like he's about to fall over any second and tumble back into the sea. He steadies himself. We all cheer and shout and applaud as loudly as possible.

I tell Matt that David is standing up, smiling, laughing, and waving now. Matt says it still seems unbelievable and that he'll try to phone David on his

404 INSIDE LITTLE BRITAIN

mobile to congratulate him, but he imagines he will have a lot of answer-phone messages to get through.

Word comes through from David's support boat that he has achieved one of the fifty fastest Channel swims of all time. It's too much for any of us to take in. His father just shakes his head in disbelief.

When David's boat gets back to Folkestone Harbour a couple of hours after he completed the swim, a large crowd is waiting to greet him. They must have been listening to the updates on Radio 1. He never anticipated this. He didn't imagine he'd be hailed by so many people. But here they are – kids, teenagers, pensioners, drunken holiday-makers, cameramen, film crews and journalists, all whooping and applauding as he emerges from his boat and climbs onto the solid dry concrete of the harbour. Everyone wants to shake his hand or get a photo or an autograph. He greets them all. Some kids phone their mates and get David to talk to them. He does the Anne voice, then Emily Howard. 'I'm a lay-dee but I've swum the Channel!'

He's loving it. He's become the person he wanted to be: someone who can enjoy this moment and celebrate with all these people, and be totally comfortable with the attention, and do whatever they want him to do. After all, David hasn't ever been that comfortable being David, let alone David Walliams from *Little Britain*. But now he looks totally at ease with the situation.

Someone thrusts a pint of beer in his face and ask if he wants to join them for a drink. David politely declines. He whispers to me that he's fucking hungry. He hasn't eaten solid food apart from one Tracker bar in over thirteen hours. 'I could murder a cheese sandwich,' he says.

Eventually, after an hour of autographs and then media interviews and another desperate thirty-minute wait back at his hotel with his friends and family, he gets to enjoy the cheese sandwich. Followed by a dish of sea bass with salad, and a glass of champagne, and some water with no ice. Or salt.

In the car on the way home from Dover, David checks the messages on his phone.

There's one from Caroline Aherne, who sings her own version of 'Congratulations', aided by Craig Cash: 'Congratulations and celebrations, we want the world to know David has swum the Channel!' She stops singing to say, 'David we're so proud of you!' then embarks upon a version of Rod Stewart's 'Sailing': 'We are Day-vid, we are swim-ming, for the women of the world, we are Day-vid . . . swim-ming the Channel!' After that song, she says, 'We love you, David, and I couldn't be prouder of you; I would have been proud of you if you hadn't made it, but let's not put a dampener on it! You'll be pleased to know I raised £17.80 from the people of Manchester for your Channel swim. David, you must be like an old prune . . . your dickie must have shrivelled, and about time too!'

Dale Winton: 'David! Un-fucking-believable. Well done, darling. What a fucking incredible time! It's amazing. Big kiss, darling, I must give you a contribution when I next see you, darling. Fucking brilliant. I'm so proud of you!'

Jonathan Ross: 'David – congratulations, that is fucking fantastic. You are obviously now more of a man than I or any other of your friends will ever be. How fucking fantastic.'

Steve Coogan: 'David – absolutely fantastic. I was quite emotional when I found out. It's a tremendous, tremendous achievement. You deserve huge, huge respect from people. It's inspiring. Let's go out and have a naughty evening to celebrate you being so virtuous!'

And there are the texts: 'Congratulations. We love you. Elton and David. PS from now on you will be known at our house as Esther Walliams.'

Robbie Williams: 'Fucking brilliant, mate . . .' followed by lines and lines of exclamation marks and kisses.

And Rob Brydon: 'You are still fundamentally a bad person.'

I ask David if completing his Channel swim in that incredible time is the greatest moment of his life. He looks me in the eye. 'No,' he tells me, 'my greatest moment was seeing X naked.' He cackles with a mixture of exhaustion and elation.

'Seriously though,' he says, grinning still, 'I can't believe it. I am one of the top fifty Channel swimmers of all time. And I have solved all of the problems of Africa too.'

The next day David's agent receives an email.

Hello Conor,

I imagine you are being inundated with requests for David Walliams after his amazing feat swimming the Channel. Apparently more people have made it to the summit of Everest than swum the Channel.

My reason for writing is that we are looking to make a series of programmes that takes two celebrities on what should be the adventure of a lifetime – climbing Mount Everest. It is the ultimate challenge and would require David to embark on a training regime and then the ascent itself in late March through to the end of May 2007.

If David is interested it would be great to meet up and explore this further.

David says, 'Maybe I should sit down and have a cup of tea and a biscuit first.'

Little BRITAIN

11 SEPTEMBER   13 NOVEMBER

OUT ON DVD